A BATTLE FOR THE SOUL OF NEW YORK

A BATTLE FOR THE SOUL OF NEW YORK

TAMMANY HALL, POLICE CORRUPTION, VICE, AND REVEREND CHARLES PARKHURST'S CRUSADE AGAINST THEM, 1892–1895

Warren Sloat

Cooper Square Press

First Cooper Square Press edition 2002

This Cooper Square Press edition of *A Battle for the Soul of New York* is an original publication. It is published by arrangement with the author.

Copyright © 2002 by Warren Sloat

The line drawings throughout *A Battle for the Soul of New York* come from New York newspapers of the late nineteenth century including the *Herald*, *World*, and the *Tribune*. The illustration of DeLancey Nicoll (page 13) was provided by the New York Historical Society.

Published by Cooper Square Press
A Member of the Rowman & Littlefield Publishing Group
200 Park Avenue South, Suite 1109
New York, New York 10003-1503
www.coopersquarepress.com

Distributed by National Book Network

Library of Congress Cataloging-in-Publication Data

Sloat, Warren.
    A battle for the soul of New York : Tammany Hall, police corruption, vice, and Reverend Charles Parkhurst's crusade against them, 1892-1895 / Warren Sloat.
    —1st Cooper Square Press ed.
       p. cm.
    Includes bibliographical references and index.
    ISBN 0-8154-1237-1 (cloth : alk. paper)
    1. Crime—New York (State)—New York—History—19th century. 2. Crimes without victims—New York (State)—New York—History—19th century. 3. Police corruption—New York (State)—New York—History—19th century. 4. Parkhurst, C. H. (Charles Henry), 1842-1933. I. Title.

HV6795.N5 S56 2002
363.4'4'09747109034—dc21   2002003458

This one, too, is for June Walker.

CONTENTS

ACKNOWLEDGMENTS

Thanks to the librarians who helped locate documents and offered suggestions at the sites named in the sources as well as at the New York Public Library and the Alexander Library at Rutgers University, two places at which I did much of my newspaper research and reading. Thanks also to the Authors Guild for its invaluable services.

Friends and colleagues supplied me with articles and books, advised me on production, and conversed with me about the themes of this book. Thanks from me to Christine Davies, Fred Kameny, Karen Tweedy-Holmes, Anatoly Ivanov, Kenneth T. Jackson, Jim Anderson, Roger Styczynski, Goetz Moeller, Paul Colford and George Kosinski. My appreciation extends also to my agent, Mike Hamilburg.

Michael Dorr, Michael Messina, and Ross Plotkin provided skilled professionalism at the editorial shop of Cooper Square Press, and Ginger Strader and Gisele Henry came through skillfully at the production offices of Rowman & Littlefield Publishing Group.

Thanks to my children, Lisa Sloat, Sarah Sloat, Thatcher Keats, and Shane Keats, for their long-standing support.

I would like to express my special appreciation to Shane and the late Mary Briault, both of whom read and commented extensively on the manuscript.

My deepest thanks are saved for the person to whom this work is dedicated. My wife, June Walker, helped me block out the book, plotted its arc, tore apart faulty construction and built it back more strongly, edited every word several times, and penciled out vaguenesses, obscurities, patches of bad or dull writing, non sequiturs, irrelevancies, and banalities. Her profound understanding of human motivations and behavior helped critically in breathing life into these people of an earlier century.

PROLOGUE
Winter 1891–1892

*In the lower parts of New York City, there is an immigrant pop-
ululion that has not yet got used to the ways of this country. An
impression prevails among the lower classes abroad that America is a land of license, that the people of America do exactly as
they please without any restraint worth speaking of. This impression gives the police a world of trouble.*

—*The Sun*, October 23, 1892

On a winter morning in early 1892 a host of shambling, grumbling, shuffling, weeping immigrants were gathered in a Civil Justice court in New York's Lower East Side. Having nowhere to leave their children, the women brought them along. They sat on one side of the aisle and, observing that separation by gender so pervasive in East European Jewry, the men sat on the other. A rail divided the forward seats from the rear; the immigrants waited, uncouth and outlandish, in the back, while the well-dressed litigants sat on the forward side of the rail, whispering with their lawyers.

The room was damp and unventilated, a stove threw heat at one end, and the musk of poverty pervaded the room. The men, all bearded, had bushy heads of tangled hair. Some of the women wore faded shawls or small knitted cloths over their heads. However ragged their garments, the women tried to make themselves presentable. By pinning up a tear in the dress or by tidying their hair, they had, unlike the men, primped for the occasion.

The courtroom consisted of hard wooden benches and tables, a few rails, and behind a desk on a raised platform sat the Justice. But to the immigrants, this courtroom represented all the majesty of American law, and the Justice sitting there, looking bored while smoothing out crumpled papers, was a nobleman. Every day that winter thirty or so families on the Lower East Side received an eviction notice, and twice a week the Civil Justices heard those cases. When eviction cases began an attendant would call for the interpreter and the lawyers would lean back and read the newspapers, for the tenants could not afford to be represented by counsel.

When the interpreter reached the stenographer's table, the Justice would rattle off the cases returnable that day. As he read the names a court attendant repeated them, watching the faces of the people in the rear to see if any of them responded by look. As they did so they were hurried inside the railing. "Step lively, now!" the attendant exclaimed. "Come now, is that your name, Viankowvliski? Why don't you answer quick and not keep the Court waiting? Lively, there!" This continued until there were no more in the rear who responded by look or motion. They were all corralled inside the rail, directly in front of the Justice.

The Justice pointed to one. "What is your name?" he asked. When the name was given the Justice found the papers in the case and said, "You owe eight dollars for rent. Why don't you pay?"

The Justice usually understood the answers and rendered judgment while the interpreter was still translating. His judgment was usually expressed in one

Trying Rent Cases in a City Court

word, such as "Friday." The interpreter would explain to the tenant that the Justice had granted a stay of two or three days, by which time the premises must be vacated. A Justice could normally dispose of one case per minute. Occasionally the flow was halted by a comment.

"The other tenants object to her children," a landlord said when a Justice gave a woman three days of grace. None of them went to school and they were unsupervised when she went to work.

"How many children have you?" asked the Justice.

"Four, the oldest eight years old."

"Why did you not pay rent on the first of the month?"

"My husband was sick and there was medicine to buy."

"How is your husband now?"

"Dead."

"Landlord, you must not be too hard on these people. I shall give her three days unless you insist on a warrant forthwith."

Prostitutes were seldom shown mercy. One such creature, rouge bedaubing a hunger-pinched face, came up before a Civil Justice that cold day. Outside the wind was howling.

"Why don't you move out?" the Justice asked.

"Your Honor," she answered, "if I am turned out today I would have no place to go. I have been sick. I have no money. In a few days I am promised a room."

The Justice named a date three days off. The landlord scowled.

"Oh, give the poor girl a chance," said the Justice, and called the next case.

Sickness and unemployment were the constant companions of New York's poor. When epidemics swept through tenement houses, the infected were shipped for quarantine to North Brother Island. One day the Justice held most of them over for another week in the hope that these families of coughing mothers and spindly children could come up with some money. Once in a while the Justice, touched by a hardship, would fumble under his robe for his billfold and give them rent money.

With no prospect of shelter, the immigrant tenants would take every possible hour the law allowed before the warrant for forcible eviction threw them out into the snow in their threadbare clothing.

* * *

Marcus Moses served subpoenas in the Lower East Side. He was trudging through the dirty snow on a blustery day that winter to serve an eviction warrant on one Jacob Weissler, tenant at 150 Clinton Street, up five flights, back. Apprehensive about exposing himself to the typhus that was raging through the tenements, the rotund

Moses climbed the steep, narrow stairs and knocked. Every door on the floor opened slightly but one—the door he knocked upon. A woman came down the hall.

"Where's the woman?" asked the paper server, pointing to the closed door.

"She gone."

"Where?"

"See husband."

"Where is he?"

"On the Island."

"Which island?" asked Moses, edging toward the stairway.

The woman could not say. A little girl came out from behind her skirts and said in perfect English: "She's gone to see how her husband is. He is on North Brother Island, sick with typhus fever."

Moses retreated one landing, and called up, "Was her husband taken from here?"

"Yes, in a wagon," said the little girl.

"Well," said Moses, "kindly tell her she will greatly oblige me by removing without further notice from me," and fled to the open air. The Weisslers had escaped eviction, but at a high price.

* * *

For five years the Statue of Liberty had been standing in the harbor, representing a fresh start, equality, the virtuous republic, democracy, the promised land.

But to the Jewish immigrants teeming into the reception center at Ellis Island it meant safe haven—from starvation or long military service or the brutality of Cossacks. Only a few expected to find the streets paved with gold or burned with the ardent desire to live where people governed themselves; most were just fleeing a society in which nine-tenths of the people were poor, ignorant, and oppressed so that one-tenth could live in liberty and luxury.

Yet there were other new arrivals for whom the streets *were* paved with gold. To them the lady in the harbor lifted her torch to offer a new kind of liberty—the promises of a metropolitan life that attracted the adventurous, the talented, the golden, the ambitious, the handsome, the tastefully attired.

They came to enjoy themselves and to be seen doing it. New York was America's showplace of extravagant living. In other cities, where life passed at a more leisurely pace, having money, good family, intelligence, good looks, business prominence, and conversational skill may have been enough; but in New York one more thing was required—glitter. To display themselves properly people in the swim were expected to have maids, butlers, cooks, nurses for the children, housekeepers, stablemen, and high-stepping carriage horses, and a coachman in the silliest livery, and thoroughbred saddle horses to trot through Central Park. A woman's dress had to come from one of the great Paris modistes, and was worn twice at the most. A man's clothing had to be imported from England. Ward McAllister, the arbiter of New York Society, remarked only half in jest that a fortune of a million dollars could support a family in respectable poverty.

They displayed themselves most conspicuously at the Metropolitan Opera— where immodesty, in a wicked age of bare shoulders, plunged to new depths. One always arrived late, near the end of the first act. Serious music lovers were incensed that the frivolous hubbub in the lower tier of boxes, called the Diamond Horseshoe, drowned out the arias. Those more interested in jewels than in *bel canto* could turn their opera glasses on Box 7, where Mrs. Astor blazed like a Christmas tree. Some families brought along an ostentatious valet to stand guard at the family's opera box.

The rich wanted to live on Fifth Avenue. Andrew Carnegie's steel mills smoked all over Pennsylvania and Ohio, but he lived on Fifth Avenue, and imprinted himself on the city by footing the bill for Carnegie Hall. Charles Yerkes' transit equipment wheezed through the streets of Chicago, but he lived on Fifth Avenue. Francesca de Barrios, the inestimably rich widow of a Guatemalan president, owned half of her native country—coffee plantations, harbors, and mines filled with ore—but she chose to live on Fifth Avenue.

Fifth Avenue was still the right address, but the rich were escaping the northward creep of millinery shops and showrooms by fleeing to its northern reaches. Upper Fifth Avenue facing Central Park was called Millionaireville, and its residents vied to outdo one another in resplendent homes. The contest got underway in 1882 when Alva Vanderbilt asked Richard Morris Hunt, the smartest architect of the day, to build her a three-million-dollar mansion that would intimidate everything else for blocks around.

Vanderbilt's palace spurred neighboring millionaires to engage Hunt (who that winter was doing the John Jacob Astor home at Fifth and 65th) or another fashionable architect to build them showplaces that proclaimed themselves expensive.

McAllister contended that the rich performed a valuable function in elevating and refining daily living. The fashionable life, he said, saved Americans "from settling down into a humdrum rut and becoming merely a money-making and money-saving people, with nothing to brighten up and enliven life."[1] Values had been so transformed that a brazen display of wealth, considered an offense against taste among the old-moneyed families, had become, for the metropolitan revelers of the Gilded Age, their contribution to public service.

In an age in which the gulf between rich and poor grew ever wider, some thinkers warned that such excesses stirred resentments and fostered the growth of movements devoted to overthrowing the government and the capitalist system.

Angry radicals ranted on platforms in the rear of saloons that the canvasback duck at Mrs. Astor's party was taken from the mouths of workers' families, that the bejewelled geegaws that John D. Rockefeller gave to his wife made it necessary for the daughters of the poor to sell their bodies. At Socialist rallies Jay Gould—a rogue capitalist steeped in chicanery, stock market manipulation and political corruption—was booed and reviled more loudly than was any other millionaire of the city.

Insisting that the happiness of mankind depended upon the destruction of money, one orator outlined his plans for an all-powerful world government, called Olombia, over which he intended to preside. Jay Gould and Russell Sage and their fellow-monopolists would have to throw their money into a general pile for distribution. "They will refuse, of course, but we must make them obey," he said. "We must use any means. The Irish use dynamite to fight for their liberty and we can do the same." Another speaker fancied that control of the railroads, largely in the hands of Gould and Sage, should be turned over to the government. He said that he intended to invite Sage and Gould to his next lecture on the subject, and that they would be bombed if they refused to attend.

Gould and Sage did not let rancorous orators restrict their freedom of the city. The two friends would meet every morning to walk together to the Sixth Avenue Elevated Railroad, and then ride downtown together on the transit system that they owned. They brought along their railroad passes to save the nickel fare.

Still limber at seventy-seven, Sage was working as usual at the Arcade Building on lower Broadway on a December afternoon in 1891 when his clerk brought him a business card. A man who claimed to come from Rockefeller wanted to see him about some bonds. Being a moneylender, Sage was always willing to listen to a venture. When Sage stepped into the outer office he found the visitor waiting with a carpetbag. He handed Sage a typewritten letter, which stated: "This carpet bag which I hold contains ten pounds of dynamite, and if I drop it, it will destroy this whole building in ruins and kill everybody in it. I demand $1,200,000. Will you give it? Yes or no." When Sage tried to stall him, the dynamiter took a glass globe from the bag and dropped it.

With a blinding flash, an explosion rocked the building, followed by the crash of shattered glass and splintered timbers, and shrieks of terror and pain. The scarlet blast blew in doors, broke the windows on every floor, blew a man through a window and hurled a safe into an adjoining room.

Within minutes Gould heard of the attack on his friend. He called Dr. John P. Munn and presently the physician's carriage was speeding down Broadway. Dr. Munn, physician to millionaires, had been five miles from the explosion but, since his face and coach were known to the police, his headlong drive was unhindered and he was able to reach Sage in only thirty-eight minutes. When his coach reached the scene the police opened a pathway for him and he alighted at the drugstore into which the wounded Sage had been carried. Dr. Munn picked the glass and splinters out of Sage, who was burned and bruised but miraculously was not seriously hurt.

Police Inspector Thomas Byrnes was walking only a half-mile away when the explosion occurred. At first Byrnes, known the world over as the most accomplished detective of the age, surmised that another steam-pipe main had blown up on Broadway and he had continued on his errand. But when he saw the carriage of Jay Gould's physician galloping down Broadway, he knew that someone of importance had been involved in a mishap and he hurried to the scene and immediately took charge of the investigation. While the injured were carted away to hospitals and a dead clerk to the morgue, Byrnes sifted through the ruins in search of clues. He found the decapitated head of the dynamiter.

With great interest upper Fifth Avenue watched the progress of Byrnes's investigation. The inspector worked on the premise that the dynamiter was an Anarchist. "The face is one of those which once seen can never be forgotten," one reporter wrote after viewing the head in a jar. "Meeting the owner of the face for the first time, the casual observer would instinctively associate him with revolution, anarchy, socialism, dynamite and feverish unrest."[2] Hundreds of people stopped at the Morgue to see the macabre exhibit. Several people said it was the head of a radical who, in several Lower East Side halls, had advocated government ownership of the railroads. The police rounded up a half-dozen Anarchists for questioning without cracking the case.

When the bandaged Sage returned to work, he retreated to an inner office, where no one could reach him without a letter of introduction. No longer did he walk to the elevated with Gould. He rode a carriage to the train, and Dr. Munn, his bodyguard-cum-physician, accompanied him downtown. Police detectives guarded the Sage house around the clock and followed him to and from work. The policeman on the beat had instructions to watch for cranks, and to keep human nuisances away from any contact with the wealthy.

Rockefeller engaged three watchmen to guard his house around the clock. John Jacob Astor, Cornelius Vanderbilt, and other millionaires followed his example. Soon sixty-five special watchmen were on duty on Fifth Avenue and neighboring streets from dusk till dawn.

Privilege shared the city with poverty. While the poor scavenged in construction sites, kicking away the snow to find a few boards to fuel their fires, the rich sat by their roaring fireplaces, watching the riotous flames. Every day the rich were more greatly outnumbered and more completely surrounded. They feared that each new immigrant was a potential anarchist and believed that the bomb thrown at Russell Sage was intended for all of them.

The journalists laughed at such apprehensions. They said that most ordinary blokes did not want to throw bombs but to move into a mansion, work up a coat-of-arms, and marry off their daughters to European nobility.

And so New York careened onward, its political vision in amnesia, its revolutionary tradition appropriated by those bent on destruction. "The divine fire," in Whitman's phrase, seemingly had been supplanted by an urban religion in which, a visitor wrote, "the people worship that Trinity known as the Golden Eagle, the Silver Dollar and the Copper Cent."[3]

The newspapers built their circulation on the inexhaustible round of grotesque excess—drunken fathers threw their children out of sixth-story windows, cute little girls handed out cards advertising neighborhood whorehouses, muttering strangers threw vitriolic acid on women's dresses. And New Yorkers agreed that such events were shocking, they were unprecedented, no other place had ever been as wicked as this city.

Everybody agreed that the city was the graveyard of American ideals.

Some blamed mismanagement and corruption. "There is no denying that the government of cities is the one conspicuous failure of the United States," wrote James Bryce in his massive work *The American Commonwealth*. Just across the Hudson, Jersey City was a junior version of New York—as rife with vice as its imposing neighbor. Philadelphia, St. Louis, Denver, San Francisco and other cities showed similar patterns of corruption.

Some blamed the immigrants. An influential editor confessed that "the curse of immigration" had shattered his faith in democracy. "There is no corner of our system," he wrote, "in which the hastily made and ignorant foreign voter may not be found eating away the political structure, like a white ant."[4]

Others thought cities were inherently decadent. In his best-selling tirade, *Our Country*, the Rev. Josiah Strong bewailed the perils of parochial schools, intemperance and Socialism as well as urbanization. The view was prevalent among Protestant clerics, who nodded in agreement when Lyman Abbott spoke at the Evangelical Alliance on "The Modern City as a Menace to Civilization."

Nobody had yet clearly shown that democracy could flourish in a metropolis, where a sense of community was undeveloped and politics was an insider's game run by bosses. Perhaps, it was said, Jefferson was right—that agriculture was the only honest way for a nation to gain wealth and that democracy would only work in a land in which everyone lived in roughly the same economic situation. Others felt that democracy itself was a failed experiment, that the rule of the ignorant majority was tearing apart the fabric of civilization.

The deepest problem, however, was that so few people cared. The rich lacked any roots in the city as well as any interest in how it fared. Used as pawns of the political machines, the immigrants knew nothing about how the city worked. The middle classes, who might be induced to support good government, fled to the suburbs of Brooklyn. Imported radicals tested their new freedoms by calling for the overthrow of the system. And as for the politicians, they were the butt of every concert-hall humorist in the city.

This was the nation in which the Puritans, on an "errand in the wilderness," sought to establish a beloved community. The Founding Fathers believed that Providence had designed America as a beacon that enlightened the world. Whitman believed that democracy delivered people from selfishness and vulgarity, and that the highest duty of government was to teach people to rule themselves. To William James, democracy depended upon good character and mutual respect.

Was America still the land of liberty, a haven for the oppressed, the promised land?

For more than a century America and democracy had, in Whitman's words, been synonymous, and had been related to virtue and liberty. And in this hard and glittering city, those old values still glowed. Blowing the embers ablaze, however, would take someone who saw beyond the difficulties of urban life to its possibilities, who could adapt old values to a new era, who embodied the New World creed that faith and industry could improve any situation. It would take someone who could arouse the people to take up the joys and burdens of self-government and call the institutions of the city to account. It would take courage and fidelity, vision and discipline—and, in this city, it would help to have a provocative style that created excitement. And, as so often happens in history, Providence had such a fellow waiting in the wings.

I

AFLAME WITH A PURPOSE
Winter–Spring 1892

1

DR. PARKHURST'S SERMON

Urban life on a tight island, where there is no possibility of expansion in territory, is bound to be worse in moral or immoral effects than in a community where such territorial expansion is possible. That's why New York is a wicked city.

—Rev. Dr. David Wylie, pastor, Scotch Presbyterian Church,
June 12, 1892[1]

As winter was coming into the city, Billy McGlory's saloon was roaring every night. It was situated in those days on 14th Street, not far from Tammany Hall, smack in the dead center of a strip of rampaging wickedness. To attract the thrill-seekers that roamed through the neighborhood by moonlight, McGlory hired six male transvestites as waiters who belted out songs with suggestive pauses and grinding pelvises. "Did you ever see a lassie," they sang, "go this way and that?" Private boxes were available, for a price, in which a visitor could watch or take part in acts of innovative depravity. On certain nights McGlory brought in can-can dancers who would storm onto the floor, kicking and squealing, shedding the lingerie below their waists one billowy piece at a time. At the conclusion the women raised their skirts above their waists and went whirling about to give the spectators an unobstructed view of their charms—but anyone who blinked would miss this revealing finale, for in a twinkling the lights would go out as the dancers fell exhausted to the floor.

McGlory himself, his gray hair dyed an unconvincing yellow, would stand quietly in the midst of the commotion, shaking hands imperiously and enjoying his notoriety, if the gossip sheets had it right, as "the worst man in New York."

A man to be reckoned with was Billy McGlory. He had a big political pull, although he took no direct part in politics himself. He paid his way with the police and expected to be let alone. Thieves, pickpockets and prostitutes swarmed through the neighborhood by the hundreds, and eventually most of them were drawn into McGlory's place. There was no point in closing McGlory's, a police detective said, for another place just like it would spring up in its stead, "and it is part of the police policy to leave a few places like McGlory's where you can lay your hands on a man at any time, rather than scatter them indiscriminately over the city."[2]

All around McGlory's for a mile in every direction tawdry dives called rootless men out of their dim and dingy rooms to join the hullabaloo. Men staggered out of saloons cursing or singing ribald ballads. Bouncers pushed out drunken sailors who had complained about not getting enough change. Most of the men who roamed the street appeared to be in some stage of intoxication, and they were inviting danger if they lurched carelessly into an alley, for robbers lay in wait in the shadows. Women walked on the street offering cheap delights to the men who swaggered past.

Late in 1891 the *Herald* began to pay attention to the hubbub in this district of the city. Then, on Christmas Eve, an oath was sworn in one of the saloons, a shot rang out, a body fell dead. The blood had barely soaked into the sawdust-covered floor when a posse of reporters from rival dailies galloped to the scene to join the *Herald* in exposing New York's scarlet strip on 14th Street. Then the dailies tried to outdo each other in challenging the police to raid these honkytonks. Even the *Post*, which regarded its competitors as ragbag scandalmongers, and rarely printed news about anything that occurred downtown, turned the limelight on McGlory in a front-page article. The police hemmed and hawed, lectured about the difficulty of making such charges stick, and expressed reservations about the accuracy of the information. The police precinct captain told a Grand Jury that he had been trying for months to come up with evidence against the divekeeper, and was beginning to suspect that McGlory's place was unjustly slandered. But the Captain changed his mind after he was warned that the Grand Jury had toured the neighborhood, had collected its own evidence against McGlory, and that the Captain stood in danger of being indicted himself if he failed to cooperate. Finally, word came to him that the Grand Jury was preparing to indict him on Monday morning. The Captain raided McGlory's on Sunday night.

So that's how Billy McGlory, despite his big pull, found himself in the coils of the law. So did Tom Stevenson, who kept The Slide, a late-night Greenwich Village saloon where rouged men, one of them a fat transvestite known as

Princess Toto, swayed up to customers and lisped, "Aren't you going to buy me something?" Their coquetry, according to the *Herald*, "suggested the infamy to which they had fallen." Police captains had entered its discreetly frosted double doors on countless occasions and found it orderly, though perhaps too lavender for their tastes. Yet the police raided it by order of the District Attorney that January after the *Herald* trumpeted that "vice reigned there in a hideous mien."[3] Both McGlory and Stevenson received one-year sentences to the Blackwell's Island penitentiary. Judge Frederick Smyth, who presided at the McGlory trial, called the description of activities in McGlory's place the most nauseous testimony ever heard in a courtroom, and "the worst man in New York" left for the Island cursing the newspapers that had undone him.

Chiefly because of the press attention, the French Hotel in Greenwich Village was also raided after years of immunity from arrest. Forty plainclothesmen advanced upon the building, scattering street harpies before them and tearing doors from hinges. The madame hurled Gallic oaths, the harlots screamed, and jabbering customers hid in closets. But the police, instead of receiving credit for acquitting themselves well, heard themselves berated. Unappreciative neighborhood residents complained in the wake of the arrests that the police for years had ignored and derided their demands for action. "This is only Sullivan Street," a woman said, "but parents love their children here as much as it is possible for those on Fifth Avenue to love theirs, and I cannot tell you how we have suffered in knowing that our daughters have had to witness the disgusting conduct of the creatures of that place."[4]

* * *

A distance uptown from that scene, in a brownstone district, lived the Rev. Dr. Charles H. Parkhurst. On the second floor of his rectory, Parkhurst had a study in which he read his Bible faithfully and consulted enlightened opinion on public and religious affairs. He plowed through tiresome laments in ecclesiastical journals about how the Protestant churches were losing attendance among the working people in the cities. With a snort of impatience he read articles about how Protestant clergymen were being dismissed from their pastorates for holding so-called heretical notions. And with a sense of excitement he read about McGlory and Stevenson in articles that he had snipped from the newspapers. Sitting at his desk with these articles at hand as he prepared to write a sermon, he thought about the links between these seemingly disparate subjects. If people fell away from the church, it might signify that the churches were ignoring the real problems of the city. Perhaps the churches were overly concerned about preserving a doctrinal purity that distanced them from the city's beating heart. Too

Rev. Dr. Charles H. Parkhurst

many clergymen were content merely to preach to coteries of the genteel, to the well-fed and the well-bred. He was pained to see how far the church had lost touch with the discordant and tumultuous life of the streets.

A Christian, he was wont to say, had his work cut out for him in New York. Something was amiss. America had changed so totally in so short a time, from a land of cow-speckled hillsides and aromatic barns to a bedlam of uprooted people, bizarre cultures, desolate tenements and vitiated air. As people flocked to the cities they tossed away their old moral strictures, and the litter filled the city's gutters.

Instead of observing Sunday as the Lord's Day, the saloons that stretched from one end of the island to the other merely locked their front doors, closed their blinds, and illegally admitted patrons at the side and rear. Desperate men embezzled money from their employers to cover gambling debts. Lascivious sofas waited behind respectable-looking brownstone stoops, and in the rougher neighborhoods painted Jezebels leaned out of windows to call passing men. Parkhurst wondered how he could be expected to preach purity to young men of a Sunday when they need walk only a few minutes from his church, the Madison Square Presbyterian, to reach the Tenderloin district, the city's center of gilded harlotry. He was particularly mindful of these temptations because of his recent appointment to the presidency of the Society for the Prevention of Crime.

The clergyman regarded himself as having a special mission for young men of the city. Bringing them into the fold was the most daunting task that the

Protestant churches faced in such naughty times as these, but Parkhurst had been remarkably successful at it. He took a special interest in the young men who attended his church, some of whom said that they had been roped in by his charismatic powers. These men contributed virility to a faith that was often disproportionately female in membership. Having interested them in church affiliation, the pastor felt that he had a duty to guard them from the succubus of vice.

He was convinced that ever since the Tammany Tiger had regained control of the city government in the previous mayoral election, vice had begun to parade about more openly. In a newspaper interview earlier that month he had pointed the accusing finger at Tammany Hall, that Democratic political association on 14th Street sometimes called The Wigwam.

Now he intended to broach the subject from his pulpit. His congregation was accustomed to hearing its minister, who combined rigorous thinking with impassioned delivery, speak of the glories and demands of the Christian life and the dangers and opportunities of the coming century. Public controversy would be something of a departure from his usual fare. To give it maximum exposure he made sure that the newspapers were alerted, for he expected that it would raise a ruction.

* * *

At fifty years of age Parkhurst was graced with a dark mane shading to gray and a vigorous set of lungs that could overwhelm acoustical flaws in any hall in which he spoke. That Sunday, on February 14, 1892, he turned those endowments to the delivery of a philippic against vice in the city.

The sermon began on a standard Protestant note. He chastised Christians for lack of grit. He scolded the State Legislature for considering bills to liberalize the sale of alcoholic beverages on Sundays. Up to that point it sounded much like the hectoring that went on in many a church on many a Sunday.

But the pastor was just warming up. He blamed the police for the atmosphere of vice in New York and denounced city officials as "polluted harpies that, under the pretense of governing this city, are feeding day and night on its quivering vitals" by maintaining a corrupt alliance with houses of prostitution and gambling dens. As particulars he cited the Grand Jury's efforts to get evidence against Billy McGlory, and the District Attorney's hesitancy to do so, then issued a blanket condemnation.

"The fact of it is they all stand in with each other," he roared. "It is simply one solid gang of rascals, half the gang in office and the other half out, and the two halves steadily catering to each other across the official line." He accused the bluecoats of operating a system of unofficial taxation upon illegal businesses.

The police, he charged, left undisturbed any vicemonger who could pay, and "every crime here has its price."

He called upon Christians to forego their comfort to work for municipal decency. "If your Christianity is not vigorous enough to help save this country and this city," he concluded, "it is not vigorous enough to do anything toward saving you."

* * *

The newspapers seized upon the sermon as the sensation of the day. The *Herald* and the *Tribune* ran the complete text in prominent positions. The *Herald* embellished his words with four drawings of Parkhurst gesticulating and eyeballing vice, his ministerial gown flowing, his mane touching his clerical collar. Even the pro-Tammany *Sun*, unable to ignore a sermon that called city officials "a lying, perjured, rum-soaked and libidinous lot," published extensive excerpts.

The city was rocked back on its heels. New York preachers had been denouncing city vice almost as a matter of course, but never before had one dared to blame the police for it. More shocking still, the tirade had burst from a respected member of ministerial committees, not a Salvation Army drumbeater but one who sat in counsel with financiers and industrialists. Yet the most shocking thing of all was its ring of truth: Parkhurst had shouted out loud what many others had whispered and winked about for years, that vice flourished by means of some sort of arrangement with the police, and the drawing rooms, saloons, and barber shops of New York were agog with a new scandal.

City officials were appalled. "It is a malicious and villainous diatribe, filled with outrageous falsehoods," said Public Works Commissioner Thomas Gilroy. "What makes it even more scandalous than it otherwise would be is that it comes from lips pledged to speak the truth and to preach Christianity. . . . They sound like the intemperate ravings of a madman."[5]

District Attorney DeLancey Nicoll was fuming. Under the leadership of its founder, the late Rev. Howard Crosby, the Society for the Prevention of Crime had always cooperated with the police and the District Attorney's office in uncovering violations of gambling and liquor laws. But this insolent preacher was steering the Society on a new course. The charges that Parkhurst leveled at him—that he had been reluctant to come up with evidence against McGlory—came straight out of the *Post*. Nicoll insisted that he had personally worked up evidence against both McGlory's saloon and The Slide, and that he needed no pressure from a Grand Jury to make him fulfill his public trust.

Nicoll rushed over to City Hall and into the Mayor's office, so choked with choler that he was unable to speak. Mayor Hugh Grant could not hide his amusement. "You will learn to take these attacks more coolly, Nicoll," he laughed, "after you have been in politics as long as I have." When he found his voice Nicoll promised to make the preacher regret his ill-considered words. The D.A. vowed to expose the preacher to the limelight he sought and in the upshot make him sorry he had sought it.[6]

* * *

The *Sun* demanded confrontation. "Either he spoke from knowledge and with precise facts to support his infamous charges," said the newspaper, "or he is a vile liar and slanderer, who should be driven from the Christian pulpit and subjected by the civil law to the criminal punishment he deserves. Let Dr. Parkhurst, therefore, be called upon to substantiate his charges before the Grand Jury, so that the men he denounces specifically may be indicted, tried, and punished; or if he is unable to present any facts justifying them, let him be indicted, tried, and punished himself as a wicked, malicious, reckless, and criminal slanderer."[7]

It is not possible to say whether the editorial prodded Nicoll, but the District Attorney took the matter to the Grand Jury, which called the minister to a command performance on February 23—to be enlightened, as Nicoll put it, "as to from what source he got the allegations upon which he predicated that marvelous sermon."[8]

The preacher had never before appeared before a Grand Jury—this one a different contingent of men than the group that had indicted Billy McGlory in December—and as he walked in and sat down he felt, as he later remarked, that "the atmosphere of the room was distinctly uncongenial." The Grand Jury, which included several Tammany braves and sympathizers, asked him a series of unfriendly questions. It transpired through Parkhurst's responses that he had merely repeated what he had read in the newspapers about the roles of Nicoll and the police captain in coming up with Grand Jury evidence against McGlory.

"The sum and substance of it all," he wrote, "was that I could not swear as of my own knowledge that the District Attorney had lived an immoral life, that police officers were blackmailers, [or] that Police Justices encouraged buncosteering and abortion."

Although mortified by his experience in the Grand Jury room, Parkhurst was not in the least chastened. "As I withdrew from that august presence," he wrote, "I recorded in my heart a solemn vow . . . that I would never again be caught in the presence of the enemy without powder and shot in my gun-barrel. It was severe schooling, but I shall be wiser clear into the next world for what I learned on the 23rd of February."[9] District Attorney Nicoll had extracted his official revenge and had indeed taught the preacher a lesson—but not the lesson intended.

2

SALOON POLITICS

It is impossible to understand New York at the end of the nineteenth century without a sense of the power of the saloons, particularly below 14th Street, or as everyone said, below the line. A saloon was situated on almost every corner in downtown New York, and one stood within a stone's throw in almost any street up the East or the West Side. An 1891 survey counted eighty-two saloons on the Bowery, an average of six per block.

In the German taverns of Kleindeutschland in the Tenth Ward the customers took their beer in deep-lidded tankards, lounging at tables and smoking pipes in wholesome leisure. But the typical downtown saloon lacked chairs and stools; the owners wanted their customers standing at a bar. Some provided customers with brass cuspidors for their expectorating pleasure. Occasionally a brewery sign added a splash of color to the dingy interior, but most were blighted with that paucity of decor that proclaimed a female had never set foot in the place. Sawdust was thickly sprinkled on the floors to absorb tobacco juice and spilt beer.

The crowded tenements in which they lived drove men out to the saloons, which became the poor man's club and information center. There an immigrant learned how to get uptown on a streetcar and how to contact a lawyer. Immigrants who moved frequently used the saloon as a mailing address, and the basements of some saloons were filled with unclaimed trunks and packages. At the corner saloon an illiterate man could find someone to read his letters to him and a man in need of cash could get an advance on the next paycheck. Charities passed the hat in saloons. It was the most accessible social institution in many neighborhoods. Since the lights burned late, it was the place to find a bailbondsman. And it was the only place with a safe that was available to a workingman.

The saloonkeeper knew more than anyone else of the woes, the intrigues, and the passions of his neighborhood. He was the first to hear of the dead horse in the alley that the city had neglected to cart away, the need for a park for the children to play in. The downtown saloon in which men whiled away their time was their school and the saloonkeeper their patron. Often he was their political mentor as well, and if they seemed interested in such pursuits he could introduce them to the local political district leader.

A saloonkeeper interested in political advancement cultivated his patrons, lent money and bought raffle tickets. He invited local politicians to his place and stood them a drink. As his standing in the neighborhood increased, he learned the ins and outs of ward politics, and in time, perhaps, the district leader made him a block captain—the population of the block probably being about 1,200, which included 250 men of voting age.

The saloon of a block captain functioned as a hiring hall. Whenever public work was available, the laborers were engaged by means of tickets, the possession of which entitled a man to a job "on a broom" or "on the big pipes." In addition to public jobs, the work ticket system was used for utilities, rapid transit and other private enterprise, the owners of these enterprises being ever willing to hand out jobs to Tammany braves in order to stand in well with the Wigwam.

The politically connected saloonkeeper was the local big shot. A woman would come in to ask him to use his pull to get her husband a city job. A few minutes later two ragged children would implore the saloonkeeper to help their father, who had been arrested for selling alligator shoes on 14th Street without a license. He would give them some change and would see the Police Justice the next morning to get their father off or pay his fine.

By the 1890s the saloon had supplanted the volunteer fire company as the principal institution of local politics. Political observers estimated that the saloonkeepers controlled 40,000 votes, the balance of power in the city. In some districts they could elect their candidates without the help of a political party. It was a city joke that the quickest way to empty a meeting of the Board of Aldermen would be to have a boy run in and shout, "Hey, mister, your saloon is on fire!"

* * *

The saloonkeepers were unanimous in their dismissal of Parkhurst. Some said he was another of those reformers who buzz about like a mayfly for a day and then are seen no more; in other words, just a goo-goo, a pejorative downtown expression for members of Good Government Clubs. Or maybe he was one of those upstate yokels who toured the city in a rubberneck wagon and went back to tell the hicks how wicked it was. Or maybe, the saloonkeepers said, holding a glass up to the light for inspection, maybe he was the worst species of enemy—one of those prohibitionists who wanted to close the saloons, ban any drink stronger than sassafras tea, and make everybody attend Sunday School. They were waiting to see how long it would take the Tammany Tiger to chew him to bits.

Six days after his ordeal before the Grand Jury, the resilient preacher was back in the courthouse. With him was his aide, Frank Moss, a trustee of the Society for the Prevention of Crime. They were in the District Attorney's office, presenting evidence that the Society's detectives had uncovered.

Parkhurst's political experience was limited. But if District Attorney DeLancey Nicoll thought that this inexperienced preacher was one of those sentimental pastors who worked up an enthusiasm that quickly cooled, he soon discovered otherwise. The minister had a mind as skeptical as an atheist's and a brisk businesslike style that did not fit the stereotype of the insipid Protestant cleric. Parkhurst's air of assurance said that he had already put his embarrassment of a few days earlier behind him, and he came to the point quickly.

He had brought evidence showing that a number of saloons had violated liquor laws by selling alcoholic beverages the previous Sunday to detectives employed by the Society. He wanted Nicoll to escort him into the Grand Jury room so that he could present this evidence to the Grand Jury—the same one that had manhandled him just six days earlier.

The District Attorney said he supported the Society's aims, had worked cheerfully and productively with Parkhurst's predecessor, and would be glad to confer with any other officer in the Society. "But, Dr. Parkhurst," he added in a

DeLancey Nicoll

frosty tone, "I refuse to have any official communication with you until you have withdrawn the falsehoods that you have spoken against me from your pulpit."

"That being the case," the pastor responded with an intonation that gave him away as a New Englander, "I will ask our counsel, Mr. Moss, to confer with you in my stead." Parkhurst handed the list of alleged offenders to Moss and requested that it be turned over to Nicoll. Moss ceremoniously gave the list to Nicoll and waited to see his reaction. The balding Moss and the brass-tacks minister sat there as the District Attorney read the list.

The seven saloonkeepers on that list had pulls of the sort that district leaders called "positively gravitational." The men that Parkhurst accused of violating the ban on Sunday sales were the most untouchable saloonkeepers in downtown New York. The list included Silver Dollar Smith, who bragged that he ran the Essex Market Court House from his saloon across the street. There was Morris Tekulsky, who had bought his place from a Police Justice; and Andy Horn, who kept one of the most frequented after-hours saloons in the city—where the journalists congregated after work. The biggest shot of all was Barney Rourke, who practically ran the Third District, a former Republican who had gone over to Tammany Hall. How important was he? Well, on one occasion he was visited in the back room of his saloon by Chester Arthur, the President of the United States, since the press of business had made it inconvenient for Rourke to call at the President's hotel suite.

When the District Attorney saw this roster of influential names he felt the heat of Parkhurst's challenge. He realized that the Parkhurst sermon was not the misstep of an overzealous cleric, but an invitation to combat—that new hands had taken over the Society for the Prevention of Crime, which Nicoll and everyone else in New York would thenceforth refer to as the Parkhurst Society. He handed back the list and told Parkhurst and Moss that they could take their evidence upstairs to the Grand Jury and that he would give them the immediate opportunity to do so.

"I was admitted to the Grand Jury," Parkhurst later related, "but upon stating my errand was courteously informed that attending to such matters was not exactly in their line, and was invited to move on, and first try my luck with the police court."

* * *

Although it was not mentioned to him at the time, the Grand Jury did have something for Parkhurst. It reached him later that same day. Nicoll had known about it while he and Parkhurst were glaring at each other in the District Attorney's office, but the Grand Jury had exclusive provenance until it was handed up to a Judge and made public. It was a presentment—a special Grand Jury action that did not indict the Presbyterian pastor, but officially censured him, stopping just short of calling him a fool and a blatherskite.

"We find the author of the charges had no evidence upon which to base them," the presentment stated, "except alleged newspaper reports, which in the form published had no foundation in fact. We desire further to express our disapproval and condemnation of unfounded charges of this character, which, whatever may be the motive in uttering them, can only serve to create a feeling of unwarranted distrust in the minds of the community with regard to the integrity of public officials, and tends only to hinder the prompt administration of justice."

The presentment looked like Nicoll's handiwork, a twist of the knife to gouge out a full measure of revenge. Although he lacked any evidence, Parkhurst believed forever after that Nicoll had done it under orders from Tammany Hall.

Nicoll had misread his man if he expected Parkhurst to slink away just because a Grand Jury had scolded him. The next day the undaunted preacher asked Lawyer Moss to take the saloon cases to the police courts, on the premise that the evidence might count for more before a Police Justice than it had with the Grand Jury.

Furthermore Parkhurst was putting together a daring plan to acquaint himself with the dens of vice of the city, to see the interior of places like McGlory's. And he asked David Whitney, a prosperous merchant and a trustee of the Society for the Prevention of Crime, to help him.

Whitney looked at his graying friend. He feared that the pastor had lived too sheltered an existence to embark at the advanced age of fifty on such a venture. He agreed with Parkhurst that being able to speak of the vices of the city from personal investigation would be an advantage, but he warned against the perils of such an undertaking—not just physical dangers, but attacks upon his virtue and misrepresentations of his motives.

In the end Whitney yielded to Parkhurst's ardor, promising to contact a private detective who could guide the pastor in his slumming or, as the smart slang of the day put it, his elephant hunting.

3

FORAYS INTO
THE NETHERWORLD

Charles Gardner, who had recently established his own private detective agency, received a letter in late February from Whitney, for whom he had done some sleuthing in the past, concerning "a very delicate matter which I wish to place in your hands." Gardner learned that the Society was looking for a detective to guide its president, a certain Rev. Dr. Parkhurst, about the netherworld. Whitney advised the detective to "be careful and not shock him too much, as it might sicken him of everything for all his life." Charlie, who had a whimsical streak—before the spring was out he and his bride would be married in the Statue of Liberty—was charmed by the prospect of such a delightful assignment, and Whitney gave him a letter of introduction to the reverend.

When the young detective called at the rectory one evening soon thereafter, a servant led Gardner upstairs to the minister's study. Getting promptly to the point, the minister said that he wanted to see the underside of life. He did not want to be spared anything, however hellish. But he wanted to tour incognito, and was concerned that drawings of him in the newspapers had broadcast his features throughout the city. Gardner responded that a disguise could be worked up. To his relief Charlie found that the minister was not a stuffy sort and, quickly at ease together, they mapped an itinerary. Charlie said they would begin that Saturday night by touring the downtown Oak Street precinct, near the Brooklyn Bridge and the East River. While they were talking a tall delicate fellow about twenty-five years old joined them. Parkhurst introduced the new arrival as John Langdon Erving, a member of his congregation, who had volunteered to accompany his pastor in his midnight forays.

In the days that followed Parkhurst and Erving worked together on a plan of operation. Parkhurst was glad to have Erving's help, especially since the young man came from a distinguished family, and therefore the city would regard his word with more credibility than it would the word of a hired detective.

By the end of the nineteenth century a lot of people who considered themselves up-to-date had decided that Satan did not really exist. Parkhurst was not one of them. He was sure that Satan, the Prince of Darkness, was a slick and cunning fellow who could dress up Sin to give it allure, and Parkhurst knew enough about his own weaknesses to take prayerful precautions against being tempted. On the other hand, he knew that Sin was apt to appear in loathsome forms that might overpower his demure young volunteer, whose safety lay in his keeping, and before they ventured out he warned Erving to steel himself against displays of ghoulish foulness.

* * *

When Charlie returned to the minister's study on March 5, he found the pastor and Erving dressed in homemade disguises. With his hair parted in the middle, Erving looked, Gardner wrote, "like a dandy one year out of fashion." Parkhurst wore a broadcloth suit of clearly ministerial cut, with a clerical collar. "I think we will do," Parkhurst said.

"Do!" Gardner chortled. "Good gracious, sir, clergyman stands out all over you. Why, we couldn't get into a Bowery lodging house the way you are dressed."

They stopped at Gardner's apartment to find something seedier in his wardrobe. He gave the minister a pair of loud black-and-white checked trousers so oversized that Parkhurst had to hitch them under his armpits. Then Gardner tied the sleeve of an old red flannel shirt around the preacher's neck. Next he added a brown slouch hat. But Parkhurst still had the air of a cleric about him. "Dr. Parkhurst, I think that hair of yours queers you," he said. "Let me fix it for you." He rubbed a bar of soap into the minister's hair, taking out the curl and overlaying it with an oily shine. That did it.

Then he made over Erving. Gardner stuck rubber boots over his shoes to hide his dainty feet. He fitted him in a pair of patched trousers that ended above the boots. He mussed Erving's hair, gave him a soiled shirt and a puffy satin red tie. "I say," Charlie chortled, "your red neckties are a passport into any place we are going to visit tonight. Come on."

They climbed up the stairs to the platform of the Third Avenue Elevated Railroad and took a train heading downtown. When Parkhurst sat down, a woman sitting nearby drew her skirts away, and the pastor suppressed a grin.

They were riding south on the East Side, where, between Houston and Fortieth streets, human beings were packed together more densely than had previously ever been experienced in a civilized country. As the steam locomotive pulled them downtown, they caught fleeting glimpses of women stooped over sewing machines in tenement rooms, working late into the night. Below them, homeless children slept in benighted alleys after a day's training in petty theft. Weary wives shrieked. Garbage clogged the streets. This was the part of town where people reeked so insistently that their presence in a crowded courtroom could halt the proceedings, nauseating the lawyers to such a pitch that the Justice would issue an official judicial order for the offender to bathe and return in a presentable condition.

Cherry Hill, where Gardner brought his two novice revelers that first night, lay in sorry disrepair along the East River. Its ruined houses near the riverbank had been proud dwellings during the War of 1812. President George Washington lived on Cherry Street when New York was the national capital, John Hancock had lived here, and the American flag had been designed here. But the area had become one of the most pestilent slums of the city. Typhus and smallpox stalked the tenement houses. Bleeding men reeled out of alleyways to fall and wallow in a chorus of hiccoughs. Raucous song was swallowed up in a scream.

They got off the elevated at Franklin Square, their red ties proclaiming them to be roosters out to crow. "I suppose this is the slums," the minister said.

"Oh, no," Gardner responded, "this isn't the real slums. We are in a bad enough locality for the average man. But wait until later."

He took them into Tom Summers' saloon on Cherry Street, which offered liquor that men in the swank clubs would call undrinkable. The entrance of three strangers evinced interest among the pool players, who kept bobbing their heads over a partition to sneak glances at them.

"What are you going to have?" Summers asked.

"Drink with me," Charlie responded, "and with my South Carolina uncle and my cousin."

Summers shoved three glasses in front of his patrons, took a bottle from behind the bar, and put out a glass for himself. He adhered to the custom of downtown saloons that whiskey was never measured out to a customer; the bartender delivered the bottle and the customer poured. Parkhurst poured himself a stiff drink. So did Erving. Gardner, a survivor of previous encounters with Cherry Hill whiskey, poured a smaller dose for himself. When Parkhurst downed his drink it brought tears to his eyes. Erving gasped and poured himself a large water chaser. The hint of a contemptuous smile flicked over Summers' face, as though Erving had done something unmanly.

"That's good stuff," Gardner said. "Isn't it, uncle?"

Parkhurst gurgled, nodding speechlessly in agreement.

Producing forty cents from his pocket to cover the bill, Gardner said they were interested in buying a pocket watch and chain with a gold case. The bar owner said he did not have any in stock but that the boys might be coming in with some goods in a few days.

While they stood at the bar, young children came and went, rushing the growler—New York parlance for buying beer by the pailful. They also bought whiskey and beer in bottles, pans, tin cans and pitchers. The trio had a second round of drinks and left.

When they were outside Parkhurst reminded Gardner to keep notes for the Grand Jury about everything that happened, and commented that Summers seemed too intelligent to be working as a fence. Then he suggested that Gardner show them something worse.

They strolled down a block of Water Street to find at least fifteen women interested in getting to know them better. When they stopped for a moment beside a group of whores, two of them caught Parkhurst by the arm, whirled him indoors and sat him in a chair. A fat greasy woman pulled Erving in, and Charlie was steered in by an elderly prostitute. The sparsely furnished room in which they found themselves had formerly been used as a retail store of some kind; a faded rag carpet covered the floor, and tired whores sat at a table. Resisting their advances, the men drank a glass of beer and left.

Gardner led them back to a saloon on Cherry Street. In a corner a Negro played Strauss waltzes on a wheezy accordion as couples danced. The room teemed with sailors, cartmen, burglars, gamblers and pimps. Men and women smoked while they danced.

Beginning to feel comfortable in his role, Parkhurst walked up to the bar and asked Charlie what he would like. Gardner ordered a beer and Erving a ginger ale. The bartender shook his head in denial of his request and drew Erving a beer. "Hey, whiskers," a young woman called to Parkhurst, "going to ball me off?" Parkhurst looked puzzled. Again she asked him, this time in terms he was able to understand, to dance, and Gardner called upon Erving to take her around the floor.

The evening grew late. Parkhurst concluded the night by buying a drink for a two hundred-pound whore who invited him to stop by her place and ask for Baby. Gardner, whose experience with pastors was limited, amended some of his preconceptions that night. Although Erving swayed unsteadily, Parkhurst, who had drunk deeply enough to drop a sea captain, first mate and galley cook, was still holding his liquor superbly as the night grew late.

The alcohol may have loosened his tongue a little, for the minister, his greasy hair glistening in the flickering gaslight, maintained that he was taking extreme measures to vindicate himself only because he had "practically been called a liar." The slim detective saw a sudden show of wrath pass over the expressive face of the clergyman.

To Gardner this preacher seemed out of the ordinary. He wanted to shake things up. Perhaps he was ambitious, for he clearly carried a large ego around with him. And he had strong views, as he exhibited when four Salvation Army women in bonnets asked Gardner to buy their organization's paper. When he reached into his pocket for change, Parkhurst gave him a glare of protest.

"I do not believe in the methods of the Salvation Army," Parkhurst explained. "They do more harm than good, and I do not propose to aid their exchequer by buying their foolish paper. A Grand Jury indictment is the only paper that hell-hole needs to convert it."

Parkhurst did not like the Army's narrow focus on salvation. He had brought with him from New England the idea that righteousness was a community matter, that God made His covenants with a people, not with individuals. He was not prowling at midnight to save some quavering drunk with sentimental rubbish, but to fulfill the pledge of his people to God.

The minister was flying high that night on more than alcohol. At that point in life at which most clergymen start touching up their old sermons for redelivery and begin to sink into an indulgent decline, he was convinced that the work for which he had been born was arrayed before him. Having come late into his calling, he knew that he was at last being tested, that his life would never again be the same.

An adventuresome nature animated the owlish pastor. He might look studious and speak with gentlemanly delicacy, but he spent his summers as an Alpine climber, and he was hard and tough. Parkhurst knew that a mountain guide was chosen by a leap of faith and that, as he wrote of it, "you by the act commit yourself, your life, to the keeping of a man whom you do not know, a man whom perhaps ten minutes before you had never seen." He was taking a similar chance on Charlie, who was guiding him not upward to more rarefied air but downward, into rathskellers where vice abandoned all camouflage. For a foothold he had under him his Christian faith and his New England mettle. What drove him onward may well have been an ego, as his enemies would so often charge, that matched his stentorian voice, but whatever the source of his energy when he took hold of something he could not be forced to let go. Parkhurst's nose had been tweaked for the city to mock at, and he would respond in kind. The political powers of the city thought that they had heard the last of him. But they had been only barely introduced.

* * *

Over the following week they prowled five more nights under the damp light of the moon. When they saw harlots gesturing to them from windows they were amused to find a big-bellied cop nearby twirling his nightstick. Fifty whores accosted them on a single block of Bleecker Street, in the shadow of Police Headquarters. "I suppose that none of the police officers in yonder building," the pastor laughed, "knows what is happening on this street." Charlie whisked them behind concert-hall curtains like Stage-Door-Johnnies to meet actresses who doubled as prostitutes—one of whom smoked a cigarette while standing on her head and offered to show them some other tricks. They visited a "tight house" (where the whores wore tights), a favored resort of soldiers stationed at Fort Wadsworth. They went to a French brothel where Parkhurst bantered with the mademoiselles in their own language and shook them with Gallic laughter.

One night they went to The Bowery—a long corridor of saloons, concert halls, tattoo parlors, barber shops that specialized in disguising black eyes, and dime museums full of waxworks displays and freaks, including the Dog-Faced Boy, the Wild Man of Borneo, the Human Turtle, the Missing Link and the Bearded Lady. New Yorkers were singing about "the things they say and the things they do on The Bowery." Recounting in quick three-quarter time a tourist's misadventures, each stanza ended fervently: "I'll never go there anymore!" Once a fashionable part of town, by the end of the century The Bowery had tarnished, attracting for the most part tramps, sailors on shore leave and tourists.

As darkness fell The Bowery's concert saloons opened and turned on their gaslights. Signboards cluttered the sidewalks. Barkers declaimed their attractions—free music, a long bar with a half-dozen highly skilled bartenders, and attractive waitresses eager to meet virile gentlemen. Parkhurst, Gardner and Erving tried to see inside the Windsor Concert Garden, but a screen hid the interior from the sidewalk. As they passed inside they saw that a bar stood to one side and a stage dominated the far end with a woodland scene painted on the curtain. The Windsor's owners had a pull, and ignored closing laws. The owners also failed to recognize the law against boxing matches, and presented prizefights on the stage.

When they sat down at a table, a rouged woman in a low-cut dress joined them. Her coarse and joyless features added a pathetic touch to her impassive manner. Gardner invited her to drink with them.

"Brandy," she told the pomaded waiter.

"Three brandies," Gardner said. Like roosting birds, three other painted women sat down with them at the table and, although they had not been invited nor had drinks been ordered for them, the waiter with the soiled apron brought brandies for them as well and looked to Gardner for payment.

Around them in the smoky hall beer glasses were emptied at a gulp. Singer-actresses were parked at tables with men, and from time to time they walked on stage to try to make themselves heard above the din. In his later account Gardner did not say what songs were sung, but many of the songs of the day were sentimental, about a baby who had joined the angels on the golden shore, or about a violet placed on Mother's grave.

After singing, the performers returned to the tables, leaning on their elbows or sitting on men's laps. Their voices were shrill and burbling with drink, and their laughs sounded forced. The women received 20 percent of the bill they were able to run up, and on a reasonably good night could make six dollars—excellent pay in an age in which the average workman made one-third that for a day's work. In some concert halls the women were actually served tinted waters, although their hosts were billed for alcoholic drinks all the same.

It was Parkhurst's first trip to the Bowery, and like every tattooed sailor who went there, he learned that its reputation as a place of revelry was misleading. Behind all the cheap merriment it was a dreary place, filled with begging tramps, with bouncers armed with brass knuckles, with forlorn women who drank for a living, with barkers trying to invest the banal with thrills, and with divekeepers who enforced the house rule that customers were to be bamboozled whenever possible. The Bowery exposed the vapid quality of evil, that Satan's flashing whirligigs were nothing more than noisemakers. No wonder the visitor who learned by his mistakes never went there anymore.

"Strange as it may seem to you, all of this tour was not a pleasure to me," Charlie wrote in recounting his adventures with Parkhurst. "In the first place not only did I have to keep the Doctor from trouble, but he was a very hard man to satisfy. 'Show me something worse' was his constant cry. He really went at his slumming work as if his heart was in his tour."

Charlie decided to test the pastor's limits by taking his companions to Scotch Ann's in Greenwich Village. He did not tell them that it was a highly specialized brothel. Its basement was divided by partitions into a series of small rooms. In each room sat a youth with a painted face and painted eyebrows, and the airs of a young woman. Each talked in a falsetto voice and called the others by female names. Parkhurst stared uncomprehendingly until Charlie explained what kind of a place it was. The pastor turned and fled from the house. "Why, I wouldn't stay in that house for all the money in the world," Parkhurst panted when they met in the street.

On another night the excursionists picked up their Italian interpreter in a Bowery saloon and headed for Mulberry Street, a street so narrow at some points that a walker's outstretched arms could almost rake the grimy buildings on either side. They walked past narrow passageways called Bottle Alley and Bandit's Roost. After reaching Mulberry Bend, a crooked turn in the street, the interpreter led them down a malformed alley, then walked down three steps to reach a basement door. They entered a stale beer dive—the proprietor dispensed stale beer, drippings left in used barrels from more affluent saloons. Whiskey sold for two cents a cup, and was served in earthenware picked out of a garbage barrel.

Four Calabrian brigands with gold earrings sat on the dirt floor playing cards. Lombardy ruffians, sitting on benches lining three sides of the cellar, scowled at the intruders. Scarecrow women in tatters sat on the benches too; subject to arrest as vagrants if they ventured outside, these women stayed in the cellar almost constantly.

Gardner ordered three beers, which were served in old tomato cans. When he invited the ladies to drink, they scurried over to the bar. One of them tried to embrace Parkhurst. He could smell her sickening breath. "You'll treat me again, won't you, pretty?" she asked, smiling at him past scaly and toothless gums.

"No, he won't," a second woman shouted. "He'll buy me another drink first."

The first woman grabbed the interloper by the throat and the two became locked in combat. The minister backed away in dismay. While the women tore at each other with their nails, Gardner, afraid that their screeching would bring the police, grabbed Parkhurst by the arm and hurried him out. "That was a narrow escape!" the white-faced preacher said. "It was horrible, horrible! I had no idea such places could exist in a civilized city. Death and disease are stamped all over this section of the town. Oh, what a misgoverned city!"

* * *

Fearing that the police would set a trap for them, the detective and the pastor grew more apprehensive with each passing night. Charlie was sure that the police were trailing them, and warned that being arrested in a whorehouse raid would be calamitous.

He thought he spotted the police on the last night of their forays. He and Erving were sitting in the bar at the Hoffman House, one of the city's best restaurants. Charlie was intending to take his companions over to The French Madame's on 31st Street, and they were dressed in finery, as befit a pair of dudes headed for the tonier side of the vice scene. While they waited for Parkhurst to join them—the restaurant was directly across Madison Square from his church—they whiled away their time, glancing at the Bouguereau painting, "Nymphs and Satyr," that dominated the wall opposite the bar—a twelve-foot-high oil of a woodland scene in which four nude pink-and-pearl nymphs disport with a satyr.

Gardner happened to notice two men watching him furtively from across the room. He believed them to be Central Office detectives or, as he called them, flatfoots. He led Erving out a side entrance. The two strangers promptly followed. Gardner and Erving rushed to the Sixth Avenue El, ran up the stairs, bought tickets, and jumped into a railroad car. Their pursuers entered the car behind them. Ignoring the protests of a railroad guard, Gardner slammed open the gate and he and Erving disembarked just before the train pulled out. The shadowy men headed uptown.

Charlie sent Erving over to Parkhurst's study with revised plans for the evening, while Charlie and one of his hired detectives made arrangements at another brothel, changing the evening's itinerary.

He had a wide assortment from which to choose. Unlike lesser cities that hid all their brothels on mean streets and in back alleys, New York strung its gaudiest baubles in one of its best neighborhoods. Its Tenderloin sporting houses were set amid brownstone town houses surrounding Madison Square, in the center of the quality hotel district. The Fifth Avenue Hotel, with its imposing white marble facade, and the Hoffman House both fronted the Square, and other first-rate hotels were located nearby. The heart of the city's shopping district was only minutes away on Broadway. When the hotels had moved uptown to escape from the encroaching tenements, the premier restaurants followed, including Delmonico's, the main dining room of which overlooked the Square. The hotels kept prostitutes out of their lobbies, but courtesans and madames sat in Broadway restaurants at tables adjoining those of women of the highest social standing. The demi-monde also mingled with The Four Hundred on "the ladies' mile" of department and specialty stores.

Many visiting salesmen lived in little towns where librarians considered it indecent to stack a book written by a man next to one written by a woman, and the townsfolk referred to pregnancy as "a delicate condition." Yet when they checked into New York's best hotels they found themselves in the heart of the Tenderloin, where vice was glorified in French fashions; where gay women (the expression, used in a sexual sense, meant wanton) were introduced to men in patchouli-spiced parlors decorated with fresh-cut flowers and carpeted with Turkish rugs; where, after slaking his lusts, the customer would be invited to partake in a midnight oyster supper. One string of houses, called "Sisters' Row" because the madames were sisters, on designated nights admitted only gentlemen in evening clothes and on Christmas Eve donated the night's proceeds to charity. The notorious "House of All Nations," a legend all over the Midwest, offered ornamented women of an intriguing variety of races and nationalities. And in the midst of this bazaar of erotic wares stood Hattie Adams's bordello—which, as if proclaiming its insolence by its very location, was situated on 27th Street, midway between the Parkhurst home on 35th Street and the Madison Square Presbyterian Church, where Reverend Parkhurst thundered every Sunday.

An hour past midnight Mrs. Adams went to the vestibule and found four men waiting with the Negro woman who kept the door. She recognized three of them—they had been at her place a short time earlier. They had promised to return when they found their friend. They said that they had been out touring gambling houses, and that their boon companion, whom they called "a gay boy from the West," had slipped away to the six-day bicycle races at Madison Square Garden, just a short walk away. Now they had returned with him, a bespectacled old boy with chin whiskers and a moustache. Hattie Adams led her guests to a rear parlor and called out a group of young women to meet them.

"This is rather a bright company," the gay gentleman said with a cheery lilt to the scantily clad young whores. He smiled with a stagy manner that suggested he might be an actor. His long hair was disarranged. Something about this fellow did not ring true for her. Hattie Adams kept squinting at him with the suspicious eyes of an experienced madame.

When the men expressed an interest in seeing something unusual, she suggested "a dance of nature," and they agreed to pay $15 to see it. The five women undressed except for their garters and stockings. Mrs. Adams had to blindfold her piano player, whom they called The Professor, because the girls would not dance if he could see them. He struck up a quick tune on the tinny piano and the women began to can-can.

"Hold up your hat!" shouted a tall blonde dancer. One of the three visitors took a black derby and held it six feet from the floor. The dancer kicked, sending the hat spinning away. The men applauded. The whores cavorted one or two at a time, never in ensemble, and one of the five did not dance at all, but stood naked before the men. The women made sexual offers, but refrained from coarse language. One of the customers, the tall dainty one, danced with the naked women.

During the twenty-minute "dance of nature," Mrs. Adams kept watching the "gay gentleman." Much of the time he did not even watch the ribaldry. He kept his eyes cast downward, sipped a glass of beer, and glanced up only occasionally. Mrs. Adams sidled over and tried to pull his whiskers, but he straightened so rigidly that she did not attempt such familiarity again. "Are you a professional?"

she asked him (meaning an actor), but did not get a satisfactory answer. One of the whores tried to get him to go upstairs and "have some fun," but he displayed no interest.

When the dance ended the men drank some beer before leaving. "Come again!" Mrs. Adams called out as they left.

By now it was quite late, but under the canopy of night the four companions, including a detective from Gardner's agency, decided to make one more visit, one last stop in their moonlit explorations into the fleshpots of the city. And so they headed downtown—Gardner and his assistant, Erving and the gay boy from the West—to the French whorehouse of Maria Andrea on West 4th Street in Greenwich Village.

They were startled when they arrived to find a burly policeman standing at the bottom of the steps. But he was not disposed to interfere. A girl whistled to them from an upper window and the Madame answered the door and let them in, asking if they had come to see "a French circus." After settling on a price, they watched an exhibition so raw that Gardner feared that at any moment the minister was going to bolt out the door and down the steps. But Parkhurst stuck it out, to the end, when the women smiled and took bows as if they had performed a ballet.

Gardner said it was almost too much even for him. Parkhurst stayed in the corner smiling, and signaled that it was time to leave. As they emerged Gardner asked Parkhurst: "What did you think of it, Doctor?"

"Think of it!" the shaken pastor said. "It was the most brutal, most horrible exhibition that I ever saw in my life!"

* * *

Thus ended their revels. For those who lived in the genteel parts of the city, Parkhurst's downtown adventures had taken place in another country. But he looked at the city as all of a piece. To neglect the regions below the line, a train ride away, was like assuming that the typhus raging downtown would never creep northward to the upper reaches.

Parkhurst had lifted glasses in saloons so filthy that he could not tell whether the floor was wood or dirt, where tobacco juice yellowed the bar and a residue of smoke hugged the walls, where bartenders wiped glasses with a dirty rag and served whiskey that tasted like a concoction of soap, kerosene, cleaning chemicals and molten lead, and his stomach had proven equal to it. Now his words—and his deeds—had to do the same.

4

THE SECOND SERMON

On Saturday, March 12, Parkhurst was working at his typewriter in his study. On his desk lay a stack of letters from "A Mother" or "A Concerned Father" asking him to continue his campaign for purity so that their young sons might be delivered from temptation. He was writing a sermon that would respond directly to these letters, and would also report to his flock on his field investigations and reply to his attackers of a month earlier.

He wanted to put into his sermon every ounce of his Christian optimism and hope—and a teaspoonful of his Christian vinegar. God had bestowed upon him the twin talents of an orator: deftness with words and a personal power of persuasion. What he was writing that Saturday would not be the most lustrous sermon of his life, since he lacked the time to polish it—indeed, he barely had time to wipe his wire spectacles—but he had to finish it quickly in order to send advance copies to the newspapers. Once he had spent whole summers thinking long thoughts, and now it seemed as if he barely had time to absorb the rush of events.

* * *

Charles Henry Parkhurst grew up on a farm on the stony ground of Western Massachusetts. Recognizing his mental gifts, his parents sent him to Amherst College, where he excelled. All the knowledge that he acquired, however, failed to give him a sense of direction, and he remained baffled about the path that he ought to take and felt isolated from his fellow men. He taught Latin and Greek at Amherst High School and later at a preparatory school in the area. He married one of his former students. He studied the connection of language with history and published a respected book of philology. He studied in Germany. But the world only grew more remote. Still floundering at the age of thirty-two, Parkhurst revisited his alma mater to seek counsel from a trusted professor, who sensed that his former student had developed too cerebral a personality and ought to breathe life back into the warmer side of his nature and become involved with people. Knowing of a church in the Berkshire Mountains with a vacant pulpit, he persuaded Parkhurst to apply for the position.

Parkhurst became pastor of the Lenox Congregational Church in 1874 and he and his wife, Nellie, moved to the Berkshires. At first Parkhurst failed to commit himself wholeheartedly to his occupation and regarded his pastorate as a waystation on the road to something else—possibly a professorship in comparative philology. But the spirit took him over, and gradually he became devoted to the ministry as his true calling. Encompassed by those worn mountains on the western border of Massachusetts, Parkhurst came to realize that he had been summoned to forsake the cold and austere life of the mind, and that this was not a free decision but the call of God.

With his change of heart came a shower of gifts. In his pastoral duties he wrote his name in the simple annals of the village, while on Sundays he delivered pithy sermons—earnest and yet droll, mordant and yet kind—reading them word for word, bending over his manuscripts with intense absorption.

For six years he ministered to the community. The church stood on the town's highest hill, and from the rectory he and his wife watched as Lenox was transformed from a farm village to an agreeable retreat for the new princes and princesses of Gilded America. Post-Civil War America was ringing in many such changes as fortunes were amassed, and even pastors were induced to regard their calling as a career and their talents as market commodities. A clergyman like Parkhurst with so seamless a blend of charismatic power and intellectual rigor could eventually expect to be called to a more conspicuous pastorate. Summer residents impressed by the country preacher introduced him to the Madison Square Presbyterian Church, where he delivered a guest sermon. And in 1880, when its pastor retired, Parkhurst accepted an invitation to replace him.

But Parkhurst was not just leaving one church for another; he was crossing denominational borders. He left a Congregational meetinghouse that ruled itself, and sailed into the purview of the New York Presbytery, which maintained tight control over all the churches in its sway. That Parkhurst had never studied formally for the ministry was nothing exceptional for nineteenth-century pastors. His disinterest in the bureaucratic intricacies of the church, however, was deplored. "It was also against me," he noted, "that when asked if I believed in the Presbyterian polity of government I replied that I knew little about it."

Everything about Parkhurst rubbed the Presbytery the wrong way. Its elders stressed the Triune Nature of God, transubstantiation and predestination as dogma. He looked at many theological concepts as tentative conclusions. The elders were concerned above all with eliminating heresies; he spoke a religious language centered on action, and laughed at their gloomy formulas. The elders maintained in the grim tradition of John Calvin that most humans, including unbaptized infants, were damned to Hell for eternity. Parkhurst thought that a person's religious impulses could be best developed by cultivating what was noblest in him. He practiced an optimistic Christianity. He was impatient with "pillars of the church" and hoped to change the focus of the church from self-absorption to the raucous life outside.

Some of these elders opposed Parkhurst because they discerned in him a spirit so recklessly ecumenical that it reached out even to the Roman Catholic Church, which they regarded as akin to the Antichrist. They also felt that Parkhurst lacked a sense of mystery, as if religion were to him just an application of trigonometry.

Despite their misgivings, Parkhurst had also attracted supporters, and he was appointed. The Presbytery discovered, beneath his unbecoming cheerfulness, a vein of orthodoxy. Parkhurst never felt a need to cling to doctrinal correctness because he doubted nothing. His trust in God was total. Parkhurst stressed commitment and service. One day in a meeting at Chickering Hall about "the problem of poverty" he said sharply:

"What if, when the poor leper came to the Lord to be healed, he had said, 'Here, Peter, you go touch that fellow and I'll pay you for it'? Or what if the Lord, when he came to earth, had come a day at a time and brought his lunch with him, and had gone home to heaven overnight? Would the world ever have come to call him brother?" Old clothes, soup, prayers, and money, he said, are cheap to give. "Just so soon as a man feels that you sit down alongside of him in loving sympathy with him, notwithstanding his poor, his sick and his debased estate, just so soon you begin to worm your way into the very warmest spot in his life."

As he wrote his sermon in the study that Saturday, much of the city was wary of his lack of discretion, but he thought that most people valued respectability over the Holy Spirit. He assumed that God had exposed him to rebuke for a reason. Its sting had stirred him to action, and God intended to change the cheap wine of his human ego to the blood of Christ, to use him in a righteous cause.

He clicked away at his sermon, sticking in new information that Gardner only that day had given him from the gambling dens—the numbers runners, the horse-betting parlors and the faro banks. His sermon would respond to anguished parents seeking his help, but he would show that he could not close down the commercialized vice of the city, for that power lay with the police. He had visited saloons and brothels in search of the enemy, but the real enemy stood outside, guarding the steps, twirling a nightstick and watching the gay gentlemen ring the whorehouse buzzer.

* *

When the doors of the church opened the next morning, a crowd had already gathered on the sidewalk. Barring entrance to all but pewholders, the ushers advised that there was no free seating in the church, the congregation renting its pews by annual subscription. Families alighting in tasteful luxury from the carriages had to pass through a throng of onlookers. As the time for services drew near the growing crowd grumbled. Some who persisted managed to find a parishioner who would invite them to sit with the family, while others made it clear with defiant stares that strangers were unwelcome. After the pews were filled the ushers allowed some to enter, and at 11 A.M. the church was packed, with crowds standing in the aisles and in the galleries.

It was the largest crowd in the history of the church. Important civic figures were in attendance. City editors had sent reporters bearing advance copies of the sermon. Eyewitnesses later swore that some ladies of the evening slipped in to enjoy the fun. A few Tammany men scurried in, curious to hear the outspoken preacher. And Charlie Gardner was ready with a counterfeit coin for the collection basket.

Although Tammany Hall regarded Parkhurst as an insignificant parson, those in the city's eminent circles were well acquainted with him. He had recently served with the Chamber of Commerce's Russian Relief Committee—along with such financiers as J. Pierpont Morgan and Mortimer Schiff—to alleviate hunger among Jews in the Pale of Settlement. As befit a solid and established spiritual leader, Parkhurst lived with his wife in a burnished home with servants. But to regard him as merely a society pastor would understate the standing of his church, which dominated the city's greatest square, and his congregation. The pewholders included Louis Comfort Tiffany, the leading force in American decor; Martha Lamb, a highly esteemed historian; and John Crosby Brown, a partner in Brown Brothers. Collectively they comprised the most imposing congregation in the city—not the wealthiest but the brainiest.

Wearing a black Geneva gown and surrounded by sympathetic listeners, Parkhurst stepped to the pulpit.

Beginning with a review of what had happened to him before the Grand Jury, he quickly made it clear that he would not retreat from holding Tammany Hall responsible for vice in the city. He attacked tainted city officials "against whom the most damning and excoriating thing that can be done is to publish their history."

"A while ago the treasurer of a certain bank downtown, who was not even suspected of being dishonest, but whose name, through no fault of his own, had become associated with a disreputable firm, was thrown out of his position. The reason stated by the directors was, that while they cordially and unanimously recognized the integrity of the treasurer, they could not afford to jeopardize the interest of the bank by having associated with them a man that was tainted even to the slight degree of being mentioned in connection with dishonest dealing. Now, that is the way you run a bank. . . . But when you come to run a city, with a million and a half of people, with interests that are a great deal more than pecuniary, and a city, too, that is putting the stamp of its character or of its infamy upon every city the country through, then you have not always shrunk from putting into positions of trust men that are ex-divekeepers and crooks and ex-convicts, and men whose detailed written history would be tremblingly near to the verge of obscene literature."

It was charged, he noted, that his sermon of four weeks earlier was general and lacking in details. "Now details, I confess, were the last things that I supposed the virtuous people of this city would need, or that the administration of this city would want. . . . I did not imagine it would be considered a part of my ministerial duty to go into the slums and help catch the rascals, especially as the police are paid nearly five million dollars a year for doing it themselves. But it is never too late to broaden your diocese."

On the previous Sunday, Parkhurst said, he sent out five detectives to check on whether the police were enforcing the excise laws. "I have here," he said, gesturing at a stack of papers, "the results of their day's work, neatly typewritten, sworn to, corroborated, and subject to the call of the District Attorney. There is here the list of parties that last Sunday violated the ordinance of Sunday closing."

The pastor explained that the affidavits listed names and dates, "which is what I understand our municipal administration desires to have this pulpit furnish it. Of course, I am not going to take up your time by reading the names." But for those demanding particulars, "well, there are 254 of them—not pulpit grandiloquence nor ministerial exuberance but hard, cold affidavits." If the city's leaders want more, "we will guarantee to grind them out a fresh grist every blessed week. Now let them take vigorous hold of the material furnished above, or quit their hypocritical clamoring after specific charges."

After that Parkhurst brought up prostitution and gambling in the Tenderloin district, in which the church was located and, without giving details, revealed that he had visited brothels in person.

"And now, fathers and mothers, I am trying to help your sons . . . I never knew until two weeks ago how almost impossible it is for a young man to be in the midst of the swim of New York City life under present conditions and still be temperate and clean. I had supposed that the coarse, bestial vices were fenced off from youthful tracks with some show at least of police restriction. So far as I have been able to read the diagnosis of the case, I don't discover the restriction.

"Don't tell me I don't know what I am talking about. Many a long, dismal, heartsickening night in company with two trusted friends have I spent, since I spoke on the matter before, going down into the disgusting depths of this Tammany-debauched town, and it is rotten with a rottenness that is unspeakable and indescribable, and a rottenness that would be absolutely impossible except by the connivance, not to say the purchased sympathy, of the men whose one obligation before God, men and their own conscience is to shield virtue and make vice difficult."

At this point some men's faces clouded, and some women hid their faces and blushed, stirring in their seats with a rustle of skirts.

The pastor said that many letters he had received were "written by people who did not dare to append their own signatures," in sympathy with the cause but afraid to offend the police. "I want to say that now is a good time to speak out; an excellent opportunity for moral heroism to come to the fore and assert itself. Nothing frightens so easily as vice," he said, clasping the rail of the pulpit with one hand as he prepared to quote Proverbs. "'The wicked flee when no man pursueth'—and they make still better time when somebody is pursuing.

"I never dreamed that any force of circumstances would ever draw me into contacts so coarse, so bestial, so consummately filthy as those I have repeatedly found myself in the midst of these last few days. I feel as though I wanted to go out of town for a month to bleach the sense of it out of my mind, and the vision of it out of my eyes. . . . Horrible though the memory of it must always be, I know it has earned me a grip on the situation that I would not surrender for untold money. But the grim and desolate part of it all is that these things are all open and perfectly easily accessible. The young men, your boys, probably know that they are. Ten minutes of sly indoctrination, such as a tainted comrade might give them, would afford them all the information they would need to enable them with entire confidence to pick out either a cheap or an expensive temple of vile fascination, where the unholy worship of Venus is rendered. The door will open to him, and the blue-coated guardian of civic virtue will not molest him. I spent an hour in such a place yesterday morning, and when we came down the steps I almost tumbled over a policeman who appeared to be doing picket duty on the curbstone."

New York's police, he said, were guilty of either incompetence or complicity and the ability with which they discharge "certain portions of their official obligations" suggested that the fault was not incompetence. On behalf of the public he insisted that the police "close up gambling-houses, houses of prostitution, and whiskey-shops open in illegal hours. If this is what they cannot do, let them concede the point. . . . If this is what they will not do, let them stand squarely on the issue and be impeached.

"In a closing word, voicing the righteous indignation of the pure and honest citizenship of this tyrannized municipality, let me in a representative way say to Tammany: for four weeks you have been wincing under the sting of a general indictment, and have been calling for particulars. This morning I have given you particulars, 284 of them. Now, what are you going to do with them?"

Charlie Gardner couldn't remember when he had enjoyed church so much.

5

PARKHURST SUNDAYS

Volleys of protest against Parkhurst's sermon rang out all over New York. City officials accused the preacher of dragging New York's reputation through the mire. Politicians charged him with bearing false witness against his neighbor. Fellow pastors labeled him a sensationalist. "It is hard to believe that a sane man, and especially a minister of the Gospel," said Jimmy Martin, president of the Board of Police Commissioners, "would so far forget himself as to talk in a manner that would cause loving and anxious mothers to look with alarm on the faces of the daughters who accompanied them and to find thereon the blushes of shame caused by his improper remarks."[1]

Morris Tekulsky, a spokesman for the liquor interests, could hardly bring himself to believe that such subjects were broached in a church. Tekulsky, one of the seven untouchable saloonkeepers on Parkhurst's list for District Attorney Nicoll, observed that the talk about liquor violations had bored the younger congregants, but that they listened avidly when the clergyman started in on naughtier topics.

Even in the fancy houses, shock was registered at the risqué sermon. "I wrote a letter to Dr. Parkhurst the other day, and told him what I thought about him and his crusade," said an indignant three hundred-pound madame. "I told him in my letter that one sermon by him such as I had read in the papers last Monday, preached to a congregation in which there were hundreds of pureminded boys and girls, did more to corrupt the minds of his auditors than any five or six of the worst dives in New York."[2]

Police Inspector Alexander Williams cautioned that the reverend's pulpit hijinks provided brothels with free advertising. "Thank God that vice is so hidden that Dr. Parkhurst has to get detectives to find disorderly houses," he prayed, "and that thousands of wives and daughters do not know of even their existence."

Williams, known as Clubber, maintained that periodic visits to a brothel for a young man of normal glandular development staved off the madness that resulted from self-abuse, and noted: "Such places have existed since the world began and men of observation know that this fact is a safeguard around their homes and daughters."[3]

Clubber's live-and-let-live philosophy was more in the spirit of New York than were the sanctimonious attacks on Parkhurst. Men about town believed that most Manhattanites did not want the sidewalks rolled up after dark and would soon tire of the puritanical pastor. New York was a good-time place. Men wanted to laugh, drink, see high kickers in tights, and hear lively songs like "Ta-Ra-Ra-Boom-De-Aye."

The song was fresh, cheeky, and syncopated, as the girl described herself in the lyrics:

I'm not too young, I'm not too old,
Not too timid, not too bold.
Just the kind you'd like to hold,
Just the kind for sport, I'm told.

It was the song of the day. Working girls sang it on the street. As the girls walked past, police, bus drivers and clerks joined in. Actors convulsed their audiences by working the phrase into the dialogue of a play.

Mayor Grant responded in the spirit of the hit song. While "incredibly scandalous scenes" occurred openly every night in the great European cities, he said, decorum reigned in New York. "Nothing is flaunted. The innocent are not contaminated against their will. Respectable citizens need never be offended."

The Mayor added that a large segment of New Yorkers claimed the liberty to patronize saloons on Sunday. "Popular sentiment is responsible for the fact that it is impossible," Grant said, "to keep all saloons tightly closed on that day."[4]

* * *

There was another reaction to the sermon, and this one was strictly business.

When the servant girl at the Parkhurst home answered the front door she found two women standing there. The bejeweled and painted one looked about forty years old. The other, dressed in a flashy style, was young and pretty. They asked to see the minister. The servant girl asked for their calling cards or their names.

"Oh, that makes no difference," the older woman said. "The doctor does not know me. Just tell him that a lady wishes to see him."

As the servant girl walked up to deliver the message the older woman glanced into the parlor. "Look, Annie," she said. "That's the man. There's his picture."

"That's the man, sure," the younger agreed.

The minister came downstairs and asked how he could be of help. Somewhat excited, the older woman stammered that she sought his aid in placing an aged woman in a Presbyterian home. Parkhurst said this was his wife's department and walked back upstairs to fetch her.

The older woman was Hattie Adams. His sermon had mentioned a bordello near his church, which was, she suspected, her place, and the newspaper drawing of Parkhurst resembled the gay boy from the West. Bringing along one of her high-kickers to help confirm the identification, she was calling to complain that, with all the brothels operating in the Tenderloin, it was unfair to single out hers. She ran a quiet place and made no trouble, and he had to come along and spoil it.

When the minister returned with his wife, they held a hurried conversation about a Presbyterian home that Mrs. Parkhurst recommended. Hattie Adams left with her suspicions confirmed, but without springing the confrontation that she had planned.

* * *

After delivering the sermon, Parkhurst was off and running. Since Thomas Edison had begun to wire the city for light and power, electrical metaphors had come into vogue, and those who commented on the pastor that week called him "a dynamo," after the machine that the great inventor used to dispatch the current through his wires.

On Monday he appeared before the Board of Excise, which licensed saloons and regulated the sale of alcoholic beverages. Bringing with him Society agents to present evidence, the minister argued that the seven saloonkeepers on the list he had originally given to the District Attorney ought to forfeit their liquor licenses for selling alcohol on Sunday.

On Tuesday he attended Police Court to watch Lawyer Moss present evidence against those same seven saloons in an attempt to get their bartenders charged with Sunday sales. The Police Justice dismissed two of the cases for lack of proof. The remaining five cases were forwarded to the District Attorney for presentation to a Grand Jury.

Moss had accorded himself well in keeping five of the cases alive. Most excise cases were dismissed at the police court level. Every Sunday the police arrested a number of bartenders for violations of the Sunday closing law, and every Monday the Police Justices threw most of the cases out, sometimes resorting to fanciful legal interpretations. In past years Justices had ruled that lager beer was not "beer" under the terms of the law. Some had ruled that if Sunday drinking occurred behind closed doors and did not annoy churchgoers the law's intent had not been transgressed. Others ruled that just because the liquid sold in a saloon was amber in color, had a head on it, came out of a barrel, and tasted cool and smooth, did not constitute proof that it contained alcohol. The police generally accepted the dismissals in good humor, since they could write up a report that showed a respectable number of arrests.

Even when the Police Justices sent the cases on to the District Attorney, and even if the District Attorney secured an indictment, they rarely came to trial. Since the District Attorney had bigger fish to fry, excise matters were stored by the thousands in his filing cabinets for long periods until they turned to dust and were dropped on grounds of advanced age.

* * *

Those who had attacked Parkhurst in February for being too general and speaking from hearsay were not all that pleased by the bill of particulars in his March sermon. District Attorney Nicoll did not call for the evidence and, as Parkhurst later recalled, "never gave me any indications of his gratification."

Although Nicoll seemed disinclined to summon him, the Grand Jury took the matter into its own hands, prevailing upon the incurious District Attorney to "request Dr. Parkhurst and his agents to appear before this Jury at the earliest practicable moment."

On Thursday Parkhurst brought his affidavits to the Grand Jury. He soon discovered, as he put it, that this Jury was "quite a distinct species" from the one that had branded him a fool in February. Although Grand Juries functioned independently of the District Attorney, in effect they usually were passive, sitting in judgment on cases that the D.A. brought to them and deciding whether or not an indictment was warranted. Its active role in calling him suggested that it might be what District Attorneys call "a runaway Grand Jury." The jury foreman had previous experience that, in Parkhurst's words, "made him familiar with the fact that a Grand Jury does not fulfill its functions by playing tail to the District Attorney's kite."

When the jury members asked him for evidence that the Society had gathered regarding prostitution, gambling, and excise violations, he was armed with powder and shot in his gunbarrel. After presenting his evidence, Parkhurst added:

"Gentlemen, I have no interest in the conviction of these parties. Evidence has not been secured against them for the sake of inducing you to indict them. My object has been solely to secure in the general mind an indictment against the Police Department."

He later commented: "Whether this statement of our desire and purpose had any influence on the jurors is of no particular importance, but it is of importance to notice that the work which they did was thoroughly consistent with our own plan of campaign, and that the remainder of its time it occupied for the most part, not in indicting individual violators of gambling and excise laws, etc., but in prosecuting its inquiries into the matter of police negligence and criminality."

Grand Jury proceedings were secret, but nothing prevented the interested from observing who was called to testify. Parkhurst was seen taking a stack of documents into the room with him. Gardner entered and left. One day several Police Inspectors waited their turn, each going in separately. It was whispered about the corridors that they had been asked to explain why the police had not cracked down on illegal activities in the city.

Other Police Department officials were subpoenaed to appear on various dates in March. Some were taken ill and failed to recover until the Grand Jury was discharged. Those who testified swore that they had never received any hush money, nor did they know of a police official who had. None offered the Jury a shred of evidence.

The Jury called in John P. Smith, editor of *The Wine and Spirit Gazette* and the source of published charges that the standard police rate for allowing saloons to operate on Sundays was $30 a month. But the trade paper editor told the jurors that he had only secondhand accounts to offer. Saloonkeepers also denied knowing anything but hearsay. Frustrated at every turn, the Grand Jury failed to uncover any direct evidence of bribes.

* * *

On the afternoon of April 1 the Grand Jury handed up a presentment that accused the Police Department of failing to enforce the law against brothels and gambling houses.

"They are either incompetent to do what is frequently done by private individuals with imperfect facilities for such work," the foreman read, "or else there exist reasons and motives for such inaction which are illegal and corrupt. The general efficiency of the department is so great that it is our belief that the latter suggestion is the explanation of the peculiar inactivity."

The Jury called upon the authorities to investigate its charges and halt the corruption in the Police Department.

Police officials were aggrieved by this insult from an ungrateful populace, and Inspector Thomas Byrnes was angry. "The fact that a body of men constituting a Grand Jury, which only sits for a month," he said, puffing on his pipe, "have brought in such a presentment against a Police Department whose efficiency cannot be equaled in this

Supt Byrnes

or any other country, is a gross outrage."[5]

Soon street corner newsboys were urging New Yorkers to read all about the most sensational Grand Jury presentment in the city's history, and the barber shops were buzzing with jibes about how a preacher had turned the tables on his accusers.

Both those who applauded and those who cursed the Presbyterian minister began to take him more seriously. Yet even that newfound respect did not take his full measure. Although he lacked training and experience in leadership, Parkhurst had remarkable persuasive powers. The first evidence of his potential in public life, for those who looked closely, was the work of the Grand Jury, which set off in the direction in which he pointed them, and produced a presentment that restated the theme of his sermon.

* * *

On Saturday morning, the next day, messengers were dispatched from police precinct stations all around New York to tramp from one saloon to another, warning saloonkeepers that any trafficking in liquor on Sunday must be attended by extraordinary precautions.

In some precincts the messengers paid return visits on Saturday night to advise saloonkeepers, even those with pulls of Herculean proportions, that it would behoove the Captain if they would refuse to admit any customers the following day under any circumstances.

The Liquor Dealers Association met in the afternoon, and after hot argument advised its members to keep closed the next day. On Sunday, April 3, four thousand saloons were locked up, most for the first time in several years, some for the first time ever. Parched men, spurred by warm weather, knocked and kicked and banged their empty tin pails on the unresponding doors. Extra trains were run across the Brooklyn Bridge and the thirsty sojourners headed into the closest saloon available. Thousands ferried across the Hudson to drink in Jersey City or Hoboken, where saloonkeepers toasted the New York clergyman for sending them boatloads of customers.

On the following day the people who lived in the brownstone districts read with approval in the morning papers that the police had made sixty-seven arrests for violations of the Sunday excise law. Alcoholism, as far as Parlor Sentiment was concerned, was the plague of the late nineteenth century, and the effects of drink upon the lower classes was deeply deplored. The Better People hoped to encumber the saloon with limitations—hours of sale, days of sale, number of licenses, high license costs—to restrict trade and reduce the number of saloons in the city.

The crucial time for the tenement wives was Saturday evening when their husbands were paid. The saloon lay between the workplace and the home, and inside it stood the bartender in his apron, his hair parted in the middle, rinsing a tumbler. The worker, happy at the prospect of a day off, stopped on the way home to get his paycheck cashed and to have one quick drink; but one would lead to another and by late in the evening his week's earnings would be gone. Then he would go home where his wife would shriek at him for coming home empty-handed, the children needing new shoes, the rent due, and himself recking and foul-mouthed into the bargain. He would consider these remarks such an affront to his dignity that he would beat his wife and perhaps the children as well.

Alcohol was the cause of unemployment, of crime, and of the misery of the slums, according to uptown thinking, for if the husbands did not spend their money on drink they would not be in such difficult straits: solve the drink problem and the social problems that embittered the age, even the yawning disparity between rich and poor, would be alleviated.

"Let us consider the influence of the dram shop on the workman," a silk-stocking pastor sermonized that Spring. "It is from this class we hear the outcry every day that the rich are growing richer and the poor poorer. It is this class which is responsible for our strikes, our lockouts, and which puts dynamite on the doorsteps of the man who has presumed to keep sober and save his money."[6]

On the day after the excise law crackdown, Protestant clergymen thanked their Maker that some good had come of Parkhurst's craving for sensation.

* * *

The excise law that the police had suddenly begun to enforce was a product of the State Legislature, which over the years had enacted statutes restricting

Sunday activities, requiring New Yorkers to spend their day of rest without theaters, concerts, most retailing operations, or most sports and pastimes. These Sunday laws codified the mores of upstate New York, where it was feared that urban life was subverting American civilization—that wicked city dwellers had cast the old religion aside to embrace Popery and paganism and regarded Sunday as a carnival day. Some even suspected that foreign Anarchists were conspiring to destroy American principles by desecrating the Sabbath.

Sabbath defenders hoped that New England's observance of Sunday in devotion to religion and the pleasures of the hearth could allay the city's debauchery. City people rambled about getting into mischief when decent folk were abed. New York's elevated railroad could be as crowded at one in the morning as at midday. Some of its restaurants and gambling halls never closed, and in them people smoked cigarettes, that quick, nervous smoke of the dude, the pimp, the sissy and the underworld. With these considerations in mind the rustics who dominated the State Legislature tried to shut down Manhattan on Sundays, governing their urban cousins with the same firm hand that the Federal government maintained over the activities of reservation Indians, whose susceptible minds might be inflamed by tribal dances.

In the State Legislature alcohol was a political issue, with upstate sentiment running against "Rum Power" and Tammany Hall defending "personal liberty"—the liberty of New Yorkers to drink whenever they chose.

When Tammany legislators fought for the interests of the Liquor Dealers Association, temperance forces counterattacked, attributing the pressure for Sunday sales to immigrants. Invariably Tammany Hall lost the legislative battle, and Parkhurst was not alone in wondering how sincerely the Wigwam wanted a liberal excise law that would legalize Sunday sales. Losing was more to Tammany's advantage.

That April the liquor interests were beleaguered. Not only had they been frustrated again in Albany, but a change was brewing in police ranks that could only create more difficulties for them. The Grand Jury presentment had overturned the status quo at Police Headquarters on Mulberry Street, and the cop who had come out on top spelled trouble for the city's saloons.

* * *

The cop was Chief Inspector Thomas Byrnes, fabled head of the Detective Bureau. Whenever Superintendent William Murray was ill or on vacation, Byrnes would take acting charge of the Police Department, and that always meant woe for the saloonkeepers. Byrnes would call in the precinct captain and, while thumping the table, warn him that by God his men had better make more arrests the following Sunday. The saloonkeepers lay low until Murray returned to service.

On the first weekend in April, the saloonkeepers heard to their dismay that the ailing Murray might never return to duty, and that Byrnes might soon succeed him as administrative head of the Department, a post called Chief of Police in many other cities but Superintendent in New York.

As a new week began Acting Superintendent Byrnes met with the Board of Police Commissioners to discuss the presentment and emerged with a new resolve. "I will do everything in my power," he said, "to ascertain what truth there may be in the charge that policemen are failing to enforce the laws properly in some parts of the city and that there are corrupt motives for such failures."[7]

New Yorkers were generally pleased. Confidence swelled as people expected that Byrnes, the leading light of New York's police force, would set things right. Byrnes was a tough administrator who had molded the Detective Bureau into an extension of his own personality—fearless, tenacious, and obsessed with details.

When he was appointed Chief of Detectives, twelve years earlier, the financial district was rife with crime. His first act was to rent quarters on Wall Street. He assigned ten detectives to that office under orders to arrest on sight any criminal found south of Fulton Street. Invited to outline his plans to the Stock Exchange governing board, Byrnes said that men engaged in enterprises so vital to the city's prosperity merited special care. The telephone had been invented only four years earlier, but Byrnes was far ahead of the rest of the Department in using it as a law enforcement tool, and he assured the financiers that if they placed a call, he could have a detective anywhere in the financial district within five minutes.

Byrnes's Fulton Street "Dead Line" was strictly enforced. Anyone who failed to pass the visual inspection of police was asked to state his business in the district. Suspicious people who failed to turn north or blustered about their rights were arrested, sent to Blackwell's Island, and held for days without charges. In 1884 the Chief of Detectives reported that not a postage stamp had been stolen in Wall Street since his tenure began. Byrnes developed a special relationship with the city's wealthy, and the Stock Exchange showed its gratitude with a testimonial dinner for him in 1886.

New Yorkers admired the sterling Detective Bureau that Byrnes had fashioned. They read of how Byrnes's men were staked out under the shadow of a wall a whole winter night in sleet and wind. His detectives would stand in front of a pawnshop all day waiting to spot a certain face. Byrnes's bloodhounds could sift arson from a building's ashes, and sensed in the squiggles of a pen the tracks of a forgery, or in a distinctive gait the return of a hotel thief. One Byrnes detective tracked a forger from Lima through the Straits of Magellan to Montevideo to Buenos Aires and collared him in Rio de Janeiro. Byrnes assigned his detectives to specialties—jewelry, banks, the Chinatown beat, Little Italy, the Jews of the Lower East Side. His Central Office detectives were storybook heroes straight out of the writings of Jules Verne.

Now, according to the newspapers, Byrnes was using these same detectives to investigate the Grand Jury's allegations.

During the next week it was announced that Inspector Byrnes would replace Murray, and the newspapers rejoiced. Editorials reviewing his exploits reminded readers of his capture of the men who robbed the Manhattan Savings Institute of three million dollars, America's biggest bank robbery. They also recalled his work in making the Detective Bureau a model for the nation. "That force, under his order," said the *Post*, "has made the New York police famous the world over for its thief-catching skill and dexterity."[8] There could not be a more welcome appointment to head the Department at this critical moment than the man called The Great Detective, who ranked in the public imagination with Sherlock Holmes.

Byrnes said he had not sought the office, but that doing his duty would be his only aim. On the second day after his appointment, Byrnes called a meeting of Captains and Inspectors to demand strict enforcement of the law. The third Sunday in April was again marked by a rash of excise arrests and New Yorkers began to wonder aloud if, as one saloonkeeper put it, they were in for "a steady fare of Parkhurst Sundays."

The prevailing view was that the work of Parkhurst and the March Grand Jury had already been accomplished—that the public had been alerted to the need for a cleanup in the Police Department and that Byrnes had emerged as the perfect man for the job.

"The days of what few gambling-houses and disreputable resorts that are still open in the city are numbered," predicted the *Herald*, "and every saloonkeeper who has heretofore obliged his thirsty patrons on Sunday morning will be arrested the moment his doors are opened."[9]

* * *

A few days later, four men gathered in Police Headquarters. With their oversized moustaches they resembled a barbershop quartet, and for the moment they were in harmony. The fullest moustache adorned the face of Byrnes, and the others were three-quarters of the four-man Board of Police Commissioners, which had just appointed him the new Superintendent.

They met in the third-floor office of Jimmy Martin, the Police Board President and Tammany Hall district leader. Although he misconstrued his English in a dese-and-dose dialect that amused the Better People, the fleshy Jimmy dressed expensively, wore his derby tilted at a rakish angle, and was partial to glistening patent leather shoes that proclaimed how far this Irish immigrant and former streetcar driver had come in the world.

The quartet was discussing a shakeup. Formally the power to transfer captains rested with the Police Commission, but Byrnes was eager to begin his reign with a flourish that signaled a break with the past, and had recommendations to make. According to him, a mass transfer of captains would upset arrangements that police might enjoy with madames and gamblers. When the conclave ended, all but one of the thirty-six captains had been shifted to new precincts.

The newspapers hailed the reassignments as a healthy purgative. The *Post* called them "the best possible proof that Dr. Parkhurst has rendered the community a great service." The daily said that Tammany influence stood in the way of "a model police force" but that "we do expect to see the police force become, in Superintendent Byrnes's hands, as efficient in all respects as it can be made under a partisan government of this description."[10]

Superintendent Byrnes promptly issued an edict ordering precinct captains to write weekly reports on all dens of prostitution and gambling in their precincts and to explain what they were doing about them. Byrnes placed the captains under arrest quotas for violations of Sunday closing laws, and the number of arrests increased each Sunday in April.

President Martin, of the Board of Police Commissioners

* * *

Police Board President Jimmy Martin was a talented political figure who made up for his lack of education with a cunning street intelligence. And in the wake of Byrnes's debut as Superintendent he needed every resource at his command, because the pressures exerted by the saloon interests were squeezing out beads of moisture on his balding head. Every Tammany district leader in the city had warned the rough-hewn Police Commissioner that the saloonkeepers were inflamed about the crackdown—threatening Aldermen with political defeat, begging Assemblymen to do something, reminding city department heads to pass the word along that if Tammany wanted to remain in power it had better let up on its friends. Some of them also offered suggestions about what ought to be done with the Rev. Dr. Charles H. Parkhurst. Heeding their warning, Board President Martin ordered an Inspector to call all the Police Captains together in order to read a rule to them.

The Inspector mustered the Captains. "I am instructed to remind you," he read, "of a resolution passed by the Police Board in September, which disapproved sending men in plain clothes to act as spies in getting evidence of violation of the excise law."[11] There were no questions, and it did not take the Captains long to get the point—that it was time to let up on the saloonkeepers.

On Sunday, May 1, the sounds of alcoholic revelry were heard again all over the island.

In saloons and clubs the political wiseacres said that Byrnes had been overruled. "Tammany has decided to protect the unlawful sale of liquor on Sunday," the *Tribune* editorialized. "It is likewise apparent to everybody that Tammany, through the Police Board, has deliberately signified to the Superintendent its purpose to control him for its own ends."[12]

Tammany approved of Jimmy's move. "I do not believe in the spy system," said Richard Croker, the Tammany boss, "and the Commissioners, in my opinion, should enforce that rule."[13]

Byrnes kept his temper in check. "I deemed it wise and necessary," he said, "in cases where men persistently violated the law to send policemen in plainclothes to get evidence against them." But if the Commissioners forbade it, "I cannot do it, that is all."[14]

The liquor interests had regained the momentum. Although the new excise law did not permit Sunday sales of alcohol, Tammany Police Justices interpreted it to mean that the saloonkeeper had every right to be open on Sunday as long as he sold non-alcoholic drinks and cigars. When police brought excise cases to court, they testified that they found the saloons open and customers inside, but—since they were in uniform—they were not served a drink and did not see anyone else served a drink. The Tammany Justices gaveled the cases out of court.

New York quickly reverted to its old ways. NOTHING VERY DRY ABOUT THIS SUNDAY, the *Herald* headlined on May 9. Of the eighty saloons lining Third Avenue between 59th and 92nd streets, only two were closed on the second Sunday in May. Commissioner Jimmy had appeased the saloon-keepers, and in the saloons the revelers clinked glasses to toast a city where trousers, not petticoats, ruled. Parkhurst Sundays had disappeared with the coming of May.

Parkhurst contended that the real winner was Tammany Hall, since the saloons would continue to operate under legal restrictions that made blackmail possible. "Tammany does not propose to cut off its own means of support," he said. "Shut up the saloons, the brothels and the gambling houses and Tammany would starve."[15]

6

DR. PARKHURST'S
CIRCUS

Although the preacher did not bring charges against the madames whose premises he visited, a Grand Jury indicted them, and their landlords went before Civil Justices to evict them—to protect themselves against charges that they had knowingly rented premises for immoral purposes. With reporters seizing upon any news available about Parkhurst's investigations, these "dispossess hearings" became the most thoroughly covered eviction proceedings in the city's history.

During the hearings the lawyers for the madames placed Parkhurst and Gardner on the stand, and enough racy details were revealed to lead the *Times* to admonish the pastor for not delegating the dirty work to agents. But more damaging revelations were still to come, in the looming criminal trials, and Parkhurst prepared his congregation and supporters for the worst with a sermon.

"There is only one means by which a man can become thoroughly qualified to fulfill the functions to which he is divinely ordained," he said. "He must put himself in that spot, body, mind, and estate, in which Christ put himself in the discharging of the commission with which God the Father loaded him."

That commission, Parkhurst said, was an earthly one:

"Christ came into this world aflame with a purpose . . . the attempt, burning and all-engrossing, to take this world as it was and make it into what it was not; to clean it, to beautify it, to make it over from a damnable world into a blessed world.

"And the first step that Christ took in his career of redemption was to quit Heaven. . . . The world's salvation costs, and we don't want to pay it. . . . It is serious work; it is expensive work; it is self-sacrificing work; it is Heaven-abandonment work, and there is no getting round it.

"Christ not only put Heaven away behind him, but he came into the very closest touch that was possible to him with the grossest depravity that was on earth. He made himself one of us and moved about in the immediate intimacies of sin. . . . If you want to be a means of saving the world just understand that you cannot do it at arm's length."

* * *

When Hattie Adams found herself under indictment for keeping a disorderly house, she went to the place that most madames, pimps, murderers, sandbaggers, cracksmen, adventuresses and thieves went—to the law firm of Howe & Hummel, conveniently located across the street from the Tombs police court. William Howe and Abraham Hummel were the most celebrated criminal lawyers of the time, recognized experts in the science of cheating justice, suborning witnesses and bribing judges. During the trial of one of the most corrupt of the Tweed Ring judges it had come to light that Howe & Hummel on more than two hundred occasions had plied the judge with gifts that resulted in light sentences for their clients; yet the slippery pair somehow escaped censure from the Bar Association and thereafter found more clients than ever waiting in their anteroom. Their respective skills were wedded in partnership, with Howe, a blustering spellbinder of enormous girth, working the juries while Hummel, a scholarly runt, flipped through the lawbooks in search of loopholes.

Hattie Adams claimed that she ran a respectable boarding house for ladies, and that on the night in question, her tenants had been modestly dressed and behaved decorously. She noted that Parkhurst, who claimed to have had dealings with her, had not even recognized her when she called at his rectory. After hearing her version of events, her lawyers averred that she stood a chance at acquittal only if they could reduce the cleric to a figure of contempt and ridicule. Howe, who had the knack of shedding tears at will when his clients stood in need of sympathy, also had a look of outraged righteousness that he kept in good repair, and for this trial put it to extensive use.

Mrs. Adams Testifying

52

Howe began his assault on the pastor while the jury was being selected. In his questions to potential jurors the huge attorney, fitted out in a shower of diamond bijoux and clothes of clashing stripes and plaids, referred to the events in the brothel as "Dr. Parkhurst's circus" and sneered at Parkhurst as "one who calls himself a clergyman." When one jury panelist said he had heard Parkhurst preach, Howe asked, "Did you go from devout motives or to hear something sensational?"[1]

When the testimony began in the first week of May, Hummel subjected Erving to the torments of cross-examination. Overcoming his early doubts about how well Erving would hold up, Parkhurst had been impressed by the young man's purity, and had nicknamed him "Sunbeam" because nothing that Erving touched defiled him. He held up poorly, however, under questioning. Having to recount the events of the evening over and over were torture to him. Hummel lingered over Erving's description of how he waltzed around the parlor with a naked whore.

"Did you have your arm around the woman?" Hummel asked.

"I do not remember," Erving said, blushing.

"I believe you were once a Sunday School teacher."

"I was."

"Will you swear that you didn't put your arm around her?"

"I don't think I did," Sunbeam said.

At Hummel's insistence, Erving ruefully demonstrated his posture in the dance. He said he took the prostitute's hand and put his other hand on her shoulder. After this evening, he said, he was in bed for two weeks with nervous prostration. Later Parkhurst was questioned about the same scene.

"Did Erving put his arm around the waist of the girl with whom he danced in the Adams house?" Howe asked.

"Yes, he did," Parkhurst replied.

"Did you deem it a part of your duty as a minister to go to these places and drink beer and contribute money for these sad and degrading spectacles?"

The court ruled the question out of order. Howe went on.

"Did you not go there in disguise?"

"I only changed my coat."

"Did you tell Mrs. Adams you were a minister of the Gospel?"

"I did not."

"Did you remind these poor creatures that they were misbehaving?"

"No, sir."

"Did you tell them to put on their clothes?"

"No, sir."

"Did you see them undress?"

"I did not. I turned my gaze away."

"Did you play leap-frog?"

"No."

"But you drank beer?"

"Yes."

"And you are a minister?"

"Yes."

"Think," Howe told the jury in a voice keening with outraged virtue, "think of Parkhurst, the minister of the Gospel, as an instigator of crime, roaming about the city, paying with his own money poor, degraded women to disgrace themselves! I declare to you that by the law of God, by the moral law, aye! by the statutes of the State of New York, Parkhurst, the minister, is a criminal!"

The assistant district attorney tried to intervene but the wrathful Howe read the State Penal Code: "Any person who directly or indirectly commands, induces or procures another to commit crime is a principal therein."

The pastor was forced to deny the testimony of a prostitute who claimed that the reverend, his nostrils flaring with lust, grabbed her by the front of the dress and ripped it asunder, and that she ran away in alarm. Her story lost much of its credence, however, when she claimed that the trio that evening were the first men she had ever seen in the Adams bordello.

Hummel dramatized the scene in his closing remarks: "'Come to my arms!' said Dr. Parkhurst. 'I am here to suppress vice. On with the dance! Let joy be unconfined!' And glass clinked against glass, and they drank together." He called Erving "that saintly Sunday School teacher, that nice, effeminate, ladylike dancer."

Despite these efforts, the jury convicted Hattie Adams, who was sentenced to nine months in the Blackwell's Island penitentiary.

Throughout the trial the courtroom was packed nearly to suffocation. Several swells in the back of the courtroom watched through opera glasses, hoping that what they would see and hear would live up to their lascivious expectations. Judge Fitzgerald, peeved to find a woman in attendance in the courtroom, remarked aloud that he thought this was no place for one of her sex but that he lacked the authority to have her expelled. The woman looked at the ceiling as if she had not heard him and kept her seat. The testimony of the chief witnesses for the district attorney—Parkhurst, Gardner and Erving—was more lurid, the newspapers said, than had ever before been heard in an American courtroom. The details that Parkhurst had excluded from his sermon—the flowing beer, the naked can-can dancing, the sexual solicitations, the high kicker who kicked hats out of the revelers' hands, the blindfolded pianist, all tickled the public fancy—especially a game of leapfrog played with five naked prostitutes. Asked if he joined in "this leapfrog business," Gardner replied: "I was the frog."[2]

Charlie's reply amused a public that had begun to wink at such delicious scandal. As the nineteenth century drew to a close, Victorian strictures were dissolving. The bold dress of certain actresses, nudity with a pagan flavor in painting and sculpture, and Loie Fuller's skirt dancing all suggested unbridled sensuality. But nothing in that year of misbehavior burst upon the scene with such thrilling effect as the trial of Hattie Adams.

Although he had managed to remain self-possessed, mild, dignified and earnest before his courtroom attackers, the trial left Parkhurst shaken. Perjury had been brought to bear against him. The next trial was ready to start and the details involving the French bordello of Maria Andrea in Greenwich Village would be even more scarlet. Were Parkhurst prosecuted for inducing prostitutes to commit crimes, his vocation as a preacher would end.

In his book, published two years later, Gardner stated that when the time came to choose the girls at Maria Andrea's, Parkhurst had made the first selection, and that a naked prostitute had sat on the pastor's lap. If this were so, both Gardner and Erving perjured themselves during the trial. His book also states that witnesses agreed during a pre-trial meeting at Moss's office to try to counter "all attempts to show that the Doctor had witnessed French vice, for fear that the District Attorney ... would try to bring out the point that we were committing a misdemeanor in witnessing the exhibition."

When the Andrea trial began, the crowds were even more excited. Gardner said that Parkhurst, Erving, and a detective named William Howes accompanied him to the West 4th Street bordello, where they were invited to see an exhibition. Seven whores were brought out and each man was to choose one. The cost was $4 each. "She said that this price would include going upstairs with the girls afterward," Gardner testified. "She asked us to pick out our girls. I picked out one, Erving picked out one, Howes picked out one and—and that left one for Dr. Parkhurst." The reverend, according to Charlie's testimony, did not even bother to pick a girl.

The women gave what the prosecutor called "exhibitions of a degraded and beastly character" on a yellow spread placed over the parlor carpet. Afterward, still naked, Gardner said, they sat on the men's laps—except for the lap of Parkhurst. Under further questioning he amended himself to say that if a prostitute had perched on the preacher's lap, Charlie had not seen it happen. "Dr. Parkhurst did not look at the exhibition much after a while," Gardner said. "He looked the other way. Once he tried to go, but I motioned to him to stay." It was not the whole-hearted Parkhurst that he later depicted in his book about their midnight adventures.

Erving seemed feverish on the stand, and started to come unwrapped under cross-examination. He said the exhibition had disgusted him and that he had turned his head away. First he testified that he repelled a prostitute when she kissed him, then that he had submitted to the kiss, and third that he could not remember. His moment of maximum strain came with a question as to whether any of the nude women had sat in Parkhurst's lap. Erving first swore that none did, but eventually, under cross-questioning, he retreated, and said that he was unsure about it.

Sunbeam wobbled when he left the stand. "What have I been doing?" he asked. "Where am I?" Assistant District Attorney John F. McIntyre asked the defense attorney to look at Erving. They sent for a carriage. "What day is this?" Erving asked, and said several times that he had let Parkhurst down. McIntyre accompanied him down the steps and took him to Parkhurst's home.

Early the next morning he was taken to his parents' country home in Rye. A family member told McIntyre that Erving had to retire from the case for the sake of his physical and mental safety.

The defense attorney declared in his summation that Parkhurst went far beyond what was necessary to prove that Mrs. Andrea operated a brothel. All he had to do was enter and be solicited—there was no need for him to hire prostitutes to perform vile acts. "To dance with naked women," he said, "to indulge in the most frightful orgies, to kiss with harlots, to hold them in lap, and receive their kisses even after such revolting scenes—how can you say there is any sort of pure or proper motive suggested in the acts of this Christian gentleman?

"See the results of Dr. Parkhurst's work on this crushed, dispirited and broken-down boy Erving," the defense attorney went on. "Imagine the effect upon his life Dr. Parkhurst has produced. . . . Is it any wonder the poor boy's mind has given way under that frightful strain?

"In the thirty-five years in which I have practiced at the criminal bar never have I heard such frightful testimony as this. . . . Did he urge them to abandon evil? Not he. 'Here is my money,' said he. 'Come, strip your persons, pollute your womanhood, show me to what depths woman can fall, and then we'll drink together and I will put you in jail.'"

Despite a powerful defense, Maria Andrea joined Hattie Adams on Blackwell's Island. The outcome of these trials created consternation in the bordellos, since a conviction usually brought only a fine.

But the shock of the trials reverberated far beyond the parlors of Tenderloin madames. Those clergymen who only a few weeks earlier had regarded the pastor as a champion of purity began to waver. Those who opposed him had been issued fresh ammunition, and those who continued to support him now considered it prudent to do so at arm's length.

Clergymen charged that his tactics would further erode the waning influence of Christianity. A Methodist conference withdrew a resolution praising Parkhurst's work. A Baptist conference divided into pro- and anti-Parkhurst factions. It was reported that the Roman Catholic priesthood "do not as a body approve of Dr. Parkhurst's methods for the suppression of vice," and a Jesuit attacked him for arousing "a morbid curiosity" among young people. District of Columbia clergymen clashed over whether Parkhurst should be invited to speak. Among his opponents was a former Chaplain of the Senate, who said, "I thought that in his fiery zeal for reform he had gone mad."

His clerical friends took up his cause at ecclesiastical gatherings, but he was disappointed at the depletion of their ranks. The general effect of the trials, he said, was "to weaken the support of uncertain friends and to arouse our enemies to a frenzy of affected loathing and hypocritical indignation."

If the trials had been endured in order to send a few pitiable women to the penitentiary they were, in Parkhurst's view, not worth the ordeal. Such an outcome had changed nothing. The role of the police in protecting vice had not been mentioned, and the real criminals had not been placed on trial. The problem was not a matter of purity but of politics, and the solution had to be political as well.

7

THE COMING CENTURY

Two days after the Maria Andrea verdict, a crowd of seven hundred young men packed the Scottish Rite Hall on Madison Avenue, eager to see and hear the preacher who had suddenly become the talk of New York.

"A while ago," Parkhurst told them, "I was visiting a house in the course of my nocturnal exploration—."

The audience heartily laughed.

"No, it is not laughable," he shouted, "it is horrible!"

The hall shook with his lungpower, mighty as a blacksmith's bellows. For a second there was a stunned silence, and then a torrent of applause.

"My party and myself came to the foot of the stairs, leading up to a temple of Venus, and we pushed against a policeman," he continued. "While we were in the house the doorbell rang. One of my friends was in another room nearer the entrance door than myself, and he heard a conversation which passed between the person who came to the door and the girl in attendance. It was a policeman taking care of the house. Now, that is the kind of policemen we have."

He told them that on the previous evening, eighteen gambling houses in the Tenderloin, including the highly protected den of John Daly, were raided. "You have read in the Scriptures about the house that was empty, swept, and garnished. There is nothing so clean as a gambling house before a raid. . . . There was a gentleman in my house last evening while this was going on. He had been out gambling. He said that he went up to Daly's. They told him, 'We would like to take you in but we are doing nothing now.' I could have told Mr. Byrnes myself that Daly's was not running."

Again the young men laughed.

"They told this gentleman, 'We know you well, but we received instructions from the authorities to keep very close until the storm blows over. But,' says the darky who had his eye in the slot of the door, 'I'll tell you what you can do. There is a place where, until the storm blows over, we are sending our patrons.'

"We who are evangelical believe in a man's being born again. The city of New York administratively has got to be thoroughly born again. No slight modifications of policy that may be made, like the sending of a police captain from the Fourth Precinct to Goatville will suffice.

"The fault with you and me is that we do not recognize our own civic obligations to the city of which we are residents. In one sense of the term I have a profound admiration for Tammany Hall." Tammany, he said, guarded its interests and kept its obligations, and deserved the power it had won. "There is a lesson in that. You can learn lessons even from the devil, in the point of fidelity and unswerving devotion to the one object that is in view. That same kind of fidelity . . . you and I have not exercised, and that explains our present situation."

As he spoke he gestured, sometimes gently and sometimes with sweeping passion, and the audience cheered as if he were a musical conductor. Afterward about two hundred men filled out cards expressing a wish to enroll in the cause of municipal reform. With more than forty organizations represented at the meeting, with cheers ringing the hall and young men volunteering their services, it seemed to Parkhurst that "the time had come for commencing to organize the earnest sentiment of the town into action."

A few days later he spoke at the Bloomingdale Reformed Church, where he again called for volunteers and handed out pledge cards for young men to become active in cleaning up the city, with another enthusiastic response.

Having been abandoned by many of the reformers and opinion leaders of the city, the embattled pastor had decided to take his crusade directly to the people and to enlist them in it. This people's movement would not be run through the Society, which was a small organization of trustees and agents, but through grass-roots groups of ordinary citizens who would keep a vigilant eye on the police.

Parkhurst and his Board of Trustees hesitated when suggestions rose for a rally to bring together advocates of reform. The trustees feared that the trials had aroused repugnance among many who ought to be allies, and that attempts to muster a broad base of support would, in the pastor's words, "draw more sharply the line of demarcation between those who sympathized with us and those who did not." But as pressures mounted among the city's reform-minded civic leaders, he and the Society relented. A rally was scheduled for May 26 at Cooper Union.

As he mustered his thoughts for a speech, Parkhurst decided to muffle the Byrnes issue. Most of the reformers who would be joining him on the platform would be speaking in praise of the new Superintendent. From the first he had harbored doubts about the value of the Great Shakeup, and within a month he had concluded that it was "a colossal piece of police posing." He feared that misplaced confidence in Byrnes would mislead the reformers; yet he felt it would be impolitic to divide them by expressing his growing distrust of Byrnes.

Nonetheless Parkhurst intended to warn his audience to beware of the police. Every speck of information coming from his agents confirmed that the police raids upon streetwalkers and gambling dens staged over the preceding few days were fakery. He wanted to say that any campaign he would lead would be aimed not at suppressing vice but at exposing the police as the overlords of blackmail, that the underlying problem was corruption. And corruption was not just a scourge threatening one city at one moment in time but part of a larger canvas. Angels and demons were wrestling in New York and the prize was twentieth-century America.

* * *

A hopeful expectancy about the coming century pervaded the *fin de siecle*. "Progress is the law of life," the *World* observed in an 1892 editorial. "Every generation is a step in advance of the former."[1] Jules Verne said the new century would have flying machines running on electricity. Some said people would live to be several hundred years old. Others said that men would loaf and watch machines do all the hard work. Edward Bellamy had written a best-selling novel called *Looking Backward* that depicted a future society of 2000 A.D. in which all want had ended and men shared the earth's prosperity as equals. Although the details differed, all of the predictions forecast better times on the way.

In step with the optimism of the times, Parkhurst regarded progress as the inevitable outcome of cosmic law. He set his sights on the continuous improvement of society. He agreed with the *Christian Union* editorial that called urbanization "part of the providential plan for the building up of the kingdom of God."[2] The coming century would be the Age of Cities, and technology would furnish the cities with marvels, for the city represented the future of America as surely as the villages represented its past.

And yet the actual cities that Americans saw spread before them, awash with poverty, homeless waifs, and reeking air, mocked the sunny forecasts. It was a strange paradox. Instead of progressing according to plan, everything in the cities seemed to worsen from month to month. Parkhurst had seen the immensities of waste that squatted in the recesses of the cities—the airless and joyless tenements, the miasma of hopelessness, the nurseries of crime, the violent philosophies, the tramps selling their votes for rotgut liquor.

He warned from his pulpit of the perils that accompanied the great changes to come. His optimistic vision of America was tempered by a rising lawlessness, hordes of indigestible immigrants of the less advanced races pouring into the city, and a pervasive atmosphere of corruption—dangers intimately linked with the growth of urban life. To counteract these tendencies he favored limits on the numbers of immigrants admitted to the United States annually.

A new world had swept away the old America of Washington and Jefferson. Corruption crept into American life during the Civil War when contractors sold defective rifles and moth-eaten uniforms to the Union Army. After the war the rot spread. Threats of impeachment drove judges of high federal courts from the bench. Even the glory of a transcontinental railroad was tainted with the disclosure that, as a Senator put it, "every step of that mighty enterprise had been taken in fraud."[3] President Grant's Secretary of War resigned when accused of taking bribes. Members of the New York State Legislature time and time again sold their votes to big companies. Most brazen of them all, Tammany Boss William Tweed and his gang of pirates pillaged the New York City government for years before evidence of their misdeeds brought them to the bar of justice. The corruption that followed the war brought Henry Adams to the borders of despair. "Are we for ever to be at the mercy of thieves and ruffians?" asks the heroine in his 1880 novel, *Democracy*. "Is a respectable government impossible in a democracy?"

* * *

On the evening of May 26, Gardner and another detective called at the rectory to accompany the pastor to the Cooper Union rally. They had been pressed into service to guard Parkhurst, who had been receiving threats via the mail, and they rode downtown together in a carriage to Cooper Union. More than a thousand people filled the hall. They included people of all religions and of none at all. There was a sprinkling of trade unionists and hard-handed mechanics, but most of the audience consisted of the Better People from the brownstone districts where goo-goos were bred. Gray heads among the audience testified to the presence of weathered veterans of the campaign against Boss Tweed who were again answering the call to the colors. Some of the young people were the spiritual, and in some cases the actual, sons and daughters of those campaigners—rosy-cheeked youngsters full of untried idealism, eager to quit their hothouse environment for the discordant life of the streets.

For hour after hour the oratory of ministers, rabbis, union leaders and old adversaries of Tweed filled the night with biblical quotations, mythological analogy, and references to the Grand Jury's presentment attacking the police. They defended their champion against "those gentlemen of the cloth who come forward to condemn Dr. Parkhurst so vigorously." A rabbi advised that in order to get in a telling blow between the eyes it might be required to "throw conventionalities to the winds and roll up your sleeves, even though all the old women in the community cry out Alack! and Alas!" The audience cheered and stamped. Men rose to their feet with cries of "Hurrah!" and women waved their handkerchiefs, and over the course of the evening they adopted resolutions demanding that the District Attorney and the police enforce the laws and "bring to speedy justice such officials particularly as fail to discharge their duties because of complicity with evildoers."

The speakers devoted much of their attention to the new regime in the police department. Just two days earlier Superintendent Byrnes had issued an interim report to the Police Commission in which he cited great increases in arrests for Sunday excise laws, gambling houses, and disorderly houses. Rev. David Burrell spoke of the report as the "First Epistle of St. Thomas Byrnes to the Gothamites." He called it "the sincere manifesto of an earnest, honest man" and said it promised a bright future for the city.

Parkhurst listened attentively to the hopeful speculation about Byrnes, for he had with him twenty-two pages of reports from Gardner and other Society agents on police activity of the preceding few days. They had seen the police stroll into whorehouses; they had seen prostitutes bringing customers inside while the police were there. In one instance the police remained for twenty minutes. When they came out once again they passed through the whores soliciting outside and arrested a strange woman on the other side of the street. The reports showed that bawdyhouses raided only a day or so earlier were already back in business. Parkhurst felt like the agnostic at the prayer meeting.

He was introduced to tumultuous and prolonged applause, and his speech was interrupted so often that eventually Parkhurst asked his hearers to desist from cheering. Summarizing the reports coming from his agents, he advised his allies to remain vigilant and not to be thrown off the scent.

"Superintendent Byrnes six weeks ago made repeated assurances that he was going to execute the law without fear and without favor," he said. "If I have read his report right he confessed that he can't. He has run against a wall, and that wall is Tammany. There exists in the mind of the community since the reading of Mr. Byrnes's report the impression that all the results that need to be accomplished have been accomplished; that there is an entirely new animus in the administration of the police. With the facts that are at my command I unhesitatingly and unequivocally deny that. The shifting around of the police has not in the slightest degree changed the spirit or the purpose of the police.

"It's the duty of the policemen to watch the people, and it's the duty of the people to watch the policemen. It's the duty of the judiciary to sit upon the bench, and it's the duty of the people to sit upon the judiciary."

He said that he had recently been asked what candidate he intended to back in the coming elections, but that he had no such intentions. "This is a long movement," he said. "We are not working for next November. There is nothing worth working for that does not reach away into the future. Let us not be discouraged. Defeats are sometimes the very material of victory. I do profoundly thank tonight the February Grand Jury for the defeat that it dealt out to me. If it had not been for DeLancey Nicoll and the February Grand Jury I should not have been here tonight. It takes sometimes a quick lash to stir up the serious part of our nature."

He stood in the dimly lit hall, behind the gaslit footlights, on the same stage on which Abraham Lincoln had made his great anti-slavery speech of 1860. "Not only am I impressed with the presence of this magnificent audience," he said, "but I have before me the image of an audience far larger than this. Do you know, friends, that this nation is watching us? I know it. In all that I have said and in all that I have tried to do I have been strengthened by the realization that the eyes not only of our great city, but that the eyes and earnest thought of all the larger cities of our country are upon us. Whatsoever good is done in New York is done for the whole country." He looked out into the sea of faces turned toward him, and he knew that a campaign had begun—a battle for the soul of New York and for the kingdom of God.

II

TAMMANYVILLE
Summer 1892–Winter 1893

8

POLICE PARADE

The scurry and hustle of the people [on the Lower East Side] were not merely overwhelmingly greater, both in volume and intensity, than in my native town. It was of another sort. The swing and step of the pedestrians, the voices and manner of the street peddlers, and a hundred and one other things seemed to testify to far more self-confidence and energy, to larger ambitions and wider scopes, than did the appearance of the crowds in my birthplace.

Abraham Cahan, *The Rise of David Levinsky*

In those days, newly arrived immigrants were called greenhorns, and as soon as he was released from Ellis Island, the typical Jewish greenhorn began learning about New York power.

Perhaps in his imaginings about freedom in America, the greenhorn had thought nothing about it. Now he had to deal with power in unfamiliar new contexts. In Russia power had been absolute and undivided; here it was segmented and spread about. Here the rich had power which they reserved for themselves, like the rare vintages in their wine-cellars; the politically connected had power which they guarded jealously; the cops held sway over the streets; and the people had a power that the immigrant from the little town in the Pale had never known before—the power of public opinion.

The first thing the greenhorn ran smack into was the police. His fellow immigrants told him to have no truck with them. Do not speak to them, do not brush close, do not lounge while one is passing. Let your motto be "Run rather than be clubbed."

Overall the cops—or the buttons, as they were called downtown—were more likely to club an Italian than a Jew, because Italians were regarded as treacherous, and undoubtedly armed with a stiletto. But the activity of the Jews in garment-industry strikes made their heads frequent targets for cudgeling. "There is more law in the business end of a nightstick than in a decision of the Supreme Court," was the motto of Clubber Williams, the maestro of the nightstick who had risen to the rank of Inspector with few questions raised about his philosophy of law enforcement.

The police clubbed all they wanted because they always got away with it. Even when they rushed into the wrong apartment and beat up the wrong person they got away with it. Even when they beat an elderly physician who tried to help a tramp they had beaten, they got away with it. They would even sneak a poke in the ribs of a defendant as he stood before the Police Justice. Far from being secret events, accounts of such behavior were published in the newspapers. If they could deal with impunity with respectable members of the community, they had no fear whatever of clubbing a trembling Hebrew immigrant.

They had the power to club at will. It was not a power that a Czar had given to them, but a power that the public had conferred upon them.

* * *

Up until recent years New York had been a lawless place. For one fifteen-year period a five-story tenement house in the Five Points area averaged one murder per night, and when the cops ventured into the area, or into alleys known as "Murderer's Row" or "The Bucket of Blood," they entered only in squads.

The criminals feared nothing. Bandits would roll their plunder through the street in daylight. One gang transported its loot in a hearse over to Mother Mandelbaum, the city's leading fence, whose connections extended through the country into Canada. Enterprising men set up stills in buildings along the Hudson River, with scouts posted to throw into the river intruders who might venture into the area at night. Revenue officers investigating liquor law violations were killed.

During the Civil War, thousands were killed in a draft riot, Negroes were lynched on lampposts and a Negro orphanage burned to the ground, and Union troops had to be called from the battlefield to restore order.

After the war, street gangs like the Rag Gang of the lower Bowery and the Boodle Gang around Centre Market controlled parts of the city, overwhelming the police by force of numbers. Men dressed in decent attire considered it foolhardy to walk in many areas of the city at night, sometimes only a block from Broadway. A man who trespassed into such dangerous byways might have a bucket of ashes overturned on his head from a window above and, before he could recover from his surprise, a half-dozen thugs would jump upon him, beat him to insensibility, and throw him into the harbor to drown. Gangs formed alliances with political organizations, and battled on Election Day with enemy gangs allied to rival political groups. Eventually the public declared its patience exhausted and granted free sway to the police to use any means necessary to make the streets safe.

Suppressing these gangs became the top priority of Byrnes and Clubber and the generation that rose through the police ranks after the Civil War. Most of the Department's captains and inspectors took part in that bloody campaign, filled with as many war-whoops and ambushes as the campaign in the West to subdue the Indians.

The police resorted to a tactical force that they called Strong Arm Squads. Dressed in citizens' clothing, these mobile squads swept through designated areas accosting known criminals and knocking them senseless without provocation. Uniformed police walking regular patrols were provided with the names and descriptions of gang members, with instructions to beat them on sight. Relentless clubbing was also used to stop the street fighting of rival gangs.

No cop was more closely linked with this era than Alexander Williams, known as the King of Clubs. When Clubber Williams was assigned to a down town precinct in the area of Houston Street he made his mark by picking fights with the two most vicious thugs in the precinct and beating them limp with his club. Then he hurled their unconscious bodies through the plate glass window of the Florence Saloon, their customary hangout. When their friends came out to remonstrate with Clubber, he left a half-dozen of them bleeding and groaning on the curb.

Promoted to captain in 1871, Clubber was assigned to command the East 35th Street precinct—the bailiwick of the Gas House Gang and the most onerous assignment in the city. Within the area that the gang claimed as its territory, its most frivolous whim was considered more binding than the sternest law. The gang looted houses, broke into stores, and fought battles with other gangs with impunity. Upon taking over, the up-and-at-'em Captain organized a Strong Arm Squad that stormed out looking for any Gas Housers who dared show themselves, drove them into hiding and restored decorum in the streets.

When some citizens complained that he had fostered a spirit of police brutality in his precinct, the outrageous Clubber responded by inviting reporters to a demonstration. He took them to the corner of 3rd Avenue and 35th Street, which had been the center of Gas House Gang activity, and hung his gold pocket watch and chain on a lamppost. The men then left and walked about the precinct, and when they returned to the lamppost, the Captain's watch was ticking away undisturbed. For citizens who demanded safe streets at any cost Clubber was their kind of cop.

Through the late 1870s and early 1880s the police mercilessly stalked one band of criminals after another, and with their dissolution it appeared that the era of the gang was passing into history. But not without a final challenge, as the most ferocious gang yet rumbled out of Mulberry Bend.

The Whyos were the boldest, the largest in membership, and the best-connected politically of the street gangs. On most nights they gathered at Billy McGlory's saloon, then located on Hester Street. No man was accepted as a Whyo until he had "done up his man"—committed murder. "It is not always the love of money that spurs them on to the breaking of the law," the *Herald* wrote, "it is an instinctive desire to be thought well of, to be esteemed, honored by their fellows as the performers of deeds that others dare not do. Many of these rowdies would rather break a policeman's head, or a citizen's, than make an easy capture of somebody's money."[1]

They were available as mercenaries for political machines. The Whyos intimidated shopkeepers into supporting the candidates who had hired them. The political connections that they formed with ward politicians helped extricate them from trouble.

An elite corps of officers was assigned to the precinct to run the Whyos out with strongarm tactics. In 1888 two Whyo leaders were hanged in the Tombs, and the once-feared gang began to unravel. With the passing of the Whyos the great metropolis had been pacified.

Glowing magazine articles made them famous for their derring-do, and the New York cops represented the standard by which police forces were measured. "I have walked through every part of the city within late years," Howard Crosby, Parkhurst's predecessor as president of the Society for the Prevention of Crime, said in 1889, "and I should not fear now to walk through any street at any hour of the night. New York is the safest in the world in this regard."[2]

* * *

As the Jews poured into New Israel, they came up against a police force that had become a law unto itself. The police ruled the streets, searching at will whomsoever they wanted, declaring curfews when they chose, restricting areas to those whom they allowed to enter, and dispensing summary justice.

Visitors from other nations were shocked by the alacrity with which New York police used clubs. "If one calls the attention of a New Yorker to it," one Briton wrote, "the invariable answer is that as the city is a gathering-place of the scum of the Old World it will not do to check the authority of the police."[3]

If the greenhorn wandered from the Lower East Side a mile or so uptown to Madison Square he would be in the hub of the city. Around the little park of shrubs, benches and statues lived many of the city's most elegant and important people. A majestic statue of Admiral Farragut, the work of Augustus Saint-Gaudens, adorned the square. On the east side of the square stood Parkhurst's church, and north of the church was Stanford White's new Madison Square Garden, designed in the Moorish style with a tall dominating tower. A few blocks away was the brownstone where until recently Hattie Adams had operated her parlor house.

And at that renowned square, on Decoration Day of 1892, under a silken, plush-bordered, gold-embroidered canopy, the chieftains of Tammany Hall waited for the annual police parade. Police Board President Jimmy Martin, in a frock coat, light trousers and a shiny black top hat, was leaning from the reviewing stand into the street, instructing a police sergeant about some point or other concerning the march. His fellow Commissioners and Mayor Grant sat nearby.

A varied assortment of New Yorkers—gentlemen and immigrants, shopgirls and merchants, children with their nannies—mingled there at the parade's terminus. While waiting they were preoccupied, as New Yorkers always were, about who currently ruled the roost.

It would probably go something like this. Two uptown lawyers deplored Irish control of the city. An Italian newcomer pondered whether the Greek Revival bank building that he had seen on his way uptown was the Duke's palace. A well-dressed matron expressed the hope that the next Mayor could be persuaded to appoint a woman to the Board of Education. The wife of one of the parading cops hoped that her husband would join one of the Tammany Hall social clubs, so that he would get promoted. Their thoughts flew in all directions but all their faces were turned south as they waited for the parade to reach them. In the distance they discerned approaching shapes and heard the strains of horns playing *America*. Cheers broke out as the marching men neared the square's little park.

Bedecked in a black uniform trimmed with gold buttons and gold cord, and capped with a white helmet, Superintendent Byrnes led the parade sitting astride a dark-bay charger like a Commander-in-Chief at the head of his army.

Immediately behind Byrnes came 120 mounted police and a regimental band, and after the first horse-drawn patrol wagon came the magnificent Inspector Williams. As Clubber strutted past the spectators nudged each other in delight, and when the parade halted for a moment he posed for the camera fiends who hastily set up their tripods or kodaked him with their new "snapshot" box cameras.

Twenty-five hundred of New York's finest trooped behind Clubber, marching up Broadway on the cobblestones twenty abreast. Each policeman wore a gray helmet and a summer suit. Each marched proudly, displaying in his bearing the reputation of the force that had tamed the streets of New York. On nearing the reviewing stand at the square, where Broadway meets Fifth Avenue, the police swaggered just a tad more.

"Say what you will about New York's policemen," the *World* observed the following morning, "they're a gritty and a wholesome set of men."

9

DYNAMITE

The Anarchists were a new downtown presence. According to drawings in the newspapers, they had spiky hair and beards, wore menacing scowls, carried sputtering dynamite bombs in their hands, and said in strangled foreign accents: "A pound of this stuff beats a bushel of ballots!" That depiction was not entirely fanciful, since the quote came from the lips of one of the hanged Haymarket Anarchists, and the standard cartoon Anarchist looked much like the leading Anarchist in America, Johann Most.

In April he completed a ten-month sentence on Blackwell's Island. It was not Johann Most's first prison term. It was his second in America, and he had also served time in European prisons. This time, however, the agony of his confinement had quite unnerved him. Had it not been for the saloonkeeper Billy McGlory, he said, he would have been bereft of any interesting company at all.

His friends and followers celebrated his release with a rally at Cooper Union. Four huge red flags bedecked the platform, and the applause was tumultuous as he tested his oratorical skills.

"I am an atheist!" Most proclaimed. "I believe in no God! But I am not satisfied to deny God alone. I also deny the right of any man to govern me. . . . I am a revolutionist and a believer in the doctrine of force because I know history. I know that no ruling class has yet been driven from power without bloodshed. I know it must come and I ask you workingmen to prepare for the catastrophe which cannot be avoided." Every government in Europe was quaking before the columns of the advancing proletariat, and he promised that the same would soon be occurring in the United States.

Johann Most was shouting, but not exaggerating. Headlines kept American newspaper readers apprised of Anarchism's siege of Europe. In France a bomb blew up a restaurateur who had delivered an Anarchist leader to the police. Juries acquitted Anarchists rather than suffer the retaliation that would follow a guilty verdict. "Everybody feels in his bones that something is going to be blown up," the New York *Times* reported from London in the month of Most's release.[1] Many on the continent feared that a secret International League of Anarchists would destroy the world.

Rootless and soapless immigrants had smuggled the doctrine into the United States, and its dangers were growing. During a labor rally in 1886, in Chicago's Haymarket Square, a bomb was thrown at a phalanx of advancing police, resulting in a fusillade of police bullets and the death of seven policemen. As a result of the Haymarket riot, four Anarchists were hanged for murder, a fifth cheated the hangman by committing suicide in his cell, and three others were serving long prison terms.

Superintendent Byrnes warned that Anarchists "display a fondness for taking up residence in New York City."[2] Once there they repaired to smoky saloons where, in Russian, German, Yiddish and a thick English they discussed the big blast to come. They owed much to Alfred Nobel's invention of dynamite, which conferred upon the Anarchist a power that matched all the massed forces of state oppression.

* * *

Alexander Berkman and Emma Goldman were committed to the cause of Anarchism. They had come to court to support Most when he was sentenced. Goldman had taken his hand and said she would give anything to take his place. Johann Most asked her to write. Berkman accompanied Most on the ferry to Blackwell's Island, and returned deeply impressed at his bearing. Angered by cartoons of Most in the newspapers, Emma suggested to "Sasha" (his Russian nickname) that they blow up one of the newspaper offices. Sasha dissuaded her, pointing out that the newspaper employees were just lackeys and hirelings doing what the capitalist bosses told them to do. But he loved her passion for justice.

Emma sneered at the genteel view that women did not belong in saloons, and used them as her salons. She despised marriage because it embodied capitalist possessiveness, and she had left behind a husband in Rochester. Women were not supposed to smoke, so she smoked forty cigarettes a day. She and Berkman encouraged each other to overcome the constraints of conventional society. They expressed their convictions so explosively that they made even their Anarchist comrades uncomfortable. The Jewish Pioneers, after admitting Emma

Goldman as the first woman member of their little Anarchist band, barred her from their meetings because she climbed on tables and shouted for blood. Goldman responded with the taunt that Judaism was just another outdated concept to be tossed into the dustbin of history.

When Most was released in April, Emma and Sasha were no longer living in New York. They were operating a coffee shop in Worcester, Massachusetts, and living an untrammeled life with Modest Stein, an artist. Whenever Stein sold a painting, he brought Goldman a floral bouquet. Berkman deplored such extravagance while the Anarchist movement stood in need of funds, and Stein mocked him as a fanatic. Emma confided to Berkman her attraction for Stein and suggested a *ménage a trois*. "I believe in your freedom to love," he responded, while admitting his possessiveness. Berkman hated such lingering bourgeois traits. He and Emma hated a lot of things. They hated the Wall Street they had left behind in New York. They hated the spire of Trinity Church, the church of the Astors that pointed heavenward from Wall Street. They hated Byrnes, who had sent Most to Blackwell's Island. But above all else in the Massachusetts summer of 1892 they hated Henry Frick.

Emma Goldman polished the coffeepot and flipped the pancakes to make their venture prosper. But the picayune successes of the well-run coffee shop held no thrills for Emma and her complementary pair of lovers. They avidly followed events in the labor struggle at Carnegie's steel plant in Homestead, Pennsylvania. Henry Frick, board chairman of the Carnegie interests, had called a lockout. Frick served as Andrew Carnegie's Minister of War in the battle against unions. When a labor dispute erupted over his insistence on reducing wages, he vowed to break the union. He had the plant converted to a fortress of barbed wire and barricades.

At the break of day Stein or Berkman would rush out to buy the early editions of the papers. They sat up nights poring over the situation in Homestead, so excited that they could not fall asleep.

One afternoon Emma Goldman was serving a customer when she spied a Homestead headline in the newspaper he was reading. She cajoled the paper from his grasp. She read that the families of strikers were being evicted from company houses and that sheriff's officers had carried a sick woman out and dumped her in the street. She flushed with indignation at Frick's callous inhumanity. She shooed out the customers, closed the shop and ran to the flat. Her lovers sat up as she burst in waving the paper.

Berkman jumped to his feet on reading the account. "Homestead!" he cried. "I must go to Homestead!" She flung her arms around him, exclaiming that she would go too. "We must go tonight," he said, "the great moment has come at last!" Nodding in agreement, she felt certain that the American worker was about to wake from his slumber.

Abandoning the coffee shop, the trio began formulating plans on a train chugging toward New York. They would write a manifesto to the steelworkers and, since they were clumsy with English, would find someone to translate it for them. They would have the German and English texts printed in New York and then distribute them in Pittsburgh.

Events in Homestead, meanwhile, had taken a nasty turn. Frick telegraphed the Pinkerton detective agency to hire a private army of three hundred strike-breakers, which disturbed many Americans. "Is it right that a private detective agency shall maintain a standing army, a thing forbidden even to the several States of the Union?" asked a *World* editorial. "Is it well that a body of armed mercenaries shall be held thus at the service of whomsoever has money with which to hire them?"[3] Defying public opinion, Frick arranged to have his army subdue the strikers and restart plant operations. The strikers were determined to drive them back. When the Pinkerton operatives arrived the workers had the plant surrounded and were prepared to resist. Shooting broke out and men were slain on both sides. When the Pinkerton mercenaries failed to recapture the plant, Frick prevailed upon the governor to call out the state militia to put down the steelworkers.

Faced with this crisis upon arriving in New York, Goldman and Berkman realized that a deed of ultimate political seriousness was demanded: they must kill the tyrant. Following the recipe in Johann Most's *Science of Revolutionary Warfare*, Berkman tried to concoct a bomb. "Sasha's experiments took place at night when everybody was asleep," she wrote. "While Sasha worked, I kept watch. I lived in dread every moment for Sasha, for our friends in the flat, the children, and the rest of the tenants. What if anything should go wrong—but, then, did not the end justify the means?"

After several failures at bomb manufacture, Berkman decided that a bullet would kill Frick just as thoroughly. He would take the train to Pittsburgh, the headquarters of the Carnegie interests, where he would buy a gun and shoot the capitalist dog in his office and he would then bite open a glass vial of nitroglycerine and blow himself up.

Although Goldman wanted to partake in the kill, they had only enough money for a single railroad ticket to Pennsylvania. Berkman said that Emma, being the more accomplished speaker, should stay behind to explain the significance of his act.

Sasha left with her the task of raising funds to forward to him so that he could buy a revolver as well as a suit of clothes to make him look acceptable when entering Frick's office. Emma Goldman bought herself high-heeled shoes and fancy lingerie and on Saturday night she joined the walking sisterhood on 14th Street. The whores, some barely into puberty and others masking their gray hair with garish dye, took their customers upstairs and returned to saunter up and down the block, accosting every man who passed and shouting remarks at men who would not pause to speak with them. The policemen exchanged badinage with the cruising women.

Emma Goldman had several offers but the customers failed to meet her standards. With the evening almost spent, her feet aching from their ordeal in high heels, she made one last try, accosting an elderly man who took her to a saloon on 13th Street and 3rd Avenue, bought her a drink, advised her that she lacked any knack for streetwalking, and gave her some money. She asked him if he were one of those Parkhurst types who were trying to cleanse the city of vice. He laughed and said he was not a professional busybody.

* * *

Berkman walked through Homestead, a mill town near Pittsburgh, to find it in shambles. Disheveled men walked about carrying shotguns or revolvers and the ground was strewn with burnt sticks, empty shells, oil barrels, broken furnace stacks, piles of steel and iron. The plant, strung with barbed wire, bristling with watchtowers and ramparts, had been transformed into Fort Frick.

"The time for speech was past," Berkman wrote. "Throughout the land the toilers echoed the defiance of the men of Homestead. The steelworkers had rallied bravely to the defense; the murderous Pinkertons were driven from the city. But loudly called the blood of Mammon's victims. . . . It is the People calling. Ah, the People! The grand, mysterious, yet so near and real People."

Berkman regarded himself as a doomed man but consoled himself with the knowledge that his eloquent lover in New York would explain his sacrifice. His deed would resound in the poorest hovel of the enslaved proletariat and would make the capitalists tremble. The slaying of Frick would light the torch that would consume an oppressive America—a society ruled by police clubs in the service of a specious democracy.

He wanted to sweep away all government, as well as property and religion. He believed that when all that had been shed, like an old skin, the world would lie moist and glistening, ready for a new start. His highest aspiration was to sacrifice his life "for the great suffering People."

* * *

The people, unaware of the great upheaval about to occur, chased frivolity.

From New York's upper Fifth Avenue the women and children had skipped away to summer in their country cottages at Newport, or the Berkshires, or the New Jersey shore.

South of Millionaireville, the larky set amused itself without a thought for the morrow. On the roof garden of the Casino, men in summer straw hats drank beer under Chinese lanterns and laughed at a Parkhurst imitator. A comic played the minister dancing and singing "Ta-ra-ra Boom-de-aye" in gay abandon while his face maintained a demure and dignified mien.

Farther downtown in a Bowery concert hall the tough blokes, dancing with their bundles (slang for their girlfriends) displayed gap-toothed grins when chorus girls in tights tacked on a new verse to the biggest song hit of the year:

> Dr. Parkhurst on the floor
> Playing leapfrog with a whore,
> Ta-ra-ra Boom-de-aye
> Ta-ra-ra Boom-de-aye.

In the rathole saloons and the concert halls offering "Entertainment for Man and Beast," The People bought hot corn and threw the cobs in the gutter, won kewpie dolls in the shooting galleries, cursed and sang and drank, oblivious of the deed that Berkman was about to commit on their behalf.

* * *

On the evening of Saturday, July 23, Modest Stein rushed into Emma Goldman's room waving a newspaper. An intruder had shot Frick in his office! Berkman had done it! At last their anxious waiting was over! In their excitement they praised Sasha as a hero who would be numbered henceforth among the immortals. Powerful emotions clashed within Emma Goldman; while she feared for her lover in the custody of the Pittsburgh police, she wanted to celebrate with the working class of the world. She reminded Stein that Johann Most was scheduled to lecture that evening before a group of German Anarchists. "He will surely speak of Sasha's act," she said to her artist-lover. "We must go to the meeting."

She had not seen Most since his release from Blackwell's Island. He had not answered the letters she had written to him in prison. Most had made it clear that since they had allied themselves with a rival Anarchist group he wanted nothing further to do with them. On the way to the meeting, it pleased her to think that while Most stood on the platform busying himself with mere words, the joyous workers in Homestead would be shouting their praises for Berkman's deed.

But as she sat in the hall, looking nothing like the Anarchist stereotype, re-sembling a schoolmarm in her starched blouse and pince-nez glasses, her antic-ipation turned sour. This was not at all what she had expected—this sodden crowd which ought to be cheering and calling for a general strike. She squirmed, fighting the impulse to pounce as Most raved on. Her anger welled up as it be-came clear that he was deliberately going to ignore the most momentous revolu-tionary event of the age.

She found his lecture threadbare. Although he roared as loudly as ever, there was more venom than ferocity in his delivery. She heard a guttural weariness that matched the lines that his time on Blackwell's Island had deepened on his care-worn face. Almost as an afterthought, tossing it as a tidbit to the audience, Jo-hann Most casually alluded to the shooting, admitting that he had only skimpy knowledge about the event and suggesting that it was hardly worth anyone's at-tention. "It is probably the usual newspaper fake," he said. "It must be some crank or perhaps Frick's own man, to create sympathy for him. Frick knows that public opinion is against him. He needs something to turn the tide in his favor."[4]

Rage suffusing her face, she rose from her chair and accused him of using the peoples' money for liquor. All the ridicule that she usually applied to the enor-mities of the ruling classes was leveled at him.

Her hostility further entangled a knotty relationship. The object of her attack had once been a demigod to Emma. In the smudgy pages of his newspaper, *Frei-heit*, he had hailed the assassination of Czar Alexander II in 1881 by inviting his readers to employ the same measures upon the other crowned heads of Europe. The Johann Most that Emma Goldman once revered would have gone off after the lecture to join celebrants at downtown Anarchist bars to raise a stein in trib-ute to the hero who shot Frick.

Emma and Sasha had adopted the views of Johann Most as their own: that in striking down tyrants the revolutionary acted as an avenging angel; that one dar-ing act could awaken the people more effectively than oceans of speeches. In-spired by his assurances that a great cyclone was gathering force to sweep away the desiccated dogmas of the past, they espoused Most's doctrine of propa-ganda-by-the-deed.

* * *

Stunning news followed in the Sunday newspapers.

Berkman had failed in his mission. Henry Frick was expected to recover from his wounds. The vial of explosives in Berkman's mouth had been discovered and taken from him. He assured reporters that "the workingmen of this country are with me in this affair," but in principle only—he had no accomplices in his deed.

The New York newspapers did not accept his word, and as soon as it came to their attention that Berkman was a well-known figure in the subterranean world of New York Anarchism, they sprang into action. Reporters raced out to dig up every fact they could find about this Russian Jewish immigrant. The press worked on the premise that the radical underworld of New York was teeming with Berkman's accomplices, and the hasty exit of practically every known Anarchist from the city was taken as evidence that they knew something they would rather not talk about. By the following day the newspapers reported that the police had come up with a list of Anarchists associated with Berkman, and that all of them were being checked for links to the Frick shooting. Most intriguing, the newspapers had learned that Berkman lived with a female Anarchist, also a Russian Jewish immigrant, who made fiery speeches to crowds of screaming radicals. It was said that the overbearing woman wielded influence in radical circles. By the time the day was over city editors were instructing reporters to get hustling and find the woman they had dubbed the Anarchist Queen.

They reported that the police had found a notice of an Anarchist meeting to be held the day after the shooting and had become convinced that the Anarchist network had scheduled rallies in advance to shriek in bloodthirsty celebration. One newspaper said that a policeman searched a downtown Anarchist and found a press clipping listing the city's millionaires and their estimated worth, which might be a death list. Another said that the police regarded the attack on Frick as the opening splash of a bloodbath to avenge the Haymarket executions by killing the rich.

Little in the way of solid facts came out of the newspapers' headlong rush for news. But the figure of Emma Goldman emerged boldly as the newspapers exaggerated her influence. A week earlier few people outside Anarchist ranks had ever heard of Emma Goldman, and within a week the newspapers had made her notorious.

Cutting short his vacation, Superintendent Byrnes returned from the New Jersey shore to investigate links between the Pittsburgh shooting and New York terrorists. He sent Central Office Detectives into the Lower East Side in search of evidence against Goldman and against Johann Most. The detectives worked on the theory that the shooting was part of a larger plot, and that Berkman was an ignorant triggerman assigned to kill Frick.

One evening when she returned to her apartment from a meeting she found that someone had broken in through a fire-escape and taken all her pamphlets, photographs and letters. But at the first mention of her name in the papers she had destroyed anything incriminating, including the material left over from Berkman's attempts to make a bomb.

However hard he puffed on his pipe, Byrnes could not find evidence linking Most or Goldman to the shooting. Perhaps the strong-willed Goldman had dominated the pliable Berkman, and had sent him to Pittsburgh, but he could not prove it.

Two reporters found her at Zum Groben Michel's, the favorite saloon of the Autonomist Anarchists with whom she associated. While other customers hissed the reporters, she denied getting money from Johann Most to give to Berkman and accused Most of living handsomely on the contributions of working people. "Most is a coward and simply talks," she said. "He would not dare to go out and kill a capitalist, as did the brave Berkman."[5] She denied that she and Most had ever been lovers.

"I suppose you will write a lot of lies," she glowered, "because your people must pander to the capitalists who give you bread, and the capitalists like to read the lies about us Anarchists."[6] Finally the reporters left in the face of threats, the Anarchists helping them out with pushes and blows to the back of the head.

But perhaps that was just their way to show contempt for the press, which dared to claim that the workmen themselves overpowered Berkman in Frick's office after the shooting and held him until the police arrived. According to the reports in the capitalist press, as the police hustled the gore-covered Berkman into a patrol wagon, workers shouted "Shoot him now!" and "Give him what he gave Frick!"; and a crowd followed the patrol wagon to the lockup where the police struggled to shut the gates to protect the Anarchist from the people.

* * *

Emma Goldman's conspiracy with Sasha Berkman to kill Frick was the defining moment of her life. "You are mistaken if you think that it was only 'the humane promptings of a girlish heart' which impelled my desperate act," she later wrote. "It was my religiously devout belief that the end justifies all means. The end, then, was my ideal of human brotherhood."[7]

Goldman's banalities about her love of humanity, however, were the products of later reflection, after she had owned up to her part in Berkman's deed. For many years she dealt with the issue by proclaiming her innocence and by prompting fellow Anarchists to speak indignantly of hateful police attempts to implicate her in the assassination plot.

Furthermore, the attempt on Frick's life was not only a crime, it was also a mistake, grounded in assumptions about power brought over as baggage from Russia. There terrorism had been fostered out of desperation, a resort to violence in the face of absolute denial of political dissent.

As Trotsky noted, in Russia even capitalism was a creation of the Czarist State. But Frick was not a creature of the American political apparatus. And neither Byrnes nor the exasperating newspaper reporters were part of a chain of command that reached its pinnacle in the White House; that was a misreading of American politics based on Russian conditions.

Emma Goldman's refrain that there was no difference between Russia and America—that all governments were alike because they all oppressed the people—was based on ignorance and lack of understanding of how power worked in New York.

In the city, power was limited and counterbalanced among Fifth Avenue clubs, saloonkeepers, the police, the newspapers, manufacturing interests, the Republican minority—and last but by no means least, Tammany Hall.

10

A BIG WIN FOR
TAMMANY HALL

In the Third Assembly District men came to the saloons of Barney Rourke and Silver Dollar Smith in search of jobs. In the Second they stopped by the Tammany social club of Police Justice Paddy Divver, known as "De Judge." Men also waited in the Sheriff's office for John Sexton, the Undersheriff, who led Tammany's 23rd District. They sought audience with Jury Commissioner Barney Martin, who was captain of the 8th (as well as brother of Police Board President Jimmy Martin); or with Deputy Court Clerk P.J. Scully, captain in the Fifth District; or with Police Commissioner John Sheehan, who ran the 13th district. They fidgeted in Special Sessions Court waiting for Maurice Featherson, who was just a subpoena server at the court, but also the Tammany captain of the 22nd District.

Every day the anterooms and corridor benches of the municipal buildings swarmed with ward heelers and job-hunters. Greasy men with bumpy noses and bull-necked men in baggy trousers spruced themselves up as they waited to be ushered into the presence of an assistant department head who might have something for them if they came in with Tammany approval.

The district captains listened keenly to the entreaties of the unemployed. The reason they held public office was not to oversee the work of their departments, but to crowd more names of Tammany men upon the city payrolls. The more jobs Tammany could hand out, the more votes it would command and the more power it would have.

* * *

The uptown gents, the property owners who paid the city's taxes, derided Tammany as a clubhouse of sports, ex-pugilists, saloonkeepers, gambling touts, men of shady backgrounds—as one of them put it, "a government of the worst, by the worst, and for the worst." They complained that the Wigwam levied taxes to provide make-work jobs for an army of drones—Irish immigrants, most of them, or their misbegotten offspring. Yet, according to the taxpayers, the municipal employees did not actually work; they could be found on the street corners of an afternoon, smoking high-flavored cigars, wearing loud suits, large diamond rings and diamond stickpins, and speculating about how many more jobs there might have been had New York been chosen over Chicago for the Columbian Exposition.

The downtown blokes had a more favorable view of Tammany Hall. Boss Tweed had won their hearts by sending them a turkey every Christmas.

Twenty years earlier the silk-stocking people had united to ruin Tweed, but as soon as he was disposed of they abandoned politics and returned to their usual pursuits. The Wigwam, however, regrouped its forces and within a few years was thriving once more. In 1889 Hugh Grant took office as Tammany's mayor and, as Silver Dollar Smith put it, New York was Tammanyville again.

Defying press attacks and scorning pretense, Tammany worked diligently, year in and year out, for its own interests. It operated on the basis that politics was a form of war in which the spoils belonged to the victor. Richard Croker, the Tammany Boss, put the doctrine bluntly: that "all the employees of the city government, from the Mayor to the porter who makes the fire in his office should be members of the Tammany organization."[1]

* * *

Like all power in America the power of Tammany Hall was limited. But Tammany's power was aggressive, its leaders convinced that if it failed to advance it would wane.

That summer the police force, which had never been free of politics, began to feel the creep of Tammany encroachment. On several occasions the two Tammany braves on the Police Board interfered with Byrnes's stabs at reform. Even when confronted with incontrovertible evidence of wrongdoing, the Police Board tended to go easy on cops with Tammany credentials.

Byrnes feared that the Department was "verging on demoralization" because whenever a cop arrested a saloonkeeper with pull the Board transferred the cop out to Goatville. When Byrnes protested to Jimmy Martin he was told to mind his own business, transfers being the purview of the Board, not of the Superintendent.

* * *

The Big Boss of Tammany was Richard Croker, who as a small child had emigrated from Ireland with his family. The Crokers had lived as squatters in a wooded area of Central Park. He started in politics as leader of the Fourth Avenue Tunnel Gang, a group of brawlers-for-hire in the pay of Boss Tweed. Although in his mid-fifties, Croker could still strike fear in anyone who saw his eyes glint and his hands ball into fists.

Slow-witted, devoid of intellectual interests and lacking social skills, Croker nevertheless was treated in the city with singular deference. Any policeman who recognized him would flourish his baton. Saloonkeepers all but kissed his ring at the liquor dealers' ball. When Croker entered the dining room at Delmonico's conversation halted at some tables until he was seated. When he paused before a table of Tammany men the diners rose. His frown caused others to lose their appetites.

Boss Croker was chunky, about five feet, nine inches in height, weighing about 180 pounds. He was disconcertingly mild of manner and soft-spoken. He swelled his chest perceptibly when he boasted that men who stuck with him were never in want. He denied being a Boss but admitted that it was his good fortune that his friends from time to time asked his advice. Of course, he agreed, Tammany Hall was a tightly run organization. Organization, he said, was the trend of the times—everything was based on it and nothing in these days could be done without it.

The Better People compared Croker to Boss Tweed, but except for their humble origins the two men had little in common. Tweed was a schemer and a trickster, distrusted even by his associates, while Croker was incapable of deceit. Tweed reveled in his roguishness, while Croker believed fervently in his virtue. He believed himself and his Tammany underlings to be men with the interests of the common people at heart.

* * *

The captains of Tammany sprang from the working class, immigrant boys or the ragamuffin sons of immigrants. Most had little schooling and while still small children had been apprenticed to carpenters, grocers, tanners, stonecutters. They went to school nights, or never went at all, and never got past the elementary grades.

Timothy "Dry Dollar" Sullivan of the Third District grew up with holes in his soles. His father died when he was seven, leaving a penniless widow with six children. As a little tyke he brought home a wet beer revenue stamp and dried it, having mistaken it for money, an enterprise that earned him his nickname. Little Tim got himself a blacking-box, walked into the Oak Street police precinct, and arranged with the Captain to black the boots of policemen in the precinct. He grew into a tall, slim, handsome young man—totally corrupt and inclined to use strong-arm tactics on his opponents, but he had a sweet side to his nature and often helped poor newsboys.

Men like him owed nothing to the uptown gents, whom Dry Dollar called "silk hats and silk socks and nothing in between." They stood before the membership on their own merits. They rose or fell on their popularity, their local strength, their knowledge of men, their executive ability, and their devotion to the cause.

Some of them moved to better neighborhoods, but they all were expected to remember that they had learned to crawl and walk on the earthen floors of shanties. They looked after those down on their luck, made sure that widows had food and fuel and that orphans had shoes. They thought of Tammany as an instrument of democracy both for the native-born poor and the immigrants, whom they introduced to the city and American ways.

The typical constituent was not looking for comprehensive solutions to governmental problems but for help in meeting his pressing needs. If a family was burned out, the local Tammany district leader promptly reached the scene to offer shelter, a meal, and money for clothing. The district leader provided employment; if there were no city jobs available, Tammany would call on a contractor favored with city contracts to hire a few willing workers.

Tammany men could never depend on a night's sleep. A local leader might be shouted out of bed at 2 A.M. to put up bail for an arrested bartender, or to go to a tenement fire where a dozen families shivered in the cold. He would pay the rent of a family about to be dispossessed, or would send one of his men for a word with the Justice to keep it from happening. The district leader went to weddings, funerals, and Bar Mitzvahs, rejoicing with them that rejoice and weeping with them that weep. He attended church fairs, neighborhood dances and boat excursions. He bought raffle tickets. His social club provided chowder parties in the summer and balls in the winter. And he was always ready to listen to complaints—of saloonkeepers against street cleaners, storekeepers against pushcart vendors, tenants against landlords. Because Tammany's leaders did not forget their roots, the common people remembered them on election day. And in their favor lay Tammany's power.

* * *

In October campaign fever struck the city. Brass bands played on bandwagons on behalf of Candidate So-and-So, followed by torchlight processions of marching men who chanted: "What's the matter with So-and-So? He's all right!" The dailies, which delighted in campaign folderol, printed as much as could be squeezed into the columns. Everyone took elections seriously in New York, and voters could always be expected to turn out at a rate of more than 80 percent.

At election time the greenhorn saw the spirit of American gaiety. In the old country, government officials were arrogant and dour, and he had approached them hat in hand. But in this land the municipal officials courted him with flattery and pageantry, clapping him on the shoulder and buying him a drink. What a country!

Aware that public opinion was capricious, Tammany was determined to keep control of City Hall at any cost, willing to go to any lengths to get the required votes—even if that meant buying them outright. Patrolling the lodging houses, the all-night Bowery bars and the side-street bonfires where scarecrows warmed their hands, Tammany ward heelers recruited voters in the closing days of every election campaign not by the recitation of political platforms but by the promise of payment in silver.

As the election drew nearer two opposing forces were bivouacked in the city. One was comprised of the tramps that arrived every October, skulking about the Bowery while they waited for Tammany to buy their votes, a transaction that also included a meal ticket and a few days of free lodging. But these fleabitten hobos looked almost respectable when compared to the opposing army, the grog-blossomed men that the Republicans were assembling as Federal Deputy Marshals. The Marshals consisted of 3,000 saloon brawlers and eye-gougers, recruited in the same districts of Philadelphia in which the Pinkerton Detective Agency signed up the strikebreakers that it had sent to Homestead.

The Republican administration in Washington had dispatched the Deputy Marshals to guard polling places on Election Day and question men about their eligibility to vote. Tammany Hall protested that the Federal Deputies had no right to go behind the guardrail at the city's polling places. They could be arrested, the Wigwam said, like any ordinary citizen, and could be ejected from polling places.

The Federal Solicitor General responded that anybody attempting to interfere with the Marshals would be arrested. "Keep them out at your peril," said the National Republican chairman, "and you will be taken to prison cells with broken heads."[2] The drumbeats of the two armed camps jittered the citizenry who, remembering bloody campaigns of old in which rival political gangs killed each other in the streets, feared that election day would bring out bayonets and brass knuckles.

* * *

Like fireworks, political campaigns in New York were loud, flashy and brief. On October 18, three weeks before election, Tammany convened to nominate candidates. Two hours before the meeting began, the Wigwam on 14th Street was packed with braves. As the hubbub on the floor gained volume, Boss Croker mustered the district captains in his office to tell them that he had decided to replace Mayor Hugh Grant with Thomas Gilroy. When the district captains emerged and placed Gilroy in nomination, several hundred men cheered lustily on finding out whom they wanted to lead them on the ticket.

The decision on Grant had come about a few weeks earlier when the mayor, summoned to the Wigwam, found the deep-chested, broad-shouldered Boss seated at a desk facing the 14th Street windows.

The Boss told the Mayor that he wanted John J. Scannell (his best friend) appointed as a fire commissioner. Grant responded that the appointment would evoke tremors of public disfavor. Not only was Scannell the Tammany liaison with the illegal gambling interests of the city, but he had stalked a man and emptied four chambers of a revolver into him in an act of cold-blooded murder and then escaped punishment on a phony insanity plea. The Mayor expressed concern that the press would flay him and that his political career would be ruined. Unable to get Croker to relent, he refused to honor the Boss's command.

Croker accepted Grant's decision with that impassive mildness and calm that unnerved his adversaries, but once left alone he commenced making plans to discard Grant for a mayor who would do his bidding.

Gilroy, who had distinguished himself as Director of Public Works, was regarded as an okay candidate. "The worst that can be said of him," the *Times* noted, "is that he is a thoroughgoing Tammany man; but he has shown himself capable and energetic, and apparently zealous for efficiency in the public service."[3]

His Republican opponent was Edwin Einstein, a German Jewish manufacturer who chided Tammany Hall for bossism. Focussing exclusively on the presidential campaign, the Republican machine ignored Einstein so openly that the *Post*, divining the true situation, called Tammany's Gilroy the real Republican nominee. Those who worked with Republican Boss Tom Platt knew that he put no effort into the local campaign and in fact encouraged some of his associates to support the Tammany ticket.

With the advantage of a heavy Democratic majority, its reservoir of purchased votes, its grip on the votes of immigrants, its accomplished use of patronage, and the drag of Republican apathy, Tammany Hall (as the odds-makers put it) "had a dead bead" on the mayoral election.

The only remaining obstacle for Tammany was those Marshals, strutting about as election day drew near while their supervisors bragged that they would make thousands of arrests for voting fraud—men who had registered to vote in several districts, men who did not actually reside in the city, and immigrants who had been illegally naturalized.

Tammany officials wanted the police to crack down on the Marshals. At the police muster on the Sunday before election Police Board President Martin told the senior officers that he would brook no interference from these usurpers, who had come only to intimidate honest New York voters. Byrnes responded that the use of Marshals in polling places on Election Day was a legitimate exercise of federal power and advised his men not to interfere with them.

"After the meeting," Byrnes recalled, "two police captains returned to my office and kissed my hand for what I said. I believe that if I had not said what I did at the time of the difference with Martin, in the presence of the captains, that there would have been serious trouble in many parts of the city."[4]

There was not a single instance of police interference with Federal Marshals on Election Day. However, alcohol probably deserved more credit than did Byrnes for the peace that prevailed, for after intimidating a few voters in the morning, many of the Marshals were drunk by midday and sleeping it off in an alley by midafternoon. While they snored Thomas Gilroy swamped his opponent, giving Tammany Hall control of the city for two more years.

The imbroglio between Byrnes and Martin was another indication, like the struggle over arrests for Sunday sales of alcohol earlier in the year, that Tammany politics was encroaching upon police affairs. After the election a rumor circulated that Byrnes was ready to quit, and that Grover Cleveland, the Democratic President-elect, would offer him the job of heading the Secret Service. But Byrnes, who was getting Wall Street stock tips that were making him rich, chose the financial over the governmental capital.

*　*　*

After the election Tammany Hall seemed impregnable. In prior elections the Third District had been one of Tammany's few trouble spots, but Croker fixed that by robbing Platt of his most effective allies.

"The Thoid," as the residents called it, was the most volatile district in the city—a place where intimidation, patronage and loyalty counted for all, issues and political labels for naught, where grudges survived beyond the grave. And the toughest political captain in that part of the lower East Side was Barney Rourke, whose saloon on Forsyth Street had become Tammany's district headquarters.

Barney headed a political club with a bottomless reservoir of votes. Were a voter too sick or too drunk to walk to the polling place, Rourke dispatched one of his henchmen to hoist the voter on his back and stagger off to the polls with him. His association provided free coal every winter to nine blind men who were led into the voting booth. If his candidate won an election by one thousand votes to six, Rourke was unable to sleep until he found out which six men had voted against him. Short, rotund, and nondescript in appearance, a man who shunned notoriety, politics was his only interest.

Over the years Rourke had been on retainer for the Republicans. After the previous year's election, however, he had fallen out with Republican Boss Platt. When Rourke transferred his services to Tammany Hall his entourage included two colorful protégés—Silver Dollar Smith and Timothy "Dry Dollar" Sullivan, saloonkeepers with their own political following. All three of them, in fact, had been on the list of untouchable saloonkeepers that Parkhurst had handed to a hostile District Attorney a few months earlier.

Alderman Smith's saloon was headquarters for the thugs of New Israel—a viper's den of Jewish arsonists, fences, usurers and their strongarm enforcers. Silver Dollar's real name was Charles Finkelstone, but he had thrown it overboard on the way to America.

Smith usually sat performing his aldermanic duties at one of the tables in the front of his saloon—a tall, portly fellow with a distinguished mane of silver hair. He could be smooth and gregarious, but those who had mussed with him found that if Rourke was the toughest political captain in the Thoid, Silver Dollar was the meanest. He relied on thugs to drive out his political rivals by force, and he resorted by reflex to violence. In 1889 he gouged a critic in the eye in a confrontation at a political meeting. Silver Dollar protected several brothels in the New Israel and owned a number of tenements that he kept in disrepair and for which he charged exorbitant rents.

Ruthlessness of the same kidney had marked the political rise of another Rourke protégé—the young, guileless and impatient Timothy "Dry Dollar" Sullivan. The brass-knuckle squadrons of the Irish Tammany captain included remnants of the Whyos, who had used his Comanche Club as headquarters in the gang's active days.

Croker was delighted with his new allies, for they had been hard-fisted opponents in the past. Working to marvelous effect, they had brought in lopsided margins of victory in the Thoid.

Tammany Hall's adversaries had been beaten so soundly all over the city that many of them were hoisting the flag of surrender. Some of the old faithful complained that it seemed more advantageous to join Tammany at its moment of triumph than to have labored in its behalf through thick and thin. But Croker saw political advantage in showing old foes that quick rewards awaited them in Tammany Hall.

As a political leader Croker was a power broker who choked on his own words and wisely refrained from tongue-tied political speeches. He lacked the magnetism and the passion of Goldman and Parkhurst. Even his value as a leader was disputed. Some of his contemporaries regarded him as an illiterate tough and a pig-headed dullard. Others saw in Croker a brilliant field marshal who had led Tammany Hall to an unbroken string of victories. Whether he deserved his position or not, the ex-pugilist was the most powerful Boss in the city's history, commanding a Tammany Hall more tightly organized than Tweed could have imagined.

His power disturbed many New Yorkers, who saw in it the paradox of a democracy that led to one-man rule.

"There is no more democracy about a really efficient boss than about the Khan of Tartary," bewailed a speaker at the Commonwealth Club, a group of silk-stocking anti-Tammany Democrats. Machine politics, he added, led inexorably to bossism "so that, finally and logically, an autocrat is at the other end of the road of complete organization just as surely as a mob is at the first end."

The power of a political boss was so limitless, said another speaker, that the only effective counterforce was a rival organization. "But the counter-organization, initiated for purposes of correction, is liable, if left to itself, to quickly run to a like excess," he warned.

A Tammany spokesman, invited to join the evening's debate, responded that Croker was working for the same social aims as were the club members—and more successfully. He advised reformers to join Tammany Hall, which, he said, "always keeps its doors open" to welcome those who espouse democratic principles.

Mr. Croker, he explained, stood for "organization," the emerging force that was reshaping business into giant companies. He valued the loyalty of a disciplined cadre. Naturally someone had to march at the head of the column, and that role had fallen to Croker.

Debaters disagreed on many points that night, but they agreed that Tammany had harnessed the power of the people and that nothing—no club, no movement, no competing machine—had shown the strength required to wrest it away. A downtown political observer put it this way: "Tammany is the real stuff. The rest are like the foam on a glass of beer—mostly air, and soon to go flat."[5]

11

THE AUTONOMIST

The city that Croker had mastered was oversized. Even the anti-Tammany papers told his story in terms of American success—the shantytown immigrant who had risen from poverty to power. The city was America in concentrated form, so crammed with boundless ambitions, incandescent personalities, unlimited resources, and wondrous machinery that it appeared to many people that anything was possible in this Baghdad-on-the-Hudson.

An English writer observed that New York attracted "men with iron in their blood, the girls whose pulses leap and tingle with the eager flush of adventure and ambition, [who] desert the village and the farm to crowd the roaring mart and glaring street."[1] Rich families from the heartland flocked to the city, as did tycoons who were taking charge of the new giant corporations, immigrants of high and low degree, political refugees, thinkers promoting their political ideas and philosophies. In New York, said another, "life is so intense and so varied and full of manifold possibilities that it has a special and peculiar fascination for ambitious and high-spirited men of every kind."[2]

That same pull had drawn Emma Goldman. From Rochester, where her immigrant family had settled, she had journeyed south to the metropolis, fleeing a dreary marriage, escaping from a provincial city of busybodies.

Hers would not be a life of ease and gay dinners at Delmonico's. But she too was mastering the city.

* * *

Notoriety had become burdensome. After the police raided her apartment, her landlord evicted her, and she found that no one wanted the Anarchist Queen as a tenant. Goldman spent her nights in all-night cafes or riding a train back and forth from the Bronx. She lost weight and developed a chronic and worsening cough (eventually becoming incipient tuberculosis). Finally she found a boarding house on East Fourth Street where she was able to rent a room.

On her first night knocking and a man calling for Viola awakened her. Every night thereafter men came by asking for women. "It finally dawned on me," she said, "that I was living in a brothel." Thereafter she made a good living by mending and making clothes for the prostitutes. Living in anonymity, she walked past policemen without being recognized.

Miss Emma Goldman

She vowed that if Sasha Berkman were condemned to death in the Allegheny County Courthouse she would blow it up; and she extracted a promise from Modest Stein, her alternate lover, to aid her in the deed.

As she was waiting to speak at a Baltimore rally in the middle of September, a telegram was handed to her. Sasha had been convicted and sentenced to twenty-two years in prison. She became dizzy; someone took the telegram out of her hands and helped her to a chair. She heard someone speak of canceling her speech, but she would not allow that. "I looked wildly about me, gulped down some water, snatched up the telegram, and leaped to the platform," she recalled. "The yellow piece of paper in my hand was a glowing coal, its fire searing my heart. It caught the audience and raised it to ferment. Men and women jumped to their feet, calling for vengeance against the ferocious sentence." As their shouting grew more raucous, police burst into the hall, wielding billyclubs and driving the Anarchists out into the night.

Back in New York, Goldman threw all of her efforts into speaking engagements to protest the severity of the sentence. She decried the injustice of the punishment meted out to the brave revolutionary.

She cherished the romantic notion that a handful of people could provoke revolution with a daring act. Goldman continued to wait for word that Berkman's deed had struck the opening tocsin in the struggle of workers against owners. She and Sasha had believed that killing Frick would lead to further activity—marches, protests, a general strike against American oppression. She was beginning to realize that the American working people failed to understand Berkman's selfless act on their behalf.

From every quarter of the city and the nation, among every social class from millionaire to pauper, arose a vilification of Berkman, the workers more extreme in their condemnation than were the owners. He was portrayed as a coward and a lunatic. At rallies to raise money for the families of the Homestead strikers, labor union officials attacked the Anarchists for fomenting violence and called for severe punishment for Berkman. The Homestead steelworkers cursed Berkman and expressed hope for Frick's speedy recovery. Even the Socialists, even Marxists, even some Anarchists condemned Berkman for his attack. None of the radicals shed any tears for the industrialist, whom they regarded as a brutal despoiler of workers, but they called the shooting a misstep of abysmal stupidity.

The hostility extended to her as well. Socialists censured her and labor leaders crossed the street rather than be seen with her. The followers of Johann Most blocked her entrance to Anarchist meetings and chased her with a curse.

This was the unkindest cut of all. Nothing that she had ever known of the great Anarchist orator had remotely suggested that he would belittle Sasha's great act.

* * *

Goldman had become a disciple of Johann Most after her arrival in New York. She heard the story of his life as a radical on the Continent, and his flight from Germany to escape arrest—a caustic tale of Olympian revolt.

He demolished the pretenses of American democracy. Its proponents claimed that the people ruled, but the people were merely manipulated by the lies of newspaper editors, politicians and business leaders. The people did not truly rule themselves, but were led around by the nose. The capitalist rulers did as they chose, reduced the wages of their workers when it suited them, increased work hours and speed-ups at will, hired and fired as they liked, and the people had nothing to say about it. The rich who owned America crushed anyone who stood in their way. These owners could not be changed or influenced; they could only be defeated in battle, scattered and exterminated.

She admired his intransigence. Inevitably she and the grizzled veteran, old enough to be her father, capped their political affinity with a garland of love. But in time the authoritarian Mostian style that had exhausted the patience of so many fellow Anarchists eventually grew intolerable for the free-spirited woman.

Anarchism had developed as a doctrine that stressed cooperation in voluntary associations in revolt against centralized authority. Some Anarchists identified with the working class and called for a proletarian revolution. More conspiratorial Anarchists built tightly organized secret organizations. And by the 1870s a virulent strain of terrorism had found its way into Anarchism. This emphasis fascinated Most, who longed to avenge himself on a society that had oppressed others and wronged him, and whatever noble sentiments he found in Anarchism were mixed with a dark desire to exterminate "bourgeois vermin." Emma Goldman had also been captivated by Anarchism as vengeance, but above all she sought in her politics an ideal to ennoble her life, to lift her above the mundane into the realm of the extraordinary.

With Sasha Berkman's help she found this in the Autonomists, a strain of Anarchism that stressed absolute individual freedom. She found her element with them, for the more boundlessly Emma Goldman expressed her outrage at the false values, injustice and corruption of the existing order the more the Autonomists applauded her. Filled with mutual spite, Autonomists and Mostians refused to recognize or even greet each other at meetings.

Finally Most demanded that she choose between him and Berkman. Goldman protested that he sounded like a bourgeois husband and that she would not be possessed.

* * *

The furor that followed the attempt upon Frick's life tore away any remaining ties of civility and respect between Goldman and Most. She was shocked when Johann Most mocked Berkman as a bumbler whose aim was politically as well as literally askew. Most's initial suspicion, propounded on the night that the extra editions first carried the story—that the shooting had been faked to benefit the Carnegie interests—was mistaken as to the facts but politically astute. Johann Most had come to grasp the power of public opinion in America, and he understood that Berkman had reversed the nation's sympathies, that the fool had fired his gun at a heartless tycoon and had wounded a hero. Within days Americans were praising the brave and magnanimous Frick, who had comported himself with honor when he was attacked; for according to the news stories Frick called on the men who captured Berkman not to harm his assailant and he seemed more concerned for the gunman's safety than for his own wounds.

Johann Most also had expedient reasons to denounce Berkman. Although an intrepid revolutionary, Most was suffering a crisis of nerve. He had been in prison twice in America, had been denied citizenship, and the newspapers were calling for his deportation. If deported to Germany, he would be arrested for a charge still hanging over his head—high treason. And he was in these straits because of the clumsiness of Berkman, who had converted his woman to a heretical school of Anarchism.

Under these pressures Johann Most, for the first time in his life, changed his views. Dynamite was not the answer. Terrorism was futile in America because the workers lacked class-consciousness and did not understand the proper use

of violence. In some countries, he said, "propaganda of the deed" was appropriate; but in America, propaganda of the word was legal and permissible and
should be adopted as the Anarchist method for propagating its ideas.

Goldman was as scandalized as would be a Catholic had the Pope declared
the Virgin Birth a hoax. Berkman had become for her the great revolutionary of
the age, and those who bespattered him committed a blasphemy. She would not
let Most's betrayal go unavenged, and by now she was so overwrought and un-
controlled that she might do anything.

When Most spoke at Odd Fellows Hall on December 18, Goldman brooded
in the front row, close to the low platform. She was seething, her heart was
thumping, and a whip was concealed under her long gray cloak.

If Most delivered his standard speech that evening, he exposed the
hypocrisies and lies of capitalism, rejected American society, jeered at its rancid
fixed elections, the moral bankruptcy of its leaders, and the sham of civil liberties that the police annulled with cudgels whenever the workers fought for their
rights.

Then Emma rose. "I came to demand proof of your insinuations against
Alexander Berkman," she shouted. The hall fell silent. She pulled out the whip
and leaped at him, lashing again and again. She broke the whip over her knee
and threw the pieces at him. Someone grabbed her from behind. "Throw her
out! Beat her up!" people yelled, and a threatening crowd began to move toward
her. Friends picked her up bodily and forced their way to safety outside.

* * *

There was more to her assault on Most than just her hunger for notoriety. It was
an expression of the immense value that she placed on integrity as the essence of
politics.

To her the allure of Anarchism lay in its grand sweep, its fire and brimstone,
and to suggest that in America it should confine itself to speeches and editorials
conjured up for her a politics that would replace the thrills of battle with the
humdrum talk of the negotiating table.

She would defy them all, champion Berkman, tell his story and take his part;
this was her rationale for remaining at large while he suffered in prison.
Although she had seriously considered leaving America, she stayed for that
purpose.

But only New York would do; no wonder that many years later, in her memoirs, Emma Goldman opened the drama of her life neither with her birth nor her
passage to America but with her arrival in New York in flight from Rochester.
The metropolis provided a forum in which to present her ideas, a milieu for the

intoxicating liberty that she sought. Individual expression was the motif of Goldman's life—not winning over the majority to her point of view, nor domesticating Anarchism so that the bourgeoisie would accept it. That, she suspected, was the true reason why the Homestead strikers were wringing their hands over the shooting of Frick—to pander to public opinion. She despised public opinion. Whether the police clubbed Anarchists into insensibility by order of the Czar, or to satisfy a public that demanded safe streets, their heads were just as bloody in either case.

At this moment in 1892, she believed that her political future rode the crest of the coming wave. Everywhere in the cities intellectuals and artists were confronting the dying century with new ideas and new movements; the challenge that they made against established institutions in the name of individual vision was becoming the very definition of what we have since come to call modernism. This idea of a total revolt against the old order was closely allied to Emma's view of Anarchism. A new century was coming, and Emma Goldman would be in the vanguard.

12

THE WORK OF THE KINGDOM OF GOD

When Jay Gould died in December, New Yorkers shrugged. "He has done nothing but to heap up money, often by dishonorable means, and leave it in trust for his children," the *World* said. "It is not a death that will cause any public sorrow."[1]

Gould, the Wizard of Wall Street, was beyond editorial barbs at last. A flim-flammer who bribed judges, bought politicians, and fleeced the public, he had devoted his life to stock-market trickery and company raids. His demise was greeted with hoots among the city's lowlife, who flocked to his mansion where the body was laid out.

At first only a few knots of people, staggering with drink, stood about the streets, but more joined them, and soon a rummy crowd filled the intersection of Fifth Avenue and 47th Street. Men began to mock the black streamer on the door of the mansion, and the crowd laughed idly. A wild-eyed man inveighed against the trusts that set prices and controlled industries, and others, taking up his cry, began to curse the capitalist system. A gathering of crackbrains was turning Gould's wake into a macabre carnival. Police arrived in force to keep order.

Magnificent carriages, bearing millionaires in black and footmen dressed like ringmasters, rolled up to the curb. Policemen shoved back the masses to let them pass. Barges of flowers arrived, borne up the steps and fading from sight behind the frosted glass doors.

By dusk, when the numbers of the idlers had thinned, Superintendent Byrnes alighted from a carriage and was greeted at the door of the mansion. An hour later he emerged with George Gould, the oldest son. The pair walked together up Fifth Avenue, deep in discussion, undoubtedly reviewing details of how Byrnes would continue to guard the safety of the beleaguered family.

* * *

Byrnes had first been summoned in 1881, when Gould received a letter accusing him of robbing widows and orphans and threatening his life. In a masterpiece of detective work, Inspector Byrnes enticed Gould's tormenter into revealing his aims through a personals column in the *Herald*. As Byrnes had guessed, the blackmailer had been ruined financially by speculating in Gould stocks and wanted the Wizard to rescue him by means of inside tips. Byrnes trapped the blackmailer in a dragnet as he dropped a letter to Gould into a mailbox.

The capture of Gould's blackmailer became celebrated in the annals of crime, and forged Byrnes's national reputation. It also put him on intimate terms with the Gould family which, because of recurring threats of kidnapping or blackmail, required his services often.

Having twice been publicly assaulted, Gould lived in fear of a violent death. Radicals assailed him as a symbol of the fraud of capitalism. Naive people thought he controlled the stock market and blamed him for their losses. Even at home he was besieged by demented callers.

Most unnerving to Gould was the bombing of the office of his friend and associate, Russell Sage. George Gould was in the adjacent room at the time, and barely escaped serious injury. In the rubble of the blast Byrnes found the head of Sage's attacker but was unable to identify him. The Inspector placed the decapitated head in a jar and rounded up a half-dozen advocates of dynamite in the hope of uncovering an Anarchist plot. The head in the bottle remained a mystery, however, until a reporter traced the dynamiter to Boston and discovered that he had been a bond broker who had suffered financial reverses. He was described as "a fine, respectable, gentlemanly looking fellow."[2] Newspaper accounts explained that the head had been mistaken for that of an Anarchist because it had been placed in an undersized jar, which distorted the features.

News of the Sage bombing stirred the cranks out of their quarters to leer and menace anew, and several began to pester their perennial target, Jay Gould. The family sent for Byrnes. Gathering in the drawing room, they recounted their problems with an extortionist, and Byrnes with the help of his Detective Bureau was able to scare him off.

But the incident, following so closely upon the bombing of Russell Sage, left Jay Gould unnerved. He removed his name from his office door in the Western Union Building. Two muscular bodyguards guarded his doors at all hours. He placed a man in the Windsor Hotel, across the street from his home, to watch for prowlers. City detectives were assigned to protect the family when a reception was held for Gould's daughter. His health declined and he grew more timorous, but in the end he escaped the violent death that he feared, dying of natural causes in his bed.

Gould was buried in a family mausoleum in Woodlawn Cemetery, in a lead coffin soldered tightly to make it unassailable, and placed inside an oaken box. A cadre of watchmen was hired to patrol the area day and night to protect the body of the patriarch from kidnap. Its location—on the highest knoll in the cemetery, devoid of bushes and shrubbery—had been chosen for purposes of security.

* * *

New York could be a frightening place for the wealthy. Cranks muttered to themselves about the imagined wrongs that millionaires had done to them and radicals pasted notes to doors on upper Fifth Avenue threatening DEATH TO THE RICH!

This was where Inspector Byrnes came in, for protection of the rich had long been his stock-in-trade. Whenever a millionaire faced threats or blackmail Byrnes would soon be on his way uptown in a carriage. He would examine the note, pocket it for closer perusal back at his desk, and with confident authority assure the assembled family that detectives would be assigned to protect them from harm. Then he would excuse himself and order his waiting carriage back to Mulberry Street while the family, watching his departure from a window, would sigh with relief.

It was believed that Inspector Byrnes whisked the culprits into his net by calling upon shadowy sources who provided him with names. His deepest secrets of detection were employed in the cellar of Police Headquarters, where Byrnes had perfected his exquisite means of extracting confessions. His study of the criminal mind had showed him how to use mental torment to break the will, a method he called The Third Degree.

The rich found Byrnes reassuring, and made up his chief constituency and base of support. Otherwise they did not involve themselves in the city and contributed little to it. It was said that the Goelet family patriarch cancelled a half million-dollar bequest for a hospital because he feared that Tammany would siphon off the money. Moses Taylor, president of the City National Bank, told friends he would never bequeath anything that Tammany could plunder. As a consequence of such mistrust, philanthropy in New York was parched, and the great metropolitan center of the Western Hemisphere lacked a great public library, a great hospital, a great zoo and a great art museum.

In general the rich regarded politics as a dirty business and refused to become involved in political debates in which they might be insulted by their inferiors. Abstaining from the exercise of their power, and interested only in their safety, the rich acquiesced to Tammany rule.

* * *

Sophisticated tolerance prevailed at a welcoming banquet for Mayor Thomas Gilroy at the Lotos Club, a Fifth Avenue haven for rich men with literary and artistic interests who liked to gather in evening dress to clink champagne glasses together.

These men agreed that the new mayor was tough and smart, and they were prepared to live with him. Over after-dinner coffee, brandy and cigars one speaker expressed his sympathy with Gilroy for having to endure the slings and arrows of those who took public officials to task. No wonder then, he said, that "many distinguished and good citizens take so little interest in politics and are so unwilling to be identified with any party or the holding of office."

Chauncey Depew, the railroad executive, turned the group's attention to Edwin Einstein, the unsuccessful Republican candidate for mayor, who was seated beside Mayor Gilroy at the head table. "Office is an honor which speedily dies," said Depew, "but to run for mayor in the city of New York as a Republican is a decoration which, like the Order of the Legion of Honor, lasts forever." His listeners chuckled at these sallies from Depew, known around the nation as a crackerjack after-dinner speaker. Congratulating Einstein for keeping on friendly terms with the new Mayor, Depew jested that Tammany had favored the loser with a respectable showing in the vote tally since "it was in the power of Gilroy and his friends to mark down any amount they pleased." The men laughed again.

Then civic leaders, wealthy merchants, and the gentry rose from their seats to toast a Tammany Mayor.

* * *

All over the city the bells of reconciliation tolled. Tammany welcomed to the fold the former Republican leader of the Tenth District, who brought his social club with him. And when the General Committee met for the first time in 1893, there were so many new members that some could not get into the Wigwam on 14th Street. The scene, said the *Sun*, represented the arrival of the political millennium.

Silver Dollar Smith, who used to denounce Tammany Hall, now proclaimed that it had "the interests of the people at heart." The silk-stockings, he said, had long been predicting that Tammany would destroy New York, taxes would empty the purses of the property owners, and the financiers would desert Wall Street. But these dire forecasts had rung false, and New York had flourished under Tammany stewardship.

Triumph, however, did not slacken Tammany's efforts. At the Hoffman House, Boss Croker conferred with officials of the saloonkeepers' trade associations on a secret but historic deal: the saloonkeepers who were members would not have to worry about police visits on Sundays if the association contributed regularly to Tammany's political campaign chest.

Croker gave little thought to the reformers—the gents who had been waving banners and cheering a few months earlier when Parkhurst stirred them at Cooper Union. For a few days they had talked excitedly about cleaning up the city, but their enthusiasm quickly ebbed. Reform was a wave; Tammany, the sea itself.

* * *

But in that city of singular destinies there was one citizen whose diligence matched that of his enemies. All through the fall and into the wan light of the new year, the gaslights burned late at the rectory as the pastor of Madison Square mapped out the defeat of his foes.

He spoke wherever and whenever he was asked. He oversaw the work of Parkhurst Society agents in presenting evidence to Police Justices and securing warrants. He talked with men all over the city, passed out cards and collected names. He urged his listeners to form neighborhood associations to keep pressure on the police to enforce the law, and he created the City Vigilance League to aid in the nurturing of such groups. "Wherever the administrative blood beats in this city," he said, "the finger of the Vigilance League shall be upon it, counting its pulsations." He suggested that League members learn about their neighborhoods, keep vital statistics, voting records, keep tabs on saloons, gambling houses, brothels, and even on the cleanliness of local streets.

So many concerned people from all over the city began to visit his rectory that he had a hole drilled in his study floor so that he could look into the parlor downstairs and see who was waiting. He had brought with him to the metropolis his memories of the New England town meeting, and he listened carefully, to learn from the concerns of his visitors and then to shape and direct public opinion in his cause. When he spoke of the task ahead, he spoke of "a long hope" and of the patience that would be required. Newspaper stories referred to his cause as The Parkhurst Crusade, but to him it was his mission—the work of advancing the kingdom of God.

HUSH MONEY

Winter–Spring 1892–1893

13

CHARLIE IN A FIX

That is what the Church is for, the establishment on earth of the kingdom of God, not merely the rescue of a few individuals, but the sanctification of the very framework of society and making holy all its administrative machinery.

—Parkhurst, *My Forty Years in New York*

Thomas Jefferson had called New York "the sewer of all the depravities of human nature." Even in his time the prevailing ambition in the city was not to make a living but to make a fortune and its politics was neither art nor science but merely a scramble for advantage. And by the end of the century the city that Jefferson loathed had spawned a gutter politics that erased the line between politicians and hoodlums—like Tammany Boss Richard Croker, who stood trial in 1874 for killing a political foe. (His trial ended in a hung jury and he was not tried a second time.) Godkin, the *Post* editor, charged Tammany Hall with "the transfer of government to the hands of the criminal class."[1]

Rev. Dr. Charles H. Parkhurst had been raised in a different world. Like other Protestant churchgoers of New England, he had been brought up to believe that the United States played an ordained role in history. In the churches in which young Charles Parkhurst had spent his Sundays, pastors compared George Washington to Moses. In Sunday school he learned that American history revealed (as McGuffey's Fourth Reader put it) "the divine scheme for moral government." Just as Providence had guided the three ships of Columbus to the shores of the New World, he believed that Providence had blown into his sails to take him to New York.

Now one might think that this New England outlook would impede his understanding of a city that embodied concentrated power. But the star-spangled piety that Parkhurst had absorbed during his upbringing helped prepare him for the mighty task he had undertaken, for it was nothing less than saving the city. Parkhurst believed that a current had sent him to New York for a purpose, like a leaf bobbing in a stream, and he found himself suited for the duties assigned to him, because saving entire cities was the kind of missionary work that matched his ambitions. The endeavors of his fellow clergymen to save souls singly seemed inefficient to him when by thinking and acting systematically he could help bring about the salvation of a whole society.

As he attempted to master the city that he intended to save, he found that he had a lot to learn. He quickly came to respect Tammany Hall as, in his words, "a superbly organized band of brigands." It was organized not for the public good; nothing could illustrate that more appropriately than the horse droppings that Tammany's Street Cleaning Department left undisturbed until they turned to dust and blew in the teeth of the public. Tammany worked only for its own pocket, but it worked hard, and Parkhurst was annoyed to hear men grouse about the Wigwam when they were themselves unwilling to roll up their sleeves and take on The Work.

Sometimes he accompanied Lawyer Moss and Agent Gardner to police court. Moss and Gardner went there for search warrants so that they could raid a brothel, while Parkhurst wanted to see how the courts worked. As the bottommost rung on the ladder of criminal justice, the Police Justices wielded considerable power. They issued search warrants; they set, increased, or reduced bail; and they arraigned virtually everyone accused of a crime. Police Justices would send felonies and other big cases up the ladder to the Grand Jury, but they had the authority to dispose of minor criminal matters—simple assault, disorderly persons, public drunkenness, prostitution—and could pronounce sentence for these offenses.

Watching Police Justices in action was instructive to anyone who sought to understand how the city worked. One would begin to get the picture upon hearing a pushcart peddler complain that he should not have been arrested because he paid his protection money every week, while the Police Justice continued to sift through court papers, apparently deaf to the tune being played.

The pastor discovered that a Police Justice could pluck whores from the very gates of the penitentiary as neatly as a pickpocket could lift your gold watch from your vest pocket. Charlie Gardner had netted prostitutes at a brothel, then had taken the case before a good Police Justice (not a Tammany man) uptown in Yorkville, who sentenced them to six months on Blackwell's Island. Since it was too late for the whores to be ferried to the island they were held overnight in a courthouse lockup. The following morning one of the Tammany Justices set them free with a release form; and when a storm blew up over his action, claimed that it was all a misunderstanding.

Police court justice even looked shabby. Disheveled men huddled in conferences, their lips puckering like goldfish as they whispered into hairy ears. There were always a few Irish and Jewish lawyers, dandruff on their shoulders and gravy on their vests, their voices and fingers raised in perpetual advocacy as they sidled along the benches from one of their clients to another. The Irish court attendants, ruddy and hiccoughing, looked but a half-hour removed from a saloon, an ethnic failing that had once spurred Parkhurst to venture the opinion that if the nation rid itself of rum and Irishmen "we could tear down half our prisons and shut up three-quarters of our almshouses."[2]

The most godforsaken courtroom was the Essex Market Courthouse, in the heart of the lower East Side. The smell of feathers and blood wafted over from the kosher poultry market across the street. The court attendants were gruffer there, the loiterers in the foyer and on the stairway uglier. Lawyer Moss maintained that the Jews produced the most brutal thugs—perhaps because they were laboring to overcome the commonly held view that Jews "didn't have de stuff." He added: "There is a marked tendency among these Hebrews of criminal instincts to cover up their Jewish origin and to disguise their names; thus Rosenthal becomes McCarthy, Rosenberg become Rose, Solomon becomes Smith, and the traveler meets men of unmistakable Hebrew features, who bear such names as Cooper, Butler and Lent."

Moss was especially wary of Max Hochstim, a Polish Jew about thirty years old. Hochstim and Silver Dollar Smith jointly ran the thriving bail-bond franchise in the Essex Market Courthouse. Bail bondsmen were supposed to measure up to high civic standards, but Smith and Hochstim held the bail-bond monopoly by breaking the legs of anybody who dared to move in on their territory.

Silver Dollar Smith acted as if the courthouse had been annexed to his saloon across the street. Striding to the bench through the crowd of waiting prisoners and lawyers, he would bow to the Police Justice, then lean forward to whisper to His Honor. Those in a position to know such things said the *sotto voce* remark was usually about the weather or an unctuous trifle. On one occasion the raspy-tongued Hochstim, emulating his mentor, flattered a Justice for "looking swell in the judicial vermin." By such boldness Silver Dollar and Hochstim contrived to convey the impression to the credulous folk in the courtroom that they had "fixed it with de Judge." That was not always possible—even Tammany Police Justices sometimes had to take account of public and judicial opinion—but Alderman Smith enjoyed enviable pull with several of the Justices and on occasion he made his power felt.

* * *

The pastor learned about this flea-bitten milieu from attending police court, from the newspapers, and from Charlie Gardner, with whom he had collaborated so fruitfully on his midnight forays. Sitting with the preacher in the rectory study, the detective imparted valuable background information about those fastened to the city's underside.

Parkhurst had spent enough time with Charlie to know that the detective was not a candidate for the church choir, but he found Gardner competent and ingratiating. For weeks after the first assignment ended the Parkhurst Society had supplied Gardner's detective agency with steady work. Eventually Parkhurst asked Charlie to come to work for the Society as Chief Detective, and the lanky young detective agreed. It was a good deal for Charlie, who had just married and needed a guaranteed salary.

Over the next few weeks, Charlie became an expert on the gambling dens called faro banks (named in honor of a favorite New York card game). Some faro banks operated openly, behind the disguise of an express delivery company or cigar store. Others locked their doors and hired a Negro doorkeeper with a prodigious memory for faces who inspected every potential customer through a small aperture and turned away those that he failed to recognize or who "looked fishy."

A fly mug, Charlie was accomplished at joking his way past lookouts. Uptown and downtown, his practiced eye watched dealers pop plaid-backed cards out of silver boxes. In some of the houses, the dealers spoke as loudly as they dressed, and the customers, standing three- and four-deep, played for nickels. At Eugene's, located near Police Headquarters, the favored game was craps. Sheeny Jake, who was Eugene's lookout, also functioned as a puller, grabbing the lapels of passersby and convincing them by the force of his will to try their luck. He also jollified the cop on the corner with cigars and other small honoraria. The most elegant gambling house in the city was John Daly's. The tall, gray-haired, distinguished Daly was often on hand to show his paintings and sculptures to his patrons before they took an elevator up two flights to an elegantly carpeted gambling room that occupied the entire floor. Big shots in politics and business lost at blackjack or baccarat and then supped from splendid plate and drank rare wines as Daly's guests. Charlie preferred the swank Tenderloin faro banks, where a fireplace crackled with merry logs, where attendants padded about supplying the wants of the well-dressed clientele, and where the smallest denomination on the table was a one-dollar purple chip.

Gardner liked to buy drinks, on the Society's expense account, for whatever jovial companions he had picked up over the course of the evening. If he lost money in the faro banks or the horse betting parlors, he sent a bill for the expense to the Parkhurst Society; but he kept the winnings for himself.

On many a midnight Florence Gardner, his pretty nineteen-year-old wife, waited patiently for Charlie to come home. When he had his own agency Charlie used to lurk all night in doorways, watching the flat where a philandering husband kept a rendezvous. As Parkhurst's Chief Shadow, he was involved in intrigues that kept him out drinking in bars with odd blokes until all hours.

Gardner combined a lighthearted approach with a serious interest in gathering information about police wrongdoing. He kept track of the storefront numbers parlors and could estimate the handle in the horse-betting rooms; and he familiarized himself with the police precinct detectives (called ward detectives or wardmen) who rang the doorbells of brothels on their monthly collection rounds for the precinct captains.

Charlie was also an effective knight-errant, imparting a push-and-get-there pace to the formerly sleepy offices of the Society. Early in the day he dug up evidence on numbers parlors, and in the evenings he switched his attentions to brothels. Sunday after Sunday he slipped past beefy pickets into side doors to drink in the city's saloons. Every week he brought in evidence for Moss, the Parkhurst Society's leading lawyer, to take before a Police Justice. Because the Tammany police justices often found fault with the case and refused to issue search warrants, Gardner and Moss found it advantageous to take the evidence uptown to secure warrants from the city's two non-Tammany justices. Usually Gardner enlisted court officers to serve the warrants rather than placing any trust in the precinct police.

When he started looking around in Captain Devery's precinct, Charlie was warned. Big Bill Devery shook a finger in Charlie's face and admonished him not to monkey in the West Forty-seventh Street precinct. They disputed this and other matters with oaths and breast-beating and baring of teeth, but perhaps it was nothing more than a male territorial ritual, since they were sharing a bottle of wine at the time.

* * *

Charlie liked to dress up his stories with embellishments, but the pastor did not seem to mind, and their working relationship flourished. Gardner was the only agent whom Parkhurst trusted. The pastor suspected that his other agents were not devoted to The Work but to some angle best known to themselves. Some, he feared, might even be passing information on Society activities to the police.

Charlie warned the pastor that Agent Chauncey Grant, who sidelined as a cigar salesman, blackmailed saloonkeepers, proposing that he would lose the evidence he had against them for excise violations if they would place a big order with him. It was also learned that the Society for the Prevention of Cruelty to Children had fired Chauncey for taking bribes. Parkhurst dismissed Grant and several other agents and the office locks were changed.

Some weeks after Grant had been fired, Charlie reported to the Parkhurst Society's Executive Committee that Chauncey, passing himself off as still a Society agent, was blackmailing madames in the row of brothels along West Fifty-third Street in Big Bill Devery's precinct. Charlie was instructed to come up with evidence against Grant.

One of the women Grant was trying to shake down was Lillie Clifton, a madame in her mid-thirties who kept a discreet fancy house in a brownstone in the shadow of the elevated railroad on West Fifty-third Street. Selecting Madame Clifton as the most promising source of evidence against Grant, Gardner took her for cab rides, bought her champagne, and cultivated the handsome madame with other attentions.

* * *

Although Parkhurst and Byrnes had not clashed in the eight months of Byrnes's reign as Superintendent, the pastor had not once crossed his threshold or sought his advice. Parkhurst believed that Byrnes was indifferent to reform and that Lillie Clifton, like her scarlet sisters in other precincts, was plying her trade without the least hazard of police interference. A break seemed inevitable.

It came when Byrnes asked the police justices to stop issuing search warrants to "irresponsible parties"—by which he meant Parkhurst agents. Responding quickly, Parkhurst told reporters he was glad that Byrnes was flying his true colors at last, "because it separates us . . . from those whom we wish to fight." In Parkhurst's eyes, Byrnes had sided with the corrupt faction of the city.

But Parkhurst was swimming against the popular tide. Rallying reformers against Tammany Hall was one thing, but it was quite another to take on a public figure with such an ironclad reputation.

Although Byrnes had been Superintendent for more than half a year, in the public imagination he was still Inspector Byrnes, the legendary sleuth whose gaze could bore deeply into the criminal brain to unearth its secrets. For many journalists he was the ultimate authority on crime detection.

Merchants told stories of how Byrnes was called in when their homes were robbed. After listening for a while he would give his assurance that the missing diamonds would be returned in three days. And on the third day, not the second or the fourth, two detectives would knock at the door and deliver the diamonds, courtesy of Inspector Byrnes.

When a pickpocket stole Lincoln Steffens's pay envelope on a streetcar, the young reporter called Byrnes for help. The Great Detective asked how much money was in the envelope, how the envelope was addressed, and what streetcar lines Steffens had taken, then said, "I'll have it for you Monday morning."

On Monday Byrnes handed him the envelope with the money just as the reporter had received it from the *Post*. The puzzled Steffens asked another reporter how Byrnes had done it. "He knew what pickpockets were working the car lines you rode," the reporter said, "and he . . . passed the word that he wanted that dip back by Monday morning, and so, of course, it came back Monday morning."

* * *

Devery was a rising star of the Byrnes regime. In the Great Shakeup, Byrnes's main exhibit as a reformer, Captain Devery had been moved from a slow east side precinct to the West Forty-seventh Street precinct. Parkhurst viewed with suspicion this transfer of Big Bill to a much more lucrative assignment.

The precinct was blessed with rows of whorehouses that operated without trouble and never robbed patrons. The madames, as the police put it, "did the right thing"; they paid protection as promptly and regularly as if they considered it their civic duty. Devery's new precinct also had a number of classy gambling houses, including John Daly's.

Captain Devery, a former boxer and bartender, was a cocky street fighter who seized opportunities as they were offered. He made it his business to know everything that was going on in his precinct, and was especially interested in the comings and goings of Charlie Gardner. There is reason to think that Devery had informants among agents of the Parkhurst Society who helped him collect such information, but his most invaluable ally—and that alliance is thoroughly documented—was Lillie Clifton. On four occasions over the course of several weeks she called at the precinct station to apprise the Captain about the activities, the boasts and the intentions of the glib private detective. Big Bill intended to convince Gardner that he was playing leapfrog in the wrong precinct.

* * *

The trap snapped shut on Charlie on the evening of Sunday, December 4. Big Bill Devery dropped his hammy hand on the Parkhurst detective's shoulder and took him into custody.

The police made him as inaccessible as they could. Efforts were made to keep the arrest quiet until Superintendent Byrnes was ready to broadcast the news.

On the following morning Charlie's captors took him to the Tombs police court for arraignment. Charlie was moping in a downstairs cell in the Mulberry Street headquarters when, two floors above him, at four in the afternoon, Byrnes was denouncing him to the press as a blackmailer.

"All these amateur police societies fall into the hands of blackmailers," Byrnes said. "Dr. Parkhurst's organization has been used almost solely for blackmail purposes and we can prove it." Many madames, he said, had come to the police to report that Parkhurst detectives had squeezed money out of them. Gardner, he said, was a master at intimidating his victims, carrying around blank warrants that he would fill in with whatever name suited him.

The Gardner arrest underscored his warnings about issuing warrants to "irresponsible parties." Because a warrant was such a powerful weapon for blackmail, Byrnes said, it should be entrusted only to the police. "If there is anything wrong with the Police Department let the reformers go to the Legislature and have it remedied," said the Superintendent. "There should be one police force only, and the efforts should be to improve that force and not to start a lot more forces. . . . I challenge anyone to bring charges against the force that will not be investigated. There is nothing that I will not do to purge the department of dishonest men if there are any such in it."

* * *

As soon as they heard the news, Parkhurst and his fellow Society trustees, Frank Moss and Thaddeus Kenneson, hurried to the lockup. Because it was after hours, they had difficulty in getting to see Gardner; after much argument only Moss was allowed in to see him.

They expressed their skepticism to the press. "The police can work up evidence and get witnesses to swear to almost anything," Moss said. "The perjury of policemen is notorious."

"Is it not a remarkable thing," Parkhurst asked the gathered reporters, "that when an abandoned woman complains to a police captain that she has been blackmailed the Captain does not stop her from continuing to carry on her illegal business? Instead of doing so he turns all his attention to the blackmailer.

"The whole matter has a very strange look. We have always found Gardner to be an honest man. Since he has been in the employ of the Society there has never been the slightest breath of suspicion against him. I shall continue to believe him to be thoroughly honest until the contrary is proved to my satisfaction."

On the following day Gardner was arraigned in police court on charges of extortion and attempted extortion. After hearing the testimony the Justice set bail at $7,500. Moss was unable to furnish bail immediately and Charlie was removed to The Tombs.

Charlie had fallen into the hands of his enemies. The charges against him were felonies. He had good reason to fret, for he was in what downtowners called "a pretty considerable fix." As he lay on his hard cot in the Tombs that evening, woebegone and presumably wishing for a drink, mugs were being clinked together and libations poured in Tammany saloons for Big Bill Devery, the thirty-eight-year-old darling of the force. They made crude jokes about the bamboozled pastor who had vowed to clean up the city. Big Bill was not finished with his work yet, they were crowing, he would not stop until he chased that goddamned Protestant preacher back to Massachusetts.

* * *

But the damage done thus far to the Parkhurst Crusade was hardly enough for Byrnes. He summoned the police reporters to his office on the evening of December 6. On duty he often dressed in uniform, with brass buttons and six gold bands on each sleeve. But that evening he wore civilian clothes, probably one of the salt and pepper suits that he favored, with a derby hat and salmon gloves. His drooping moustache suggested languor and his body suggested hidden reserves of power—an athlete's body still trim in middle age. In all public appearances he was never in a hurry, always ready to take a kindly interest in a newsboy or a retired cop, yet there was a hint of affectation about his placid style. On this evening, although he tried to appear calm and controlled, it was evident that his blood was up. Byrnes had an acquired voice, which imitated the inflections of his Wall Street friends, but his original thick Irish street brogue came through in moments of stress and emotion, as it did on this night.

He called Parkhurst a hypocrite embroiled in a petty vendetta against the police force. The preacher sought revenge, Byrnes claimed, because a cop had testified against the interests of a young lady in his congregation who was seeking a divorce. He charged that Parkhurst had tried to induce the officer to perjure himself.

Parkhurst and a silly society woman who was his close ally, he went on, were scheming to entrap leading city officials. "By intrigues with women," he said, "they seek to compromise the Chief Magistrate of the city, our prosecuting officer, a number of judges, and prominent municipal officials." Society agents were assigned to shadow office-holders, he said, to see if they went to brothels or kept mistresses.

At the conclusion of his remarks Byrnes banged shut his rolltop desk, rose abruptly and announced that he had said all he wished to say. Ignoring a volley of questions, he stepped toward the door with a mild "Good night." As his hand touched the doorknob he turned with a parting thought.

"Well, boys," said he, "I will tell you one thing more to show the contemptible character of this man Parkhurst. After the arrest of Hattie Adams and while her trial was pending, Parkhurst asked this (society) woman to get him some of the vilest French pictures. His friend readily consented, and with another woman secured the beastly prints and took them in great glee to her pastor. Parkhurst's object in securing them was to offer them as pictorial evidence of the scenes he had witnessed in the Adams house. When, however, his faithful parishioner delivered them the wily doctor hesitated. 'Suppose,' said he, 'that some inquisitive juror asks me where I got these pictures. I had better not take them from you now. You carry them home and put them in a big envelope and get some woman whose handwriting I do not know to address them to me. Then I can say conscientiously that I don't know where they came from.' It was done. Now, that gives you an idea of Parkhurst's high character."

* * *

Through most of the day the maid at Parkhurst's rectory turned away reporters and visitors as the pastor typed up a reply to Byrnes's charges. When he finished the statement, a tired and flushed Parkhurst met with the press at the appointed hour. He began by pleading guilty, for the sake of argument, to everything Byrnes had brought up.

Let us assume, he said, that my motives were mean-spirited. What of it? "How does that help Mr. Byrnes any? Does that fact close up any of the gambling houses that he is allowing to run? Suppose I have been dealing in 'French pictures' and that I had all my pockets full of them when I went into the courtroom on a specified occasion, what of it? Does that fact suppress any of the vile dens of infamy in this city that exist because Mr. Byrnes and his department are viciously neglectful of their duty?

"Supposing I have availed of members of my congregation . . . and put them upon the track of city officials, set them studying up the unwholesome record of any who are today in positions of municipal authority, and arranged with all my elders, deacons and deaconesses to discover the facts as to the domestic life of the Police Commissioners, police magistrates and police captains, what of it? How does that help Mr. Byrnes?

"Mr. Byrnes is trying to shift the issue from his shoulders to mine. . . . He thinks that by showing the community what I am doing, he will make the community forget what he isn't doing."

* * *

MR. BYRNES DECLARES WAR, said the *Times* headline. PARKHURST HELD FOR PUBLIC SCORN, said the *Herald*. Editorials took the side of the Superintendent, citing his statistics of increased prostitution and gambling arrests. One stated that he was carrying out his "promise to improve the efficiency of the force and to earn a fair reputation for himself."[3]

The press coverage damaged support for the Parkhurst Crusade, and the pastor was put on the defensive. A *Times* editorial suggested that Parkhurst ought to back the Police Department's "better element . . . allying himself with a man whose power for reform was a thousand times as great as his own, and working in co-operation with him, instead of indiscriminately attacking the police force in general and its chief in particular. The controversy between himself and Mr. Byrnes illustrates the greatest of the many mistakes of Dr. Parkhurst."[4]

14

FOR THE GOOD OF
THE SERVICE

While attacking the Parkhurst Society as pseudo-reformers, Byrnes was taking steps to enhance his own standing as a force for reform. First he assigned several Central Office Detectives to reconnoiter various precincts where gambling appeared to flourish, and bring him their findings. Then, unbeknownst to the precinct police, he sent out the same detectives to conduct gambling raids. Thirdly, as a journalist put it, he "threw a large and heavily charged bombshell into the ranks of his subordinates"[1]—accusing several high-ranking police officers, including Inspector Clubber Williams, with having neglected their duty.

This affair gave the editorial writers fresh evidence that a new broom was sweeping clean. The press was especially excited about the case against the flamboyant Clubber, who had never been accused of showing the least interest in reform.

It was the first time in the history of the Police Department that an Inspector had been brought up on charges. While serving in a lower rank, however, offenses aplenty had been ascribed to Clubber. In 1887, when he faced dismissal on serious charges, it was reported that throughout his career there had been 358 complaints lodged against him—at least 100 ahead of anyone else in the department—and he had been reprimanded or lightly fined 224 times.

His admirers laughed at the suggestion that he would get any punishment worse than a slap on the wrist. To them, and to just about everybody in the Tenderloin, Clubber cast a shadow larger than life.

* * *

Stretching from Fourteenth Street to Forty-second and from Fourth Avenue to Seventh, the Tenderloin was the wickedest part of the city. One day, according

Inspector Williams

to an old legend, when a horse-drawn streetcar reached the heart of the Tenderloin, a passenger yelled from the window, "There's the man who stole my watch!" and a half-dozen men loitering on the sidewalk broke and ran in various directions. Swells wearing gloves and smelling of toilet water ogled passing women. Actors and actresses could buy breakfast at two in the afternoon, a steak cost thirty cents in the cheaper cafes, and a schooner of beer, almost a quart, cost a nickel.

Wherever they might begin, the sporting crowd and the visiting salesmen ended their day there. Bent on mischief, college students ran amok through the Tenderloin after football games. Most of the fancy brothels were situated there, as well as high-toned gambling dens and all-night Turkish baths.

Clubber had given the Tenderloin its name. When he was transferred to command the West Thirtieth Street precinct in 1876, the young Captain, dazzled by his good fortune in being sent to so lucrative a post, told a friend, "I've been living on chuck steak long enough—from now on it's tenderloin." Or so the story went as recounted in the *Police Gazette*, a magazine of crime and boxing news found in every fully equipped barbershop.

Transferred after three years, Williams returned in 1881 for another lucrative stay, and over the following six years he appeared to be accountable to no one. If citizens called his attention to a house of prostitution he would lecture them on the laws of slander and demand to see their proof. Although a Grand Jury presentment in 1883 recommended his dismissal the Police Board did nothing to restrain him.

In 1887 the Clubber was commanding another precinct, the nineteenth. When Frank Moss, representing landowners and merchants, called upon the police to clean up a vice-ridden neighborhood, Williams insulted him, and a police emissary warned Moss that he and his allies would be clubbed out of the area. Although then Mayor Abram Hewitt advised Moss that the two Republican members of the Commission would back the Republican Clubber no matter how compelling the evidence, Moss took his case to the Police Board. Mayor Hewitt supported Moss with a letter to the Commissioners complaining that Williams could not be induced to suppress vice in his precinct. After a Police Board trial the two Democrats voted to dismiss Williams, but the two Republicans voted against the motion. Since a tie vote did not carry, the Clubber survived, and soon thereafter was promoted to Inspector.

He grew even bolder. Cops under his command let it be known that saloons would be immune to raids were they to favor Hollywood Whiskey as their house brand. In return, Clubber received emoluments from the president of the whiskey company.

Clubber had countless friends and supporters who admired his leonine courage and his struggle to reclaim the streets for the law-abiding public. Visitors from all over the nation were impressed when a New York friend would point out the broad-shouldered giant with the remark: "There goes Clubber Williams." Far from being a pariah, he was a Republican mainstay, a valuable counterbalance to Tammany control of the Police Department.

* * *

Byrnes and Clubber were old foes, and it was rumored that Byrnes had blocked his appointment to head the Central Detective Bureau. Attracted by the possibility of confrontation, the press turned out in force for the Police Board hearing.

After the commissioners took seats around the table Byrnes presented the case against Williams and Captain Michael Doherty, which involved the same evidence. Central Office detectives had been sent out to raid a place on The Bowery and another on Fourteenth Street, and gambling paraphernalia had been seized in each. Byrnes contended that Captain Doherty should have raided these places himself and that Williams, his supervisor, should have seen to it that the Captain did so.

Everybody in the room leaned forward to attend carefully as Inspector Alexander Williams strode up in his dress blues to put questions to his superior. At fifty-three his "magnificent audacity," as one newspaper put it, radiated as powerfully as ever. The recording stenographer plunged his pen into an inkbottle. The reporters opened their notebooks. Williams rested his clenched right fist on the table and leaned on it. Byrnes tugged at his moustache.

"Does the Superintendent know that I knew that this place in the Bowery existed?" Williams defiantly asked.

"No, I do not," Byrnes said heartily.

"Do you know that I knew that the place on Fourteenth Street existed?"

"No, sir."

"Did you ever specially draw my attention to either one of these places?"

"I am quite sure I did not."

Clubber asked the Superintendent if he thought that Clubber would have made the raid "if I had had the information you possessed about the place in Fourteenth Street."

"Do you want me to answer that question?" Byrnes responded.

"Yes, sir."

"No, sir," Byrnes said emphatically, "I do not."

"Why?" asked Williams, taken aback.

Byrnes said that on an earlier occasion he had alerted Williams about plans to send Central Office detectives to two other suspected gambling dens. By the time his men arrived, the gamblers were gone. "Then I concluded that I'd better do these things myself. Now that is the reason I did not tell you."

Under questioning from Board President Jimmy Martin, Clubber said that he received information about activity in the precincts from the captains under his jurisdiction, but did not know what the captains did not tell him, nor whether the information he received was true.

"That's a matter of discipline," Byrnes snapped. "I have men under me and I make them tell the truth."

"You have not time to find out whether they tell the truth," Williams rejoined, "and neither have I."

This defense cinched matters with the Police Board, which dismissed the case against him. Captain Doherty got off with a reprimand.

"The result shows that the charge against me was unjust," Clubber told reporters. "There is still on the statute books of Connecticut a law which prohibits a man from kissing his wife on Sunday. You might as well try to enforce that law as to stop gambling in New York."

It was a defeat for Byrnes, but an honorable one, and in its aftermath, at his request, the Police Board transferred five captains "for the good of the service." Some said that Byrnes was making Herculean efforts to stop police corruption, others that he was merely trying to rid himself of an old enemy. One high police official was quoted as saying that "the Parkhurst crusade" forced Byrnes to "make a showing" by moving against his subordinates. Whatever his motives, through the rest of the year Byrnes brought no more charges against Captains or Inspectors.

* * *

Meanwhile Byrnes's attack on the Parkhurst Society rolled on. With the example of the wretched Gardner before them, the Board of Police Justices adopted a resolution that search warrants could be issued only to police officers, not to Parkhurst agents.

As a way of bypassing Tammany's grip on the courts, Parkhurst agents had developed relationships with two holdover non-Tammany Police Justices, to whom they took their evidence for warrants. The Police Justice Board blocked that practice by stating a new policy, that warrants could only be issued in the district in which the offense was alleged to have occurred.

And, to round out a dismal week for the Parkhurst Society, the Grand Jury indicted Charlie Gardner on two separate counts.

The first count was extortion, based on Lillie Clifton's statement that he had blackmailed her at the rate of $50 a month. The second count was attempted extortion, based on her accusation that Gardner demanded $150 from her to keep her case from going to a Grand Jury.

The second count (the demand for $150) was the more dramatic one because it was his alleged collection of this money that trapped him, and the prosecution decided to try him solely on the second count without dropping the first.

Madame Clifton said Charlie made his demand on Sunday evening, November 20, after telling her that the Parkhurst Society was ready to take a large number of cases to the District Attorney to seek indictments. This is how she told the story at the arraignment:

"There's going to be a terrible rumpus in this town," he said, "and I'm sorry, Lil, to say that you're on the list."

"Surely you wouldn't do anything to me," said the woman, "after promising to be my friend."

"No, I wouldn't willingly," replied Gardner, "and to prove I'm your friend we'll go over to the Society's office together and I'll show you something."

They reached the building on Broadway and climbed the five flights of stairs to the Society headquarters, whereupon he opened a bottle of champagne.

"Lil," Gardner chuckled, "what do you think of these psalm singers? I blew in $300 for expenses last week and $200 the week before, but they're good for it. I'll get it."

Charlie produced a bundle of about one hundred folders. "These are for indictments," he explained, "and they've got to go down to the District Attorney's office in the morning." He took out one marked number twenty-two. "That's yours, Lil, and it's a hard one to fix."

"Why do you treat me like this?" the woman demanded. "Don't I pay you enough?"

"I can't help it," he said, sipping his champagne. "It's my duty."

But, he promised, he could fix things up for $150.

By the time they finished the bottle she had consented to pay. Charlie gathered the empty bottle and the glasses and climbed a ladder to leave them on the roof, hidden from the eyes of the psalm-singers.

* * *

The saloons, where the drinkers tried to anticipate the moves in the upcoming trial, were abuzz with stories about how much money Charlie Gardner was carrying when he was arrested. It was said that although he worked for the modest salary of $25 a week, his pockets bulged with bills of large denomination.

But if unaccounted wealth raised legitimate questions, Clubber Williams had some explaining to do. His home, in which reposed a full-sized safe for cash, jewelry and other valuables, was far beyond the reach of an ordinary public servant. He also owned a place in Connecticut, where he kept a steam yacht at dockside. When questioned about how a police officer could afford such a vessel, Williams called it rather an ordinary yacht, not to be compared with J. Pierpont Morgan's. His dock, a stone sea wall running 160 feet out into the water, had cost him $39,000.

Nor was Clubber the only rich cop. William Murray, who had preceded Byrnes as Superintendent, had retired to a palatial estate. Captain Allaire had recently purchased a fine home on East Nineteenth Street for $18,000, and also owned a summer home on Long Island as well as a $15,000 three-story bay-window brownstone on West Ninety-first Street. Inspector McLaughlin owned a four-story building of apartments with stores on the first floor on West Fourth Street, and early in 1893 he purchased yet another valuable property.

Precinct detectives, who earned only $1,200 a year, were buying real estate in Westchester County. Their wives wore diamonds and rode about in marvelous equipages, maids arranged their hair and manservants answered their doors. The men in the brass buttons and blue uniforms came home to mansions where servants drew their baths and started their fireplaces. Such displays of wealth, breaking out even in the lower ranks of the force, were a far more significant public question than the money in the pocket of a Parkhurst agent. They were examples, Parkhurst said, of "honesty converted into dollars, female virtue into corner lots."[2]

A PUT-UP JOB?

After raising money from its backers to mount a defense for Gardner, the Parkhurst Society hired not one but two lawyers who specialized in criminal law: John W. Goff, who functioned as the principal counsel, and W. Travers Jerome.

Although they both were former Assistant District Attorneys, their backgrounds contrasted markedly, Goff having come to America as a poor Irish orphan in the keeping of his uncle, while Jerome, a cousin of the society beauty Jenny Jerome, came from a well-connected family.

On the last day of January the defense attorneys arrived at the Court of General Sessions to find a blazing stove crackling in the courtroom. They also found a familiar figure, donnish and bland, sitting at the opposite table. The lawyer was Francis Wellman, the most accomplished assistant D.A. in Nicoll's office—a Boston blueblood who had taught at Harvard Law School. It was Wellman who had prosecuted Billy McGlory, a trial that sent the divekeeper to Blackwell's Island.

The presiding judge was the sixty-one-year-old Recorder, Frederick Smyth. Born in Ireland, Smyth was an inflexible judge of rigid demeanor, one of Byrnes's few close friends, a staunch Tammany man. Every year at police banquets at Delmonico's, Smyth was seated in the place of honor at the head table, and in the course of the evening he would eulogize the police as the keepers of civilization in the city.

* * *

Within a day twelve men—women did not serve on juries—were selected. In its opening remarks, the prosecution made it clear that Gardner was on trial for a single offense: that he attempted to extort money from Lillie Clifton by telling her that evidence to bring about her indictment would be presented to a Grand Jury unless she gave him $150. Thus threatened with blackmail, Madame Clifton went to the police for advice. The prosecution stated:

"Police Captain Devery then marked $150 in bills . . . and gave them to Lillie Clifton. On December 4 she . . . gave Gardner the $150. Of this he put $50 into a basket on his table and put the other $100 in his pocket. He then got into a cab with Lillie Clifton and started off to get something to drink. When he got out of the cab and

Gardner—"He Cried 'See There.'"

turned to help the woman out, he was arrested. He threw the money into the street. It was a part of the marked bills, $100. Officers of the law . . . went to Gardner's rooms the next morning and in the basket found the rest of the marked bills, $50."

The witnesses for the prosecution began with Chauncey Grant, the renegade Parkhurst agent. Chauncey admitted that he was trying to shake down whorehouses on West Fifty-third Street, but claimed that he was following a script written by Gardner, who had enlisted him as a go-between. In that role he called on the house of Madame Clifton, which Gardner allegedly told him was one of the most promising because she kept a stable of eighteen whores. Cross-examination forced Grant to make damaging admissions about his honesty and his history, but did not destroy his credibility as a witness.

Lillie Clifton made a star witness, performing perfectly and saying all the right things. The bejeweled Madame Clifton admitted to running a brothel—she described it as a cozy, homey place, operated only on a limited scale for old and trusted customers and with only three or four girls. She denied, however, that she paid any protection to the police.

On October 12, she said, Chauncey Grant had come to her place, representing himself as a Parkhurst agent. He asked her if Captain Devery had been around asking for money, and she said he had not. "If he has not he will be," she quoted Grant as saying, "and I and Mr. Gardner can be just as good friends to you as he can be."

But two days later Gardner met with her in a saloon where he told her that he had nothing to do with Grant. When she went to his quarters a few days later, she testified, Charlie asked her for money. "He asked his wife to excuse herself. 'Must I leave the room, Charlie?' says she. 'Yes, you must,' says he. When she was gone I asked him how much it would cost me to be protected. He said $50 a month. I then put $50 on the table and told him that I would call every month with the money."

One day when the two of them were riding uptown in a hired cab and drinking champagne, he offered to steer customers to her place and asked for a commission for any business he brought her. Then, she said, she asked him if he would protect her from arrest and he replied that he would be happy to oblige, for a price. She claimed that at this point, with the champagne embubbling his brain, he boasted of protecting others, in these words: "I have fifty in my Sunday School class and you make fifty-one."

Three days after she made her first payment to Gardner, she said, she stopped by the precinct station for the first of a series of meetings with Captain Devery. "I told him what I had done," she testified, "and said I was friends with Mr. Gardner and the Society would not trouble me and wouldn't he allow me to open." But, she added, the honest captain was having none of that and warned her in stern tones not to try to "open your doors for that purpose while I am in this precinct." Nevertheless he told her to continue making payments to Gardner and asked to be apprised of her dealings with her blackmailer. She and the captain met on three more occasions.

Meanwhile, the madame, resplendently dressed in silk, velvet and diamonds, continued to visit Gardner's apartment. Charlie was often out and Lillie would stay to console Florence Gardner, who was forever waiting for her husband to come home.

On the evening of December 4, she brought the money that Captain Devery had marked. "Mrs. Gardner was not at home. Gardner was on the sofa. I gave him the marked bills. The roll of $50 he put in a workbasket. The $100 roll he shoved in his outside coat pocket and then told me that I was a good girl and that he would take me out and treat me. We got into a cab and drove to the Twenty-fourth Street and Fourth Avenue saloon." When they arrived Charlie was arrested.

Clifton was cross-examined with a disdain meant to impart to the jury that the word of a whorehouse madame was incredible, but Jerome's attempts to disturb her calm were fruitless.

"Then you were laying a trap for Gardner when you went driving with him on October 26?"

"Why, certainly."

"But you drank his wine?"

"Yes, and rather enjoyed it, too." With that the flouncy madame winked slyly at the jury with her left eye, on the side that Recorder Smyth could not see.

* * *

Next the police took the stand to tell how the trap was sprung. Detective Sergeant Michael Crowley said he stopped at the madame's house on December 4 to tell her that the police waited in readiness—that as planned, she should take the money to Gardner at his apartment. When she went in, Devery and Crowley waited outside. When she and Gardner emerged and got into a hack that had been waiting for them, Crowley and Devery followed at a jog. When the cab pulled up at a saloon and Gardner got out they collared him.

"I walked out over the sidewalk," Crowley testified, "over to where he was standing and I took him on the shoulder and I said, 'I arrest you.' And he turned around to me and he says, 'All right.' So I looked at him for a second or two and he put his left hand in his pocket and I saw something drop. I said to him, 'You have dropped something. Pick it up.' He says, 'I don't want to. Pick it up yourself.' I said all right. It was a roll of bills.

"I said, 'Get hold of him, Captain,' and we walked him from there to the corner, and I counted the money in his presence and in the presence of Captain Devery. As we were going down in the cab he says, 'You've got me now, and I suppose you will pound me.' I says, 'No, I will not pound you anymore than anyone else.' He says, 'Will you leave me have a drink?' I says, 'It's Sunday night, old man, and I wouldn't leave you have a drink.'"

Cross-examination failed to shake Crowley's story. He denied being "unfriendly" to Gardner but admitted that they had clashed in court years earlier and had never spoken since.

Big Bill Devery's testimony corroborated Clifton and Crowley. After the arrest, the Captain said, he searched Gardner's pockets to find more than $1500 in cash as well as a deed to a lot in New Jersey. But the other $50 in marked money was not on Gardner. "I said to him, 'You had $150 and you have only $100 of it here, where is the other $50?' He said, 'I have not got anything to say.'"

The prosecution's case snapped shut with the testimony of Inspector William McLaughlin who led a party on the following morning to Gardner's quarters where, he said, the missing $50 was found in a sewing basket.

* * *

Early in the trial the defense attorneys became convinced that they had incurred the enmity of the Recorder. Almost all of the Recorder's rulings went against the defense, and they protested each adverse ruling in strong terms. Goff, a highly strung man who brought to the courtroom an almost inhuman intensity, was incapable of hiding his resentment.

As the trial went on the civility between the defense lawyers and Smyth was frayed to the breaking point by objections that grew ever more venomous. The animosity grew strident when the cabman whom Madame Clifton had hired to wait at Gardner's testified that he had seen the bills drop from Charlie's pocket. He was asked to identify the Parkhurst detective.

"Gardner," the Recorder barked, "stand up!"

Gardner began to rise from his chair.

"Sit down!" Goff shouted.

He began to settle back in his chair.

"Gardner," the Recorder repeated, more severely, "stand up!"

"I object!" Goff shouted. "Gardner, keep your seat!"

"I have ordered you to rise, Gardner," Recorder Smyth said.

Gardner obediently began to rise again, but Jerome pushed him back down into his chair.

"Your Honor," said Goff, his face flushed with anger, "this prisoner cannot be made to stand up for identification. It is a violation of his constitutional rights. He will sit down unless Your Honor directs that this prisoner be made to stand up by force."

Three court officers stood behind Gardner's chair. Smyth was glowering. Goff looked defiant. Gardner wore a sickly smile.

"Well, then, officers of the Court," Recorder Smyth said dryly, "lift the prisoner to his feet if he will not stand otherwise."

Catching Gardner under the armpits, one of the guards easily raised the prisoner to his feet and the cabman identified him.

"Now," Goff said, still furious, "we move that Your Honor will discharge this jury from the further consideration of this case, because the prisoner's constitutional rights have been violated."

The Recorder dismissed the motion, and Goff took exception not only to his ruling but also to his "unjustifiable tone." From that point on the defense grew more acrimonious.

* * *

Lavish press attention, playing up the animosity between the Recorder and the defense team, fanned an already strong public interest in Charlie's trial, and by the fourth day the area around the courthouse was a mob scene. The public construed the trial as a fight between Parkhurst and Byrnes, and it was the most sought-after ticket since Gentleman Jim Corbett challenged John L. Sullivan for the heavyweight boxing crown in New Orleans a few months earlier.

It was customary in those days for the defense to make its opening statement just before it presented its case. So, after Goff made a motion for dismissal on several grounds, all of which the Recorder waved off sternly, Jerome followed with an opening statement in which he told the jury that it had not heard true evidence, but the perjured testimony of people with "personal grudges" against Gardner. Sergeant Crowley and Gardner had quarreled in a court case years ago and, according to Jerome, Crowley had been plotting revenge ever since. Gardner had also crossed swords with Captain Devery, who had tried to bully the detective out of his precinct. And Jerome contended that Grant "was once an agent of the Parkhurst Society, who had been discharged by Gardner because it was suspected that he was really a spy who was working for the Society only that he might tip off the police as to the houses which were to be raided and to keep the police informed as to contemplated movements."

Jerome argued that the case against Gardner was "a put-up job" to throw discredit on Parkhurst's society, which was closing gambling houses and houses of prostitution and thus drying up police revenue. He attempted to make the police into the defendants, charging that they systematically blackmailed the industry in which Lillie Clifton toiled.

* * *

After this provocative opening the defense called Charlie as the first witness. As the young detective told it, he had spent time with Lillie Clifton with the sole aim of collecting evidence against Chauncey Grant, and had played upon her weakness for drink to get it. Lillie had two incriminating notes from Chauncey but had given only one of them to Gardner, and his continued attentions to her were designed to get the second. According to Charlie their first meeting went like this:

"She said he [Grant] had come to her and represented himself to be an officer of the Society and had asked her if she would not like to make some arrangement with the Society like that she had made with the police. She had said to him that she would, but then she got suspicious that Grant was not a Society agent, and he then promised to introduce her to me. I never had authorized Grant or anybody else to make an arrangement for me to see the woman, and told her so."

Charlie said he next saw Lillie several nights later when she showed up unannounced at his place. "She said she had been unable to find the other note Grant had written to her. I asked her if she was ready to make the affidavit she had promised to make concerning her dealings with Grant. She said no, as Captain Devery had told her that if she did so he would close her house and send her to prison. I then reported the entire case to Dr. Parkhurst and Mr. Moss and received my instructions from them how to act."

On November 20—the night when, according to the indictment, he attempted to blackmail her for $150—he said that he went home to find Lillie Clifton sitting with his wife, and once again he asked her to sign an affidavit against Chauncey. He testified that he told her to stop coming to his home, that if she wanted to see him they could meet at a saloon. He denied having taken money from her on any occasion.

On the night of his arrest, he said, she came to his home and said: "'Grant's been around again. What shall I do?' 'I don't care what you do,' I said. 'You're a nuisance—running around my house like this.' I don't know exactly what I said, but I abused her pretty well. She cried and said she was sick, and would I give her a drink of whiskey? I said I had none in the house, but I'd go out with her and get her some whiskey."

They left the apartment and went in the cab to the saloon, whereupon Sergeant Crowley arrested him as he alighted from the cab. "Captain Devery ran over and Crowley said, 'Search his left-hand pocket.' Devery put his hand in my overcoat on the left side and found nothing. Lillie Clifton had got out of the cab meantime. As I turned when Crowley pulled me around, I saw Devery knock something out of her hand. It fell on the sidewalk. It was money. Devery picked it up, handed it to a policeman who came along, and told him to count it." Then Crowley hissed, like a villain in a melodrama: "We have got you and Parkhurst where we want you now."

* * *

Wellman subjected him to a severe cross-examination, bringing in witnesses who claimed that Gardner had blackmailed them when he was an agent for the Society for the Prevention of Cruelty to Children. None of the witnesses enjoyed high reputations for their probity, and they were shaky on dates. Charlie was also forced to deny that he was fired for knocking down fares while he was a streetcar conductor.

"You say you saw Captain Devery knock the roll of $100 in marked bills, which it is alleged you dropped, from the woman Clifton's hands?"

"I do."

"Why did you not assert your innocence then and there?"

"I did tell them that they could not put up a job like that on me."

Florence Gardner made a good defense witness. The pretty nineteen-year-old mother-to-be said that the first time Madame Clifton came to the apartment,

Charlie asked the woman whether she had brought Grant's letter with her. Lillie Clifton responded that she had not brought it, but promised to do so.

When Madame Clifton called on a second occasion, Charlie was not at home. Mrs. Gardner said Lillie chatted at length about the luxury in which she lived, comparing it to the humble circumstances of the Gardners. "She told me that I did not have my husband with me much," Florence testified. "I answered that it was business and not pleasure that kept him away. She told me that next year at the same time I would have my husband with me more; that I would not hear any more of Dr. Parkhurst and his Society. I asked her what she meant, but she told me not to mind about it."

* * *

Ill at home, Parkhurst testified by means of a deposition prepared at the rectory and read to the jury. In it the pastor described meetings with his Chief Detective about Chauncey and Lillie, and reported that the trustees of the Society had instructed Charlie that "he should seek to make a case against these women, and that he should also seek to secure from them at least an affidavit to the effect that Grant was, in the name of the Society, attempting to levy blackmail against them."

As the testimony ended, rumors flew about the city that Recorder Smyth was livid with anger at the antics of the defense, and all those following the trial wondered whether the threat of a contempt of court citation would soften the defense summation.

It did not. Goff delivered the rampaging summation, in which he charged that Gardner was not on trial for blackmail, but for interfering with blackmail. Throughout the trial, he fiercely proclaimed, a collective effort by means of sneers, nuances and expressions had been made to create an atmosphere suggesting Gardner's guilt—"that even though the accused was innocent he must be convicted." He stopped short of accusing the Recorder of being part of a conspiracy, but he cast aspersions at "the Recorder's most remarkable memory, which enabled him not only to suggest points that helped the prosecution, but those that hurt the defense."

The intent to frame Gardner was, he said, evident in the source of the case— a woman "who for nine years had thrived and fattened as a lawbreaker" yet at the first sign of trouble ran for help to Big Bill Devery. "She says she went for advice. Do lawbreakers go to Police Captains for advice?" Although Lillie Clifton pointed the finger of accusation, he said, "Superintendent Byrnes runs as the understratum in this whole case."

Why, he asked, were there two rolls of marked bills for one payoff on December 4? "There were two rolls of marked bills so that one of them could be placed, as it was placed, in Gardner's house by this woman Clifton, and so that the other could be placed by her on his person, if she was smart enough to get them there, which she was not. It is in this overzealousness that the conspirators defeated themselves. They made their case too well. Liberty was ignored, and decency was set aside because Czar Byrnes had ordered that a case should be made against Gardner."

When Goff was finished, Wellman rose and began his summation:

"What does Mr. Goff urge as his defense? Simply that there is a conspiracy between the police and other officials to railroad an innocent man to State Prison. He asks you by a vote of acquittal to brand the officials who represent you as guilty of a conspiracy of this kind. He says that this case is only a determination on our part to destroy Dr. Parkhurst and his Society.

"They say that the police set a trap for Gardner. Well, it is the duty of the police to catch criminals by setting traps for them. Were the Parkhurst people not setting traps when they went around to brothels and bought wine and saw circuses to procure evidence on which to convict keepers?'"

Wellman raised questions about Gardner's sources of income: "He tells you that he owns lots in Westchester valued at $9,000. Altogether it appears that this man owns more than $11,000. Where did he get it? He is 27 years old. . . . His largest salary has been $25 a week, and he has been twice married. Has he saved $11,000 out of his small salary? Then why cannot he explain his wealth?

"Will Gardner lie? . . . Why, in his affidavit to the court to reduce his bail on this very complaint he swears that the only property he owns in the world is his wearing apparel. That is an absolute lie. He intended to deceive the court, for here he has shown us that he is worth at least $11,000. Think of Dr. Parkhurst and other honorable men being dragged into such despicable work as this man was practicing!"

Finally the Recorder explained the law, and sent the jury away to reach a verdict.

* *

While the jury deliberated, men who discussed the trial in saloons and barbershops agreed with Goff that Byrnes was the force behind the Gardner trial, as he had been in proceedings against Captain Doherty and Clubber Williams.

From what they could observe and learn through the newspapers, Byrnes had not let that earlier defeat change his aim to make corruption more difficult by transferring captains, replacing wardmen, and breaking up old alliances.

Although Captain Doherty had gotten off with a reprimand at the Police Board hearing, Byrnes had seen to it that Doherty's precinct detective (called a wardman) was returned to street duty. At Byrnes's request the Police Board replaced Barney Meehan as wardman with John Hock, a red-haired German cop who had been on Bowery patrol for the past year. Byrnes, said his defenders, was looking for honest cops but could only play the hand he was dealt.

The image of Thomas Byrnes was beginning to change. No more the mysterious legend, he was now seen as a mundane figure—a choleric man, standing before his Inspectors and Captains in his inner sanctum, balling his fists, swearing a blue streak, pounding the table and insisting on results and on answers. But no answers came from the silent officers standing at attention.

When the jury returned, the foreman said "guilty." Florence fainted and Charlie was sent to the Tombs.

To those who saw it Byrnes's way, it was another blow against corruption. But to the trustees of the Parkhurst Society, it was a victory for corruption. "It was not Gardner that we were trying to defend, nor was it Gardner that they were trying to convict," Parkhurst wrote. "The sense of this intensified all proceedings, and explains much of the passionate interest with which the case was watched, and the passionate energy with which it was conducted."

16

CITY OF RASCALS

The verdict emboldened both police and criminals. With the Parkhurst Society in disarray, prostitution and gambling increased and the police strutted about more confidently.

The pastor was dismissed as naive. "If Dr. Parkhurst believes in the honesty of Gardner, after a long and close association with him," the *Times* said, "he will believe anything, even that he is himself an efficient and successful detective."[1]

Time would reveal, however, that the supposedly naive Parkhurst was aware of the dimensions of corruption in the police force, while the supposedly shrewd Byrnes was either deluding himself about the extent of police criminality that he faced or cynically overlooking it.

Even the instrument that Byrnes was using, the Central Office Detective Bureau, was thoroughly rotten. As he had done in checking on Clubber, Byrnes continued to send the detectives out as an internal investigative force, but they were more tainted than the precinct police that they investigated. The most shocking example of their relationship with criminals was their alliance with bunco artists.

The top bunco men belonged to Jimmy McNally's greengoods gang. To see how McNally's men operated, you would hie yourself to Grand Central Station. Every day McNally and his gang, smelling of bay-rum aftershave, waited there for their victim to come along—a man whom, although they had never seen him before, they recognized immediately, the mark who was rich, gullible, and greedy enough to be guyed.

Each gang member played his part in convincing the mark that what he was being offered—a chance to buy counterfeit money—was risk-free and that he was justified in taking it.

McNally, known as the King of Greengoods, told the victim that in one sense the counterfeit money they were offering was real money—in the sense that it was made from plates stolen from the U.S. Mint. He would show the victim a bogus news item in which it was reported that plates for printing currency had been robbed from the National Treasury, that someone high in the Treasury Department was believed to be in cahoots with the rascals and that it was surmised that important political figures were involved in protecting the criminals, so that making arrests was regarded as nearly impossible.

The gang played upon the theme that corruption in high places was so rank that it was perfectly okay for a plain citizen to get in on it and take a few measly thousands for himself. Eventually the victim would declare that if such were the case he had no scruples in the matter.

The guy bought what he supposed was a satchel of money made from stolen plates, for which he paid ten percent of the face value. But when the guy's attention was diverted for a moment the satchel was switched. By the time he opened the satchel and found it stuffed with sawdust, the greengoods men were a safe distance away. If he decided to make a fuss about it, the greengoods men had nothing to fear, for the Central Office Detectives, who took over all these bunco cases, were in cahoots with them, and in fact took a cut for themselves.

The detectives would scare the guy out of town by reminding him that he had been conspiring to commit a federal crime and if he were indiscreet he could draw a prison term for it. The detectives always warned the victim to say nothing, for "if the newspapers get hold of this we will never find the swindlers."

The Central Office detectives forbade the bunco gang to swindle city residents; the guys had to be visitors. As a bonus, the police regulated the trade, enforcing territorial arrangements between gangs and scaring off usurpers who tried to move into a territory already claimed.

* * *

The bunco game—and every other criminal enterprise from which the police took a cut—continued unabated, although for some months before and after Charlie's arrest, the police insisted that the whorehouses proceed with caution. That was the experience of Augusta Thurow, who ran a boardinghouse for prostitutes on Second Avenue.

One day that winter (probably the first of February) a big man with a red moustache knocked on her tenement door. He was John Hock, hand-picked by Byrnes to be the new wardman of the East Fifth Street Station. Hock took out a memorandum book, ran his finger down a list of names, and said that Captain Doherty wanted to see her.

Augusta and her husband, Ernest, tried to get along with Doherty, the precinct commander at the East Fifth Street Station, and indeed they found him genial, as long as they paid their hush money regularly. But around the time that Charlie Gardner had been thrown into jail, some of their girls were arrested, apparently so the Captain could compile an arrest record that would mollify his superiors at Police Headquarters. Augusta and Ernest grumbled that it was unfair that they paid protection yet their girls were arrested anyway—but they paid the fines, and continued to pay blackmail to the police; and they did as they were advised, closing when the Captain sent word to close, and reopening when the Captain sent them the wink.

The summons to the precinct house that winter day worried them, and Augusta talked it over with her husband, a minor Tammany official who spent at least a portion of every day in a boozy haze. They had no idea why the stout Captain wanted to see Augusta, but they expected that money would solve whatever problem had arisen.

She was already throwing the wardman a $10 perquisite every month to keep on his good side. She gave every policeman on the beat $2 a week, and every time a new face came on the beat he had to get his $2 immediately. He would stand in front of the stoop until she came down and paid him. If she did not pay him, the girls would not be allowed to stand in the doorway and strike up conversations with passing men.

According to the story that she later told to Parkhurst, she put $25 in her pocketbook and made for the station house. When she got there she found others waiting ahead of her, and she recognized one of the ladies as a bawdyhouse keeper. When she finally got in to see Captain Doherty, she told him that she wanted to do the right thing, and was paying the wardman $25 every month, but business was not that good.

"You see, Madame," Captain Doherty reportedly told her in his office, "I have received orders from the Central Office to close up all the disorderly houses in this precinct. But I think it can be arranged so that you can go ahead. But be sure to receive only old friends, for if you don't do so you are liable to fall into the hands of a Central Office detective."

Augusta Thurow said she then told the captain she had the money with her and wanted to pay him now. "Oh, I am not supposed to receive money myself, you know," he hastened to explain, as though it were against police regulations. "However, as long as you have it with you, you may leave it. Just put it in an envelope and mark it 'Hock.'" He took a pencil and a blank envelope from his pocket and handed them to her. She placed the $25 in the envelope, penciled "Hock" on it, and tucked the envelope in a pigeonhole in the Captain's desk.

With that Augusta hoped that things had been smoothed over. But soon the red-haired wardman stopped by with an alarming message: the Captain sent word through him that he would not stand for the notoriety of her "joint" at the bargain price that she was paying.

Mrs. Thurow responded that this was unfair, since she had always cooperated with the Captain. Hock failed to sympathize. A "ranch" like hers, he said, should be worth $60 to $70 a month in protection, and if she could not do better she would be raided. For taking increased risks the captain needed additional recompense.

Neither the pastor's crusade nor Byrnes's shakeups closed up the gambling houses and brothels, but both made the cost of doing business more expensive. Gardner's activity had forced the police to conduct more raids and drove up the cost of protection. Byrnes's shakeups were costly too. The transfer of a captain from one precinct to another always involved the transfer of money from one pocket to another. After The Great Shakeup every whorehouse in the city had to pay an "initiation fee" to the incoming precinct captain. And Byrnes's latest round of five reassignments of captains after the Clubber hearing meant that the whorehouses in five precincts were saddled with the same expense again just a few months later. This, as Parkhurst acidly noted of the transfers, "will give to the unsophisticated reader a new conception of what Mr. Byrnes means by 'the good of the service.'"

* * *

The Parkhurst forces had been dealt a severe blow at the trial, but Recorder Smyth was not through yet. A week later he announced that he intended to cite Goff and Jerome for contempt of court. The legal establishment was shocked, for it was the practice of the courts to deal with contempt immediately. Furthermore, Smyth had never cautioned the pair, as was invariably the practice, that they were risking a citation. Even lawyers who believed that the defense lawyers had gone overboard were inclined to suspect that Recorder Smyth had been biding his time and planning revenge.

Jerome rendered a full apology while Goff, refusing to grovel, denied any intention of disrespect and expressed regret for having offended the court. But their peace offerings were not received graciously, although Smyth relented on his intention to pronounce immediate punishment, agreeing to hold it in abeyance for several days.

Goff and Jerome found an advocate in Joseph Choate, who volunteered his services. When he appeared on behalf of his beleaguered colleagues, the courtroom was packed with lawyers who wanted to see Choate, the quintessential big business attorney of the Gilded Age, in action.

Choate told the Recorder that he had known Goff and Jerome since their admission to the bar and held them in the highest regard. He asserted that in the aggressive defense of his client Goff had properly objected when the Recorder supplied an answer to Lillie Clifton while Goff was trying to catch her in a lie. He admitted that his client had overreached himself in his summation and had used "language that was disrespectful to the court," but called it an excusable lapse committed at the end of a heated trial.

The most serious charge was that when the Recorder had ordered Gardner to stand up for identification, Goff and Jerome had attempted to prevent the attendants from carrying out the order. But Choate furnished affidavits from several witnesses, including members of the jury, that nothing of the sort had occurred, and he respectfully suggested that Recorder Smyth was mistaken.

"Well," said the Recorder, "I sat here and saw Jerome and Goff put their hands on Gardner."

"In spite of that," Choate dryly responded, "all these witnesses, who were sitting here also, did not see what you did."

Surprised by Choate's unabashed defense, Smyth dismissed the charge against Jerome. He dismissed the same charge against Goff but fined him a total of $200 or thirty days in jail for three other instances of contempt. The incensed Goff, his dark blue eyes burning, insisted upon serving the jail term. Only at the last moment did Choate and other attorneys talk the stubborn Irish attorney into paying the fine.

* * *

The lawyers and the criminal justice system soon suffered another jolt when Barney Martin was named a Police Justice.

Barney, the brother of Police Board President Jimmy Martin and the former associate of sneak-thieves, bank robbers, pickpockets and Whyos, took office to a chorus of boos and hisses from most of the city's newspapers.

He was nearly illiterate; he once owned a saloon used as a hangout by the Whyos and the Swell Mob; while Coroner he engineered the release from custody of a member of the Swell Mob accused of murder, and Barney's political connections had to be put into play to help him dodge an indictment. While Deputy Sheriff he was indicted for bribery, but was never tried because the indictment was erased on a technicality. A year earlier the Wigwam might have hesitated to favor Barney for so sensitive a position but, like the police, Tammany Hall was growing more brazen.

Barney told "the boys" that being a Police Justice would change nothing— certainly it would not interfere with his political work in the Eighth District for

Tammany. He owed as much to the men who had toiled on his behalf. "They done noble," he said.

Croker too was casting off restraints. As chairman of the Finance Committee of Tammany Hall, he received no salary, and he had no paying job. Yet the Crokers had just moved into a new home on Seventy-fourth Street near Central Park, said to cost $200,000, and when they entertained a French Admiral in May, the Dresden china and silver service were of enviably high quality.

He had recently plunked down a quarter-of-a-million dollars for a half-interest in the horseflesh at the Belle Mead Stock Farm, for more than sixty years a leader in breeding the American thoroughbred horse. He followed that purchase, the largest in American turf history, by buying some of the top horses in American racing at breathtaking prices. The Tammany Boss paid $30,000 for Longstreet, $24,000 for Yorkville Belle, and $22,000 for Dobbins. He became a partner in Monmouth Park in New Jersey and Gravesend Racetrack in Brooklyn. The Tammany Boss had become a power in the Sport of Kings. A few months earlier no one in racing had ever heard of him. Now men deferred to him when he arrived at racetracks, and he went to the track almost every day.

* * *

Recorder Smyth sentenced Charlie to three years in Sing Sing, but while Goff and Jerome pursued an appeal the convicted man languished in the Tombs—framed, in the view of the Parkhurst Society, for interfering with police corruption.

Even so ingrained an optimist as Parkhurst was hard put to find solace when the dust settled after the Gardner fiasco.

Obstacles had been raised to obtaining search warrants, and the Society's freedom of action had been hampered.

Furthermore, public support for the Society had dwindled. Former backers had lost heart or trust. "On the fifth of December," the pastor acknowledged (citing the date that Gardner's arrest was announced), "the Society for the Prevention of Crime stock was very low and continued falling for months."

Press disapproval was virtually unanimous. The *Times* called the Parkhurst Crusade "a complete failure."[2] The *World* warned that if "Dr. Parkhurst's methods against vice are to be encouraged" and "irresponsible hired detectives" perform police work, the city would be the worse for it, even were the pastor's charges true.[3]

For another thing, the city seemed more resigned than ever to Tammany rule. The Republicans continued to play dead for the sake of whatever bounty the Wigwam might bestow upon them. The rich were content, so long as their personal safety was assured, to adorn the city as ornaments, waiting for the opening bars of the next cotillion. And the menacing growls of the Anarchists only made the police more indispensable and unassailable.

Nevertheless the pastor continued to hope. As Tammany showed more effrontery in its disregard of public opinion, Parkhurst saw it sowing the seeds of its defeat. He believed that in their seeming triumph his enemies had ironically confessed their guilt, a confession embedded in the central roles played by Byrnes, Devery, Lillie Clifton, and Recorder Smyth; and that in time these roles would suggest "to the community, under startling colors, the organized combination seeming to exist between the police, the prostitutes, and the Bench."

Buoyed by this belief, and stirred by an ego trampled and stomped in the editorial columns, he was ready to wage a counter-offensive. According to his plan, the Society's agents would be sent out to saturate one selected precinct. They would not concentrate on raids but on amassing evidence. His fellow trustees, in his words, "agreed that our next step must be to make a solid case of malfeasance against a police captain."

The Society's governing board narrowed the possibilities to the three most vice-ridden precincts in the city.

One was the Tenderloin precinct, which Clubber Williams had made famous.

A second was the twenty-second precinct, from which Devery was departing (leaving instructions for the new precinct captain to take good care of Lillie Clifton "on account of the services she had rendered" in the Gardner case).[4]

The third, in the heart of the Lower East Side, was the Eldridge Street precinct—a turf that belonged to Barney Rourke, Dry Dollar Sullivan, Silver Dollar Smith, and Max Hochstim, and was dominated by the Essex Market Court House.

Eventually the Society chose Eldridge Street, in Parkhurst's words, "as being the precinct where, as it appeared to our detectives, gambling and disorderly resorts were being conducted with a more shameless and blatant openness than in any other."

Perhaps it was sober judgment that induced Parkhurst to pour all the Society's energies into the Eldridge Street precinct. Or maybe he had an appetite for revenge. Whatever the reason, he was heading for a scuffle with the new captain of the Eldridge Street precinct—Big Bill Devery, the cop with the brightest future in New York.

THE ELDRIDGE
STREET PRECINCT

Spring, Summer, Fall 1893

17

THE FAT PRECINCT

He was not lacking in a certain kind of genius, but it all ran on depraved lines.

—Parkhurst on Devery, *My Forty Years in New York*

By 1893 the Eldridge Street precinct, teeming with what Teddy Roosevelt called "ethnic turnover," was becoming the New Israel.

Even for a city used to unsettling waves of immigration, the Jews were a special problem. Some New Yorkers objected to the influx of non-Christians into a Christian land. Others raised the old canard about the Jews' love of gold and silver. Many laboring men feared that the Jewish influx would drive down wages, since the Hebrews were reportedly ready to work longer hours for less money.

And there were those who felt that the Jews lacked "the stuff" to make it as Americans. The managing editor of a Swedish weekly newspaper in New York called them "utterly incapable of understanding this country."[1] Frank Moss of the Parkhurst Society mused that "it seemed a hopeless task to fill them with any such controlling love of liberty as would work their deliverance and make them fit to enjoy the freedom designed by American institutions."

* * *

A visitor glancing into the doorways of the Lower East Side would see dirt-caked floors in the dark hallways and walls grimy with smoke. Ragged children played in sticky alleys. According to a census, 3,600 Russian Jews lived on a single square block, making it the most densely populated spot on earth. Families sold sleeping space on their rented floors to single men. "There's one family of four people upstairs who have two rooms and keep seven boarders," a staff housekeeper told a reporter, "four women and three young men." Jacob Riis, a *Sun* reporter, found a room with five families living in it, a total of twenty people. In such cramped quarters the ingrained modesty of the Eastern European Jews eroded. During the day their mattresses were stored with the kitchen utensils on the fire escape. When summer arrived the people slept on roofs and fire escapes.

In Ludlow and Allen streets, where the signs were inscribed in Hebrew, the insectivorous sewing machines whirred incessantly from every window. Families, including children, toiled in the needle trades, stitching all day and half the night. Dim-sighted old men with shaking hands drove the needles into their fingers. Middle-aged women racked with coughing sewed tuberculosis into the fabric. At the sewing machine, in the dark corner in the dim light, joyless young girls worked hour after hour to survive.

In Hester Street the sidewalk merchants set up their stands at five in the morning. They sold used overcoats, cloth remnants, candles, chickens dead of

The Most Densely Populated Block

malnutrition, strings of garlic bulbs, lead cutlery, oilcloths, tinware and shoes. Cracked eggs sold for a penny. Mushy peaches and limp turnips competed for stray pennies. Those without pushcarts strung trays from their shoulders or sold out of aprons, or dropped a plank astraddle two ash barrels, or laid goods on an oilcloth on a stoop. As the sun climbed in the sky the streets filled with the stench of rotting fish and vegetables.

Women ventured into the mire to shop with a few copper pennies. By the age of thirty they looked old, with lined faces, toothless mouths and sunken eyes, and walked with an ungainly gait. They wore shaitels, ill-fitting wigs that covered the hair they had cut short at marriage as pledges of fidelity. "Come by me and get a good bargain," a pushcart merchant would cry. A woman would stop to offer half of what he asked. He would screech that his family would starve were he to accept her bid. She would say that he must take her for a fool to buy such overpriced goods. He would suggest that her children should die of cholera for trying to make a beggar of him. She would reply that he was a thief and gesture as if to spit upon his wares. He would grab them and throw them on a heap for protection.

Ugly beyond pretense, the Lower East Side hardly seemed like a prize for a rising police captain. But there must have been something more to it than met the eye, for this was the precinct to which Big Bill Devery was sent after the Gardner conviction.

* * *

Men passing time in saloons were arguing whether the Columbian Exposition was worth traveling to Chicago to see, and if so whether it was worth the extra price to ride the new express train that could get you there in nineteen hours, and whether Croker was collecting payoffs from George Gould, Russell Sage, and the other streetcar magnates. And the Devery reassignment also became the subject of lively debate, the core of the argument hinging on the cash value of being assigned to one precinct or another. One group held that the fattest precinct in the city was the Tenderloin. That was the ideal assignment, they said, for a captain who wanted to fit his wife out in jewels. Others argued that the Tenderloin's day had passed and that the best pickings lay in the Lower East Side. Those precincts—the Eldridge Street, East Fifth Street and Delancey Street precincts—enjoyed a bonanza of blackmail from the brothels, gambling dens and saloons.

Of the three the fattest was the Eldridge Street precinct. Saloons came six to a block. Gambling operations were conducted out of storefront locations, and the prostitutes clustered as thick as the roses of Sharon. This area lacked the ruffles of the Tenderloin, but it made up in quantity what it lacked in style. Furthermore, it abounded in "fences"—receivers of stolen goods who placed the loot in pawnshops or resold it through a secret network. They operated by sufferance of the police, with whom they divided their gains. It was also the precinct that contained much of "The Thoid," the most hard-fought political district in the city. Every Christmas the Eldridge Street wardman took up a collection among the saloons for the precinct captain. In recent years the Christmas fund had exceeded $8,000, more than three times a Captain's annual salary.

The thirty-eight-year-old Captain Devery, who wore his moustache curled like a dandy and his hair cropped close like a tough, quickly made his presence felt. Donning civilian clothes, he paid calls on the gamblers and brothel-keepers in his protectorate. His behavior was startling, but Devery lived by a code of alarming openness. Direct contact helped him to size up his clients and to estimate how well they were doing. He did not discuss money, of course, but a few days after Devery's visits, a brothel-keeper would be summoned to the precinct station to see Devery's wardman, Edward Glennon. When Carl Werner arrived the wardman told him that the "initiation fee," which every Captain exacted upon being reassigned to a new precinct, was $600.

"I said to him that it only used to be $500, and asked him why the price had been raised," recalled Werner, a stout bespectacled man with a gold watch chain who looked more like a professor than a whoremaster. "Glennon only laughed at me, and said he couldn't help it. I told him I was a little pressed for cash just then, but would try to get him his money in a few days. He appeared satisfied, and I left." He paid the initiation fee in two installments over the next month and continued to pay the standard $50 per month.

Rhoda Sanford had a brothel on Bayard Street. "I was operating openly in February 1893, when Captain Devery took charge of our precinct," she recalled. "Glennon came to my house and asked for the madame. I went to the door. I knew what he come for, for I had read in the papers that there was a new captain in the ward. He told me he was Captain Devery's man. He said, 'I suppose you know what I am after?' I said, 'Yes, what's the damage?' He told me it was $500 and $50 a month."

Capt. Wm. S. Devery

Devery extracted every cent he could squeeze out of the brothels, but he did not take blackmail and then conduct raids anyway, as did Captain Doherty in the adjacent East Fifth Street precinct. He took pride in his straight dealing; once you bought Devery he stayed bought.

He was ready with any answer that would serve to confuse or placate his questioners, and he harbored a contempt for respectability. "All righteous men deplored his happy, honest wickedness," wrote Lincoln Steffens, who came to know Big Bill well. "The wicked deplored his shamelessness, which frightened them." Devery, he said, mocked everything.

"Say, boss, there's a question I got to ask you," the captain exclaimed one day to Steffens. "You know so much more than I do, specially crooked knowledge about crooked men and things, I got to ask you a question that's been bothering me some of late." Big Bill grabbed Steffens by both shoulders to get his undivided attention, and asked with a serious look: "What I want to know is, have you noticed any stray graft running around loose that I have overlooked?"

* * *

Everybody said Devery had been sent to Eldridge Street as a reward for trapping Charlie Gardner. There is, however, another plausible explanation for the transfer.

He was a great cop. Devery was widely regarded as the best cop in New York—the most effective and intelligent, and the most fearless. He also had highly developed political instincts, and in being transferred to this precinct he was being sent into a delicate political situation.

The Lower East Side was a volatile place. After a decade of immigration, unions had gained a foothold among the Jews in the garment trade. The cauldron was bubbling even more violently of late, since the Czar had virtually barred Jews from colleges. Joining the ranks of immigrants, the young intellectuals imbued the Lower East Side with a radical hue.

Just as poor as their fellow Jews, the students were compelled to eke out a living under the same conditions, working in the garment trades. In a short time they had become the editors, the organizers, and the agitators for better living conditions.

Appalled by working conditions in the industry, where sixteen hours a day failed to supply enough money for a miserable existence, they fought for better wages, shorter hours, and more humane working conditions. The Jewish workers, who had great respect for learning, acknowledged their leadership. The Jewish trade unions grew apace, and won a number of victories.

The Lower East Side needed a precinct captain with political skills as well as courage. Tammany Hall was inclined to be indulgent with the working class, and did not want a captain who spoke only with his nightstick, but the excitable nature of the immigrants had to be held in check, especially with the Anarchists at large. Diplomacy was needed.

Most police captains of the time, unable to disguise their contempt for the Eastern European Jews, were unsuited for such work. But Devery shook every hand offered to him. When he called upon Max Hochstim and Silver Dollar Smith, or upon union leaders like Joseph Barondess, he combined the right mixture of irreverence and good-fellowship. As much politician as he was cop, Devery was gregarious and ingratiating, and while it was his nature to razz, he did it with a disarming wink. He was the perfect choice for the job.

DEVERY AND THE DIVA

Big Bill Devery was just getting settled into the precinct when hard times arrived. The first warnings—news items about Midwestern banks failing and railroads tumbling into receivership—came as the rumble of distant thunder. Then New York business began to feel the pangs. On June 27 the stock market all but collapsed, and "the stringency," as it was called, began to hit home. The downturn, later known as the Panic of 1893, caused unprecedented economic suffering.

The Republicans blamed it on the follies of President Cleveland. The Democrats charged that the high tariffs of the preceding Republican administration were to blame. The American Iron and Steel Association blamed "thousands of idle and vicious foreigners who have not come here to work for a living but to stir up strife and to commit crime."[1] On the Midwestern plains the Populists blamed the Eastern moneychangers. And in the East, as factories closed and the jobless found their pantries empty, as misery struck the Lower East Side, the Anarchists and Socialists blamed the capitalist system.

Downtown New York went through a surly summer. As hunger grew among out-of-work garment trade workers, Anarchists praised "the mighty speech of bombs."[2] Women cursed the police from stoops on Rivington Street, and on Allen Street, the bloody-minded shouted for the people to arm themselves. Recalling the fate of the seven cops killed in the Haymarket riot, the police grew anxious.

At a rally in Walhalla Hall on an August afternoon unemployed men began breaking chairs and gaslights. The men included a lot of cloakmakers, whose union leaned toward Anarchism, and the men engaged with the police in a bloody battle that ended when vigorous clubbing drove the men into the street, where they vowed to return better prepared to take revenge.

Nightstick still in hand, Big Bill sympathized with the plight of the workers. "The men are both light-headed and hotheaded," he told reporters. "If they would go at it in the right way, I would like to see them hold meetings. Instead of breaking them up the police would give them protection. I would contribute towards hiring a hall. After all, the men are in a bad way. I am sorry for them."

New York provided a steady stream of surprises, but to hear a police captain speaking thus was truly startling. Nor was that the end of Devery's diplomacy. He turned up at labor meetings to shake hands with the workers and advise them that if they were peaceful their demonstrations would be respected, but that if they intended to advocate combat with the police, it would go badly for them. His cool manner impressed and sobered the most pugnacious radical.

When Anarchists began to foment disorder at a Socialist meeting in Pythago-ras Hall, Big Bill showed up to issue a warning: if the police took action, people would be hurt, and a panic might result. Therefore he suggested, with a grin, that the meeting be adjourned. After some face-saving bravado by the Anar-chists, it broke up.

On another occasion Devery had a group of troublemakers brought to the precinct station, where he spoke through an interpreter.

"You are all respectable-looking men," Devery told them. "I know you are out of work, and that is unfortunate. I do not intend to lock you up and make you pay fines, for you have no money; but you must not stand at the corner of Essex and Broome streets and block the way. Now all of you go home, and if you are caught there again, I'll certainly lock you up."

Even the arrested men may have been surprised at this, since the usual method the police used on belligerent workers was to take them to a secluded place and beat them.

One can only conjecture about his motives and under what orders, if any, Big Bill worked. It is possible that Devery, whose politics were of a progressive bent, was improvising on his own, although it appears that the police in adjacent precincts were also approaching the workers in a style somewhat mellower than had been the case in the past.

Big Bill tended to be tougher on the dynamite-happy Anarchists than on the more law-abiding Socialists. This was a matter of some weight, for the marches and the speeches against hunger and homelessness that summer, while sincere expressions of crisis, at the same time were bids to win the loyalty of garment workers. The Socialist leaders of the United Hebrew Trades were winning that struggle, and the frustrated Anarchists were growing more bloodthirsty. One of the few tactics left to them was to unmask the State's repressive role by goading the police to violence, and profiting from the resulting havoc.

After months of having lain low, Emma Goldman hurled herself into the fray. She discovered that during her absence her fame had grown. All kinds of stories had been circulating about her, including a rumor that she had beaten Johann Most with a horsewhip, though that mighty orator—while conceding that she might do anything to attract attention—denied that any such thing had happened.

A band of devotees surrounded her as she called upon workers to fight with the heroism of Berkman and the Haymarket martyrs. "Wherever that woman went," the *Herald* said, "her voice was raised to inflame the simple and easily misguided minds of her hearers against capital and property."[3] The *World* said the plump little woman was "breathing words of slaughter and phrases of incendiarism, and appealing by invectives, taunts, and persuasion to the feelings of her hearers."[4]

Many saloonkeepers were refusing to rent their halls to Anarchists—not only because of police pressure, but because the Anarchists were inclined to express their political views through wreckage. One expedient of the Anarchists to surmount this problem was to pack Socialist meetings and try to take them over—often by making a continual clamor to give the podium to Emma Goldman.

When unsuccessful in getting the platform at one hall she would lead the march to another, demanding to be heard as the voice of the people. The men

*"There are people who will not be afraid to head your march under the black flag. The flag of danger to our foes,"
said Emma Goldman.*

followed. A short time earlier, when they lived in the shtetls of Imperial Russia, these men would have laughed had they been told that they would be taking advice and instructions from a woman. But this was America, and all was topsy-turvy here.

On reaching the next hall, they would shout out her name and suggest dire consequences if their entreaties were ignored. When it worked Emma Goldman would be invited to the platform.

She spoke in a disjointed, hectic style unified by its mocking spirit. She hectored her audience like a schoolmarm whose patience has worn out, belittling her listeners as stupid and gullible men to whom religion had taught the virtues of slavery. As in Russia, so in America, where the capitalists ruled them. Even their own union leaders cracked the whip over them. "Get rid of your leaders," she said. "You have shown by entering Walhalla Hall that you are men enough without leaders."

Even the police who monitored her speeches testified to her passionate sway over crowds, projecting herself so that what was remembered afterward was not the message but the spell that she cast. She did it with the simplest of materials, appealing directly to the emotions of her listeners. It was useless, she said, to talk seriously to her audiences about ideas. Instead she spoke of hungry wives and children, of evicted families soaking in the rain, and contrasted their plight with the pleasures of the rich—their homes, their banquets, their equipages and fine blooded horses.

Goldman praised those who had attacked the police in Walhalla Hall, and deprecated as cowards those who counseled caution, and urged those who went to rallies to carry weapons. She set her supporters to harassing the press and often tried to have them physically ejected. During one speech discord broke out because a worker had been detected talking to a reporter, which she had explicitly forbidden to her audience.

Angry men made for the offender, who turned pale, held up his hands and begged for mercy.

"Stop!" exclaimed Goldman. "Don't lay hands on him! Let the miserable, traitorous wretch get out."

The Anarchists stepped back, opened the door for him and he rushed out.

Wherever she spoke, those conducting the meeting felt the need of an antidote. Even Joseph Barondess, the Anarchist head of the cloakmakers' union, was stressing patience, determination, and discipline, and trying to distance himself from hothead oratory. He hoped to shift his union's emphasis to demands that Mayor Gilroy persuade the Civil Justices to stop evicting families for the duration of the stringency.

On the day after the Walhalla Hall battle, a crowd of tattered men, some with bandaged heads, stood in front of the Essex Market Court House to see their friends brought to arraignment. Barondess told the arrested men he would help them as much as he could. Then he walked over to Devery.

"Captain," said Barondess, "you don't blame me for yesterday's work, do you?"

"Why, no," Devery replied, shaking his hand and taking him by the shoulder. "And I don't blame the men either. They must learn to respect the majesty of the law, however, and not take matters into their own hands."

Most of the men were fined small amounts which Barondess paid. When he ran out of funds, Barondess went into Silver Dollar Smith's saloon, cadging coins that he brought back to the court.

Goldman's inflammatory speeches created problems for Devery, who came under fire for permitting her to speak. The captain had to explain to his critics that he was having her speeches monitored, but that he did not wish to create sympathy by appearing to persecute her for speaking on behalf of starving children.

* * *

Superintendent Byrnes returned from vacation to muster police activity against fulminators of violence—to the relief of the wealthy, notes threatening death by dynamite having been left on the doorsteps of Fifth Avenue mansions. "In the future I shall have officers carefully report all speeches, and if I find anyone inciting people to riot, I'll arrest him without further delay," he told the press. "I can stop this sort of thing and I'm going to do it."

Finding his own precinct policy superseded, Captain Devery implemented Byrnes' orders. All the meeting halls in the precinct were closed, and janitors were advised to alert Devery immediately if an Anarchist meeting began.

The *World* protested in the name of free speech. "We think the police have made a mistake in attempting to stop the holding of these meetings," Pulitzer's paper said. "The blatant utterances of a notoriety-seeking virago like Emma Goldman do nobody any harm, convince nobody, stir nobody to passion." But the *Herald*'s headline promised that BYRNES WILL SHUT ANARCHY'S MOUTH, and the *Tribune* said that "it cannot be doubted that affairs were getting into a doubtful and dangerous condition, and that the Superintendent has done well to call a halt along the line of disorder."

Byrnes promised that if Goldman persisted in insurrectionist oratory the consequences would prove "very unpleasant to that young lady." But Goldman did not cool her message. On several occasions—at Golden Rule Hall and across the river in Newark—she advised the hungry to arm themselves with ample ammunition and to go to the bakeries to take bread.

Similar words were set down in news accounts of her Union Square speech on the night of August 21. In the *World* she was reported to say: "Unite and go from street to street. Go among the capitalists and rich people and ask for bread, and if they do not give it to you peaceably, then take it by force." She advised workers that they "have as much right to use arms as the police."

During that speech, the police decided that they could make a case, and an order was issued for her arrest. Detective Sergeant Charles Jacobs and other police followed her that night when she boarded a streetcar but, to avoid causing excitement in a crowd, they stopped short of arresting her. By the next morning she could not be located.

When the police traced her to Philadelphia, Sergeant Jacobs was sent on the Pennsylvania Railroad to bring her back. He arrested her just as she was about to enter a hall for a rally.

According to Goldman's version of the story, she learned to her amusement that she would be riding back not in handcuffs, but in one of the train's private compartments. She might be returning in captivity, but Jacobs had arranged for their mutual comfort.

As soon as they boarded Jacobs set about ingratiating himself with Goldman. He said that he had nothing against her, but was only doing his duty and supporting his six children. She asked him why he had not chosen an honorable occupation and why he had to bring more spies into the world. He replied that police were necessary to protect society.

He ordered dinner for two brought to the car. During the meal he praised her braininess but warned that she would never make a bundle of money in her present vocation. He said unctuously that he would be sorry to see a fellow Jew go to prison. She could get out of it and even get paid well if she would "look out for number one."

"Out with it," she said, "what's on your mind?"

Well, he explained, Superintendent Byrnes had instructed him to tell her that charges against her would be dropped and a goodly sum presented to her if she would supply the police with periodic reports about what was going on among East Side radicals.

At this point, she said, she threw the water from her glass into the detective's face. "You miserable cur!" she shouted. "Not enough that you act as a Judas, you try even to turn me into one—you and your rotten chief! I'll take prison for life, but no one will ever buy me!" Jacobs, his tail between his legs, meekly reached for a napkin to dry his face.

* * *

It sounds like a cheap period melodrama. Nevertheless it is probably truthful in its essentials. Verifiably Sergeant Jacobs specialized in recruiting and maintaining a circle of informers vis-à-vis downtown radicalism; they reported to him in a Bowery restaurant at midnight, passing along word of what transpired at union meetings, on the foibles of labor leaders, and items of information overheard in the shops and meeting halls. It is credible, therefore, that he would have tried to recruit her, and her response sounds completely in character.

After she was delivered to New York she was taken to Byrnes in the subterranean rooms in Police Headquarters in which the Third Degree had been perfected. His penetrating eyes glared as he threatened to have her put away for years. She responded that the whole nation ought to find out how corrupt he was. He raised a chair as if to strike her with it, then, thinking better of it, he called for a detective to take her back to the cell. In the afternoon she was charged with inciting to riot at Union Square and was placed in the Tombs to await trial.

Her enemies were glad to have her in custody. There were even some radicals who were not unhappy to see her behind bars. And, although she never said as much, not even in her memoirs, she was probably not completely displeased either, for her debt to Sasha Berkman had at last been paid.

19

"A COLOSSAL ORGANIZATION OF CRIME"

While Devery wended his corrupt way through the precinct, Parkhurst agents trailed his footsteps. They also reconnoitered the mean streets, looking for vice—a snap in this part of the city, where it beckoned from the windows. Seeking no warrants, the agents concentrated upon documenting the open luxuriance of vice.

Devery, meanwhile, was claiming that he had run vice out of his precinct. According to his weekly reports to headquarters, brothels and gambling houses had gone smack out of business. Every week Inspector Clubber Williams, his supervisor, endorsed Big Bill's hokum and sent it up to Byrnes.

Of course Big Bill's men made arrests from time to time. The cops never raided a brothel—Devery would not allow his contracts to be violated—but attempted to run up an arrest record by collaring the most powerless kind of prostitute, the streetwalkers.

* * *

Parkhurst worked on the premise (although he lacked evidence and was probably wrong) that Big Bill "had to pay roundly for his precinct" and therefore fostered the spread of vice in order to get his investment back.

When the pastor left with his wife for the Alps in June, The Work continued under his instructions, and in July Thaddeus Kenneson and Frank Moss presented the Society's evidence of corruption in the Eldridge Street precinct to District Attorney Nicoll. Admitting that the facts looked properly documented, the D.A. promised to get them to the Grand Jury. But he reneged, then assured them that he would bring the evidence to the August Grand Jury. When that

Grand Jury was winding up its business and preparing to disband, Moss, convinced that Nicoll was dawdling, threatened to bypass the D.A.'s office and go straight to the Grand Jury with his evidence.

Nicoll arranged a conference with the jury foreman, Richard Cross. A friend of the police department in all weathers, Cross had misgivings about jarring police morale while Captain Devery was defending the ramparts against Anarchists. In Cross's view, the precinct was a tinderbox and the bluecoats needed all the backing they could get. Kenneson and Moss were unable to budge him. Nicoll promised to get the Society another chance early in the term of the September Grand Jury.

Again in September and again in October, Nicoll decided that with the threat of insurrection hanging over the city, the times were too unsettled to permit evidence demoralizing to the police to go before a Grand Jury. He continued to promise access, however, to the next one.

* * *

After Nicoll failed to come through in August, Moss and Kenneson warned him that rather than dangling on his string, they would take their evidence to the press. And in October they did, issuing an official report, formally to the Board of Police Commissioners, although it was first released to the newspapers. The report listed fifty-three whorehouses and eleven gambling dens that were operating with impunity in the Eldridge Street precinct.

The report accused Devery of having agreements with brothels and gambling houses that allowed them to operate "with no more concealment than if it had been a drygoods store or a butcher shop." It called Devery a liar and concluded:

"Devery could not maintain this protective attitude toward crime were it not for the backing which he gets from the superior authorities to which he is amenable. He is simply one factor in a colossal organization of crime by which our unhappy city is despotized. The precinct swarms with boys and girls, and is a superb fitting school for adult depravity; it is a sort of devil's seminary, in which the vicious negligence of Devery constitutes him a kind of first trustee."

The report made a splash in the press, which played up the animosity between the Society and the captain, and Big Bill cut short his vacation to respond. Devery said he was aware that Parkhurst had taken particular interest in his precinct; on the night of June 3 he had followed the preacher and another man, whom he supposed to be Moss, for three hours. "They walked through Forsyth, Christie, Stanton, Canal and other streets, but did not enter any house, nor could they have seen anything to shock them," he said. "I was within a half-block of them all the time and four of my men were with me." Shamelessly, he wondered aloud why

Parkhurst was reluctant to work with him. "I will be only too glad," he said, "to make use of any evidence that Moss might have." But he added that it would be difficult for him to make any arrests, were any warranted, since any wrongdoers were probably lying low because of the newspaper hullabaloo.

The Board of Police Commissioners met a few days later. When the Society's report came up, the Board mocked Parkhurst as an opportunist and sensationalist and refused to examine information that had already been in the newspapers.

"I think that it is not worthwhile to waste time in reading it," said Commissioner McClave. "I move that it be referred to the Superintendent for consideration."

Perhaps coincidentally, arrests for prostitution tripled in the precinct after the supposedly worthless report was made public. As before, the unfortunate prostitutes were all streetwalkers.

* * *

In October, after Parkhurst's return, the Society again tried to alert the Police Board and the public to the reign of vice in the precinct. Updating their information, Parkhurst agents gathered new evidence against forty-five resorts, either gambling dens or whorehouses, operating openly under the nose of Captain Devery. Copies of the report were sent to the Captain; to his superiors, Williams and Byrnes; and to the Police Board.

This time the official response was even more inhospitable. Police Commissioner Sheehan admitted that in the past he had given Parkhurst credit at least for sincerity, but had wised up after reading interviews in which the pastor admitted that his goal was to bring down Tammany Hall. The so-called crusade, Sheehan concluded, was merely a political campaign to defeat Tammany in the coming election and should be ignored.

Byrnes reported that he had put two of his trusted Central Office detectives on the case and had been assured that the Society was flailing about wildly. He had also instructed Williams and Devery to investigate these charges—and, as might have been guessed, Clubber and Big Bill found that they were baseless. "Any person who would make such a statement," Clubber Williams said scornfully, "in the face of the actual condition of the precinct, has no regard for truth or his moral obligations." Clubber said the charges were nothing more than an attempt to get even with the Captain who had captured Parkhurst's top detective.

The newspapers gave their full attention to the controversy, but Parkhurst was out of press favor. Even the *Post*, a pillar of anti-Tammany feeling, took an arm's-length approach, counseling the Police Board that the pastor's motives ought not to interfere with a serious look at the reports. And a *World* editorial lambasted Parkhurst's homecoming sermon, in which he reminded his fellow preachers that Jesus was not afraid to dirty his hands in the world's work. "But it is nowhere recorded that the great Teacher ever went spying after nastiness," the *World* said, "or that he ever sought to reform the unfortunate fallen by hiring some of them to commit criminal indecencies in his presence in order that he might get them sent to jail and make himself talked about."

* * *

In the aftermath of Charlie's conviction, the Society suffered from a continuing lack of public support. Contributions slowed to a trickle. And yet the Gardner fiasco, upsetting though it was, worked as a tonic inside the organization. For one thing, it flushed out a cabal of treacherous agents cast in the mold of Chauncey Grant, hostile to Gardner and possibly even informers and turncoats. For the second time in less than a year virtually the entire staff was purged.

Then the Society put together a more trustworthy collection of agents who worked harder, were more talented, and were more devoted to their mission. "In point of effectiveness we were in finer shape shortly subsequent to Gardner's arrest than we had ever been before," Parkhurst wrote. "How much we owe to the vicious opposition of the enemy!"

The new agents had their work cut out for them. The Society's reports, attacked as gross exaggeration, had only begun to probe the depths of corruption. In the Lower East Side the cops shook down everybody and everything—not just purveyors of vice, but also bootblacks and restaurants, haberdashers and produce markets. Even the pushcart peddlers were extorted every week. On Hester Street, site of the largest such market, the police took their cut every Friday. Rather than collect it themselves, they recruited peddlers to do it for them. Joseph Goldstein, a hardy young Jew, was one of those designated to make the rounds, an honor that he was powerless to decline. From those at the best locations he took a dollar. From those with corners in less favored streets he demanded $.75. The lowest price was $.50. When he completed his rounds Goldstein stepped into a doorway and gave the money to a cop, who gave him $2 as a fee and exempted him from tribute. If anyone refused to pay, Goldstein pointed him out to the cops. The "politzmen," as Jews called the bluecoats, shook them, shouted at them, and cuffed them over the ears. Should a bold spirit stand up to them, he would be beaten and kicked, his pushcart overturned and his goods trampled in the mud.

For that matter, there were a few cops in those Lower East Side precincts who drew the line at nothing. The worst of them worked closely with Max Hochstim, the Jewish saloonkeeper who, with Silver Dollar Smith, controlled the bail bond business in the Essex Market Court House.

Max Hochstim

Hochstim and his police accomplices manufactured false evidence solely for the purpose of blackmail. On several occasions, for example, they rented a room, sent young men with prostitutes to occupy the room, and then swooped in to arrest the owners of the boardinghouse. On other occasions they induced young men (stoolpigeons who loitered in the precinct stations or thugs who frequented Hochstim's bar) to make false charges against women. The cops conveyed to their victims that the charges could be dropped if money changed hands, and these cases rarely came to court. Yet even when faced with the power of the police a Tammany captain, and Tammany-appointed judges, a few of them occasionally fought back. When such resistance developed, Hochstim's thugs were sent to administer a beating or a stabbing.

It was a devil's seminary indeed. But were such conditions not more likely to prevail in districts of the city in which people failed to understand the glories and duties of American civic virtue? The pastor believed that the Jews could be gradually assimilated, but that at present they were being absorbed in indigestible amounts. He feared that American values would be eroded by these

In Max Hochstim's Saloon

immigrants, "distinctly of the less advanced races, people who are aliens, not only in respect of their place of birth, but as regards everything that is constituent of personal value." The problem, according to his fellow trustee Moss, was that "they bowed so humbly to the yoke of their oppressors."[1]

Whatever the cause, something worse than ordinary corruption was abroad in the Eldridge Street precinct.

* * *

By the end of October the Parkhurst Society had amassed so much evidence against brothels in the precinct that it could pick and choose which would be most opportune to raid. In order to arrange the raids without a warning shot going off to the whorehouses, however, it would be necessary to keep the precinct police in the dark—which could be done if the Society could prevail upon a sympathetic Police Justice. Moss had found one in Justice John Voorhis. With solid evidence in hand the Society might convince Voorhis, who was not a Tammany man, to make an exception to the new rule that only precinct police were empowered to serve warrants. Voorhis might be persuaded to assign court squad police to accompany the Parkhurst agents to the brothels to serve the warrants, make arrests, and bring back the arrested women without alerting Devery.

The agents took their evidence to the Essex Market Court House on the morning of October 27. After winning the cooperation of Voorhis, they made arrests in three brothels and were back in court before Captain Devery knew what was afoot.

The Parkhurst agents had struck quickly, but it did not take long for word to spread. While the detectives and their counsel, Frank Moss and Thaddeus Kenneson of the Parkhurst Society, presented their evidence, the streets began to fill up around Silver Dollar Smith's saloon. The group, "about as low and disreputable and criminal a body of men as ever got together in New York," according to the *World*, gathered in the surrounding streets, hoping to accost the Parkhurst agents as they left the courthouse. They "uttered curses and threats as loudly as they dared. There were thieves, gamblers, ex-convicts and those wretches who live upon the melancholy earnings of lost women."

The stage was set for a spectacular confrontation—some called it a riot—pieced together here from news accounts and affidavits later given to the police.

* * *

Inside, Moss learned from Parkhurst agents that one of the men sitting in the courtroom had tried to interfere with their arrests, warning one of the women so that she had evaded capture. Moss pointed out the man to Justice Voorhis, and the Justice directed the court officers to bring him to the bench. They started toward him, but when they saw him they turned pale and refused to go further. "Why don't you bring that man here?" Moss demanded of the head officer. "If you don't bring him I will bring him myself." Still the officers stood in their tracks. Moss, taking the man by the arm, ordered him to advance to the bench, and pushed him forward when the man hung back.

"You are accused of having warned a defendant in this case that the officers were after her," Justice Voorhis said. "What do you say to that?"

The man would not answer.

"What is your name?"

"Max Hochstim."

There was a stir in the courtroom. Hochstim! Everybody feared his power as a leader of a gang of Jewish thugs, and as owner of The Thirteenth Ward House, a saloon with a back room for gambling. Hochstim was establishing himself as a wholesaler in prostitution, supplying downtown brothels with whores shipped in from other parts of the nation or imported from Europe. The Justice admonished Hochstim to keep out of his courtroom. Then Hochstim walked over to the attorney for the defendants and asked if he thought it would cost him more than a one hundred dollar fine to demolish Moss' face.

Justice Voorhis held the madames on $500 bail for trial. In the courtroom all had gone well, but as the hearing wound up Moss became alarmed at reports that a "large number of idle men of forbidding appearance," as he put it, were congregated near Silver Dollar's saloon. Moss suggested that they might prudently slip out one at a time to avoid notice. But others argued for the opposite approach—that they should leave in a body, relying on the safety that lay in numbers.

Moss and Kenneson left separately and unnoticed, then waited across the street to see if the five detectives escaped safely.

There was a sudden stir as the Parkhurst agents emerged together into the street. Immediately some in the crowd pressed upon them, cursing and brandishing their fists. They were particularly hostile to John Lemmon, the Parkhurst agent most active in assembling the case against the disorderly houses. Several men surged forward as if to punch him, and one who waved a knife at Lemmon was forcibly restrained by others in the mob.

The agents turned in a body and began to walk away from the courthouse, and the crowd set out behind them. There were about 150 to 200 men in the mob, and the detectives began to walk faster, glancing from time to time behind them. Some of the toughs shouted to men lounging on corners. "Those are Parkhurst's men, and we are going to do them up," they yelled, and others joined the fun. Men from the dives and gambling dens, pimps and burglars joined the gaiety. The detectives reached Broome Street and headed for the Bowery. Some of the toughs grew bolder, ran up at them from behind to taunt them with a shout. When a detective's hat was knocked from his head he did not stop to retrieve it.

At the corner of Allen Street they met a policeman on duty. "I call upon you to disperse this mob," one of the detectives said to him, "or we shall have a man killed here!" The cop laughed and ignored them.

Behind them the mob stopped and tried to put on a collective look of innocence. The agents paused only for a moment, and when they were sure that the policeman would not help they continued again, faster than before. The mob had begun to press them closely and had turned from laughter and taunts to an expressive silence. "The crowd was not the usual howling mob, which expends most of its energy in wind," Lemmon said, "but had a decidedly business air about it."

When they reached the Bowery, Lemmon suggested that they take a Fourth Avenue horsecar. They had just missed one and had to wait for the next. The mob grew bolder. Rocks and bricks flew at the agents. As another horsecar came in sight, it appeared that the mob would at any moment assault them. When the streetcar arrived the other four agents boarded it, but Lemmon became separated from them by a passing beerwagon. He made a dash for it, jumping on the front of the car. A man leaped on it, striking at him. Lemmon ducked and struck his assailant, knocking him off the car. The crowd surged around the car, two men stopping the horses by grabbing their bridles. Four other men were trying to board the rear of the car.

The passengers inside were frightened. Men jumped on the car at both ends and tried to force their way inside, but the detectives stood at the doors and held them back. At that moment two policemen ran up and the two men holding the horses released the reins. The horsecar driver whipped his horses, and the streetcar went up the street at a run, leaving a mob that scattered and ran from the police.

* * *

The newspapers played it up. "Many shopkeepers in Broome Street and along the Bowery in that neighborhood excitedly repeated the story of the assault, as they had seen it, to all comers," the *World* reported. "Some of them said they were willing to repeat it in court if they could be sure the police would not take revenge by annoying them in such petty ways as a revengeful policeman can use against even the most carefully honest shopkeeper."

Moss called at the office of an angry Police Superintendent. Byrnes was thumping tables with rage. "He said that he knew who committed the outrage," Moss said, "and damned them roundly, and said that he would sift the matter to the bottom, and would have the guilty parties, no matter who they were or how high they were. He said it was a bad condition of affairs if a mob could drive our men half a mile through the streets without interference, and the honor of the Police Department was at stake. He was earnest and profane."[2]

After expressing eagerness to get to the bottom of the matter, however, Byrnes unaccountably placed Captain Devery and Inspector Williams in charge of the investigation.

According to Lemmon, Big Bill proved uncooperative. When the Parkhurst agent went to a police lineup at the Essex Market Court House, he found it almost in darkness. With inadequate lighting it was hard for Lemmon to see the features of the men, who stood with the light at their backs and their faces in shadow. Despite these disadvantages Lemmon said he picked out two of the mob from the group, one of them the man who had brandished the knife at him. Lemmon said Devery was astonished, and asked, "Who gave you the pointers so as to identify these men?" Another Parkhurst agent identified a third man. All three accused men were active members of the Hochstim gang.

* * *

A few days later Big Bill and Clubber turned in a report to Byrnes that contradicted virtually everything that the Parkhurst agents said had happened.

According to their report, there had been no disorder in or near the court, no Society agent was assaulted nor did anyone appeal to the police for protection. No brick had been thrown at a horsecar. No one had grabbed the reins of a horsecar and stopped the horses. All the police and every witness they interviewed said that there was nothing to it.

Big Bill reported that his men had interviewed twenty-seven businessmen on Broome Street between Essex Street and the Bowery and on the Bowery from Grand to Delancey Street, all of whom were in the neighborhood and about their places of business at the time, and each said that no breach of the peace occurred.

Three members of the Essex Market Court squad all said that there was no disorder in or about the court and that no Society agent was assaulted or appealed for protection.

Two patrolmen reported that a band of boys ranging in age from twelve to sixteen were following the Parkhurst agents for a time. One of the patrolmen said that when he started for the boys, they scattered, and none of the men had asked him for help. A lawyer who was standing with him corroborated his story.

The streetcar conductor said in his affidavit that when the Parkhurst agents boarded they advised one of their number to draw his revolver. "I took him by the shoulder and said to him, 'If you are going to do any shooting you will have to get off this car,'" the conductor said. "I saw no violation of the law by anyone except these people [the agents]."

Captain Devery suggested that if the people of his precinct were losing patience with high-handed Parkhurst agents, he could readily sympathize. "If his agents come here, spying and terrorizing, causing violations of the law, they will get their deserts," he said. "It's a shame the way they force themselves into peoples' houses, and in some cases they have even made threats of breaking in doors. They stand upon stoops and terrorize everybody, if they think they can do so safely. I think Dr. Parkhurst is bringing disgrace upon his cloth."

Parkhurst responded that the incident underscored the corruption of "Devery's diocese, which he claims is remarkable for its immaculate purity. . . . The fact is that we were attacking the police and the thugs attacked us, which conclusively proves the affiliation between the two—that is, between those under Captain Devery and the thugs in his precinct."

Since he had no witnesses or evidence, Byrnes declared the investigation closed, noting that the Society was free to lodge complaints against the three accused men.

"I understand that the police call the riot a fake," Moss responded. "It is evident that the police want us to take the brunt of this complaint against the prisoners and put upon us the burden of proof. That is absurd."[3]

Both sides left it to the public to decide whether what happened on Broome Street was a near-riot, or a group of youngsters making mischief.

20

THE RULE
OF THE PEOPLE

That fall an Anarchist bombed the Chamber of Deputies in Paris, injuring four legislators and others. In New York, Inspector Clubber Williams halted a Middle Eastern belly dance presented at a midtown theater, and the celebrated bluenose Anthony Comstock objected to a wax statue at the Eden Musee of a gorilla carrying off a woman.

After listening to John Goff's argument, the State Supreme Court reversed the conviction of Charlie Gardner. The court agreed with Goff that extortion could occur only when fear or force was used against a victim, and that since Lillie Clifton was in cahoots with the police, neither fear nor force could possibly have been brought to bear against her. Charlie was released from the Tombs, where he had languished most of the year.

As it grew chilly, fallen leaves blew across Sheep Meadow in Central Park, and the breath of horses steamed upward as they pulled streetcars up and down Broadway. Hard times began to take on an aspect of permanence. The poor shivered, their hopes reduced to the possibility of buying coal by the pailful on credit. The rich ordered their coal by the ton for their cellar bins and awaited the reopening of the Metropolitan Opera House, which had been damaged in a fire and dark for a year.

Tammany Hall made ready for Election Day.

* * *

Like gray rats, the tramps began to stream into the downtown districts in October. District captains found them, their hair matted and their trousers baggy, in the saloons, picking up beans and stew at the free lunch counters.

They demanded free lodging, meal tickets and cash for their votes. Campaign workers signed up hotels and lodging-houses to put them up for a few days.

The activity was most intense in Paddy Divver's Second Assembly District, chock-a-block with cheap lodging-houses, with thinly partitioned cubbyholes six feet by four, hardly ample enough to contain a cot, and renting for fifteen cents a night. All the lodging-houses along Park Row belonged to Divver's allies; they delivered 150 to 300 votes per house. Divver's men canvassed the saloon-keepers; each promised to deliver fifty to one hundred floater votes to Tammany. The Tammany captains made arrangements to register them at various polling places to squeeze from them the maximum number of votes.

For many campaigns Paddy—who had operated a downtown saloon and spoke with a thick brogue that he had brought over from Ireland—had looked after the interests of Tammany Hall. Over the years he had so embossed himself on its political fortunes that the Second Assembly District was commonly called Divverdom. In 1890 his long service to the Wigwam had been rewarded by elevation to the Police Justice bench. Being a Police Justice, the boys of Divverdom said, was a soft snap—it involved little work and paid a princely $8,000 a year.

Uptown in the silk-stocking districts Justice Divver was thought of as a municipal disgrace. Paddy had been blackballed in 1892 when he applied for membership in the prestigious Democratic Club—perhaps because his ten-candlepower diamond stickpin was too loud. Paddy's candidate for the State Assembly in 1893 was Michael Callahan, a former bouncer who kept two of the most unholy dives in the city, one of them a hangout for remnants of the Whyo gang. Callahan had been accused of killing a man, although a coroner's jury cleared him, and was illiterate besides.

Almost every night the bandy-legged Paddy could be seen staggering homeward, his derby at a jaunty angle, after a night of drinking and cards in Andy Horn's saloon. Immigrants, who regarded judges as men of haughty expression and flinty manner, were amazed to learn that in New York judges caroused like tomcats by moonlight.

But whatever was said to his detriment in the oak-paneled clubs of upper Fifth Avenue, and however he scandalized the immigrants, the Wigwam was mindful that Divver controlled the most overwhelmingly Democratic district north of the Mason-Dixon line.

Paddy and other Tammany leaders were placing special emphasis on rounding up immigrants to swell the voting rolls. The Jews were available wholesale through Jewish political clubs. The Italian immigrants were under the control of padrones in East Harlem and Mulberry Bend, who oversaw every aspect of their move from the steamer ticket to the waiting job in America, and sold their votes, usually to Tammany, although the padrones had no objection to selling them to the Republicans or to both if they could get away with it.

Tammany made certain that they were quickly naturalized. The Wigwam paid application costs and marched them over to the Court House to wait on a line that stretched around corridors from the third floor to the basement. Although they had a long wait, when they reached the Superior Court Clerk's Office they had an easy time; the questions were few and simple. One Sicilian could not remember the name of the President of the United States, but he knew that Divver was the President of New York.

Invariably the registrants lied, as they had been coached to do, about how long they had been in America and, after being naturalized, all that remained was to get the election inspectors to accept their voting papers. Tammany had aides for that as well. They shepherded the immigrants through the registration offices, which had three inspectors, of which two were Tammany men, the third being Republican. (An investigating member of the city Bar Association reported later "that nearly all of the Republican election officials were either stupid or bought up.")[1]

Republicans did not even bother to set up a naturalization bureau. Their efforts below the line were thwarted by official persecution. If they ran their own lodging houses the Board of Health would close them up. When they put up a speakers' stand in the street, Bureau of Encumbrance workers carted it away to a junkyard. Nor was there any use taking a case to police court. A Tammany Police Justice considered it a betrayal of his judicial oath to render a decision that went against the interest of the Wigwam. In "The Thoid," Dry Dollar Sullivan did not bother resorting to subterfuge. Republicans who had the misfortune to see his men committing election irregularities kept it to themselves, for if they made a fuss about it Dry Dollar would have the police hound them out of business or arrest them on some charge or other.

Republican Boss Thomas Platt did not put up much of a fight. When a reformer offered to show him evidence of wrongdoing, he agreed to review it, but not in the evening as suggested, since his interest in uncovering corruption was confined to regular business hours. "I have no faith that you will be able to accomplish anything or that your reform movement will amount to anything as a campaign force," Platt responded wearily. "Votes in this city do not count unless counted by Tammany."[2] Rather than squander his resources, Platt's strategy was to win outside the city, take control of the State Legislature, and make his move against Tammany from Albany.

On Election Day the polls filled with red-nosed floaters who voted, then walked to the end of the line to vote again. They forgot their false names, or got them wrong, and had to be reminded from a list. Republican watchers were thrown out of polling places by order of Tammany officials. Men with money in their hands bid for votes in front of polling places. A Republican inspector who tried to have an illegal voter arrested was pulled out on the sidewalk, kicked, thumped, bounced across the street and warned to stay away.

A story later circulated that a Republican watcher at a voting district in Divverdom challenged a Tammany heeler who wanted to help his "deaf-and-dumb brother-in-law" vote in the booth. A small crowd collected as the Republican poll watcher argued to no avail that his alleged disability did not render the voter incapable of filling out and folding his own ballot. The Democratic supervisor overruled the objection and swore him in. "Do you swear that you are deaf-and-dumb?" he asked. The crowd laughed when the voter replied, "I do."

Tammany swept the city on Election Day.

* * *

Neither election majorities nor any other kind had the respect of Emma Goldman. She was inclined, like Dr. Stockman in Ibsen's drama, *An Enemy of the People*, to think that "the solid majority" was always wrong. They had rejected her warnings about the destructive effects of capitalism just as the townspeople in the play reject Dr. Stockman's evidence that the waters of the spa, the main economic interest of the town, are poisoned.

When friends urged her to get a lawyer for her approaching trial, she responded that trials were shams and mockeries, and defending one's self was playing by the State's rules. She intended to model herself after Berkman, who had refused counsel. But she changed course when she received a letter in which Sasha advised that while it would ordinarily be inconsistent for an Anarchist to hire legal representation, her situation was unusual. Goldman's courtroom eloquence could advance the cause of Anarchism, and a lawyer could protect her right to be heard. Following his advice, Goldman accepted when Oakey Hall, a former Tammany mayor of the city, took her case because he felt that the police had overstepped their authority in denying free speech.

Reasons of the heart had Emma Goldman looking at things differently. She had become romantically involved again. A tried and true Anarchist who had served a long prison term in Austria for publishing revolutionary material, Ed Brady supported her work on behalf of Berkman. But her new lover, who was ten years her senior, was also something unprecedented in her life—an intellectual interested in cultural ideas, the most well-read and scholarly person she had ever known. Brady had introduced her to the works of the important writers of the age, including Ibsen, who wrote of enlightened individuals who were the true shapers of events and of cultural change, and Nietzsche, who thrilled her with his passionate individualism and his contempt for religion.

She had not changed her basic views. "Everything wrong—crime and sickness—are the result of the system under which we live, " she told the *World* reporter Nellie Bly (who conducted the interview in jail, before Goldman's release on bail). "Were there no Capitalists, people would not be overworked, starved and ill-housed, made old before their time, diseased, and made criminals."

But a new theme emerged in the interview in the Tombs—the opposition between love as an empowering act and marriage as a condition of duty and servitude. "I believe in the marriage of affection," Goldman told Bly. "That is the only true marriage. If two people care for each other, they have a right to live together as long as that love exists. When it is dead, what base immorality for them still to stay together!"

Now, from her standpoint, capitalism had even more to answer for—not only did it spread hunger and suffering, but also it suppressed the human spirit. She would not make herself into a commodity, trading sex for security.

Anarchism was beginning to take on a cultural dimension for her as a general attitude toward society—the most important aspect being that there should be no limits on a person's freedom other than those imposed by her own nature. That was what Nora sought in *A Doll's House*, when she walked out of a barren marriage at the end of Ibsen's drama.

Following Nietzsche's injunction, "You must become who you are," she linked liberty with the growth of the individual. She began to insist that defiance of bourgeois conventions, which stifled individual expression and forced people into hypocrisy, was indispensable in order for each personality to develop to its fullest measure. Like many of the individualists of the age, she had come to believe that organized society was the enemy.

* * *

In October she went on trial. Emma Goldman later claimed that she was innocent and that the State was trying her for her views, not for any deed that she had committed. The trial suggests that she was wrong, or untruthful, in the first instance—that she had been rabble-rousing in her speech in Union Square, at a time when even Anarchist leaders were trying to maintain the peace. In the second instance, however, she made a good point, for over the course of the trial it repeatedly appeared that Goldman's philosophical views were really on trial, and not what she said from a platform on the evening of August 21.

Detective Jacobs, the chief witness for the prosecution, testified that he took down her remarks, expressed in German, in a notebook. According to his translation, she warned the crowd that the police were armed with clubs and pistols, but that the workers could arm themselves with clubs and stones, and urged them to make demands. "If you don't get it, take it by force," Jacobs read from his notes. "If you take bread alone you will do very little good. Go to the houses of the capitalists. Demand your rights. If you are refused take them by force." The state contended that this was a call for insurrection. Jacobs (the same detective who had brought her back from Philadelphia) admitted under cross-examination that he could not write shorthand. Other police who understood German corroborated his testimony. A defense witness, a reporter for a German-language newspaper, confirmed the testimony of the prosecution—that she had spoken of taking goods by force. Goldman denied the words that witnesses claimed she had said, and her lawyer claimed that the words had been falsely inserted in Jacobs's report.

But the facts of the case never seemed to count that much to Assistant District Attorney John McIntyre. He placed major emphasis on the political and religious beliefs of the defendant, and he spared no pains to apprise the jury of them:

"Do you believe in a Supreme Being, Miss Goldman?" he asked.

"No, sir, I do not."

"Is there any government on earth whose laws you approve?"

"No, sir, for they are all against the people."

"Why don't you leave this country if you don't like its laws?"

"Where shall I go? Everywhere on earth the laws are against the poor, and they tell me I cannot go to heaven, nor do I want to go there."

McIntyre also played on the prejudices of the jury. "She went to the Union Square meeting on the evening of August 21," he said in his summation, "to influence that crowd of aliens, who might run a knife into you or blow you up with a dynamite bomb."[3]

His presentation of the case created the impression that Emma Goldman was standing trial for not believing in law or in God. "How far this will go toward convicting her," the *Times* said in an editorial, "it is not easy to determine."

A group of hostile journalists found her, as one put it, "serene in her great satisfaction with herself" and vain. "She looked constantly as if her thoughts were the most important things on earth," one reporter wrote, "and as if it really made her tired to know so much." They also made fun of the admirers who surrounded her during breaks in the testimony.

As expected, Goldman was convicted. In imposing sentence, Judge Martine furthered the impression that he was sending her away for her beliefs. "You have testified in your own behalf that you did not believe in our institutions, that you did not believe in our laws and that you have no respect for them," the judge said. "Such a person cannot be tolerated in this community . . . look upon you as a dangerous woman in your doctrines."

As six Central Office detectives stationed themselves in the corridors of the old brownstone court house, on the lookout for Anarchists, Goldman was sentenced to a year's imprisonment. She heard the sentence with the scorn worthy of an Ibsen heroine.

21

A CITY AROUSED

In another part of the Lower East Side, north of the Eldridge Street precinct, Augusta Thurow was trying to endure the caprices of the East Fifth Street precinct. Despite her regular $25 protection payment on the first of every month, her First Street brothel had come under police siege. When she went out to talk to the cops standing sentinel, they told her they had orders from Captain Doherty to arrest any girls who stood in the doorway.

When she went to the precinct station for an explanation, the portly Captain said he was acting under orders of the Superintendent and that the Central Office Detectives would raid her place if a policeman were not stationed there. The captain complained that her place "had become notorious." Inspector McAvoy, the most pious of the police brass, had raised hell because Augusta's girls had accosted him right in front of the house. Reminding Doherty that she had closed her place for a few days in January at his request while the Police Board hearing against him was pending, Mrs. Thurow asked him to take the man away. The patrolman was gone that evening.

Every time she bailed out her girls she had to slip $5 to the desk sergeant in order to get her bail bondsman approved. One night at the station house she ran into Hock, the red-haired wardman. "We're going to raid your house tonight," he said in a nasty tone.

"If that's the case," said the exasperated madame, "I'll leave the girls here. What's the use of having them arrested twice?" Shortly after she arrived back at her First Street boardinghouse a patrolman called with a message from Captain Doherty to forgive the mistake, and to stop by to bail out her girls.

Scene in the Station House

When Augusta was herself arrested in November, she was near the end of her patience. "This is a nice thing," she remarked to the detective taking her to the station house, "after paying my money, to be arrested."

"Well, I don't know," the detective said. "You don't seem to hitch with the Boss. The Parkhurst people are making so much trouble that in a few days First Street will be no more."

* * *

Mrs. Thurow and the prostitution industry had its problems, but a supply of whores was not one of them. A hundred thousand women worked in New York offices, plants and shops, in almost all cases for less than $4 a week. They survived only by living in the meanest of circumstances, in dirty tenements in crime-ridden neighborhoods. At work they faced relentless pressure from owners, bosses and foremen to yield to male attentions. Some working women gave in to men who had the power to advance them or to influence the amount in their pay envelopes. Many a household maid yielded to similar blandishments. Unmarried women who found themselves "in the family way" went to illegal abortionists. With their reputations ruined, many drifted into prostitution as a means of survival.

Other girls stumbled into prostitution. Sometimes it started as an occasional sideline, a few quick dollars to supplement her income. Then things would come unstuck. She would contract a disease, or her cousin would see her, and when the word was spread her respectable relatives would have nothing to do with her. Then she would find herself in need of protection. The price of a man's protection, however, was high, since he took her earnings to indulge his pleasures. Then the police would notice a new streetwalker on the block and demand something to protect her from arrest. Then one night her cadet, as they were called downtown, would rough her up a bit, and another night he would beat her more seriously. She would begin to drink, smoke opium or sniff cocaine. After a few blackened eyes and a lot of alcohol and drugs, the fresh looks that had made her so marketable would begin to fade, and had to be restored with rouge, and she began to think that if she really wanted protection she ought to get into a house. And then everything was taken care of for her, the madame collected her earnings and gave her a pittance and controlled even her comings and goings. Prostitutes suffered, but the industry had always managed to survive. Now the Parkhurst Society was placing new strains on the flesh trade.

* * *

A few days after the election the three madames whose places had been raided on the day of the Broome Street riot were tried in Special Sessions Court before a panel of three Police Justices that included the former saloonkeeper Paddy Divver. "Had there been any way under Heaven that they could have been acquitted," Parkhurst said, "they would have been."[1] But the cases, worked up by the new cadre of agents, were airtight. The madames, each of whom kept a brothel in the Eldridge Street precinct, were convicted and fined.

With their most compelling proof yet against Big Bill Devery, Parkhurst and Moss again trod the well-worn path to Nicoll's office to see if entrance to the Grand Jury room were still barred.

Tammany Hall had dumped Nicoll, who was winding up his affairs as District Attorney. He was maintaining a loyal silence, but his friends said Nicoll was leaving with regret. Boss Croker had decreed his departure because Nicoll had resisted efforts to make his office into a Tammany patronage operation.

Nicoll, a well-knit, handsome man of thirty-eight years, with the light step and quick reflexes of a tennis player, had first come to public attention as an Assistant District Attorney who comported himself well in prosecuting several public corruption cases and won the support of Joseph Pulitzer, who had boosted his political career in the *World*. A direct descendant of Sir Richard Nicoll, the first English Governor of the colony of New York, the well-born

Nicoll had cast his lot with Tammany Hall but could have made a good living without political connections, for he excelled as an attorney. He enjoyed a reputation for quick wit but relied on legal acumen and diligent preparation rather than on showy oratory for effect.

Although Nicoll still regarded the preacher as a preposterous windbag mad for notoriety, he did not doubt Parkhurst's sincerity. The pastor seemed to him not a fake but a zealot, suspicious of any quibble from the District Attorney about a point of law that interfered with his crusade.

Nicoll was interested above all in furthering his career. He played the numbers game as district attorney, with the goal of racking up as close to a 100 percent conviction record as possible. His paramount rule was never to get anyone indicted who could not be convicted, since that would go down on his record as a defeat—and it was virtually impossible to convict a police captain. At least he was convinced that such would be the outcome, for an indictment of a high-ranking police officer for wrongdoing would be an unprecedented event in New York history.

Parkhurst played by entirely different rules. When Nicoll was tossed off the Tammany ticket, Parkhurst had defended him as having "done good work in the District Attorney's office and having not always proven himself amenable to Tammany";[2] but he knew that the fire that burned in Nicoll was not righteousness but ambition.

On that day in mid-November Parkhurst and Moss hoped to present the Grand Jury with evidence not only against Captain Devery but also against Captain Schmittberger and Inspector Williams.

This time, after five months of obstruction, District Attorney Nicoll presented a less guarded attitude. He confided to them that he did not regard their evidence as merely against three police officials, but as a crusade against the Department. All well and good, but he advised (as Nicoll later recalled their conference) that were so serious a matter undertaken "it was of the utmost importance to the good government of the city that it should be successful, and that it was foolish to underestimate the grave obstacles which stood in the path of success."

After wishing the clergyman godspeed in his work against corruption, Nicoll added that Parkhurst had harmed his own cause with his sweeping attacks on public officials. Some of them were not corrupt, and could even be enlisted in the crusade were they not driven away by attacks on their integrity. He continued:

In so formidable an undertaking Parkhurst would need every available ally. One might be Byrnes. Nicoll said that Byrnes had withstood "the most extraordinary political influences" and would not protect any subordinate who had done wrong. Parkhurst had failed to take advantage of departmental rifts: "You ought to know that the Superintendent is against the captains, and the captains against him." This was an opportune time to cement an alliance, since Byrnes was ready to act independently of the Police Commission. "I should not be at all surprised," he concluded, "if I could bring you together here in this office."

When this meeting was discussed publicly, several weeks later, the two men agreed about some elements of the conversation but disagreed sharply about others. According to Nicoll, Parkhurst said he would think it over, and at a later conference acceded to working with Byrnes. Parkhurst, however, said that he took the proposal to the Society's board of trustees. Then, according to the pastor, he reported to Nicoll the next morning that the Board had decided against allying itself with Byrnes.

Parkhurst claimed that as they examined the evidence, Nicoll tried to lead him away from the Devery case. Aware that Devery was a Byrnes protégé, the pastor responded: "That means you do not want to buck up against Byrnes." Nicoll reportedly returned the serve with this: "Let Devery be and take Schmittberger. I think Byrnes would go on the stand if you take Schmittberger."

Parkhurst was convinced that Byrnes had put Nicoll up to it, that it was a political maneuver by means of which Byrnes intended to destroy Clubber, and that Byrnes was willing to take the stand against Captain Max Schmittberger, a Clubber protégé.

At the conclusion of the meeting Nicoll indicated again that he would be receptive to getting the Society evidence before the Grand Jury. But this time Parkhurst did not rely on Nicoll's assurances.

With his usual disregard for legal proprieties—risking censure, reprimand and perhaps even a presentment against meddling with the secret deliberations of the Grand Jury—the minister stopped the Grand Jury foreman as he was walking in the courthouse and pleaded his case. Once again it appeared that Parkhurst's charism worked; a few days later Parkhurst and Moss were invited to present their evidence against the three police officers to the Grand Jury.

* * *

For Parkhurst this was a crucial moment in the city's history. For him the crisis hinged neither on revenge nor on redeeming the Society's good name, but on the political effect of the trial.

Politically the Devery case was a hot potato. It was Big Bill's custom to attend Tammany clambakes and boat excursions, shaking hands as if a candidate for office. Big Bill owed Boss Croker his rank, for the Tammany members of the Police Board had promoted him at Croker's insistence. An indictment of a Tammany police captain would tie all of Parkhurst's themes together.

The pastor waited hopefully until November 29, when the word came that the Grand Jury had handed up an indictment charging Devery with neglect of duty.

The initial shock was powerful. Newspaper editorials called it a red-letter day in city history, a victory for Parkhurst, and the opening shot in a fight against corruption. But the immediate reaction was just the beginning. A week after the indictment the Board of Police Commissioners transferred thirteen precinct captains in a single day, including Big Bill Devery, who was reassigned from Eldridge Street to the Old Slip precinct, a most unwanted assignment. Captain Doherty was transferred out of the lucrative East Fifth Street precinct to the dreary Leonard Street station.

On the same day, December 5, the police staged the most extensive crackdown on prostitution ever seen in New York. They halted festivities in Bowery concert halls at 10 P.M. and ordered the proprietors to admit no women after that hour. Saloons with back rooms were instructed to keep their places clear of women. Waitresses in downtown coffee saloons, a favored occupation for prostitutes seeking customers, were fired by order of the police. Severe measures were applied against streetwalkers on Broadway and in Sixth Avenue in the Tenderloin district where police swept through the streets arresting any women found loitering.

Parkhurst sardonically noted that the captains had waited to begin the "wave of purification," as he called it, until after the first of the month, when police made the monthly shakedown.

* * *

By the second day the Tenderloin resembled an epic scene out of a roadshow company. It was a cold night, snow blanketed the city, and all over the Tenderloin prostitutes had suddenly been evicted. "Had a merciless hand deliberately planned the worst time of all to drive these creatures forth, none could have been more successfully chosen," the *Herald* commented.[3] Without their belongings, lightly clad, they had been thrown out to shiver in the snow on Broadway and Sixth Avenue.

The police disavowed any part in it, but as the details came in it was established that they had pressured landlords to evict prostitutes immediately, and the police had supplied the lamenting women with the address of "Old Parkhurst," who was responsible for their homelessness. Hollow-eyed, the broken blossoms of the Tenderloin trudged through the slushy streets and up the brownstone steps of the Parkhursts, where a Christmas wreath welcomed them. Some of them arrived in an angry state, blaming the clergyman for their eviction.

They were hungry and homeless. But they found Dr. and Mrs. Parkhurst solicitous and willing to listen to their woes. Denying themselves to all other visitors, from early morning until far into the evening the Parkhursts received the women in the handsomely furnished front parlor.

The visitors knew where to sit, for at the end of the nineteenth century parlor chairs came in two models. Men's chairs had arms and were higher than a woman's chair, which lacked arms in order to accommodate full skirts. A woman's chair also reinforced her social posture—to sit upright, away from the chair back, with her hands folded in her lap. Doilies and antimacassars or tidies were attached to the backs of chairs and sofas to protect fabrics from the greasy pomades that men used.

Dressed in his street clothes except for slippers, the pastor sat in his favorite corner of the sofa, near the front window, and made them welcome while tea and toast were served. He listened with a concerned frown as they told him that every door was closed to them. If they were willing to abandon their depraved lives, Parkhurst said, he would find them food and shelter and would help get them employment. The Parkhursts had talked with a number of churches that could place some of the "unfortunate creatures" in private homes. Although he doubted the sincerity of some of the whores, many of them appeared to be earnest about turning from vice, largely because pimps and madames had treated them badly.

They left speaking well of the parson—"le ministre," as the French whores called him—and cursing the police.

* * *

For days the newspapers were full of Parkhurst's soirees with prostitutes and his observations about them. He did not think that turning from vice would be easy for them. "The fascination of their wicked mode of life," he noted, "its ease and luxury, are more alluring than drudgery in the shop or in the kitchen."[4] So many barriers were raised against them, and so little encouragement offered from the respectable world, he said, that they often lost heart and found a warmer welcome among their old associates.

He called police activity a bluff. "The police realize that there is a tide rising against them such as they cannot stem, and they are hurrying to cover as fast as ever they can," he said. "This transfer of captains is a humbug, a shallow pretense. The Commissioners saw themselves compelled to do something in self-defense and they have selected this cheapest of all methods. . . . Then there are pecuniary interests that must be respected."

He was asked what he meant by that.

"Oh, I guess you know what that means as well as I do. I have never used soft words at any time in charging the police of this city with levying blackmail."

Parkhurst charged that prostitutes had been recruited to New York. "I have had women of this class tell me in my own house," he recounted, "that they did not belong here, but that they came from outside because they knew that in New York the police would protect them. The police of this city have been enticing prostitutes from other cities and States to come to New York, in order that they might be the means of clothing their own wives and daughters and living in style, quadrupling in comfort and elegance anything they could maintain on their own legitimate salaries."

By now Parkhurst was convinced that the police actively promoted vice—furthered it, nurtured it, planted it where it was not already growing; that the police were a satanic force in the city and that Devery's precinct fully deserved to be called "the devil's seminary." And he had proved that he had learned a lot about political maneuvering.

* * *

All at once New York stirred.

Several newspapers chronicled the infiltration of politics into the police force and the burgeoning growth of police membership in Tammany social clubs. Much attention was paid to the Pequod Club, of which Police Commissioner John Sheehan was president; it was said that police felt constrained to join, and that belonging helped when disciplinary charges arose. Captains, it was said, were being reprimanded for balking at selling tickets for club chowders and punished for not meeting their ticket quotas. Byrnes favored a ban on police membership, but the two Tammany board members ignored his protests. As the newspapers put it, the cops were being Crokerized.

Other stories described the voices of the Police Board President and the Superintendent raised in dispute behind closed doors. In its lead stories of December 17 and 19, the *World* depicted a Police Commission in turmoil, quarreling with its Superintendent and ready to dump him.

It was also reported that Tammany figures at least twice had intervened with Byrnes on Devery's behalf. News stories claimed that Tammany countermanded Byrnes's order to Big Bill to close up a brothel in the West Forty-seventh Street precinct; and one paper reported that when Devery was transferred to Eldridge Street, Tammany bosses saw to it that Byrnes's instructions to clean up the precinct were disobeyed.

The underlying message of the stories was that poor Mr. Byrnes just could not get anything done. He had the best interests of the police force at heart, but he was helpless. When he attempted to impose his will, police captains went over his head to the Commissioners, and even Republican captains dutifully carried out Tammany instructions. According to the press, he had been relegated to a figure-head. For the first time, Byrnes was being examined with a hard gaze, especially when he took on an extraordinary assignment on behalf of George Gould.

It was one of those messes that entangled rich married men and young ac-tresses. This one, Zella Nicolaus, was only nineteen years old, and the willowy golden-haired beauty was suing the heir of Jay Gould with the help of Howe & Hummel, defender of wronged womanhood.

After Byrnes had a talk with her, the actress left hurriedly on the next Atlantic steamer, bound for Italy with a male companion. The superintendent took pains to explain to the press that any moves he had made against her redounded to the public good, and were not made on Gould's behalf alone. "It is impossible," he said, "to say too much against her character."[5] In the past the Great Detective had performed numerous duties for the Gould family, but this one had become a public scandal.

* * *

Suddenly Tammany Hall looked vulnerable. For the first time since the Tweed era a number of civic-minded organizations came together to combat election fraud. Taking the lead, the Bar Association appointed John Goff to come up with evidence of election wrongdoing and prepare the cases.

Goff leapt in with his usual intensity. The evidence he amassed showed that in one Assembly district, 13,000 people voted while only 7,000 were registered; that polls were kept open after the legal closing time; that honest cops were rep-rimanded and transferred for doing their duty; and that certified poll watchers were hampered by Tammany people who milled about the table five and six deep, blocking their view. "It was not really an election," Goff said. "It was an ex-ecution of the will of Tammany Hall." He compared the fraud to the enormities of the Tweed era.[6]

In December forty-four floaters and repeaters were swept up in a dragnet and charged with fraud in the previous month's election. But Goff was after bigger game. He was interested in a pre-election speech in which, it was said, Police Justice Divver had encouraged fraud by promising a patronage job to the block captain with the best showing in the Second Assembly District. Although sym-bolic awards like banners were not illegal, it was a crime to offer prizes—cash or patronage—to encourage electioneering.

In his waning days in office District Attorney Nicoll worked closely with Goff on the election fraud cases, taking them to a special Grand Jury.

* * *

Even Albany was stirring. Attracted by charges of police corruption, the legislators were peering southward to see what was up in the wicked city. The Chamber of Commerce suggested that the Legislature come down to look at the sorry state of the Police Department. Republican Boss Platt promised several people that there would be an investigation. And he could deliver, for the Republican Party had won considerable gains around the State and were ready to take control of both houses of the state legislature in 1894.

Four years earlier Platt had dispatched a similar committee to look into Tammany mismanagement. But the Fassett Committee, named for its chairman, State Senator J. Sloat Fassett, withdrew before any lasting damage resulted to Croker or Tammany, and many New Yorkers believed that Platt, while he wanted to score political points, did not want to wound Croker seriously. In two years Tammany might be back in control of the Legislature and Platt would need favors from the Tammany boss—committee assignments, deals on Judgeships, the same courtesies that Croker was currently receiving from Platt. Thus was the game played in Albany.

Although none knew what would come of such a probe, it was said that worried Police Commissioners were already choosing the Captains that would be sacrificed to the investigators to save themselves.

Croker displayed a rare eagerness to talk. The Tammany leader met with reporters from several leading dailies in mid-December to defend Tammany against a rising tide of attacks. He claimed that the tales of his riches were exaggerated, and that the city was well governed, as any committee down from Albany would soon discover. He reminded reporters that Senator Fassett had come into the city four years earlier to eradicate Tammany Hall. "The whole thing was a fizzle, of course," he mocked. "I don't know where Fassett is now. The papers said he was going West to see if he didn't have better luck in politics out there."

Meanwhile Parkhurst was making another attempt to get Clubber Williams and Captain Schmittberger indicted. He grappled again with the D.A.'s delaying tactics, and blamed Nicoll's presentation of the case when a Grand Jury heard evidence but failed to indict the pair. A public quarrel followed, in the course of which Parkhurst and Nicoll gave differing accounts of their earlier meetings. Nicoll denied suggesting that Byrnes would testify against Schmittberger but not against Devery. "What I did say," he explained, "was that, in view of the Gardner case, I thought it would be wise to proceed in the first instance against some other Captain than Devery, because I thought the prosecution of Devery would be handicapped by the suggestion of revenge."

Nicoll also advised that Parkhurst was harming his own cause by "lobbying his indictments with the Grand Jurors outside of the Grand Jury room," since his activity could "invalidate the indictments."[7] The D.A. added that the pastor seemed bent on sweeping aside everything in his zeal, including the law.

Parkhurst shrugged off reports that he was receiving death threats, but admitted that he would not accept any packages through the mail. Muttering crackpots rang his doorbell. His agents guarded him when the occasion warranted. He would not deny rumors that he was carrying a revolver and refused to call upon the police for help. "Doesn't it strike you as incongruous," he asked, "that I should look to them for protection?"

22

LEADERS

When she was a child in Russia, Emma Goldman was told that America was different. In her own experience, however, it was merely a variation on Russia: another country cursed with government, law, and prisons. Wherever she looked—in public life, in the family, in the sweatshop, in the bonds of matrimony—she found oppression.

She came from a land where secret police spied upon people even in their homes, and where enemies of the ruling class were tortured. The peasants wallowed in vodka and illiteracy; instead of rising against their oppressors they told each other fairy tales about the Royal Family. Her own parents had described the Czar to her as a kindly father who oversaw and disciplined his children.

Failing to arouse the superstitious peasants through agitation, the revolutionaries turned to sabotage and terrorism, bringing on reprisals and repression. Strict censorship, tight control of universities and police roundups suppressed the last vestiges of political expression. The Jews became prime targets. The Minister of the Interior fanned the flames of anti-Semitism. New laws sharply curtailed Jewish rights of residence, freedom of movement and occupation.

The tyranny of the society extended into the schools. Young Emma lacked a proper respect for authority and was often in trouble for speaking out when classmates were beaten.

A household czar ruled at home. Her father beat her often; on one occasion, infuriated by reports of her behavior in school, he attacked her with his fists. Sometimes she had to stand in a corner for hours, or was made to walk back and forth with an overflowing glass of water in her hands, punished with a lash for each spilled drop.

When she was fifteen years old, her father arranged to have her married. "I had protested," she recalled, "begging to be permitted to continue my studies. In his frenzy he threw my French grammar into the fire, shouting, 'Girls do not have to learn much! All a Jewish daughter needs to know is how to prepare gefilte fish, cut noodles fine, and give the man plenty of children.' I would not listen to his schemes; I wanted to study, to know life, to travel. Besides, I would never marry for anything but love, I stoutly maintained." Without any help from her mother, Emma blocked his efforts to marry her off.

Faced by oppression on all sides, she dedicated every fiber of her being to rebellion. She would love whomever she chose, would imbue the future with the force of her personality, and become what she was meant to be.

* * *

Her courage stood firm after the sentencing, when she was led out of the Tombs to the Black Maria and driven to the barge that ferried the prisoners over to Blackwell's Island.

It was a bright day, and as the barge steamed toward its destination the sunlight frolicked on the water. A few reporters went along for the ride and when they reached the island she admonished them to avoid writing more lies than were required, then she followed the Deputy Sheriff along the broad, tree-lined gravel walk to the entrance of the gray prison.

The penitentiary to which she had been ferried, the same one to which the courts had sent Hattie Adams and Maria Andrea, was used for jailing short-term convicts; had she been given a more lengthy punishment she would have been sent to a State Prison.

The island (later renamed Roosevelt Island) was a long sandbar in the East River. It also held a penitentiary for men (which Johann Most called The Spanish Inquisition in America) and a lunatic asylum; from her standpoint these forbidding monuments embodied an economic system that stunted human life. She would be there for a year.

* * *

Emma Goldman would later write that her stay on Blackwell's Island was a crucible in which she was recast, but a close look shows that the change had begun before she reached the island. Although she was one of them, Goldman had little rapport with the Jews of the Lower East Side. She thought that immigrants who failed to become committed radicals were mired in the same apathy and superstition that she had found in the Russian peasants. The virtues of the immigrant Jews—their patience, perseverance, readiness to accept suffering, and their quick understanding of how to circumvent differences and gain leverage through solidarity—lacked the impetuous dash that Emma Goldman associated with heroism. It took an extraordinary sort of person, she saw, to challenge the established order at every level, and the people she saw around her on Ludlow and Essex streets seemed ordinary.

Even before entering the penitentiary she was on her way to becoming a sectarian figure with a loyal following that to an increasing extent consisted of fewer and fewer workers and more and more intellectuals and activists, many of them friends of her new lover, Ed Brady.

She had met many of them—both émigré and American radicals—at Brady's favorite place, Justus Schwab's saloon on First Street, where the regulars included John Swinton, the radical journalist; Ambrose Bierce, a cynical writer of dark works; and James Huneker, America's leading champion of Ibsen and Nietzsche. She and Ed spent so much time there that she used Schwab's address on her personal cards and used the saloon as an office. At those beer-soaked tables, following in the tradition of Prince Kropotkin, the radical aristocrat, she pursued her vision of Anarchism as "the most complete development of individuality."

The East Side Jews, however, were engaged in a different battle. Developing their individuality, emulating Emma Goldman's struggle for self-fulfillment, was not an immediate priority for them. They were fighting for survival and dignity.

One cause that created a flurry of interest in New Israel was the hard lot of the Kievents, a Jewish immigrant couple who had been convicted in the Essex Market Court House and sent to prison for robbery. The state's case against Philip and Rebecca Kievent was based on the testimony of two men who claimed that on February 24 they were drinking in the Kievent saloon on Suffolk Street when Philip invited one of them into the basement on the pretext of introducing him to a willing woman. According to the testimony Kievent's victim was attacked and beaten, $250 was forcibly taken from him, and he and the other man were then thrown outdoors.

The Kievents maintained their innocence. They said that the men were not in the saloon at the time of the alleged robbery, and they produced sixteen witnesses to confirm that the two men (of scoundrelly reputation) were in fact drinking elsewhere.

After the Kievents were sent to prison their cause was taken up in the Lower East Side. People came forward to say that the police had induced the witnesses to frame the Kievents because the couple had refused to pay protection for their saloon. It was said that when they were taken to court the police told them that if they came up with $150 the whole thing would be dropped—the same kind of railroading that Max Hochstim and his wardmen allies were trumping up in other parts of the Lower East Side.

The Jews found an unexpected ally in Parkhurst. After becoming aware of the campaign on behalf of the Kievents and shortly before leaving for his annual summer in Europe, he asked Sunshine Erving to look more deeply into the matter.

Erving, now recovered from his mental breakdown, reported back to Parkhurst. The Kievents, he said, were not saints; Philip had served a term for keeping a house of prostitution and had been arrested for theft although the case was dismissed. Erving was sure, however, that they had been framed.

Parkhurst was convinced that the Kievents had been unjustly convicted. "I knew that wherever you dig in a case of this kind you find police rottenness," he said. "I wanted to let the downtrodden Jews of the East Side know that we would stand between them and their oppressors, who should be their protectors."

Slowly, over a period of months, the Protestant pastor gained the trust of the immigrants and, as he put it, "there came pouring in upon me confidential revelations which were voluminous and appalling."[1] The City Vigilance League, which Parkhurst had founded, alerted Lower East Side immigrants of their rights with regard to police behavior, and kept alive the issue of the wrong that had befallen the Kievents. The immigrant Jews were ready to defend their collective rights. While Emma Goldman appeared to be more interested in a different constituency, Parkhurst showed a courteous and big-hearted chivalry.

* * *

As the nineteenth century waned, the new century was taking shape. Goldman and Parkhurst were consciously shaping the kind of society they hoped to make. Although they came from highly different backgrounds and had widely varied expectations, both had the resources to lead—both were strong-willed, with courage and personal magnetism.

Both began their political careers in a state of political innocence, committing an act of political naiveté in which they miscalculated, underestimated and misjudged their foes.

For Emma Goldman the shooting of Frick had an effect opposite to the one she intended; first because it did not ignite revolution; second because her persistence in supporting Berkman's act isolated her more profoundly from the immigrant community. After failing to revolutionize the American system, partly because she lacked even a rudimentary notion of how it worked, she turned to remaking herself.

Parkhurst too began with an act of naiveté. As a New England idealist, he may have thought that mere moral exhortation would mend the city's problems. When he was burned, when he realized that he had underestimated the power and the unforgiving nature of big-city machine politics, he set out to learn how public life worked. As his mastery of politics grew, he showed perseverance, willingness to listen, flexibility, and good reflexes in returning every volley.

* * *

Because so few New Yorkers were willing to take such risks, Parkhurst was heartened that the Jews, who rallied on behalf of the Kievents, showed a singular bravery in the face of police oppression. Nothing like their protest was evident elsewhere in the city. And something else occurred as the new year arrived that gave him another reason to hope that the immigrant Jews were able to grasp, as he put it, "the genius of Anglo-Saxon institutions" and that they understood the source and the meaning of liberty.

Early in January of 1894, three cops were arrested in the Hester Street market on charges of blackmailing pushcart peddlers. The peddlers had identified the collectors and had told in detail of how they had been forced to pay weekly tribute. And the collectors, when squeezed, had named the police for whom they collected. Now two unprecedented events had occurred in the once-torpid city—a police captain had been indicted and victims of police blackmail had dared to speak up. Parkhurst could hardly be blamed if he thought that something was happening in the city at last, and that not only was there a connection between the two events, but that both events had resulted from having concentrated all of the Society's efforts on a single precinct. Things were falling into place just in time, for 1894 had arrived—the hour had struck for the campaign to drive Tammany Hall out of office in the coming election.

THE VIRTUOUS CITY
Winter–Spring 1894

23

A NEW YORK
WELCOME

*Pay no attention when you are told that it is for genius to lead.
It is not for genius to lead—it is for the multitude. I do not believe that God thinks very much of genius. If He did He would
make more of them.*

—Parkhurst, at a political meeting, November 3, 1893[1]

Its official title was the Special Senate Committee to Investigate Police Matters
in the City of New York, but people had already named it the Lexow Committee. On the train down from Albany the Republican majority had chosen the
forty-year-old freshman senator, Clarence Lexow, as chairman—the only Republican on the committee who knew the city, a lawyer who had lived and practiced in the metropolis for some years, although he now commuted from Nyack.
It was a good choice, although the Republicans had not actually made it. Lexow
was named chairman by order of Boss Platt, and that was all there was to it.

When the Republican Senators left Grand Central Station for their lodgings
at the Hotel Metropole they probably rubbernecked at the carriage windows.
Even the most urbane traveler found it hard to resist gawking at this bustling city.

A sense of hurry charged the city, a step-lively air of commerce that matched
its tall-masted sailing vessels parked among the smokestacked steamers in the
harbor, and its skyscrapers, like the golden-domed Pulitzer Building, which tow-
ered twenty stories above the streets.

From their carriages the Senators saw livery stables at nearly every other corner, for it was a city of horses as much as a city of people. They saw traffic inextri-
cably knotted—wagons, carts and delivery vans, buggies and beer trucks, funeral

corteges on their way to cemeteries. There was no place to put all these appurtenances of horsepower, and when not in use many of them were left on the street, secured by chains. The senators saw sidewalks covered with empty beer kegs, produce and impassable piles of merchandise. Above them roared the elevated trains, around them screeched wooden wheels, the air was thick with soot and dust particles, and when they glanced down they could see everywhere the origin of that dust—the road apples that the horses dropped in the streets.

Brownstone townhouses, the living quarters of the well-to-do, covered the smart part of the city so thoroughly that some people dismissed New York as architecturally dull. For others it overflowed with variety. In contrast to the coordinated look of the Paris boulevards, New York was a jumble of granite, marble, stone, brick and iron. The styles were as varied as the materials, and a hodgepodge abounded on all sides.

If they were typical visitors the upstate legislators were both fascinated and repelled by this grand and terrible metropolis. They may not have reacted as intensely as did Rudyard Kipling, who called the city "a long, narrow pig-trough."[2] But like most Americans, they probably found it wanting in civic virtue. Owing to lack of interest, New Yorkers had taken five years to put the Statue of Liberty out in the harbor; it had taken begging with a tin cup to raise funds for the pedestal. And for years some of the late General Grant's friends had been trying to raise money to put up a proper monument to him, yet it remained unfinished. People who dwelt in the same building never exchanged a hello. They didn't own their homes like upstate New Yorkers. They just rented them. No wonder these landlord-ridden folk took no pride in their city, and threw their garbage out the windows.

And if they had the usual upstate attitudes, the senators believed that this collection of foreigners, confidence men, Tammany hacks and frivolous fops could not rule themselves, and thus it was incumbent upon the legislature to set the city aright.

* * *

The New Year had brought a yearning for reform. The shocking election frauds of Tammany Hall, which Goff had outlined at a rally at Cooper Union and then had documented in a series of arrests, had aroused The Better People from their slumbers. The Real Estate Exchange charged that the city's building department was being used to harass the political opposition, that property owners who opposed Tammany were besieged by inspectors demanding repairs or declaring buildings unsound. A half-dozen other groups were stirring, and even the progressive-minded element of Tammany was raising questions about Croker's one-man rule.

Parkhurst's success in getting Devery indicted had convinced the citizenry that the uptown pastor could not be written off as a blundering zealot. His resourcefulness was acknowledged and a crusade that had once seemed quixotic was being reassessed.

Clerics who had condemned his tactics were now backing him. When the pastor of the Broadway Tabernacle Church wrote to him offering help, Parkhurst sighed in relief. "You can hardly understand what comfort and encouragement there is in such a communication," he wrote back, "especially after the experience of the past two years during so much of which my ministerial brethren hold themselves in such unsympathetic relation with the entire business."[3]

* * *

Despite the new receptivity to reform, a welcome that ranged from chilly to cynical greeted the contingent from Albany.

Tammany braves sneered at them as hayseeds who had come down to throw cowflops at the Wigwam—but none of it would stick.

Senator Jacob Cantor, one of the two Democrats on the Lexow Committee, was at a loss to see any need whatever for an investigation. The Harlem senator, a Tammany brave, expressed regret that the Police Department had been tarred with such broad strokes. "It has been for years the pride of the city," said the portly Democrat. "Throughout the country it is considered the finest in the land. It is singularly efficient."

The police themselves seemed confident that the storm would blow over. At the annual Captains' Dinner at Delmonico's, an array of city figures, led by Recorder Smyth, praised the police to the skies. Over cognac, coffee and cigars, the eyes of gray veterans misted as they recalled the men by whose side they had fought with their clubs to win back the streets from the Five Pointers, the Hudson Dusters, and the Whyos.

The cops were also pleased to learn from Police Board President Jimmy Martin that former District Attorney DeLancey Nicoll had been hired to defend them at the Lexow hearings.

* * *

Even the reformers, the ostensible allies of the senators, were standoffish. Not just because they dismissed the upstate senators as a wagonload of rustics who knew nothing of the city's workings, nor because Manhattanites smarted at being ruled from afar. No, the main reason for their skepticism was Boss Platt.

In 1889, Platt had made a deal with Croker to create more Police Justices by an act of the legislature and to divide the positions equally. When Platt was tricked out of his appointments, he sent the Fassett Committee into New York to punish Tammany Hall. But the committee withdrew after landing a few glancing blows. Political insiders said Platt had used the investigation as leverage in a secret deal and had cancelled it once it had served its purpose. The reformers assumed that the Republicans on this committee were just Platt puppets.

* * *

Unprepared for the New York welcome they were about to receive, the upstate legislators also arrived ill-equipped for their task, with no staff, no files, and a complete ignorance of the cast of characters, as well as all of the other background information essential to making sense of its politics. But they had a remedy for that. They intended to make the acquaintance of the Rev. Dr. Charles H. Parkhurst and get on friendly terms with the good man. Upstate newspapers had published accounts of his bracing campaign for the moral reform of the city. The Senators had been given to understand that the preacher had rows of filing cabinets crammed with evidence, and that all they had to do was invite Parkhurst before their committee. He would repeat his charges, supply them with his evidence, and in jig time the investigation would be wrapped up and they would be back in the bar of the Delevan Hotel in Albany swapping racy stories and enjoying the favor of Boss Platt.

Such were their expectations when Senator Lexow convened the committee on Friday night, February 2, in a meeting parlor at the Metropole. Parkhurst sat before them in the audience, a fine-boned man in a black cloak, in the company of Charles Stewart Smith, the president of the Chamber of Commerce, and other Chamber officers. Yet none of these men were smiling in welcome.

Since the Chamber had petitioned for the investigation, Smith was called upon first. To the chagrin of the Senators, he made it clear that he had no evidence to offer. "I've heard that the police were blackmailers, but I can't say that I ever saw a policeman in the act of levying blackmail," the Chamber president said.

Listening severely, Parkhurst reacted with animated expression to Smith's remarks. The preacher had small hands and feet, delicate ways, and his hair, worn long to his collar, was splashed with silver. In the two years since he began his campaign he had grown grayer.

When Chairman Lexow asked Parkhurst if he had any material to present, the pastor replied that much remained to be done before the stage of taking testimony could be reached, if the committee intended to do any serious work. Then his face darkened.

"I want to raise the question of whether these proceedings are to be secret or not," he said. He insisted that secrecy was crucial, for otherwise witnesses could not be protected from police revenge.

Republican Senator Charles Saxton replied that closed hearings would be impossible, that the evidence and findings would eventually be laid before the complete Legislature and the public. Sternly, the pastor responded that such being the case he had serious misgivings about the wisdom of their coming to New York City at all.

"I think it only fair to say to Dr. Parkhurst that we expected to rely upon him for assistance in this investigation," Senator Lexow said peevishly.

Parkhurst snapped that the Society for the Prevention of Crime was making its own investigation and that it did not intend to imperil its efforts by becoming part of a legislative show. On this sour note the brief meeting broke up.

* * *

Known to friend and foe alike as the Easy Boss, Thomas Platt was a tall, thin, stooping man with a limp handshake who conducted most of his Republican State Committee business in the lobby of the Fifth Avenue Hotel. When he turned up, the epitome of the aging dandy, every evening after dinner in the marble-floored rotunda, those waiting on the blue plush sofas rose and approached that he might give them audience. A neatly trimmed beard framed his careworn face as he whispered with Republican Brethren or answered questions from reporters.

Mr. and Mrs. Platt lived in the hotel. From their corner parlor they could see the roof garden of Madison Square Garden and, now that the statue had been returned from the Columbian Exposition in Chicago, they had a view of Saint-Gaudens' sculpture of Diana lissomely balanced on the tower. Their suite of rooms also took in a view of the Madison Square Presbyterian Church, where they rented a pew but rarely attended. Although the Platts had been members of the congregation for three years, the Republican Boss had never actually met the pastor. Asked why he had joined, Platt replied that he found the pastor "brilliant and inclined to be a little sensational."[4]

Books and magazines were piled on the tables of their four-room suite, which was bedecked with plants and flowers. They dined every evening in the public dining room, often with family or friends.

On Sundays he dressed in a black frock coat to meet with his captains and troops for sessions called Sunday School, and Platt's lessons were delivered in a secluded alcove at the hotel called The Amen Corner.

That winter he was fifty-nine years old and enjoying the recapture of the State Legislature that the November elections had won for him. Despite his successes, his prospects in the metropolis remained under a cloud. In the past Tammany Hall had allowed two Republicans to serve on the Board of Police

Commissioners. But Croker had never been happy with the arrangement, and in accordance with his wishes in early 1894 a lone Republican holdover remained. For Platt, Republican representation on the police board was a matter of utmost importance. With no chance of winning a majority in the city, it was his principal source of city patronage.

Parkhurst's crusade gave Platt his chance. He decided to have a Senate Committee created to investigate police affairs, send them to New York City, and have them conclude that what the city needed was a Bipartisan Police Commission.

Over that weekend Platt met at the hotel with some of the Republican members of the Lexow Committee to make his wishes known. There is no record of that meeting, but what Platt said is readily established from the context of later remarks.

He told them that he had to have two of his own men on the Board of Police Commissioners. He expected the committee members to come to the city, meet a few times, read a few affidavits and hear a few witnesses to be provided. Then the Republican majority would issue its report, in which it would recommend his bill. As chairman, Senator Lexow was expected to guide the Senators in this direction.

It was not to be a long process, for he wanted the bill in a matter of weeks. Furthermore, as he put it, he was "against any smelling committees at the expense of the people,"[5] and expected a limited, inexpensive investigation.

Once again the Easy Boss intended to sidestep reform. He preferred to deal with Tammany Hall, whose leaders understood the rigors of party organization, rather than with reformers, who had nothing to offer him. He expected that he would make a deal for continued police patronage with Croker.

* * *

Parkhurst believed that Tammany had nothing to fear as long as Platt controlled events. That same Sunday the pastor told a reporter that he was undecided as to whether his agents would appear before the committee. "Everything will depend upon the developments of the next few days," he said.

"I repudiate the notion that they are here to investigate charges made by me," he said of the committee. "As I understand it, they are here to investigate the Police Department, and they are clothed with full power to do so."

"But the committee evidently looks to you to present charges for investigation," the reporter said.

"If that is their attitude," he responded, "they might just as well have stayed in Albany."

24

PRESSURE

When reformers met for a second time with the Lexow Committee on Monday in the Hotel Metropole, the pressure was on.

The senators were tense and petulant, and everything that they advanced to foster confidence only heightened Parkhurst's impression that they were completely in the dark. He warned them that a proper investigation would be arduous and lengthy. "If you can't get the facts from the aggrieved parties," he lectured, "you must wring them from the police by boring down to the very quick, by thorough, prolonged and ruthless investigation. That will require much time—possibly a whole year."

When that failed to elicit a response, Parkhurst spoke with added urgency. "However thoroughly we may respect the integrity of purpose of the gentlemen of this committee," he said, "we cannot lose sight of the fate of previous investigations whose integrity of purpose has been just as unquestioned, who have been what is termed called off. In view of this, we naturally experience feelings of anxiety lest a similar fate befall this committee."

When he finished the pastor remained standing, awaiting a reply, and a silence fell upon the room. "Everyone expected that it would be broken by an explosion," one newspaper reported, "but the Senators seemed to be disarmed by the perfect courtesy of the Doctor's manner, and by his smile, which was deprecatory of any intent to offend. They seemed to realize that he merely intended to be 'frank.'"[1]

Finally the chairman spoke. "There is only one remark to which I care to reply," said the slight, nervous, trim-bearded Lexow, "his suggestion that when a line of inquiry shall have been started there is danger that the committee may be called off. I can say for myself that I cannot be called off, and that whatever line of investigation is pursued will be followed to its legitimate results."

Senator Daniel Bradley followed. "I wouldn't stay on this Committee one hour if there were any danger of its being called off," said the folksy Brooklyn Democrat. "I know the Doctor refers to the Fassett Committee, but this isn't that kind of a Committee."

An hour later the Senators were leaving the city. "When, if ever, they are to return here and pursue the proceeding which, for convenience sake, has been termed an investigation remains to be seen," the *Herald* wrote.[2] Another paper said that if the Senators did not intend to conduct a vigorous independent investigation they might as well "resign their trust at once."[3] The City Club, which had voted to cooperate with the Lexow Committee, changed its mind. The committee appeared to be losing its last scrap of public support.

Parkhurst said he would refuse to let his agents testify publicly before the committee. "We want first to be assured that the Committee means business," he said. "We cannot afford to throw away our ammunition."[4]

Nevertheless the pastor stayed in contact with the Senators. When Lexow got a bill through the Legislature providing immunity to witnesses regarding any crime revealed under oath before the committee, he was following a Parkhurst suggestion. And after consulting again with Parkhurst and other civic leaders the committee members resolved to extend the life of the investigation indefinitely, while Lexow made a point of saying that "we fully recognize the magnitude of the task we have undertaken."[5]

Senator Clarence Lexow, Chairman of the Committee

Now the pastor raised the stakes. He had his eye on the most important appointment the committee would make—counsel to the committee. Parkhurst advised that naming a city man versed in local affairs would go far to overcome the disadvantages that the committee members faced as outsiders.

He went to the committee with a bold recommendation—Goff, the lawyer who had defended Charlie Gardner. The message was implicit but clear: Goff was a serious hell-raiser and a committee that would appoint him meant business.

Parkhurst must have made a persuasive case—or the Republican Senators must have been eager to win his blessing—for on February 12 the committee wrote to Goff inviting him to serve as its chief counsel.

* * *

In Boss Platt's view, the pastor was taking over the direction and scope of the investigation. Platt also must have been chagrined to learn that Lexow, whom he was grooming for a promising future in politics, had offered the chief counsel position to a reformer, and a Democrat to boot.

But shouting was not Platt's way. Hoping to rein in his underlings in a gentlemanly manner, the Easy Boss posted a letter to Lexow. "I have some suggestions to make and I trust you and Senator Saxton will give me opportunity to present them before taking any action," he wrote. "I shall be in my room at the hotel all this evening and hope to hear from you or see you or be around when and where I can see you."

There is no record of what explanation the Republican Senators gave to Platt for offering the job to Goff. Whatever else was said, it is known that they heard Platt forward his own candidate for counsel—William Sutherland, a Rochester lawyer who was a power in State Republican politics. The Senators who met with Platt that evening heard a glowing account of Sutherland's merits. Two days later the Senators met in another Sunday school session, and after it broke up Platt sent a note to Lexow. "Mr. Sutherland will give it force and intense interest," Platt wrote. "He will make it a success and do you all credit—send for him and set him at work."

By this time several of the newspapers had decided that Platt had set up the Lexow Committee solely as a decorative touch to aid in the passage of the Bipartisan Police Commission bill, which the *World* called "the Croker-Platt Police Board bill." News stories reported the rumor that the bullnecked Croker and the chicken-necked Platt had worked out a deal: Platt would get two seats on the Police Board and Tammany would get off so lightly in the mild and brief "investigation" that its leaders would cakewalk out of the hearing room. Concerned that the bosses were up to their old tricks, the press scolded them both, the *World* warning that Tammany "can never be completely overthrown, thoroughly and permanently beaten, so long as there is a corrupt Republican machine with which it can trade."[6]

* * *

The election fraud trials were also building up new pressures in the city.

The cases were based on evidence that Goff had developed on special assignment for the Bar Association. Jailing some wretches as a warning to others who might have the same idea always quickened Goff's heartbeat, and through the winter he had kept at it diligently. He even harried the police about their lackluster results in making arrests. One of the most important suspects, a pal of Justice Divver, had been roaming at large for weeks while the police claimed they could not find him. One day Goff came upon him in the street, found two cops and ordered them to make the collar.

The tally when Goff was finished (and nothing on such a scale had ever occurred in the city before) was fifty-six men indicted for election cheating. Even more surprising than the indictments were the convictions. Several of the malefactors got off with fines, but some were sentenced to short terms, and one man, convicted of false swearing (he had claimed to be blind and to require help in voting), was sentenced to two years. The entire downtown political structure gasped in unison.

Then came consternation. Jim Dooley, a Divverite election inspector, was sentenced to five years in Sing Sing for making a false count of a district's voting returns. The next day Mike Fay, an inspector in the same district, received the same sentence for the same offense. Fay was a Republican inspector, but it was widely known downtown that he was in the pay of Tammany Hall.

Goff failed to come up with the witnesses to get Justice Divver indicted, but he had the floaters and Tammany small fry shaking in their boots. With rumors rife that hundreds more would be indicted, Divver's boys began to flee the city for Jersey City, or Connecticut, or Canada.

The downtown mugs were aghast. Boss Croker had dropped Nicoll, as they understood it, because Nicoll had indicted and prosecuted the men in his own political organization. But the new District Attorney, John Fellows, was doing the same. In that case, what was the point of having a Tammany District Attorney at all? If the Wigwam ran the city, why were these things happening?

To disturb the downtown Tammany folk even more, the newspapers were pursuing stories of Croker's wealth, his new house, his lavish entertaining and his horse farm. Divver had a similar problem. Like Croker, he had grown rich, acquiring an impressive country home in Far Rockaway and considerable business property. Now it was being said throughout the Second District that he would soon be leaving Divverdom altogether for a grander neighborhood—probably a brownstone on Madison Avenue that Mrs. Divver favored.

If these signs of upward social striving were not damnable enough, neither of the men was available while Goff was hunting down their boys. Divver was picking oranges in California, leaving his men to fend for themselves. Croker was touring the Southwest and Mexico in a luxurious private Pullman car that cost more than $50 a day, enjoying himself while Tammany braves were on their way to Sing Sing in a smoker.

The people below the line could not feel cozy with a political organization that showed weakness. When downtown people gave their allegiance to a Boss and did whatever the organization asked of them, they expected support when things went kaflooey. Instead Croker was saying in interviews from the Southwest that Tammany Hall would not stand for election fraud of any sort.

Divver faced revolt in his district. Saloonkeepers recalled his merciless array of collections: General Committee dues, Committee on Organization dues, annual election campaign assessments, benefits for the unemployed, and tickets for Divver's annual chowder—some saloonkeepers were expected to take twenty of them, and that was $100 worth of tickets.

Now the boys began to recall other grievances against the bandy-legged Justice. His sons had all the choicest jobs. Some said they had always found Divver bumptious, and wondered why the lowest elements in the Second District ranked highest with him. Although they would not have dared a few months earlier, some members of the P. Divver Association asked for an accounting of club funds. Tammany braves in the Second District were quitting, while others were announcing that they would overthrow Divver from within the organization.

These signs of katzenjammer in Tammany Hall overjoyed Parkhurst. "Our triumph is at hand," he said. "Every indication shows that the demoralization of the enemy is complete. Their ranks are wavering; soon they will break, and then the whole army of rascality will be thrown into utter rout."[7]

* * *

But while the pastor was shouting hallelujah, the forty-four-year-old Goff was trying the patience of the Senators. He wrote to the committee that he would not accept the counsel post unless a series of conditions were met: (1) that the committee would have to continue its investigation beyond the end of the current legislative session; (2) that he would be given a month's preparation time; (3) that he alone would select his associate counsel; and (4) that he would control the investigation and would not stand for having any limits placed on him.

After firing off this inexpedient note, he waited in his office in the Times Building on Park Row for a response. Meeting with committee members later, he added another condition: he refused to work with Sutherland.

Upon hearing that Goff had alienated the Lexow Committee, Platt pressed the case for Sutherland. The Easy Boss assured the senators that Sutherland had his witnesses lined up and was ready to proceed. In a letter of March 2 he impatiently called for Lexow to get the Bipartisan Police Board bill up for a Senate vote—although no hearings had yet been held. Deploring the "constant delays and unceasing concessions to the Parkhurst Party," he fretted: "It will not do to wait any longer for evidence to be brought out before the committee."[8]

On March 4, Lexow and other Republican legislators met in Boss Platt's hotel suite to discuss the mechanics of the Bipartisan bill as well as an appropriations bill to pay the counsel and for staff operations.

On the following day Goff met with Lexow Committee members in Albany. During this session he argued against a proposal to make Sutherland his associate counsel. He objected that Sutherland, who was Republican National Committeeman from New York State, was too close to "the State machine" (meaning Platt). He warned that he and Sutherland would inevitably lock horns over the direction of the inquiries. He pointed out that the Rochester attorney knew no more about the metropolis than he did about the canals of Mars.

Platt's associates whispered to committee members that Goff was unwilling to divide the honors because he was out to glorify himself. But Goff's pugnacious style had done him more harm than had his detractors. "Mr. Goff does not seem to have given the committee his full confidence, or to have felt that we intended to make an investigation which would go to the bottom," said Senator Saxton. "I do not think Mr. Goff has really had cause for doubting our sincerity of purpose. He insisted on certain pledges from the committee, which were all right and to which we agreed. He insisted on other pledges, which we thought bound us more than we felt we should be bound. . . . We told him that we thought he was asking too much."

Having made his position clear, Goff must have been astonished by a telegram from Senator Lexow on March 7 stating that the committee had appointed Goff and Sutherland as co-counsel and setting the first public session for two days later in New York. Leaping to his desk, he shot back a note demanding the right to choose his own associate counsel and insisting on a month of preparation time before holding hearings. After that he dropped all communication with the committee.

Only two days later the Lexow hearings began in a borrowed courtroom in the Court of Common Pleas in lower Manhattan, with Sutherland as counsel.

The Senators listened gravely, awaiting revelations. But Sutherland had naught in his briefcase but what Platt had provided, and it lacked any pop.

The newspapers treated the hearings as of minor interest, and one account complained that Sutherland did not properly pronounce the names of some of the city's streets. Parkhurst showed up as a spectator on the second day of hearings with Frank Moss, but the two, finding little to detain them, departed after an hour.

25

VISION AND
ELOQUENCE

The pressure continued to mount as the pastor took the Empire State Limited to Albany on March 15 to speak in opposition to the Bipartisan Police Board bill at a Senate hearing.

Some of the city's foremost citizens accompanied him. The delegation included Charles Stewart Smith, the sixty-year-old president of the Chamber of Commerce, a merchant prince who belonged to several boards of directors and was a trustee of the Metropolitan Museum of Art. It included members of the city's most distinguished clubs, like the Metropolitan Club, the president of which was the financier J. Pierpont Morgan, and the Union League Club, mostly Republicans who had no use for Boss Platt's style of politics.

The men who had made this 145-mile trip—the merchants, bankers, manufacturers, insurance executives, and railroad magnates—paid the biggest tax bills in New York. These distinguished men never talked politics in terms of loyalty or of helping pals, but of rules and laws that should apply equally to all. Believing that citizens should engage in politics out of a sense of altruism and civic duty, they distrusted mechanics and streetcar drivers who took up politics in order to seize opportunities.

Smith spoke for them at the hearing. "We believe that the Police Department of New York City is absolutely rotten," he said. "We believe it is the main source of corruption in the government. It is absolutely essential to good government that there should be a reform and a reorganization of the department." Charging that Platt's bill only divided patronage between Republicans and Democrats, Smith called for a Police Department "lifted absolutely out of politics."

Next came Parkhurst to remind the Senators that they were unfamiliar with conditions in the city. The Legislature, he said, was concocting a remedy before it had begun the diagnosis. "Better be sick a little longer than try to get well on quack therapeutics," he said. "A bipartisan bill enacts partisan politics as a constitutional ingredient of our municipal life."

On a Bipartisan Police Commission, he predicted, the Republicans would protect Republican captains and Tammany Hall would protect Tammany captains. Parkhurst wanted the mayor empowered to appoint a single Police Commissioner who would be solely accountable for everything that happened in the Police Department.

* * *

Although they would not be aware of the implications until later in the decade, Lexow and his Senate colleagues that afternoon were hearing the first distant drumbeats of the coming Progressive movement. Parkhurst and his allies were not just addressing a specific bill that day in Albany, but presenting a new vision of the city. They wanted politics out of the Police Department, of course, but they also wanted to reduce political influence generally in cities. They wanted civil service rules applied in police appointments, but also wanted all municipal workers everywhere chosen on merit alone. They wanted to take elections out of the hands of the Board of Police Commissioners, but also wanted honest elections in all the growing cities across the nation. They were declaring that forward-looking people were prepared to throw partisan politics overboard as excess baggage unsuited to the efficient city government of the twentieth century.

The reformers had lived through the era of corruption and gaudy display that Mark Twain had called The Gilded Age. A number of them had been attracted to the Republican Party by the example of Abraham Lincoln but had been disillusioned by his successors. Boss Tweed and other big-city Democratic bosses had disillusioned the Democrats among them. Many of these reform-minded people, rejecting both parties and opposed to boss-controlled, immigrant-fueled big-city government, had embraced a concept of political virginity called "the good government movement" (which is why their adversaries called them goo-goos).

The goo-goos were coming to the conclusion that political machines had no place in municipal elections; that local candidates should run on a non-partisan basis; that the good men of both parties should unite against the rogues of both parties, and that professional administrators should run the day-to-day business of the city. The party regulars called them Mugwumps, a derogatory term for those who deserted their party to vote for "the best man."

And these men, whose views would find a home in Progressivism, had journeyed upstate to speak in the Senate Chamber of the State Capitol, where the kind of political wire-pulling to which they objected was the main order of business, where bribery was so openly marketed that newspapers published the going rate for votes. The Republicans had wrenched control of the Legislature from the Democrats, and Platt had replaced Croker as the man to see in Albany, but legislation was for sale as before.

Whatever the future portended, the present was under Platt's firm control. After hearing their views, the Cities Committee favorably reported his bill to the Senate floor for a vote.

* * *

Parkhurst had gone to Albany to attend to two matters—not just Platt's bill, but the Goff business. A rift had opened between Goff and the committee, which had apparently given up on him and had already begun hearings with Sutherland as counsel.

The pastor believed that Goff was crucial to a thorough investigation. By this time Parkhurst had promised to cooperate with the committee, and provide it with material from his files, but his promise had been based on the expectation that John Goff would be leading the charge.

When Parkhurst and the uptown reformers took the Empire State Express back to the city, the Lexow Committee members were on the same train heading back to resume hearings. As the train chugged southward the minister was given a chance to speak on Goff's behalf.

Goff had never signed on as counsel to the committee and, the Senators being peeved at his high-handed demands for free rein in the job, all contact with him had ended. Edmund O'Connor, a solid Platt man, was the angriest of the Senators. "He wanted to be the Committee," exclaimed the Binghamton senator. "The Committee will direct its own course, without direction from Mr. Goff or Mr. Anybody Else." He also complained that after the committee appointed Goff and Sutherland, the latter showed up and began preparations, while nothing had been seen of Goff.[1]

During the five-hour ride back on the train Parkhurst smoothed things over. He reminded the Senators that Goff's stringent terms were drafted when everyone in the city distrusted the committee and doubted its sincerity. The resentment against Goff was strong but, by whatever gifts he possessed—of personality, guile or psychology—Parkhurst convinced the Senators that they would toss away their place in history if they did not take Goff as counsel.

By the time they reached the city, he and the Senators had rolled away all impediments. Sutherland would continue as counsel for the ensuing month, focusing on election fraud, then would yield his place to Goff, who would also get the preparation time that he wanted. It was made clear that Goff's would be what was called "the main inquiry." Parkhurst was asked to spring this proposition on Goff.

But when Parkhurst went to Goff's Park Row office, he found the Irish lawyer unwilling to serve. To Goff all the signs were adverse, from the fate of previous investigating committees to the rumors of political deals between Platt and Tammany. Goff's associates and all the wise elders of the city had warned him of the dangers he faced in taking the job and of its certain failure. "In our hands there was not a scintilla of evidence," he recounted later, "that would prove an act of corruption on the part of any member of the Police Department."

Parkhurst argued forcefully, but when he failed to overcome Goff's resistance he turned to leave in defeat. Goff later recalled the scene thus: "I said to him, 'My judgment is against you, but my heart is with you.' He turned back into my office and with a feeling and an eloquence that I shall never forget he said: 'Then let me appeal to your heart.' Immediately I was conquered." Goff agreed to take the job.

Parkhurst himself announced Goff's decision, and expressed for the first time "entire confidence in the sincerity and earnestness of purpose of the Senatorial Committee." He added: "We are satisfied that the investigation will be searching and pitiless, and we confidently believe that the committee deserves to receive the earnest support and cordial cooperation of the press and the community."

Anyone who knew the odds had to be impressed by such skillful negotiation. He had talked the Republican Senators into pursuing a course that irked their own party boss; and, since they were paid nothing extra for staying on through the remainder of the year after the Legislature adjourned in May, Parkhurst had induced them to take on an onerous responsibility involving months of hard committee work at no remuneration. It was an accomplishment many men might have boasted about. Yet in *Our Fight With Tammany*, his account of the campaign, the pastor brushed off the victory in a few words: "We told them [the Senators] that they could trust Mr. Goff, and then we came back to New York and told Mr. Goff that he could trust them."

Parkhurst knew that a measure of virtue was necessary in order for a republic to work, and he appealed to the committee and to Goff in that spirit. He also knew that virtue had to be stirred up, cajoled and insisted upon. And as a Christian he knew that people acted out of human rather than angelic motives. He himself had been first stirred to action not out of pure chivalry, but because his ego had been trampled upon. The prostitutes, small-time operators, petty criminals and saloonkeepers that would be prevailed upon to testify at the hearings were not angels—and neither were the members of the Lexow Committee. Yet all of the players in the coming drama kept in their hearts a glowing coal of nobility, and he had the gift of knowing how to kindle the embers. As a result of his solitary tenacity the Lexow Committee and the Devery trial were about to uncover police corruption that had been shrugged off for a generation.

26

TRUST AND DISTRUST

The Lexow Committee began its hearings on March 9 in a borrowed court-room in the Court of Common Pleas building. On that day and on several days thereafter the senators heard a succession of witnesses on election abuses. Their testimony would have reduced the Founding Fathers to tears, but the question that hung over the proceedings was this: what did it have to do with the police?

Sutherland strained to make a connection. He called a series of witnesses, supplied by Boss Platt, who complained that police had done nothing to stop Tammany Hall's repeaters, floaters and buyers and sellers of votes from tampering with New York's last election, but he could not get any of them to implicate the police in any active way.

His task was even harder because the committee had agreed to allow opposing counsel to question the witnesses, and Sutherland found himself confronted with a talented adversary who knew a lot more about the city than he did. Hired to safeguard the interests of the Police Department, DeLancey Nicoll raised energetic objections and firmly cross-examined witnesses. With each witness the former District Attorney reinforced his point that the police had been hapless bystanders, trained to deal with crime, not with election statutes and tangled legal points about voting eligibility. Nicoll reminded the committee that the Bar Association and a number of other organizations had appointed hundreds of pollwatchers for the election, and that although Goff had gathered the resulting evidence and had secured the indictment of several dozen election officials, not a single charge of interference had been lodged against a police officer, and with good reason: the police had done nothing wrong.

Sutherland was most successful in showing the partisan help extended by Captain Doherty's wardmen for Tammany candidates. Tales were told of torn political posters and threatened saloonkeepers, but many of them had been in the newspapers already. A wine-dealer in Doherty's precinct told of how he had been asked to "do the Captain a favor" by taking down an anti-Tammany poster and was threatened that he would be "fixed" when he refused.

"How did you know the man was a detective?" Senator Bradley asked.

"Vell," the German merchant said, "he told me he vas."

* * *

While the Lexow hearings droned on, reporters dozed, waiting for Goff to begin the real investigation. Newspaper accounts of the hearings were invariably found on the inside pages with such headlines as this from the *Herald* of March 31: "Senator Lexow's Mill at Work—The Spectacular Investigating Machine in Operation, but the Results Are Only Meagre." The apathetic public reaction bore out the warning that Parkhurst had given to Senator Lexow in Albany that the metropolis "was pervaded with utter distrust of him and of all the members of his committee."[1]

The blasé reaction was okay with Boss Platt, who was biding his time, waiting to see what Governor Roswell Flower would do with the Bipartisan Police Board Bill. As far as Platt was concerned, Sutherland had been dispatched to the city to stall until the Governor made his move.

Trying to hasten his rival from the stage, Goff charged that Sutherland was protecting Republican cops, notably Clubber Williams. As the animosity between Sutherland and Goff broke into the open, their bitter exchanges received more press attention than the hearings.

Sutherland's critics met with the Lexow Committee to demand his ouster. Parkhurst, Goff, and Moss told the Senators that unless Sutherland was spirited away they would pull out of the investigation.

The Rochester lawyer had earned no glory as counsel. Although he had done nothing dishonorable, Sutherland's role as Platt's agent consigned him to irrelevance. Even had he wanted to ask tough questions, even had he felt the urge to do diligent research, he was restricted by time. Time was required to develop evidence, but even more important, time was required to establish the Lexow Committee as a credible presence. The people who had evidence against the Police Department were the most vulnerable class of people in the city, and the people against whom evidence was sought were the most invulnerable. Those with evidence needed assurance that they would not bring upon their heads the lasting enmity of the police for nothing more than the sake of a quick and sloppy set of mock hearings rigged to get a Platt bill through the Legislature. That was the sort of commitment that Sutherland could not make, given the circumstances, and history did not give him the chance to prove that he could have done it had his priorities been different.

When Sutherland's stint ended the committee recessed for a month while its members went back to Albany. In the meantime Goff plunged into the task at hand—poring over records, trying to convince potential witnesses to testify, and establishing relations with Parkhurst Society agents willing to assist him. The Irish lawyer put together a team of associate counsel, which over the coming weeks would work closely with him. They were Frank Moss, lawyer for the Parkhurst Society, and W. Travers Jerome, who had collaborated in the defense of Gardner and who, like Goff, had been an Assistant District Attorney. They prepared diligently for the hearings, set to commence after the Legislature adjourned.

* * *

Sutherland did leave a small bonus, however. Near the end of his stint he called as witnesses Morris Tekulsky, the president of the State Liquor Dealers Association, and Jimmy Martin, the president of the Police Commission. In the public spotlight the two men revealed a lot about themselves.

Those who scorned Tekulsky as an ignorant tough underestimated him; Temperance debaters who had matched wits with him at forums knew him to be sharp-witted and informed. He may have talked out of the side of his mouth, but he knew his stuff.

Too proud of his pull to disavow it, the tough Jewish saloonkeeper, a plump man with pink cheeks, conceded to Sutherland that he was a very influential fellow indeed.

"Have you ever had a patrolman transferred?"

"Yes, Peter Carter, from my district to the First, I believe. He insulted me."

"Haven't you interfered with policemen and advised them not to make certain arrests?"

"Yes. I'd prevent them now if I could."

To the chagrin of several Protestant clergymen, Tekulsky had just been named a delegate to the state's upcoming constitutional convention.

"At whose instance were you named as delegate?" Sutherland asked.

"At the instance of a committee from the Liquor Dealers Association of New York County," Tekulsky growled. "They went to see Mr. Croker at Tammany Hall."

"Did you go to see Croker?"

"Yes, at that time and hundreds of other times."

Next Sutherland summoned Jimmy Martin with the intention of exploring his dealings with Tekulsky, his feuds with Superintendent Byrnes, and possible conflicts between his public office as Police Board president and his role as Tammany leader.

When Jimmy was called as a witness he carefully folded his satin-lined overcoat before draping it on the rail of the jury box, revealing a cutaway suit that he wore with dignified prosperity over his well-fleshed body. He took off his smooth high hat and placed it bottom up on the floor. His patent-leather shoes glistened as he sat in the witness chair. He had come a long way from his modest beginnings as a horsecar driver, and in a short time.

Although Sutherland was later disparaged for letting Martin get away with too much, the Police Board President nevertheless revealed himself as a man whose lack of curiosity about police protection of vice was almost catatonic. Jimmy Martin just sent any allegations of wrongdoing back to the Police Department so that the accused officers could investigate themselves. Nor did he ever question the inevitable outcome that the police found themselves blameless. Sutherland summed up Martin's tenure as "a case of masterly inactivity."

Jimmy explained that the Police Board had adopted the resolution against "plainclothes spying" in September of 1891 because a committee of merchants had complained about police blackmailing.

"You are telling us," Sutherland asked, "that one of your reasons for this action was that the system of allowing policemen to enter saloons in plain clothes in search of evidence would have a tendency to enable policemen to collect money from the saloon keepers?"

"Yes."

"Did they indicate who the policemen were?"

"No, sir."

"Did you ask them?"

"No, sir."

"Did you endeavor to ascertain who these policemen were?"

"No, sir."

Martin acknowledged that Tekulsky had visited his office on a half-dozen occasions to seek the appointment, transfer or promotion of police, and that he had granted "three or four" of these requests. He saw no conflict of interest in being both a Tammany leader and a Commissioner, that men looking for appointments to the Police Department came to him as Tammany leader, or that he voted on promotions for men under his wing. He admitted that captains were promoted upon Tammany recommendation and "charged up against" Tammany, confirming that the Police Board practiced a quota system, in which each Commissioner took turns in making appointments, and each protected his men.

"Mr. Martin, did you ever in the course of your career as a Commissioner secure a single promotion, or other reward, for a policeman solely upon his merit?"

"Yes, sir, two cases that I can remember."

"Only two cases in all your career?"

"I think there were more, but cannot recall them."

Martin left the witness chair unruffled. But the newspapers did not let him off easily, and a number of articles appeared about his sumptuous bachelorhood, his retinue of servants, and his brownstone home next door to the Rockefellers. Editorials questioned how he managed it on the comfortable but hardly regal salary of $5,000 a year.

His loyal followers in the twenty-first district complained that the Senators had no reason to question his record. It was perfect. Every policeman from his district ever brought up on charges had been acquitted.

* * *

Meanwhile the pressure kept growing more intense, until it reached Tammany Hall—the red brick building itself with white marble trimmings on Fourteenth Street. When the talk in the saloons turned to municipal upheaval there was no dearth of examples in the events of that spring, but the most slam-bang event of all was the resignation of Boss Croker.

Richard Croker

Tammany leaders had been hearing rumors for a week that the iron man could bear the strain no longer. His predecessors could at least escape at home, but Croker was the first Tammany leader to have one of those crackly telephones in his home, and anybody could turn the crank and ask the operator to connect him to the Boss.

Ever since his return from his vacation, he had been complaining of headaches, indigestion, insomnia and other maladies linked to urban life; and everyone knew that he bossed Tammany Hall with an obsession for detail that frayed his nerves. He had threatened to quit a dozen times. They knew that it curdled his stomach to read editorials asking questions about the sources of his wealth. They knew that he was growing weary of snide comments, even within Tammany, about King Richard the First. They knew that downtown the braves were sulking because Croker had let some of their pals go up the river. They were aware that his marital infidelity had been the subject of a sermon, that Mrs. Croker was talking of filing for divorce, and that no divorced man could lead Tammany Hall.

Nevertheless they could not bring themselves to believe that anyone would resign as the Central Power of Tammany. No one ever had. Only prison or death had pried the scepter from the hand of a Tammany Boss. Even his friends thought that his threats to quit were just blowing off steam, and that he ought to hand over some of the details to someone else. They thought that Croker wanted to make the Tammany captains grovel and beg him to stay.

They were mistaken. On an afternoon in early May the Executive Committee was summoned to the Wigwam for a special session of great moment—the acceptance of Croker's resignation as chairman of the Finance Committee, the office of supreme power in Tammany Hall.

While a plaster bust of Honest John Kelly, a deceased Tammany boss, regarded them from a high niche, Tammany's big chiefs and little braves awaited Croker in their finery. He entered the reception room wearing a long black Prince Albert coat, a waistcoat to match, dark gray trousers, a white shirt with gold studs, and a brown silk cravat. His silk hat was faultlessly ironed. His followers fell back as he approached, so that he passed between two human walls. As he headed for his office men surrounded him expressing their regrets. "It is just like a funeral," said a battle-scarred veteran of the ranks, shaking Croker's hand. Then Croker met inside for a few moments with Police Board President Jimmy Martin and other top Tammany men.

An hour later the Executive Committee was called into the Tammany amphitheater. They filed in and took their seats, while portraits of Washington, Adams, Jefferson and Jackson regarded them from the wall.

Croker lingered in his office for some time after the committee assembled, agonizing over his grammar. When he completed his letter of resignation he walked into the committee room and as was his custom seated himself among the rank and file in the front row. Jimmy Martin, at the head table, turned to him to say that the committee awaited his communication. Croker stood, walked to the table and handed the Police Board President an envelope. Martin opened it, glanced at it, and handed it to a secretary to read.

After the resignation was read the room was enveloped in a mist of humid oratory, or, as the reporter of the unfriendly *Tribune* later put it, "an hour or so of driveling eulogy, panegyric and buncombe followed."[2]

* * *

Croker told reporters that he had resigned on his physician's advice. He said he was leaving Tammany Hall standing like a fortress against its enemies; it had 30,000 active workers, more than ever before. Furthermore, the city was free of corruption; Tammany had posted 3,600 election officers at the 1893 elections, and a few of them had taken it upon themselves to break the law. Tammany deplored their crimes, for which they had been prosecuted by a District Attorney nominated and elected by Tammany Hall, and convicted before judges placed in office by the same organization. He added that those who besmirched the good name of the city injured its commerce by frightening away visitors and conventions. He reminded all that under his leadership Tammany had never lost an election.

For days thereafter the rumor mill whirred about his reasons for quitting. Some accepted Croker's explanation, recalling that he had suffered previous health problems. Others maintained that Croker had extracted all the meat from the lobster and had decided to retire, as one prominent Republican put it, "in the height of his power."[3]

His foes contended that the Boss was hiding from the Lexow Committee. He did not want to be called to the witness chair, they said, where his wealth would be examined and his ignorance revealed. They noted that he had sailed away on a long European vacation when the Fassett Committee came to town four years earlier, and contended that he had been forced to make a deal with Platt to escape a subpoena.

But those closest to him said Croker had quit because he sniffed reform in the halls of Tammany. The Boss could fight reform like the devil, but when it began to infiltrate the organization, it took the heart out of the fellow.

27

THE DEPARTMENT
ON TRIAL

The office door of the Society for the Prevention of Crime was always locked. Parkhurst agents unlocked the door when callers knocked, which occurred every hour or so. Visitors, usually sent by a chapter of the City Vigilance League, slipped in to report on policemen who failed to enforce the law or to pass on information about prostitution or gambling in their neighborhoods. The agents were wary of strange visitors who might be police spies. Everyone spoke in low tones and avoided addressing each other by name.

The office was located at Fourth Avenue and Twenty-third Street, a short walk east of Madison Square. Japanese screens divided the office into two sections. One side of the screens was covered with newspaper cartoons depicting Parkhurst as David, Don Quixote, or as an Indian brave hunting for the scalps of Tammany and the police. Marcus Wishart, the Society's executive head, a tall, thin, gray-haired man in his fifties, worked at a rolltop desk. A safe stood at one side of the room. Behind the screens two typists clattered away, answering letters and making several copies of every report the agents turned in. The reports, records and affidavits were stored in a bookcase.

Parkhurst agents said that they lived under aliases to protect them from police retaliation. There was some truth to that, but some of them had more personal reasons for using a false name—creditors, abandoned wives, former girlfriends in the family way, and outstanding warrants. Parkhurst had chosen them for their skill, not their purity.

Wishart was slow and methodical; John Lemmon was jaunty and gloried in his role like Gardner; and the regular churchgoer of the group, Arthur Dennett, had joined the staff as a matter of faith and duty. His fellow agents called the twenty-seven-year-old Dennett "a long drink of water"—six feet, four inches tall with chin whiskers. He had come down from New Hampshire, where he operated a summer resort and a general store, to enlist in the Parkhurst Crusade, and he brought with him a rustic manner that misled some of the police into underestimating him.

Parkhurst handled the detectives as if he had been managing people all his life. He met with them on a near-daily basis, often in his study at home. He knew not only the location of every brothel and gambling den in the city, but how its business was going, and had shares in whorehouses been sold on the stock market he could have played it to financial riches. He knew the quotas that Byrnes had set for excise arrests in every precinct every Sunday, and even had some sense of whose turn it was to be arrested. He was receiving an enormous amount of mail and held an amazing store of information. He had become the Grand Panjandrum of a busy and successful investigating business—a role he could never have imagined two years earlier—and in his own words he found "the excitement very agreeable."[1]

All those people who sidled up to the door and knocked quietly for admission were promised confidentiality to protect them against police reprisal. In early April the agents were especially eager to hear the knock that brought material about Big Bill Devery—for the hour had come for his trial.

* * *

The police turned out in force at the downtown courtroom near City Hall where Devery went on trial in the first week of April. A gleaming mass of burnished brass and gold braid dazzled the eyes of the jury as they looked into the spectators' gallery. From the headquarters on Mulberry Street through every precinct station from the Battery to Harlem, the word had spread that Big Bill should be supported with a show of solidarity that New York would never forget. The senior officers challenged the jury members with their stares. The trial, they expressed with their presence, was a matter not of evidence but of loyalties.

Through the trial they continued to come. Every precinct captain considered it his duty to attend at least one morning or afternoon of the trial, and the spectators also included sergeants and roundsmen, city officials and judges, Police Justices and Tammany braves. The police who would take the stand in Devery's defense were not allowed into the courtroom, so they roamed the corridors, asking every emerging brother cop how the trial was going. They would confer in the hall to make snide remarks about Moss and Kenneson, Parkhurst Society lawyers who were advising Assistant District Attorney Bartow Weeks in the prosecution.

Devery was charged with neglecting his duty by not moving against specific houses of prostitution operating in the Eldridge Street precinct. The evidence consisted mostly of the testimony of Parkhurst agents, who provided details of how they easily located, entered, and in some cases transacted business in the precinct's tawdry brothels. Sex was offered without stammer or stutter all over the precinct, they said, and women leaned out the windows to invite men in unambiguous terms. A Parkhurst detective testified that on one occasion two policemen were standing in front of the house when he and his companions left. Another Parkhurst gumshoe testified that between September 23 and November 9 he had been in twenty-five brothels in Devery's precinct. A minister testified that he had called on Devery three times about vice in the precinct, but that Devery shrugged him off.

Colonel E.C. James, attorney for the Captain, tried to use the testimony on the abundance of vice as a defense. Of course, he said, the precinct was crime-ridden, and these brothels could not be suppressed all at once, but evidence would be produced to show that Devery was making progress.

Furthermore, the colonel showed that Parkhurst's agents were not angels either, some of them having been arrested on various occasions in various cities for various offenses. Lemmon admitted having a fight with a man after a girl waiter kissed him, but denied that a married woman sat in his lap and that her husband thrashed him. Wishart owned up that he had been convicted of disorderly conduct in Pittsburgh and that he had been fined another time for striking a police officer, which he said he did to avenge an insult.

The defense attorney also tried to make as much as he could of the lies that they had told in order to get into brothels. James forced Dennett and Lemmon to admit to lying. He worked up a lather of indignation about such dastardly deceptions. And he indulged in some sarcasm about how they were now claiming to be telling the truth, and asked the jury, could a man who lied his way into a bawdyhouse be trusted on the witness stand? He expressed shock at the callousness of men who would send an innocent like Dennett into such places.

Colonel James used all of these as elements of the defense, but his main squeeze (downtown lingo for the most important thing) was that Devery was on trial only because Parkhurst was engaged in a vendetta against him. Judge O'Brien was compelled to interject that whether revenge motivated the Parkhurst Society had no bearing on the merits of the case, but the colonel continued to pound away at the motives of a spiteful preacher who schemed to trap Captain Devery because of what had happened to the Society's chief detective.

With that tactic uppermost he approached the cross-examination of Parkhurst attempting to show that the Society became extremely active in Devery's precinct after Gardner's arrest.

"Up to the time of Gardner's conviction," the colonel asked, "had you sent any of your detectives into the Eleventh precinct?"

"I think we had, but I wouldn't swear to it," said the pastor, who wore a long black frock coat, a voluminous mackintosh and dark red gloves to highly dramatic effect.

"Did you not send the detectives into the Eleventh precinct after the conviction of Gardner?"

"Yes, we sent detectives into the Eleventh precinct after Gardner's conviction, just as we sent them into another precinct."

"Was the other captain one who had taken an active part against Gardner?" the defense counsel asked.

"I don't know how large a part of the police force were active against Gardner, but it was a pretty large one, I should judge, and I'm not sure this captain was not one of them."

Then came the key exchange of the trial.

"Is the movement known as the Parkhurst Crusade directed against the keepers of disorderly and gambling houses or against the Police Department?" the colonel asked.

"It is primarily against the Police Department," Parkhurst quietly responded.

There was a stir among the many uniformed officers seated among the spectators.

"Is that the only answer you wish to make to my question?"

"If you wish me to be more specific I will say that it is directed against what I understand to be the criminal collusion between the Police Department and the criminals, as the keepers of gambling and disorderly houses are called."

"Do you include the District Attorney's office?"

"Well . . ." Parkhurst paused slightly before he answered, "yes."

The minister's assertion brought cries of surprise and laughter in the courtroom and shocked Assistant District Attorney Weeks. Parkhurst bowed in his direction and added, "Present company is, of course, understood to be excepted."

"I am afraid," the irked prosecutor remarked, "present company will have to accept the original answer."

Byrnes attended much of the trial, sitting with Weeks and never acknowledging Devery even with a nod. Upon being called to the stand, the Superintendent said that when the Parkhurst Society made its charges about the Eldridge Street precinct the previous summer, he ordered Devery to investigate all the premises cited and to arrest anyone violating the law. Although the captain was already sending in weekly reports, Byrnes called for a supplementary report every week, instructed Inspector Williams to look into the Parkhurst charges and sent two Central Office detectives into the precinct as well. He did the same when the charges were renewed in October.

Devery's reports to the Superintendent, read laboriously to the jury, provided the most damaging evidence against him. Devery squirmed a bit to hear them read back, especially after his lawyer had acknowledged that the precinct was vice-ridden. Repeating themselves almost verbatim week after week, they stated unequivocally that not a single instance of prostitution or gambling blemished his precinct. The places cited by the Parkhurst Society were, according to Devery, closed.

Under cross-examination from James, the Superintendent said nothing detrimental to Devery, giving him a terse, almost grudging endorsement.

"Are you well acquainted with him?" the colonel asked Byrnes.

"I can't say that I am."

"You are well acquainted with his conduct and general standing on the force?"

"Yes, in a general way."

"What is his reputation, so far as his conduct is concerned?"

"Good."

"Has he been obedient and attentive to his duties?"

"To my knowledge, yes."

"Have you ever known him to be guilty of willful disobedience?"

"No."

In his summation, the colonel cited Captain Devery's meritorious record and his acknowledged courage and skill. "While under the superintendency of that great and good man, Dr. Howard Crosby," James said, the Society for the Prevention of Crime "adhered to its purposes and in a quiet and unsensational manner accomplished much good. Then—an enthusiastic ecclesiastic came to the head of the society. (Laughter from the police.) He permitted himself to be surrounded by a set of vagabond detectives, and has so far committed himself to what is called The Parkhurst Crusade as to make the reckless and unjustifiable statement that the crusade is not against crime, but against the Police Department and what he is pleased to term the criminal complicity between the Police Department and criminals. And this includes the office of the District Attorney." He repeated that Devery had been singled out because he had caught Gardner, the Society's "pet detective." Of course, he allowed, anyone who looked hard enough could find vice in Devery's precinct—it was after all the Lower East Side—but the Society's leaders, since they refused to cooperate with the police, betrayed their lack of any sincere interest in stopping it.

Weeks praised Devery's past record, singling out his activity against Anarchists. "And we are proud of him," he said, "in that when an agent of this Society tried to blackmail a fallen woman he arrested him and brought him to justice. But now, we claim, he has been false to his trust, derelict in his duty."

The judge told the jury not to be swayed by the hope that a conviction would add glory to the Parkhurst Society or that an acquittal would restore the defendant to his former position. The only question for them, he said, was whether a crime had been committed.

The acquittal took longer than expected. Not until eight hours later, at 11:30 P.M., did the jury find the captain not guilty, thus saving him from what could have been a one-year jail term and a $500 fine as well as dismissal from the force. Loyally awaiting the verdict, a band of police and detectives sent up a cheer. After he had shaken hands with the jurymen, Devery was seized and carried aloft out of the courtroom by his friends and fellow officers.

* * *

Parkhurst was not the least disheartened at the verdict, and to demonstrate his energy and good spirits he went up to Harlem the following evening to speak.

It was an indication of Parkhurst's growing influence that he spoke to delegates of the New York Methodist Episcopal Conference and members of the New York Social Union—a mixed audience with as many women as men. They were meeting at the Calvary Methodist Episcopal Church which, although far uptown, was regarded as the leading Methodist church in the city.

"We have just been defeated," he told the audience. "If we had been victorious I do not think that I should have been able to come here tonight on account of shock, and yet, somehow or other, we are getting there." His listeners reacted with a cheer that did not suggest defeat.

The church held 2,500 people, and every seat was filled, and an equal number were standing outside in the rain straining to hear him through the church's open doors. The men cheered and the women waved their handkerchiefs in what was called the Chautauqua salute, and both sexes laughed at his sallies, although two years earlier some of these same men and women had probably spoken of him as a sensation-monger and a renegade.

"One expression of Mr. Nicoll comes back to me comfortingly," he continued. "It was on an occasion when I had gone to his office to try to get an indictment against a police captain—not Devery. He told me that it would do us no good to get an indictment because we would be beaten in court. I remarked that we always seemed to gain something from these defeats. 'Yes,' he said, 'you do, and you'll get there, I think.' There was a good deal of comfort in that remark, coming from Mr. Nicoll."

Thoroughly at ease, he amused as he preached with characteristic vigor, orating in his finely honed voice and delivered in his perfect timing. His manner and his voice stripped everything from his listeners, so that they forgot that they had to catch a morning train, or had a recalcitrant child at home, or that they would never be able to pay next month's bills, or any other extraneous thought. They were only in the present.

The lesson of the Devery trial, he said, was that Tammany Hall was in control of everything, from City Hall to the Police to the courts and even in the District Attorney's office, and that the only solution was political. Crooked cops and crooked politicians had to be swept from power.

The last thirty months, everything that the Parkhurst Society had investigated and all the activity of the City Vigilance League, had made no difference. Nothing had changed because justice was impossible under Tammany Hall. "Suppose we have a case against a gambler. We go before a Police Justice, and that is illustrated as well to the general mind by the late Patrick Divver as by any other example." They broke into laughter and applause. "There are only two justices in this city before whom we can bring such a case with any confidence, and the Board of Police Justices make it a point to keep those two up in Goatville."

The audience was familiar with the lack of enforcement among brothels and gambling dens, but did they know about police dereliction of duty in the matter of abortions? Some in the audience gasped, for the subject was never broached in mixed company. He read aloud from *The City Vigilant*, the magazine of the City Vigilance League, which had developed the evidence: "It seems to us that nothing has occurred that covers the Police Department with more obloquy than that a crime so heinous in its quality should have been left by the police to be unearthed by a private organization. . . . If we were Superintendent of Police and we had not been able to detect the sixteen baby slaughterers, we think we would have imitated the good example of Judas Iscariot."

He noted that the Assistant District Attorney had lauded Devery for suppressing Anarchists in the Eldridge Street precinct. Then he read a report of volunteers of the City Vigilance League who had counted the saloons open on Sunday, March 18, in that precinct, and the continuous procession of men, women, children, police, and a police captain into them. "Now that's what I call Anarchy," he snapped. "Taking the laws as they have been laid down and making a plaything of them is Anarchy. I assert that the entire Police Department are Anarchists."

All over the city he used the lesson of the trial, showing his listeners that the Central Office detectives, the Inspectors, and the Superintendent had all backed Devery against the weight of the evidence; that Devery's ridiculous reports on the suppression of vice had been laughed at in court. Everyone in the city knew that the verdict was a joke and that the Eldridge Street precinct was maggoty with vice.

Now, he added, whorehouses that had been closed for months were preparing to reopen. He claimed to know which ones they were, what they had paid in bribes to reopen, and to whom they had been paid. He also charged that gambling parlors that had shut down or had restricted their operations in recent months were back in business all over the city and that the numbers runners would soon be selling on the streets again. The growing boldness of vice in the city, he said, could be traced straight to the acquittal of Devery.

"There is no hope for us," he said angrily, "until our archenemy is done away with at the polls, and I expect that will happen next November."

28

ON THE EVE
OF A STRUGGLE

The whole city was buzzing about the verdict. "No event has transpired during the history of our work that has operated more directly and powerfully to define and compact popular sentiment than the acquittal of Captain Devery," Parkhurst observed. "It was far more to our advantage that we were defeated in our efforts against him than it would have been had we been successful."[1]

The newspapers hammered away at the crimes of Tammany. "At no time since the overthrow of the Tweed Ring have so many daily newspapers and other publications been engaged in exposing the infamies and abuses from which New York has suffered under Tammany misrule," the *Tribune* commented on May 5. "The records and careers of Tammany officeholders have been unsparingly laid bare. It has been proved beyond denial or dispute that many of the most important departments of the city are looted and despoiled by Tammany Commissioners and subordinates."

The newfound wealth of Croker and other Tammany leaders was questioned in editorials. Croker's real estate deals were exposed for public perusal. The *World* published a series of scathing profiles of Tammany leaders and their lowlife associates. The newspapers were merciless to Justice Divver, keeping a tally of the frequent occasions that inebriation or hangovers prevented him from presiding over his courtroom. The Justice was linked to a saloon purchase which also involved a master of bunco games and the owner of an illegal gambling operation. Other stories showed the Tammany spoils system at work in the schools and the Fire Department. News stories about waste, nepotism, featherbedding and favoritism suggested that Mayor Gilroy's administration was careless and mismanaged. Muckraking, although it would not be known by that name for a few more years, had begun.

* * *

Never before had interest in a coming election begun so early. By March anti-Tammany Democrats had decided to put up a slate for the fall election. In April they held a rally, with fireworks and a march to the Lyceum Concert Hall behind two brass bands. Tammany Hall was assailed for bossism, election fraud, blackmail, levying tribute from business and oppressing the powerless. The hall was filled with working people from the gashouse district, and their cheering shook the rafters.

Neighborhood associations were mushrooming all over the city. Ever since Parkhurst handed out pledge cards at the beginning of his crusade he had been calling upon people to sign up. When he had enough cards he and his friends had put together the City Vigilance League, which was designed to help start and sustain grassroots community organizations. Parkhurst's original plan had been to create a chapter in each of the city's thirty Assembly districts. The chapters, however, took on autonomous lives of their own, while the League helped whenever called upon, donating the services of Parkhurst agents for reconnoitering the neighborhood. All the chapters, however naïve their original presumptions, quickly became adversaries of the police, who insulted them or tried to double-talk and bamboozle them.

* * *

Parkhurst went to the annual dinner of the City Vigilance League with public support shifting in his favor. Two years earlier it had been said that the public would soon tire of his exhortations, and he had gone through a time when his work was considered disgraceful. But his weathering of adversity, his growing political skill, his magnetism, and his combination of tenacity and flexibility was winning over the city.

At the tables on that April evening the two hundred guests talked about whether the Governor would sign the Bipartisan Police Board bill, whether the Lexow Committee would accomplish anything, and whether Tammany could be beaten in the coming election. Reformers could win, it was said, if a united campaign could be mounted. Every previous attempt to close ranks had run up against Platt, who insisted upon running a straight Republican ticket and refused to combine with reformers—and had always been able to win something for his boys after a Tammany victory by making deals with Croker.

When the coffee was served, Charles Stewart Smith, the president of the Chamber of Commerce, struck the theme which dominated the evening.

"If the influence of our cities is to predominate more and more in the government of the country, as no thoughtful man can doubt, then the greatest concern of the lover of his country must be to inquire what is to be the character of the government of the great cities of the United States," he said. "Monarchies have endured for a long time under corrupt rulers, but corruption strangles republics, and the question of how long this Republic of ours can endure may depend upon the answer that the men of our generation give to this important question. You, young gentlemen, may hold the fate of the Republic in your hands.

"As to the policy pursued by your society, I don't imagine that you or my friend Dr. Parkhurst claim that you have never made mistakes. A man that never makes a mistake never makes anything. What I claim for the work of your society is that, notwithstanding the powerful opposition which comes from organized corruption in this city and the feeling of timid friends that you were going too far, and that the case was hopeless as far as ultimate success was concerned, yet you have conquered in this regard. Your society has now a position of respect and confidence in this community, and gratitude is fast taking the place of distrust, and this is the reason why I am glad to be here to add my testimony to the public appreciation of your good work."

Parkhurst enthralled the audience, which hung on his every word. Speaking with brio and confidence, he had the virtuosity of Anton Dvorak at Carnegie Hall conducting his new symphony, "From the New World."

"We believe in a grand future for the city of New York and before God we know it is coming," he said to a tumult of cheers. "There is no man, there is no people, who has ever accomplished anything . . . who did not have confidence in the future. There is no people who, so far as the having of a foundation for the future, has done so much as the Hebrew people—distinctively a prophetic people, with a long, clear glance into the centuries that were to come. If the Vigilance League knew that it had a pessimist in its ranks it would turn him out. No man who believes in God and has a good digestion has a right to be a pessimist." The audience laughed and applauded.

Then he called for a unified ticket to oppose Tammany Hall in the coming election: "If we want to win, we cannot afford to be divided in our antagonism to that archenemy. Any man who allows himself to be put forward as a candidate in any one of these pending reform movements without being very sure that there is going to be sympathy with his candidacy on the part of the other reform movements, is an out-and-out traitor to our municipal interests." Thunderous applause followed these words.

* * *

In the weeks that followed Parkhurst went from hall to hall and from church to church telling any group that would listen that the Devery verdict would in the end exact its own kind of justice. Speaking to working men one May night over a beer hall, he called their attention to the stir that was enlivening the city, of the "earnestness of thought" among citizens, their "devotion to a common purpose" and he said that he was "confident in the great grace that lies in the united action of resolute men." Although many of these workers had no use for religion, they felt the authenticity of his faith. They knew that he was addressing the need to make life count for good; of his conviction that nobility lay within the hearts of the people, and that not only individuals, but cities and nations would be held accountable to show what they had done to bring in the jubilee. He called for people to show their colors, step forward, and reshape a city closer to the heart's desire.

* * *

Augusta Thurow and her husband read the newspapers, but even if they did not she would have heard of Parkhurst, for everyone spoke of him now, including the Wardman John Hock. Whenever she had complained of her treatment by the police, of how she paid for protection from police raids but was raided anyway, Hock blamed Parkhurst for making things hot for the brothels.

After the raids on First Street in November, the red-moustached wardman told Augusta not to reopen, because Parkhurst's agents were active. One day Hock told the Thurows that it was impossible for them to stay at their location any longer, but that if they took a new place he would not pull them. They took rooms nearby, moving their prostitutes with them. Then, when Augusta Thurow saw Hock, he demanded another initiation fee because it

Mrs. Augusta Thurow

was a new place, and what he was asking—$1,000 for the Captain and $250 for himself—took her breath away. "Hock," she responded, "I can't pay it. I can give it to you in installments. I can give you $500 down, and after that $50 a month for protection and $50 installments on the balance."

Hock went away without committing himself. "Things are on the bummerina," he said when he showed up again. "Parkhurst's men have been around making trouble. You'll have to lay low for two months."

The frustrated couple moved their girls out of Captain Doherty's precinct and into the Eldridge Street precinct. They took a place over a saloon at Broome and Allen Streets, and the Eldridge Street wardman assessed her $250 as an initiation fee. Mrs. Thurow pawned some jewelry to come up with $150 and gave it to Hock on account. But the saloonkeeper would not let any men upstairs because he was having license trouble. The wardman, he assured her, had said all would be fine soon. By the end of February, however, they were still unable to do business. Mrs. Thurow dropped a note at the station house asking the wardman to stop by. When he came she told him she wanted her money back.

"I can't get it back," he said. "I wish I could." When March came around she could not pay the rent and was dispossessed.

Whether out of courage, or spite, or love of virtue, or to even the score with the cops—whatever it was, she decided that she had something to tell Parkhurst.

OUT FOR BLOOD
Spring 1894

29

THE FAIRER SEX

If men were angels no government would be necessary.

—James Madison, *The Federalist Papers*

One of the sensations of the spring was Thomas Edison's latest invention, the Kinetoscope. There were ten of these iron boxes in a theater in Herald Square. Inside the boxes images were projected on a small screen. The viewer watched through a hole in the box. The images were a series of still pictures, each one slightly varied, so that when they were shown in rapid succession they gave the illusion of motion. They were "moving pictures" of ordinary human actions—people running, jumping up and down, sneezing. Each of the ten films cost a nickel to see and each was only sixteen seconds long. Yet people were coming out in droves to see this latest wonder of the Wizard of Menlo Park, and the line stretched all around Herald Square. People wanted to look into those boxes because they presented, as one of the films was called, "A Peep Into the Twentieth Century."

The suffragists also afforded a glimpse into the future. Like Kinetoscopes, like the incandescent lighting that was spreading through the city, like the horseless carriage race held that year in France, the suffragists presaged a new century that lay around the corner. Believing themselves to be harbingers of change, they were instilled with high levels of energy.

"Such enthusiasm!" said the suffragist Elizabeth Cady Stanton. "Such interest! It is a revolution! Every place I went woman suffrage was the theme of conversation. It was talked of on the streets, in the shops, at dinner tables. Everyone was interested."[1] Mrs. Stanton, who wrote the speeches that Susan Anthony delivered from platforms, was a seasoned judge of such matters, for she had been in the movement for four decades, and she had never seen the like of what was happening in the spring of 1894. Cultured voices were singing songs of suffrage, and well-born women were ringing doorbells and distributing leaflets. Fashionable ladies were devoting evening gatherings to "the petition." Advocates and adversaries both clothed woman suffrage with millennial significance: according to the suffragists it marked the dawning of a new era of peace and happiness, according to their foes it spelled the end of Western Civilization.

Buoyed by the belief that they represented the future, the suffragists exuded a confidence that hardly seemed warranted for a movement that could attest to forty years of failure.

* * *

That spring a special Constitutional Convention was holding hearings and meetings to recommend changes in the State Constitution. The suffragists took the opportunity to pose their own constitutional question: now that Wyoming and Colorado had given the vote to women, should New York not do likewise?

They stepped out of the Woman's Suffrage League on Fourteenth Street into a city that was male to the roots of its being: crass and aggressive, gaudy and obvious, prodigal and rough. While women might fit becomingly into the landscape of Paris or Vienna or London, they were out of place in New York City, which lacked an architectural unity or even an imposing plaza. Everything in the city—its cluttered streets, its pressing crowds, its tall cast-iron buildings—expressed power. Elevated trains chugged along stark causeways on stilts, bombing the suffragists below with burning cinders. Wagon wheels rumbled and screeched on the Belgian block pavement, paining their ears. This rude city was entirely run by men in every respect—every bank, every factory, every city office, every newspaper, every means of transport and, except for a few retail shops, almost all business. Femininity counted for nothing there.

Yet the suffragists never faltered. In small groups they traversed the rank city, wearing what was almost a uniform of white shirtwaists, round straw hats, long black skirts and of course white gloves (in New York even working girls wore white gloves). No bustles, of course, for nothing was more completely out of fashion. They wore the clothes of the day but they represented a coming day, and the conviction that they would eventually win fueled their persistence.

Men reacted sometimes with growls, sometimes with apathy, and often with the politest of refusals. Some men who declined to sign the petition—which asked the State to cross out the word *male* as a criteria for voting—inquired as to why women, so lovely and sublime a sex, would wish to meddle in politics, which they would only find tedious and dull when it was not nasty and rancorous. Women were too good for such pursuits, the men said, and even against their will they ought to be protected from the unpleasant scenes that often took place at the polls. Entry into public affairs would only soil their innocence.

The men's refusals came in the form of bouquets; and yet the petitioners knew that on other occasions some men expressed caustic sentiments about woman suffrage. Suffragists found themselves assailed in the letters columns of the newspapers as joyless, unlovely, shrewish creatures who wanted to usurp the place of men because something in their makeup was askew. Whatever they were, angels or witches, men were unwilling to let them vote.

Of the 175 delegates at the Constitutional Convention the one who worked hardest against woman suffrage was a Tammany brave and a recent Lexow witness: Morris Tekulsky, the former president of the Retail Liquor Dealers Association.

They were trying to outcampaign him. They called upon Protestant clergymen, ringing the rectory doorbells as if they were collecting debts, asking repayment for the uncounted hours of volunteer work that women had contributed to their churches and to such interdenominational work as the Society for the Prevention of Pauperism, the Association for Improving the Condition of the Poor, the Female Reform Society, the Children's Aid Society and the Orphan Asylum Society. By this means the women enlisted some ecclesiastical support for suffrage yet something in their mien rubbed many clergymen the wrong way, and they may have stirred up a measure of ministerial opposition while trying to win support.

Whatever their effect they shook things up to so great an extent that on the second Sunday in May, just before the opening of the Constitutional Convention, clergymen all over the city devoted sermons to the subject.

Parkhurst, neither an advocate of woman suffrage nor a staunch opponent, predicted in his sermon that the destiny of woman will "savor less and less of masculinity as she approaches the perfection and consummation of her being." Clergymen who backed woman suffrage tended to emphasize the purifying effect it would have upon vice and drunkenness. Those who spoke in opposition tended toward sweeping predictions that the drift of woman's rights issues led to the dissolution of the family. "You are mad!" one Episcopal cleric clamored that Sunday, "You are mad, I say, if to the women you extend the franchise, and the welfare of our Republic!"[2]

* * *

To old political captains the agitation about votes for women was another sign that politics was losing its virility. They recalled the days when a man marched to the polls with a band of armed friends to protect him. But in these effete times there was hardly a bruise to remind men that politics was a bloody trade. Even the men too young to remember the days of street brawling agreed that women did not appreciate that politics was a rough and tricky game, played for keeps.

One instance was the rigmarole that surrounded the Bipartisan Police Board bill and the appropriations bill for the Lexow Committee. Politics was holding up everything. John Goff could not take over as committee counsel due to lack of money—the committee was still waiting to be funded. The resolution for $25,000 to cover the committee's staffing and operations lay on the Governor's desk, but nothing had happened yet.

Lying with it was the Bipartisan Police Board bill. The insiders said Platt was pressuring the Governor to get that bill, and if the Governor signed it there would be no further Lexow investigation, Boss Platt having what he wanted. But if the Governor vetoed the bill, Platt would give the signal to keep the probe going.

All through the city the men of substance who followed legislative affairs, and the men who liked to hear themselves talk, pondered and chewed over what the Governor would do, what the next move would be in the grand game of politics. Women were not expected to follow such intricate matters.

* * *

Charles Stewart Smith, the president of the Chamber of Commerce, was relaxing at his country estate in Connecticut when he learned that Governor Flower had vetoed the appropriations bill. A reporter read him the accompanying statement, in which the governor called New York City the best-governed city in the state, lauded its police force, fire department, schools, parks, clean streets and its low crime rate, and declared his intention to bar the use of public money "to pay the campaign expenses of a political party" or "for summer vacations for rural senators." In conclusion the Governor justified the veto by claiming that Republicans controlled the Legislative Committee of the Chamber of Commerce and had called for the probe to reap some political advantage. In short, he said, it was all politics.

"This is the most remarkable message I have ever heard," responded Smith. With annoyance he noted that the probe had the support not only of the Legislative Committee but by unanimous vote of the entire Chamber. He acknowledged that many members of the Chamber's Legislative Committee were Republicans, but added that the Chamber did not traffic in partisan politics and was "as clear-headed a body of men as there are in the United States." He pointed out that the press was impugning the honesty of the police on a daily basis, and that if the newspaper accounts were false, an investigation would absolve the Police Department of unwarranted charges.

Smith showed the reporter a note from Parkhurst typed up in anticipation of the veto. "I do trust that there will be those who will bridge the present emergency," the note implored. "If at this time the investigation should be interrupted or stopped a great part of the effort that has been put forth in the past seven months would be rendered fruitless."

"Dr. Parkhurst need have no apprehension," Smith added, pocketing the note. "The investigation will be neither interrupted nor stopped." He assured the public that the funds would be raised privately. "I should say after listening to that message that it would be the incentive for people to put their hands in their pockets and make up a subscription. I should say that message would make it easy for us to get more money than we need."

Within days, as Smith predicted, the Chamber had pledges for the money. Chamber members willingly dug down and contributed, although many of them, fearful of police disfavor, insisted that their contributions remain anonymous.

"If it had been the Governor's purpose to crush the investigation by one very hard blow it has failed," the *Herald* trumpeted. "If it was his purpose to put nearly all the reform and anti-Tammany men of wealth in the city on their mettle and reach for their checkbooks with the intention of raising twice the sum of $25,000, it has succeeded."

Within a day came the second big veto, as the Governor nixed the Bipartisan Police Board bill. Nobody was surprised at that veto either, although the cheer that it brought to Tammany Hall lasted only briefly. Within hours Mayor Gilroy appointed Charles Murray, one of Platt's closest aides, to the Police Board. Tammany Hall was aghast, particularly because Murray had made himself odious to the Wigwam by getting several of Dry Dollar Sullivan's men indicted for election fraud. Angry promises were made that Gilroy was through—that he would not serve another term as Mayor. Croker, who had known Gilroy's intentions, had nothing to say about the appointment, although his friends said it had been the reason he quit as Tammany Boss.

Men followed these political affairs in the newspapers; some out of a sense of duty to be an informed citizen, while others enjoyed the gambits and tactics, and liked trying to guess the coming countermove. But the women, except for a few rare exceptions, showed no more interest in these proceedings than they might in a boxing match. They regarded these legislative acts and vetoes as male concerns, and many of them, had they thought about it, would have been pleased that men exempted them from having to bother their heads about such matters. It was an exceptional woman who was distressed by the funding problems of the Lexow Committee, or worried about whether the composition of the Board of Police Commissioners worked to the public good, and few women for that matter had any conception of what the Lexow Committee was about or what the Police Board did.

30

FIRST BLOOD

He was the man of the hour, the toast of the town. Phrenologists were writing articles for the Sunday editions to explain John Goff. The distance from his ear to the top of his head, it was reported, indicated uncommon persistence. His head was narrow behind the ears, a sign that he ate for nourishment rather than pleasure. He had more reverence than faith, and his features showed all the traits and marks of the reformer. Goff was the subject of editorial cartoons, the latest name to be dropped, the new personage to be spoofed in a roof garden vaudeville revue.

In May the subject of all public speculation was holed up in his lower Broadway law office, which hummed with arrivals and departures, with conferences with Parkhurst agents, with furtive men who wished to remain unseen.

The furious activity was part of Goff's preparation for his debut as counsel for what jokers called the Lexow Club. He had been informed that all the necessary funds for the investigation had been pledged, and that the Chamber of Commerce was making splendid headway in collecting the donations. To him, the money was nothing; his assistant counsel, Frank Moss and William Travers Jerome, were prepared to defer their fees for the present, and the only immediate need for money consisted of meeting expenses and paying for secretarial help. If necessary, Goff would cover those items out of his own pocket. He intended that the hearings be resumed on schedule.

He had an assured manner that dispelled all doubt. Although only a little over average height, he had at the age of forty-three prematurely gray hair, a full beard and moustache tinged with faded traces of auburn, shaggy eyebrows, deep-set blue eyes and sunken cheeks, a head fit for a bust—in fact he looked a bit like Rodin's John the Baptist. Some reporters claimed to detect a fanatical cast to his features but, given his politics, they were predisposed to think so. His family had been Irish patriots for generations, some having died for their cause on the scaffold, and Goff had been working for rebellion since his boyhood, when he played children's games with Charles Stewart Parnell, who had since made his mark as a spokesman for Irish independence. Goff had continued to work in America with the Clan-na-Gael, a terrorist organization devoted to the overthrow of British rule in Ireland.

John Goff

In his practice Goff concentrated on criminal law. He had become steeped in it as an Assistant District Attorney, and was regarded as one of the half-dozen best in the city. His clients included the Anarchist Joseph Barondess, the "King of the Cloakmakers," whom Goff had defended in connection with charges of extortion and jumping bail in a labor dispute. Barondess was convicted, but Goff secured a pardon from the Governor, and the labor leader had returned to New York to introduce Emma Goldman to union organizing activities in the tailoring trades.

In preparing for the reopening of hearings, Goff surrounded himself with piles of lawbooks and affidavits, but his studies were interrupted as Parkhurst agents came in with shifty-eyed men with stories to tell. When the day was over he went home, but not to rest from his labors. Goff lived modestly in an uptown flat with his wife and their son and daughter. He was a scholar, and his study teemed with books, which he read voraciously—not novels or ephemeral works, but history, philosophy, and poetry. Atop a high bookshelf in his study stood a scale model of the three-masted *Catalpa*. Goff had chartered the ship out of New Bedford in 1875, supposedly in search of whale oil, but actually engaged on a mission to rescue six Irish revolutionaries from life imprisonment in Australia. Goff's Irish Rescue Party raised $30,000 to back the project financially. His admirers had presented him the ship's model as a memento.

When he arrived home Goff enjoyed listening to his daughter, Inisfall (the Gaelic name means "the land of the spirit of song"), play old Celtic melodies on the harp. He cherished the memories of the Old Country that he had left as an impoverished lad.

But as he prepared himself for the Lexow investigation he had little time for Irish folk tunes or scholastic metaphysics. Into the wee hours he labored past the point of exhaustion. He read tall piles of affidavits, climbed mountains of research, paced the floor in mental struggle.

Goff had taken on an assignment that no other prominent lawyer in the city would even consider. Many were afraid of police retribution, others of incurring the displeasure of Tammany Hall. Some were afraid of being tarred with the brush of certain defeat. Some had no appetite for the job because, having anticipated that the Governor would never fund an investigation aimed at Tammany, and because lawyers had been left dangling and unrecompensed in previous Senate investigations, they were sure that whoever took the office would be that most woeful figure, the lawyer without his fee.

In soliciting funds for the hearings, Chamber of Commerce officials assured donors that they would be repaid if State funding became available in the future, but the contributors were less concerned about reimbursement than about anonymity. They were anxious to keep their names from the police, and the Chamber officials promised to hold them in confidence. To the far-sighted businessman the contribution was an intelligent investment, since police corruption was expensive and demoralizing, although it was easier to hand out a few dollars to the police than to challenge them.

Potential witnesses were even more reluctant. Goff contacted men who said they were eager to see justice done and welcomed his efforts, but begged off from testifying because the police could "do a put-up job" on anybody they wished. Too few New Yorkers, as he put it, had yet "become vertebrate."

Not that Goff lacked informants; on the contrary, every second person he met had a confidence to whisper in his ear. The supply of anecdotes about police corruption that he was gathering could keep a committee interested for a decade. Sometimes he met with midnight visitors at his study who favored darkness so as to keep their meeting secret. None of his informants dared to step into the limelight. "One man would tell me the name of some other man who might give me something of value," he said, "and that man would tell me of some other man, but when I would see the persons named they would be horrified at the suggestion that their names should be mentioned in connection with the matter in any way. There was not a man who was willing to come forward and boldly swear to the actual giving of bribes, or that as eyewitnesses they saw bribes accepted."[1]

Saloonkeepers who were paying off the police admitted the truth to him in his office, but warned him that they would deny everything on the stand. "The Senate Committee goes away, but the police remain," one concert hall operator told him. "I would be ruined were I to tell all I know."

* * *

As Goff looked for a way to get the ball rolling, hoping that one willing witness would induce others to follow, a meeting was taking place that would help his cause. James O'Kelly, a shoemaker on the Upper West Side, was talking to a very tall fellow who had walked into his shop, introduced himself as Arthur Freeman, and said he wanted to get on the police force. Freeman had a New Hampshire twang and a country-cousin style that suggested that he had just fallen off a hay-wagon, but he was trying his darndest to sound slick, and he reckoned that ability was not enough in New York—that pull was the main thing. And he heard tell that the shoemaker had the pull. According to the version that the tall hayseed told later, when they had sufficiently felt each other out O'Kelly pulled a Civil Service examination from his desk, and said that for those in the know the exam answers were available in advance.

The tall, bearded rustic visited the shoemaker again soon thereafter, and this time, according to his account, they spoke freely about paying—somewhere between $300 and $400, with $50 as a down payment—to be appointed to the force. O'Kelly gave "the long drink of water" a city map to study while waiting to take the Civil Service examination. Upon making his payment the applicant would be provided with a set of stolen exam papers, and if this proved insufficient, the results would be doctored. Most important, O'Kelly said, the matter would be clinched by means of a letter of recommendation to Police Commissioner John McClave. The hayseed agreed to the terms and said he would return soon with the money.

As soon as he left O'Kelly's shop, the hayseed—actually the Parkhurst agent Arthur Dennett—headed for Goff's office. What Dennett reported confirmed information that had come from another source, a man named Gideon Granger who said he had operated as a liaison between O'Kelly and Commissioner McClave.

Granger was about thirty years of age. He came from a distinguished family, liked gaudy women and strong drink, and he was completely undependable as well as a thief. Although a charming and accomplished wheedler, Granger was careless and never entirely forthright. He was hardly the most credible of witnesses. If Goff had learned anything as an Assistant District Attorney, however, it was that there were few informants with haloes. Those who informed on wrongdoing were invariably those who had been present to witness it, and as a rule they were not Sunday school teachers or Goo-Goos.

Granger said he had proof that McClave was selling appointments and promotions, and on several occasions had passed along the payoff money directly to the Commissioner. More often, though, he gave the money to George Richards, McClave's police orderly, who forwarded it to McClave. Granger had a notebook in which he had written the names of appointees and what they had paid for their appointments.

But the most intriguing twist was this: Granger had just been divorced from Commissioner McClave's daughter. He had been carrying the bag for his father-in-law.

Granger's accusations sounded plausible because of numerous rumors implicating McClave. Coming up with evidence, however, had hitherto been impossible, for in briberies of this sort a go-between was invariably used to protect the official from direct contact and thus allow him to deny everything. Except for Granger, Goff had plenty of smoke about McClave but no fire.

Poking about in records, Goff discovered that the vain and dapper Police Commissioner had failed in a number of business ventures and had left a trail of bad debts behind him. But as soon as he had been appointed to the Police Board in 1884, his fortunes had begun to soar. For the next decade his lumber company buzzed with orders from the transit companies and other businesses that had contracts with the city. Other members of McClave's family had also shared in the largess—and all of this had fallen to the lot of a Republican.

* * *

Goff decided to open the hearings with McClave. Going after one of the Police Commissioners at the outset would cause the kind of commotion that would engage the public's attention. Beginning with a Republican had another value; it served notice that the Lexow hearings were more than a Platt maneuver to make Tammany look bad, that the committee was dead serious and aimed at uncovering wrong irrespective of political considerations, and that the days of Sutherland's dithering were over.

McClave was the most respectable Commissioner, with the most correct English, an example of the businessman that the reformers hoped would rescue public life from the politicians. But despite his manicured nails and his tailored clothing, McClave was just Tammany window-dressing. Although nominally a Republican, Tammany owned him. He feigned independence but in crucial votes he always sided with his Tammany colleagues and never raised embarrassing questions about the conduct of the department. And why would he? In just a few years he had acquired a country home, horses and servants, a sleigh festooned with nodding plumes, and (the token of being in the swim in the 1890s) a shower in his black-onyx bathroom, and all of this opulence could be traced to his seat on the Police Board.

There was, however, an element of risk in Goff's course. The young wastrel might be lying or exaggerating to settle a score with his father-in-law. Goff believed the main lineaments of Granger's story, but he was aware that the young man might be tempted to embellish his testimony to besmirch McClave.

Granger was a feckless truant, a flighty fellow who might change his story on the witness stand. Unless, of course, Goff and the Parkhurst agents could induce O'Kelly to confess.

Under such pressure sleep did not come easily, and so Goff worked almost all through the night. He had put all his chips on one number, and all was riding on a single spin of the wheel. If his witness turned on him, he would have to rely on his sharp sense of courtroom combat, and with the abandonment of a gambler he gathered his team together and headed for the General Session courtroom where, on May 21, the curtain went up.

* * *

That morning Goff stood about in conference with Moss and Jerome while Commissioner McClave, short and slender with gray hair that he parted in the middle, sat conferring with Nicoll. Goff had worked with Nicoll in the District Attorney's office, and knew that he had a skillful adversary. Soon Parkhurst and Charles Stewart Smith showed up at the Court House—a sign of a new era, for neither man had bothered to attend much of the Lexow hearings under the baton of Sutherland. They shook hands earnestly with Goff, apparently expecting great things.

McClave took the witness seat with a pleasant smile that signified that all this flub-dub-and-guff would quickly be set right. He was dressed like an aging dude with his hair in fluffy bangs. It took less than a minute for Goff to start wearing away his false air of relaxed amiability.

"How many times have you failed in your business?" was Goff's first question.

"I was a junior member of a firm that went into liquidation in 1870," the Commissioner responded.

"Did you fail in 1866?"

"No," McClave said, the smile beginning to falter.

"Did you not go into liquidation and offer to settle with your creditors for $.10 on the dollar?"

"Positively no."

"Has not Charles Crissman a claim against you for an old debt?"

"He has not."

"Will you swear that?"

"Yes, positively," said McClave, the smile gone.

Nicoll objected. What, he asked, did a business reversal of thirty years earlier have to do with the police investigation? But McClave, already upset, insisted upon responding. "There is nothing in my life that I am anxious to hide," he said. "Nothing that will not stand the sunshine. If you go back thirty years, why not go back to my childhood? I have nothing to conceal."

As the questioning continued Goff established that McClave's main purpose on the Police Board was to ensure that Republican cops received their fair share of promotions and choice assignments. The Commissioner admitted that he had charge of the fortunes of Republican police just as the other Commissioners promoted and assisted Tammany cops. Goff noted that Jimmy Martin had acknowledged in an earlier hearing that he kept a book in which the appointments of Captains Devery and Gallagher were charged up to Tammany Hall, and Goff asked whether McClave knew that this was a fact.

"I don't know anything about it," McClave answered. "I keep no such book. If the other Commissioners keep such records I am not aware of it. Yet I would aid Republicans if I could in preference to Democrats."

When Goff suggested that McClave might be dipping into the police pension fund to speculate in stocks, Nicoll protested that evidence of irregularities should be established before Goff dove into McClave's private affairs.

"The line of inquiry that I have adopted bears directly on the witness's official acts," Goff responded. "I do not hesitate to give warning that I will prove that Mr. McClave has banked the proceeds of bribery and corruption."

"That is absolutely false!" the Commissioner shouted.

"Now I have an adverse witness," Goff said.

He then began to ask questions about checks from policemen and applicants to the force. McClave denied that they were given to him for payoffs, and invoked the name of his son-in-law as the source of the information. "He is absolutely unreliable on the witness stand," McClave said.

Goff turned his sugar-and-venom style on his old colleague Nicoll when the former District Attorney requested a break in the testimony. "Mr. Nicoll is weak," Goff said, "and suggests that we have a recess for recuperation."

"I presume that was a pleasantry on the counsel's part," Nicoll said, rising with a look of mixed surprise and anger. "If Mr. Goff really thinks I am weak, let him come out in the corridor, and I will convince him of his mistake."

After the recess Granger was called to the stand. It was the moment of greatest dramatic tension in the hearings thus far. The Commissioner stared ferociously at his son-in-law, a pale, slender young man with brown hair and a slight moustache. Seating himself in the chair, Granger stared back with an attempt to smile that misfired as a sneer.

Granger said that he bore no ill-will to his father-in-law. Then, under Goff's direction, he began to rattle off the names of men who had paid McClave for appointments or for promotions and the amounts they had paid for them. Nicoll jumped from his seat again, shouting that the committee had no power under the Senate resolution to pursue this line of inquiry. He said the witness hated Mc-

Clave, was unworthy of credence and was giving hearsay evidence. But Lexow allowed the questioning to continue.

It was common practice, according to Granger, to overcome obstacles to an appointment with money delivered to the right place. One applicant, a half-inch below the required height, apparently grew slightly taller after police surgeons were paid. Another failed the physical examination, but was certified as qualified when $50 was sent to the surgeons. "I sent the draft to a man named O'Kelly," said Granger, "whom I knew to be the go-between of the Nineteenth Assembly District between the applicants for the police force and the men who made the appointments." Granger related an occasion when he gave $320 to the shoe-maker O'Kelly, who said, "The way you're making appointments your father-in-law will soon get rich." He also told of talking in McClave's billiards room with a policeman who was willing to pay for a promotion. Occasionally, he testified, he dealt directly with his father-in-law, but more often he worked through Richards, the orderly who accepted envelopes for Commissioner McClave and who, being dead, was beyond the reach of a subpoena.

As Granger warmed to his task, he began to enjoy it, chewing gum furiously and smiling broadly. Goff asked him for his memorandum book and questioned him about some of its notations.

"The first entry is Little, $250. What does that mean?" Goff asked.

"I meant," Granger replied, "that it cost Little $250 to get on the police force."

"How do you know?"

"O'Kelly, the go-between, told me."

Senator O'Connor protested that this was not evidence, and Goff and Nicoll began to wrangle about this point.

"May I say a word?" asked McClave, jumping up suddenly, his face white with rage.

"Your counsel—" Lexow began.

"I simply wish to say that this man on the stand is a drunkard, a liar, a thief, and a perjurer—and it has been proven." With that, Lexow's gavel began to pound and lawyers began to shout and flail the air. Granger smiled supercili-ously and said nothing.

"I hope you will not adjourn without giving me a chance to cross-examine and show the character of this witness," Nicoll exclaimed with passion. He put everything he had into it, apparently fearing that the news accounts would be highly damaging if McClave failed to get his side of the story on the record on the same day that the accusations were printed.

"I am under the impression," Lexow responded, "that Commissioner McClave has stated the witness's character as he understands it."

"I will convince you within ten minutes of the character of this man," said Nicoll, waving papers in his hand. "I have the documents right here."

But Lexow refused his request, and in the hall as the day ended McClave was, as the saying put it, taking on dreadful. Speaking too boisterously in his excitement, he vowed to have Granger arrested and charged with a dozen crimes. Members of the departing crowd stopped to look at the spectacle as McClave turned the color of a boiled lobster. Nicoll attempted to calm him while agreeing that the situation was indeed outrageous. Goff's opening shot had been a humdinger and already the feathers were flying.

31

McCLAVE'S ORDEAL

The following morning the courthouse was crowded with hundreds of men—uptown gentlemen, retail clerks and bullet-headed men from the tenements—seeking admission to the hearing. When reporters tried to push their way forward to get in they were met with hostile stares and the men refused to relinquish their hard-won places. The men, looking in their dark clothing and derbies as if they were in uniform, gave noisy analyses of the previous day's testimony. Some said that nobody believed the ridiculous story that Granger had tried to fob off on the committee, while others claimed that John Goff had McClave dead to rights.

Great numbers of men were turned away for lack of room, some only after heated exchanges with the doorkeeper.

The crowd was partisan and divided. The anti-police faction prevailed, but a minority shouted hooray for the Commissioner when he appeared in the hall. Later, in the courtroom, arguments broke out between the factions with an aggressiveness that carried over from the shoving and pushing that had taken place in the hall.

The crush of men in the corridors and the atmosphere in the courtroom showed unmistakably that the Lexow inquest, dismissed a month earlier as small potatoes, had at last aroused the populace. Even the pro-Tammany *Sun* conceded that Goff had provided a day's full measure of excitement.

* * *

The morning session began dramatically.

"May it please the gentlemen of the committee," said Goff, rising from his chair, "I am informed that the witness of yesterday is not in court. He told me yesterday that he would be here on time, but he disappointed me. I ask that the sergeant-at-arms be ordered to produce him in court if he can find him."

As soon as he sat down, Nicoll stood up. "I never expected the witness to come back," the former District Attorney responded. "What has happened is not a surprise to me or to my client. We talked it over last night, and concluded that he would never appear here again. He would not dare to repeat before you the lies he began yesterday afternoon."

As the spectators buzzed about the disappearance of Granger, Goff recalled McClave to the witness chair. He began with a series of questions aimed at showing that McClave, a man of modest means in 1884, had become wealthy over the course of a decade on the Police Board. McClave owned up to having a country home, another home in New Jersey for his aged mother, and agreed that he provided munificently for his large family, which included nine surviving children, and kept a staff of five servants, including a nurse for Mrs. Granger's children. The pretended ease with which the Commissioner had begun the first day had changed into a nervous frown that grew deeper as Goff changed the subject to McClave's ongoing relationship with Clubber Williams.

"When you were down on Long Island one summer, did not Inspector Williams send his yacht down there for your use?"

"No. I don't think he has a yacht. He has a catboat that cost about $200, and the newspapers have been trying to make out that he has a steam yacht."

"Are you a defender of Inspector Williams?"

"No, he is able to take care of himself."

"How many times has he been on trial before you?"

"Two or three times."

"You have always voted for his acquittal, haven't you?"

"Inspector Williams has not been found guilty of a charge since I have been a Commissioner."

"Yes, we recognize the impossibility of doing so."

This brought a reaction from the crowd. The anti-police faction enjoyed McClave's discomfort. They were getting back at him for the insolence that over the years he had so thoroughly demonstrated to the public. The crowd hoped for a flash of his quick temper, but through the morning, although he grew morose, they did not get to see it go off.

After the lunch break, Nicoll rose to deny a newspaper report in which it was suggested that he knew Granger's whereabouts. He said he was eager to cross-examine Granger and said he bore with him twenty proofs of Granger's forgeries.

"Mr. Nicoll, that will not do," Lexow said. "We cannot allow you to use such words. They are in the line of intimidation, and we are bound to protect our witnesses." He said that the committee would compel witnesses to testify and protect them from the results. "We know perfectly well that any man who goes on the stand takes his reputation, almost his life, in his hands."

"Mr. McClave," Goff asked, "did you not threaten last evening to have Granger arrested if he appeared in court today?"

"No, I don't think I put it in that way."

"Will you swear that you didn't say to me, in the hearing of Granger, that you would send him to State Prison?"

"No, I will not swear I did not."

"No, of course you will not. You and your counsel have talked about forgeries. Your counsel stood up in court yesterday and shook aloft papers, saying that they were forged by Granger. Don't you remember that?"

"I think I do," McClave said ruefully. He admitted that he and Nicoll had conferred the previous evening about bringing criminal charges against Granger.

Goff then asked a series of questions that established that McClave had set up his son-in-law in business, and prior to that had wangled him a job in the Post Office.

"You recommended for the service of his country a liar, a thief, and a scoundrel, did you?"

"He promised to reform, but backslid," McClave said, adding that he had done "everything I could to reform my daughter's husband."

Goff disclosed that Granger had come to his study the previous evening and stayed almost until midnight reviewing the course of the next day's testimony. He said Granger was jittery because plainclothes police were following him.

* * *

McClave's frayed temper came apart a little later when Goff began to grill him about the police pension fund. In sputters and stutters he denied the insinuation that he had dipped into the fund for his own speculative ventures. Goff then goaded the Commissioner about the increase in punishment of top police officers since the Lexow Committee had arrived.

"Is it a fact," Senator O'Connor asked, "that there has been a larger number of convictions of officers of all grades than before?"

"Yes, I think so," McClave said. "There has been more or less newspaper criticism, and the inspectors and captains have exercised more vigilance."

"That implies previous neglect, does it not?" Lexow asked.

"I should not like to say that," McClave responded.

Goff reverted to the question of Granger's whereabouts. "Do you know if anyone applied to a magistrate for a warrant for the arrest of your son-in-law?" he asked.

"No."

"Was anything said about that?"

"Mr. Nicoll spoke of it last night."

"No warrant has been obtained," Nicoll said. "I told Mr. McClave it was his duty to have this man arrested. I was going to attend to it, but I have been too busy."

Lexow interjected: "If any direct or indirect effort is made to intimidate or browbeat any witnesses this committee will stand up for them."

"I want to know if this committee would protect a man who is guilty of forgery and perjury," Nicoll responded. "No honest man would hesitate to come forward. No one should blame me if, when I discovered that this man had committed 20 crimes, and Mr. McClave hesitated to bring charges against the father of his grandchildren, I advised that he be prosecuted."

"It has not been proved that this witness lied," Goff responded. "He stands here on the same footing with Mr. McClave, because Mr. McClave threw his sheltering arms about him and continued to allow him to beget children in his house, year after year. Last night Granger said he was afraid he would be arrested if he came to court. I said that no such arrest would be made. He said that his father-in-law had threatened him."

A burst of applause greeted his words, and Lexow threatened to clear the courtroom if spectators continued to demonstrate. "You allow a man to sleep six years under your roof, knowing these charges," the Rockland County Senator said heatedly, "and as soon as he testified against you, you threaten him with arrest. It is intimidation."

At the close McClave complied with a committee request to turn over records of his private and business bank accounts, and Goff took them home with him, where he studied them through most of the night. McClave used his private bank account to deposit his salary as a Police Commissioner, keeping these earnings separate from his lumber business. From time to time, however, he had made large extra deposits. Goff compared the dates to find that they coincided roughly with dates upon which Republican police officers had been promoted. Such coincidences might not convict McClave in court, but they gave Goff the material that he needed.

* * *

On the third day, Goff began by establishing that Frederick Martens had been appointed a Captain on McClave's recommendation on May 6, 1892.

"Now, Mr. McClave, you have stated that you only deposited to your personal account your monthly salary as Commissioner and private moneys made by speculation and the like." He looked at the witness and shook his index finger at him. "I ask you how it is that on May 19, 1892, I see an item of $6,158 credited to your personal account?"

McClave took the bankbooks and after fumbling over them discovered a similar item among the return voucher items in his business account book. He could make no explanation for it, but said that sometimes he borrowed money from his personal account to put into his business account and later paid it back.

Goff then established that James K. Price was promoted to Captain on his recommendation on December 23, 1892, then added: "I find in your business account a deposit of $10,748 on November 17, just about one month before the promotion. Can you tell me anything about that?"

"No, I can't. If you mean to imply that it came from that appointment, or anything like that, it is unqualifiedly false."

"Is that all the explanation you can give? I find that on January 7, 1893, one month after Captain Price's appointment, you deposited $3,000. Can you explain that?"

McClave explained as he had in the earlier instance that he had probably transferred money from one account to another.

Goff also noted similar large deposits corresponding roughly with the appointment of Captain William Strauss, another McClave recommendation, on December 30, 1891.

By now McClave's inability to explain any of the deposits began to sound hollow, and a grimace darkened Goff's face. The spectators and reporters began to discern that this was more than a job to Goff—that he was out for blood.

After McClave, looking haggard and frenzied, denied an accusation that the owner of a hotel used for prostitution had asked him to transfer a Captain, Goff produced three letters dealing with the police appointment of the applicant who had grown half an inch after paying off the police surgeons. One of them was a note from Granger recommending the appointment to his father-in-law, a matter about which McClave two days earlier had denied any knowledge.

Nicoll became livid and for a time barely able to speak. "Yesterday I had them on this table in front of me," he said, his face growing red, "and someone, I don't know who, has taken them. I want to know from Mr. Goff where he got those papers."

"The papers reached me in a perfectly legitimate way," Goff said, also a little red in the face. "I have a right to use them."

"I ask the committee to direct their counsel to make an explanation to me," Nicoll responded.

"Mr. Goff says he got the papers in a perfectly legitimate way," O'Connor said. "He is not responsible if you lost them."

"I didn't lose them! They were taken away!"

"I received the papers in an envelope addressed to me," Goff said. "I do not know from whom they came or how they came to me. I received twenty anonymous communications this morning."

"I do not object to the use of the papers," the ex-prosecutor said. "I intended to use them myself on cross-examination. But I do not think I should be compelled to have a rail put about me to protect my property."

"Get a Gatling gun," Senator Bradley said.

"You must be careful of your company," O'Connor added.

"Here," said Goff, passing them over to Nicoll, "are your papers back."

"Put them in the bag and keep them there," Nicoll told an assistant. "I'll never take another thing out of the bag in this room."

Goff then began an interrogation of McClave aimed at showing that the Republican Commissioner was as incurious about police wrongdoing as were his Tammany colleagues. Now relying heavily on denunciation as his defense, McClave replied that the accusations of the Parkhurst Society and the newspapers were always wrong. Boiling with indignation, the Commissioner asserted that there had always been and always would be brothels and gambling dens in cities. "If there were none what would be the use of spending five million dollars on a police department every year?" he said loudly. "If there was no crime what would we need courts for?"

"You say that crime will always exist in New York," Goff responded. "Do you expect always to be on the Police Board?"

"No, I hope not. I'll give up my place to you. You'll fill it better, perhaps."

There was still more agony in store for McClave. Goff suggested via his questions that McClave and his beloved Tammany friends—he had to withdraw "beloved" in the face of objections—had harassed Superintendent Byrnes. His questions also laid down the charge that McClave had never lifted a finger to protect the public from countless instances of police brutality, and that as a consequence the police beat people without fear of punishment. By day's end McClave looked as limp as a rag doll. But his ordeal was not over yet.

* * *

John McClave appeared for his fourth stint of testimony a much different man than the dapper, well-groomed gentleman who greeted the Lexow Committee on Monday. His eyes were lusterless. His hair was tousled and he had not been shaved for a day. Even his well-cut coat seemed ill-fitting. Facing more questions from Goff about his personal finances, police promotions, and taxes, he confessed to being discombobulated after three days on the stand.

Goff showed no pity, and some of the crowd began to hiss his unforgiving approach—which brought down the gavel and a threat from Senator Lexow to clear the room of spectators.

After Goff was through with the bedraggled witness, Nicoll was given a chance to develop testimony. Nicoll did his best, plugging in the denials at the appropriate points. Yes, he had sponsored Clubber Williams for promotion to Inspector, and he would proclaim it to the housetops: Williams was a great cop and the agents of the Society for the Prevention of Crime who had brought charges against Williams were vermin like Gardner—corrupt and destructive.

McClave's last day on the stand was marked by moments of poignancy, as the beaten man related his efforts to deal with a reprobate son-in-law who had never supported McClave's daughter and grandchildren and had lived for years on his father-in-law's money. Despite the young man's weaknesses, McClave said he discerned good qualities in him. Yet a month after his marriage, Granger went to the vaults where the wedding gifts were kept in storage, withdrew the silver and pawned it. Granger had also pawned all the business equipment when McClave set him up in business, and by his own admission he began to open registered letters twenty minutes after he began working in the Post Office. After taking a job in a clothing store he began to steal and pawn cloaks. He passed forged checks. His daughter filed for divorce, he said, only after it was discovered that Granger was consorting with "disreputable women."

He regretted his failure with Gideon Granger. When McClave described a conversation with his son-in-law in which the young man promised to reform, the Commissioner's voice failed and tears rolled down his cheeks. He sobbed that he still liked Granger and would reform him if he could. The pitiful sight aroused general sympathy, and Senator Bradley, known affectionately in Brooklyn as Uncle Dan, left the hearing room and returned with a red bandanna which he used to wipe his moist eyes.

There was more badgering, more blowups, and near the end, on the brink of collapse, McClave denounced his questioners for poring over his life from the cradle onward, for holding up family matters, including his daughter's divorce, to public scrutiny, and for mulling over old debts and butchers' bills. His husky voice and rambling manner subdued the crowd.

A few days later it was reported that McClave was ill and his condition worsening. "I look for an epidemic," Goff commented, "before this investigation is through."[1]

32

THE URBAN SPIRIT

While the Lexow hearings provided astonishments for newspaper readers every day, the agitation for woman suffrage also gathered steam, and the two big stories kept running day by day side by side all the way down the big blanket-sized dailies, as if they were part of a bigger story, chapters in the episodic tale—Pulitzer called it the great unfinished novel—of the city itself.

The newspapers examined the suffrage issue from every conceivable angle. Anti-suffrage women held meetings at which they confessed that they would rather be dipped into muck than vote. Wealthy women, asked to affix their names to the woman suffrage petition, refused because they feared that their servants might sign the same document. Meetings were held at which women said that they did not want to accost strange men on the street to ask their political support for various public issues; they did not want to serve on juries, listening to indelicate testimony that they would be forced to discuss behind closed doors with strange men, far into the night.

The newspapers reported that the suffragists were making little headway with working women, that most working girls responded to the overtures of the Suffrage League's Labor Committee with indifference and regarded the issue as "a Fifth Avenue fad."

* * *

When a *Sun* reporter solicited comments from shopgirls on Sixth Avenue and Broadway, some said they were too busy to bother themselves about such fiddle-faddle, while others expressed support for woman suffrage. Their remarks, some of which follow, were unabashed:

"If the bestowal of the vote is to put women generally in authority over us, then I am against it. Women are not to be depended on, because they are naturally inclined to be treacherous. However pleasant she may be to your face, you are never sure of a woman. Give me a man every time."

"To the constant agitation for the last forty years of the woman's rights question we owe the improvement in the commercial standing of our sex. For the opening of almost all business pursuits and colleges to women, we are directly indebted to the pleaders in the woman suffrage movement."

"If we could vote many wrongs would be righted. Women in this store are paid less than men, yet we can measure off a yard of goods or match ribbons better than a man. There should be a law that women receive the same pay for the same work."

"All these women who keep blathering about getting the vote for working women do it for their own aggrandizement and not to help us. Not one of them but is carried away by a nauseating greed for notoriety. Some man supports them—husband, son or brother—they couldn't earn a living for themselves if they tried, but they don't try, but just stand up there and talk and talk until the country is dead sick of them."

"Certainly I should like to vote. It might better my conditions, for instead of selling pins and needles, which is dreadful dull, prosaic work, I might get a chance to turn ward politician, have exciting times, plenty of money and patronage, live on the fat of the land, and flee to Europe when things began to sizzle around me."

"Voting would take more time for investigation and study than women who have their living to earn could give, practically leaving the ballot in the hands of those who do not need it, the very women who have private means or male relatives to support them."

"The greatest insult our sex ever received was from our own men when they denied the voting privilege to cultured and intelligent white women and gave it to ignorant black men just released from slavery, few of whom knew their letters."

"All this hullabaloo about woman suffrage is just made by women who have nothing else to do. Why, some of the leaders of the movement have been going around to the shops asking us to attend their meetings, so that the working women may be represented. I suppose they would like us to stand on the platform with them—first working woman exhibit A, second working woman exhibit B."

* * *

Some of the shopgirls wanted to vote, others said to blazes with the vote, but theirs were city voices, and nothing like the voices of a generation earlier. Forty years earlier, when the women's rights movement began, women did not even own opinions on public questions, much less summon up the cheek to express one. Now there was, like the department stores in which these women worked, a broad selection from which to choose. And they were the words of women who were prepared to take care of themselves. They were in the game, enmeshed in the world for better or worse, as fully a hostage to fortune as any man.

For half a century the women's rights movement had pleaded for protection. They had asked only to be shielded from drunken husbands, from iron divorce laws, from laws that placed married women completely at the mercy of their husbands. For forty years their supplications had been largely unheeded while the old society in which they lived evaporated.

Now they asked for protection no longer. They worked in business offices as typists, or worked in manufacturing plants in the city. Many women roomed in boarding houses and had no fathers or husbands in the city to protect them; there was no way for them to be heard except directly.

The men saw that the women of the city were changing, and were displeased. When men had changed in response to the city, they had cast off the old ways because they were cumbersome and no longer suited them, but now that women were changing the men were suffused with nostalgia for the hearth, for the old ways, for the plain old life of the villages.

According to these men, such hateful developments were the result of woman's urge to vote. Women did not need the vote, these men argued, because in a sense they had the vote already: men cast the ballot for them, on their behalf, as representative of the family unit. Men had created a protective envelope for women in which they dwelt, and women broke it at their peril. To allow women to vote for themselves would atomize society into a mass of individuals and place a premium on childlessness and singleness.

By this time there were other men, although in a minority, who disagreed. They acknowledged that society was changing, for they saw that it was taking surprising new shapes, that old structures were collapsing, and that the individual rather than the family was becoming the basic unit of society.

Men who favored woman suffrage said that women now needed the vote for self-protection. For the first time in the history of their struggle women found a significant body of men who agreed with them. They were a small but influential minority—businessmen, labor leaders, editors, lawyers, clergymen and politicians—many of whom had once been on the other side of the fence. Their views had changed, they said, because they sensed a change in the society. "Woman herself is different in some respects from what she used to be," the railroad magnate Chauncey Depew said in explaining his own conversion. "She owns a large amount of property, upon which she is taxed. She has become a great industrial factor. She has a right to say how she shall be taxed, and under what laws she shall conduct her business."

* * *

Individualism, so tightly interwoven with the liberty, equality and democracy of American men, had entered at last into the lives of American women. By the end of the century many women were struggling for livelihood or for recognition.

The urban force of individualism fired the mind of Emma Goldman, its spirit drove her romantic rhetoric and her radical politics. During her time on Blackwell's Island she began to articulate it more clearly. She had encountered American individualism in books that admirers had mailed to her cell, books sent to her by a host of admirers, including the Swintons.

That spring Mr. and Mrs. Swinton turned up one visiting day at Blackwell's Island Penitentiary. John Swinton was an aged man, but with classic features and an impressive bearing as erect as a youth. Greeting the prisoner warmly, Swinton said he had just been telling Warden Pillsbury that during his abolitionist days he had made speeches a lot more violent than hers, and that the warden should be ashamed to keep such an innocent little creature locked up.

Coming by at that moment, the warden assured Swinton that Goldman was a model prisoner and had become an efficient nurse. The deferential warden found them a well-furnished room, with a sofa and comfortable chairs, as befit the visit of important personages like the Swintons, who moved in literary circles.

Presumably she thanked them during that visit for the books that they had sent her—books by American writers, for Swinton, who had defended Walt Whitman against detractors who found *Leaves of Grass* crude and immoral, championed the American voice. Goldman, who had almost no acquaintance with American thought and had hardly realized that there were any American radicals, now had progressed far enough in her mastery of English to read them.

American radicals tended to espouse individualism, and their views on the tyranny of the majority appealed powerfully to her. She was becoming a scathing critic of what she regarded as the banality of American life—"the mythical liberty of America," its frippery expressed in its vapid enthusiasm for the flag and parades. She despised the mass spirit that dominated America, making life "uniform, gray, and monotonous as the desert." She distrusted American popular views, and especially distrusted American women, finding them too willing to endure all, too responsive to the call of duty, too willing to live for others and to have no real notion of themselves or their own needs or ideals at all, whether they were the wives of businessmen or prostitutes serving time on Blackwell's

Island. Emma Goldman found an aimlessness among her fellow-prisoners that clashed with her sense that life should be lived to the uttermost.

If the great truth lying in wait at the end of the century was that a woman had to take care of herself in a man's world, Goldman had learned it the hard way, as an outsider and outlaw. To her the most significant political truth was found neither in the Lexow hearings nor the suffragist cause, but in the vision of the superior spirit, the iconoclast.

* * *

Social and economic conditions were shaping the twentieth century woman in the spirit of individualism. But individualism was not a persuasive argument to take to the Constitutional Convention. Quite the contrary, given the questions that bothered the delegates. Would giving women the vote create another source of discord within the family? Would it increase the already alarming incidence of divorce in cities? Would women embroiled in public affairs neglect their children, with a resulting increase in lawlessness and crime? Faced with such questions, women stressed the contributions they hoped to make to the collective good.

The suffragists countered that their cause represented social progress and the forces of good order, that when they voted they would war upon the forces of darkness—vice and the saloon power, impure food, the exploitation of child labor, and radical political philosophies.

In that light, they elaborated, women were not abandoning their traditional roles, but adapting them to new conditions. In earlier times it was thought that if a woman provided her family with good food and clean surroundings she was adequately taking care of the home. That was no longer the case. If the streets were unswept, if the garbage were improperly collected, if disorderly houses spread unmentionable diseases, if tainted meat were sold in the butcher shop, if unclean milk were delivered to the doorstep, if clothes were made in germ-ridden sweatshops, then soap and a pail would not make a wholesome home. A mother could clean every day and the children might succumb in a cholera epidemic just the same. As urban society grew more complex, the care of the family grew more related to public life. Men had been in charge of that sphere, but their stewardship had been found wanting, and many women at the hearings in Albany wondered whether men cared enough about such issues.

33

FROM THE
BOTTOM UP

The Lexow Committee was delighted with the outcome of Goff's gamble. His dismemberment of John McClave had riveted the attention of the city. With the hearings now the cynosure of all eyes, some of the committee members said, it was time to press the advantage and make more high-ranking police officials squirm in the witness chair.

But that was not Goff's agenda. His attack on McClave was only an attention-getter to convince the city that the committee was serious. He wanted to follow Commissioner McClave with a procession of madames, saloonkeepers, gamblers, Tammany sports and cops. He intended to wrest evidence from them, browbeat them into confessions, and climb step by step up the hierarchy to reach the senior police officials. Starting at the top, he argued, would never work, would harvest nothing but "a series of absolute and positive denials." If he went after the top brass, he said, by the time he got around to questioning the ordinary blokes, the victims of oppression and bribery, they would not dare to contradict the officials who had preceded them. It was through the small fry that the evidence was created that made it possible to fricassee the top officials. That was his plan, and although Senator O'Connor only half-heartedly acquiesced to it, the committee members deferred to Goff's judgment.

Thus Goff set out, as he put it, to trace "the course of bribery from the time the bribe left the hands of the bribegiver, and we hoped to show a common and well-organized system of bribery and oppression, so that when we came to examine the officers of the department the proof would be so conclusive that they could not deny its existence." The problem was that people had no reason to trust the committee. Since his appointment two months earlier Goff had been digging for evidence in vain. He was beginning to fear that he would fail, that he would not make the connections, that the misdeeds of the top people were so well-hidden that to root them out was impossible, that perhaps he should have heeded those who had advised him against taking this job.

Over the course of the week that followed McClave's testimony only one hearing date was held, on May 29, and Goff's distress outweighed that of his witnesses. The theme of the day was the market in police appointments and promotions, but the witnesses hemmed, hawed and denied everything. Goff pointed accusing fingers and took umbrage to no avail. He tripped them up in contradictions and found a remarkable pattern among young men about to be appointed to the police force to borrow $250 to $350 from family and friends, but that did not constitute evidence. He hammered away at one patrolman for so long that even the committee members petitioned for relief. "Oh, come now, Mr. Goff, what's the use of questioning this man any further?" Senator O'Connor interjected. "We are all satisfied that he is lying, but the trouble is you cannot get him to confess it."

Goff asked another cop twenty-nine times—in a slightly varied way each time—whether the witness' nephew had paid for an appointment to the force, and for his pains received twenty-nine denials. The same cop denied seventeen times that he had been instructed in what to say on the stand, and was compelled to deny eleven times that his nephew kept a brothel on Delancey Street. It was exasperating work, but even in failure Goff showed an intensity that kept the reporters scribbling and the artists drawing sketches for the dailies.

His major witness for the May 29 hearing was O'Kelly. In a meeting with the shoemaker on the previous evening Goff had succeeded in bullying and bluffing him into confessing that he had passed $175 to a Republican district leader to get someone an appointment on the police force; and the testimony established that the prospective appointee, who rose from among the spectators to be identified, was the Parkhurst agent Arthur Dennett, the long drink of water from New Hampshire, known to O'Kelly as Arthur Freeman. On the stand, however, O'Kelly repudiated everything he had admitted on the previous evening, and denied ever having said anything incriminating to the Parkhurst agent. He admitted offering to ask a Republican district leader to help the applicant with a letter, but said nothing so crass as money was involved.

Goff looked steadily at the witness and asked, "Did you lie to me last night?"

"I did," the witness replied. "You terrorized me into it. I'm on my oath now."

"Why did you tell Mr. Goff a deliberate lie?" Lexow asked.

"I told Mr. Goff when I went to his office the first day that I received no money. Last night I was bulldozed and excited and didn't know what I was saying."

Convinced that the police had gotten to O'Kelly, Goff complained about the "almost impossible" task of finding witnesses. "My subpoena servers are watched and followed," he said. "The men who receive subpoenas are approached and intimidated. The actions of my witnesses are watched even in court. There have been men in this courtroom day after day whose business it has been to keep watch of my witnesses and follow them when they leave the courtroom."

"If witnesses have been intimidated let them tell of it here," Senator Cantor said. "If subpoena servers have been shadowed let them go on the stand and say so."

"If my subpoena servers go on the stand they will become marked men openly," responded Goff. "The only way I can hope to succeed is to keep their identity as secret as possible."

Goff's only victory that day occurred in Police Headquarters. Commissioner McClave, still reeling from his encounter with Goff, became ill during a Police Board meeting and left immediately for home.

* * *

The next time the committee convened, it was the first of June, and Goff seemed more anxious than ever. Upon entering he fluttered about the courtroom, talking nervously with committee members and exchanging glances with his assistants. He winked, shrugged his shoulders, and nodded knowingly. Something was going on. Everybody was in place by half past ten, but Goff said he was still not quite ready. Reporters joked that Goff was stalling until the Chamber of Commerce arrived with the check for his services. Then a number of Parkhurst agents entered the courtroom with a man and two women, and sat down in the witness area. The Parkhurst agents sat surrounding the three witnesses, as if guarding them.

Goff had reached a turning point. He had some witnesses at last. Actually he had not come up with them himself; they were a gift from Parkhurst agents. Yet even as he made ready to put them on the stand he was not sure that they would talk. The Parkhurst men had been working on them, and Goff hoped that in the chair he could subdue them by the force of his will. They wanted to get even with the police, but they were afraid. Goff was anxious that were they to get out of custody, out of his sight for even a moment, that they would turn tail and run, or that a cop would look menacingly at them or exchange a few words with them and their resolve would crumble.

Goff's first break came with Charles Prien. The stocky, solid man who had come in with the two women and Parkhurst agents rose from his seat and walked to the stand.

Prien was a German of middle age and middle height. Proud of his service to the Union in the Civil War, he wore a veteran's button in his coat. Until late 1893, he said, he had operated "a boarding house for ladies" on Bayard Street. Goff asked if it might be more accurately described as a house of prostitution. "I think so," the German agreed.

"You have heard of what is called protection, haven't you?" Goff asked.

"Oh, yes, in some way." He looked at his shoes and the ceiling, and at everything but the blue coals of Goff's eyes.

"You have heard of wardmen going around the police precinct and getting money from various persons?"

"Ach Gott, yes!" he said vehemently.

"Did the wardman collect any money from you?"

He thought a long time about his answer. "I guess so!" he finally said, so emphatically that the audience laughed.

And then he talked. Gamely but by no means eagerly he told of the depredations of the police upon his wallet. For six years he had paid protection to the various Captains of the Eldridge Street precinct. At the beginning of every month he paid cash, beginning at $25, and raised to $50 when Captain Adam Cross took over the precinct. Every December, in the spirit of Christmas, he was called upon to share the blessings that had been bestowed upon him with the Captain, in an amount that had grown from $75 to $100. When he was raided he had to pay Cross $500 to reopen. Every time the Captain was changed, he had to pay initiation fees, his last one, for $400, going to Captain Devery. One of these payments was made in the clubroom of the John J. O'Brien Association, the political club controlled by saloonkeeper Barney Rourke. Asked if he felt that he had risked his safety by coming to the hearing, Prien replied that he was not afraid but intended to get out of town immediately.

Late in the previous year Captain Devery had sent him word to close up, "that some trouble was going on."

"What kind of trouble?" Goff asked.

"Parkhurst trouble."

Goff noted that the closing coincided with charges that the Parkhurst Society had leveled at Devery in October.

Prien spoke unashamedly of his business and claimed that he would have succeeded in it had it not been for the rapacious appetites of the police, who gouged every available dollar from him until he was left penniless.

"Did you hear anyone say anything about resuming business when this committee gets through?"

"I think there are a great many waiting until the Senate Committee goes away," Prien said. "Then they'll open up again."

As Nicoll was cross-examining the witness, Senator Lexow suggested that if Goff had any more direct testimony from Prien he should get it in before recess. Goff responded that because of the peculiar status of his witnesses the hearing ought to continue without a recess.

"What, you're going to sit right through?" Nicoll responded.

"We don't want any more Granger business here," Senator Bradley said.

"If Mr. Goff says to me professionally that there is an exigency in his case which suggests a continuous session I am willing to miss my midday meal," Nicoll said.

Goff said that he regrettably felt it was necessary to deprive Nicoll of a break. They sent to the main corridor, where tarts, buns and coffee were sold, and Nicoll resumed his cross-examination while munching on pastry. Meanwhile the Parkhurst agents continued to surround the two women, so that they could not be talked out of testifying, or spirited from the courthouse.

* * *

One of the two women was Rhoda Sanford, a stout middle-aged blonde widow, who had a place on Bayard Street near Prien's. Goff took an account book from a satchel beside him and asked with an air of triumph whether she recognized it.

The witness was staggered at first, then indignant. "Yes," she said, rising, "and I recognize the man there beside you who stole it from me." She pointed to Dennett. Further testimony showed that two men had visited her a week earlier on the pretense of buying her business and induced her to show them her account book so they would have some idea of what were the usual levels of police bribery.

Reluctant to admit anything, Mrs. Sanford lied lamely about the meaning of the entries in the account book. She said that she gave money to unknown men who came to her place, but she thought she was making a political donation.

She was asked if she remembered telling the prospective purchasers that she was being raided in spite of her payments and that she had a mind to "halloo for Dr. Parkhurst"—who by chance entered the courtroom just at that moment.

"Well, yes," she responded, "I did say that, and I said more, too, and see that you have this down." She looked straight at the pastor. "I said that the houses were not down on Dr. Parkhurst as much as upon those who extorted money from them, and I also said that when poor girls visited Dr. Parkhurst's house, after having had nothing to eat for two days, it was mighty poor consolation for their empty stomachs to be given nothing but tea and toast."

Nicoll's cross-examination consisted of a single question: "Did you pay any money to Captains Cassidy, Cross, McLaughlin, Devery or Cortright?"

"No, I gave $500 for a political organization."

* * *

Mrs. Sanford was a chatterbox compared to the next witness, Emma Jones, who was even reluctant to admit that she was married to Baldy Jones, and claimed to have no idea whether or not he was a district Tammany Captain. Only a few responses were necessary to make it clear that Emma Jones was not going to be bullied into disclosing anything she did not wish to say.

Goff asked whether she remembered going to Atlantic Garden to meet some men who were interested in buying her brothel. Like Mrs. Sanford, she was shocked to discover that she had been dealing with Parkhurst agents. After repeated denials, she admitted meeting with them. Goff attempted to get her to testify that she had told the men that they would have to put up large sums of money to the Eldridge Street precinct captain, but she denied saying any such thing.

At the end of the day Goff was visibly worn from the mental wrestling-match with his witnesses. He had not been completely successful with the women, although their testimony had helped his case. O'Kelly's change of heart and the disappearance of Granger underscored the difficulty of keeping witnesses. Nevertheless, in getting Prien to talk he had cause for cheer.

Two days after Prien's testimony the police arrested him on charges of running a disorderly house. When Prien was brought up for arraignment the Police Justice threw the charges out on the ground that the police had no valid case.

Goff and his allies were not sure how the ordinary bloke would interpret Prien's brush with the law. He might shrug and say that the police would do up anybody who had the temerity to appear against them, or he might read it as a signal that the Lexow Committee also had some pull in the police courts.

34

GOFF'S GRIDDLE

On June 4, the next hearing date, Augusta Thurow waited in the front row of the courtroom. Her husband, Ernest, sat by her side and Parkhurst agents surrounded them both. Parkhurst, who remained for the entire day's proceedings, was well-versed in the facts of the Thurow case. He conferred several times with Jerome, who had in hand an affidavit that Mrs. Thurow had made to Parkhurst agents in which she gave details of the blackmail payments she had made to the wardmen of the Fifth Street and Eldridge Street precincts, implicating more than a dozen police officials.

The *Herald* described her as a large, middle-aged blond woman and commented upon her air of determination "as she squared herself in her seat and prepared to answer the questions put to her."[1] Straightforwardly she told the story of her troubles with Wardman Hock and her trips to the precinct station to see Captain Doherty, detailing her experiences with the police from the time that she and her husband started the furnished-room brothel on Second Avenue until they ended up in the Eldridge Street precinct, evicted, homeless, and bled dry. Then Nicoll cross-examined her.

"Do you mean to say," he asked, "that the captain kept on raiding you, even while you were paying money for protection?"

"Yes," she replied, "sometimes the man was waiting at the house for the money as soon as the girls got home from court."

"Did you ever remonstrate with the policemen," Lexow asked, "because you were not getting the protection you were paying for?"

"Yes, I did. I told Captain Doherty it was a shame that my business was broken up. He said the reason was that my house was the worst in the neighborhood.

I said, 'Captain, why is my house the worst? Is there any charge against us of robbing men, or half-killing them, or did you ever hear of anybody kicking a man in my house?' He said, well, he had orders against all these houses, and mine was the worst."

Mrs. Thurow's story was so singular that it could not fail to be convincing, and when she was finished her dapper little husband took the stand to provide the first direct testimony of police interference with the investigation. Ernest, a German with thinning brown hair and a huge moustache, testified that a patrolman had called upon them over the preceding weekend.

"Did he say anything to you about how your wife should testify before the Committee?" Goff asked.

"He told me my wife should not mention names in her testimony."

"What did he tell you exactly?" Lexow asked.

"That as soon as the Lexow Committee was gone and the Captain and Sergeant were changed then we would have good times again, and my wife could open another house."

The Thurows told the committee that in their desperation they turned for help to the political boss of the district, George Roesch, who was now a Civil Justice but at that time had been a State Senator. Augusta went to see Roesch alone, Ernest having a hangover that day. She said Senator Roesch listened carefully to her complaints about the police. "He told me that he could fix it up all right for me," she testified, "but that it would cost me $150." She was able to raise only $100, which she sent over to him with a promise that she would get him the rest.

Later she mentioned Roesch's name to Hock, the precinct wardman, but did not get the awed response for which she had hoped. "Yes, that's just the trouble with you people," he said, "you give to the politicians what ought to go to the police. What do you think? Are the politicians doing for you, or are we doing for you?"

* * *

Front-page stories spread this testimony all over the city. Roesch denied everything. "I could not afford to have anything to do with such a case as hers," said the Civil Justice. "I never had such a woman for a client in my life."

For Parkhurst, the testimony of Augusta Thurow, whom he had delivered to the committee, vindicated the charges that he had been leveling against the police for two years, and he was breathing buoyant lungfuls of hope and promise.

Just before departing on his annual summerlong European vacation, he issued an appeal to the honest members of the Police Department to step forward and aid the city in ridding corruption and wrongdoing from the force.

"Careful minutes will be made by us of every blue-coated witness who has the courage of his knowledge and conviction," the pastor wrote, "and such ones we dare your polluted and gold-banded superiors to do harm or make prey of."

* * *

On the day that Dr. and Mrs. Parkhurst sailed Civil Justice Roesch came bounding into the hearing room, expressing shock that slander had defiled his name. He said that he had adjourned court for the day in order to appear and vindicate himself.

"I protest!" shouted Goff, rising and shaking his finger at the committee. "This is a bad precedent!"

"Of course we would like to extend every courtesy to Justice Roesch," Senator Lexow said. "We will hear you under oath."

"Certainly. I want to go on the stand under oath."

Goff still appeared unwilling to accommodate Roesch. "If every person whose name is mentioned on this witness stand is to be allowed to come into court and contradict the evidence against him, a bad precedent will be established," he said, and paused for a moment. "However, this, I think, is an exceptional case. Mr. Roesch is a judicial officer of this city, and I agree that he should be given an opportunity to be heard in his own defense. But we have important work in hand for today and tomorrow, and I therefore suggest Thursday morning."

Roesch continued to urge that he be allowed to go on the stand at once, but eventually agreed to return on Thursday, June 7.

* * *

Whence had come this mixture of poor judgment, political ineptitude, and dim intellect? He was a Croker man, someone whom the Boss had imposed upon the city. Hoping to placate the Germans, who were always grousing that Tammany gave them less than their fair share of jobs and patronage, Boss Croker had placed Roesch in charge of the Seventh Assembly District because he spoke German. But Roesch made enemies in the district and used the police so blatantly in the interests of Tammany Hall that he clashed repeatedly with Captain Doherty, who felt that Roesch was overriding his authority as precinct captain. After the election Croker replaced Roesch as district leader and made him a Civil Justice.

Now willing to admit that he knew and had represented Augusta Thurow, Roesch told the investigators that she had come to see him strictly in his professional capacity and had paid him a retainer of $100 because she said that the police were persecuting her and she expected to need legal counsel.

Goff smiled faintly as the spider smiles when the fly steps into his parlor. With his folder beside him for reference, he began to probe the witness, beginning with his initial denials to reporters that Mrs. Thurow had been his client. Roesch shifted his weight about on the witness chair, which appeared to be growing warmer.

"Now, Senator, you have had quite a clientele among the disorderly houses of your district?" Goff began.

"Well, yes, I have had some, but not many."

"Is it not true," Goff went on, "that you have gone about your district and tried to keep people away from this committee?"

"No!" shouted the witness, "and the insinuation is infamous, sir!"

Mrs. Thurow, who sat at the back of the courtroom, craning forward to catch every word, heard him deny that she had come to him to buy political influence. "And did you not give this paper to Mrs. Thurow and tell her to show it to the Sergeant in case any of her girls were arrested?" Goff asked. He produced a slip of paper that Roesch had signed testifying to his friendship with the madame. Justice Roesch could remember nothing about it.

The witness was then asked regarding the transfer of a Sergeant out of the Fifth Street Station. After persistent questioning the witness admitted that the transfer "might have been made" at his insistence. He also admitted helping get a promotion for Roundsman Jake Brown.

"You remember, I suppose," Goff asked, "when Brown was specially detailed to attend your chowder party and that he was selling tickets for you to saloon-keepers and keepers of disorderly houses?"

Justice Roesch furrowed his brows, trying hard to remember. He readily called to mind his political organization's chowder party, but could not remember whether the Roundsman had been occupied in selling tickets. He also failed to remember that a saloonkeeper sent back five tickets, pleading that he had already bought five and could not afford any more. He denied that he had ordered Wardman Hock to arrest a saloonkeeper who had refused to join his political association, and denied that it had taken two arrests to persuade the saloonkeeper to change his mind. He denied arguing with Captain Doherty about political interference in the conduct of the precinct. He denied receiving payments for getting men appointed to the police force. He failed to remember that he had written to the Excise Board asking that a saloon license be withheld until the applicant became his client, and that as soon as the applicant engaged his services the license was granted. He did not remember having campaign circulars sent to the brothels in his district. There was much that he denied and much that he did not remember, and the effort to call these events to mind was beginning to take its toll, for the daisy in his buttonhole was wilting.

"Can you state how many times you visited the District Attorney's office each month during your term as district leader to interfere in the cases against keepers of disorderly houses?"

"Never, Mr. Goff, except as counsel. In the last two years and a half I have visited the District Attorney's office only three times."

"Each time on behalf of a disorderly house keeper?"

"They were my clients, and I pleaded for them. Two of them were fined."

"Did it ever reach your ears that you were called a nuisance in the District Attorney's office on account of your interference in disorderly house cases?"

"Never."

Roesch admitted having policemen transferred for Election Day service but said that Captain Doherty had agreed to the transfers.

After his day before the Lexow Committee everyone agreed that had Justice Roesch any brains he would have let well enough alone and that it had been foolish of him to expose himself to Goff's merciless questioning. But by then it was too late.

Over the course of a brutal interrogation, Goff proved himself so thoroughly steeped in Roesch's history that some suspected that a trap had been set for the unwitting Justice. For most of a day he squirmed in the witness chair that the reporters had begun to call Goff's Griddle. The counsel had clearly not been frittering away his time in the weeks he was getting ready for the investigation, and it looked to the observer that he had the hearings in the palm of his hand. Goff's performance on June 7 did more than just make a Civil Justice regret his hasty rush for the witness chair; it also intimidated the opposition. After Roesch's testimony, police officers continued to express outrage at being maligned in public, but few of them demanded to go on the stand to defend themselves.

* * *

The Roesch testimony connected police corruption and Tammany Hall in the public consciousness. And while the city's attention was fixed on Roesch, the man who bossed Tammany Hall and had furthered Roesch's career slipped quietly away on a Cunard liner bound for Europe.

It was said that he intended to establish his pedigree. Family members explained that the Crokers were people of substance in Ireland. Although he had embraced the Roman Catholic Church upon his marriage, Croker was actually a product of the Protestant Anglo-Irish ruling class. The Croker family, which had come to Ireland as soldiers in Oliver Cromwell's occupying army, included a surveyor-general, a poet and wit, and enough courtiers, barristers, soldiers and gentlefolk to populate one of Shakespeare's historical dramas.

Croker intended to visit his distinguished relatives in Ireland, including his uncle, a blue-ribbon stock breeder in County Limerick and a brother who owned an estate in Askenton. After that he would tour the Croker ancestral home and intended to return with photographs of the old ruined castle, the coat-of-arms, and family portraits to substantiate his claim that he descended from stock that occupied several pages in "Burke's Landed Gentry."

Dr. William T. Jenkins, his physician brother-in-law, said that he had sailed quietly so as not to bring out all the Tammany braves to bid him *bon voyage*. "He is no longer the leader of Tammany Hall, yet there are those who persist in thinking so," Dr. Jenkins explained. "He was constantly visited by persons asking his advice and requesting him to do things for them. He wants to avoid this care and worry, and get away from it all."

The doctor claimed that Croker had been planning the trip for months, but friends knew that he had rented homes near the Gravesend and Saratoga tracks during their racing seasons, and had been talking about attending the races only a few days before sailing.

Everybody talked about his departure. Republicans said he had been frightened away by mounting pressure for the Lexow Committee to call him to the stand. Others said he had left when the Chamber of Commerce raised the funds necessary to pay the committee's expenses for an ongoing investigation. Some Tammany braves said Croker left to avoid an imbroglio over his successor, while others whispered that continuous strife with Mrs. Croker had driven him away.

A week earlier torture would not have wrung a word of blame from any Tammany man, but once Croker sailed his immunity to criticism wore off. The braves said that he had left them in the lurch, and had given the enemy a club with which to beat the organization.

The *Commercial Advertiser* reported Croker's departure under a two-line banner headline across the front page in the largest type available as follows: THE WICKED FLEES WHEN NO MAN PURSUETH! BUT RUNS FASTER IF SOMEONE IS AFTER HIM!

But the Boss had defenders. "Why should he stay?" asked Silver Dollar Smith, floating in the pool at a Turkish bath. "Every child knows that this is all politics. If you were Mr. Croker and had all the money you wanted, would you stay to have hayseeds ask you questions that would insult you?"

35

REVENGE

By late June the momentum was running in Goff's favor, and each day's session elicited testimony more damaging to the police than what had come before.

One day Frank Moss brought in George Appo, a professional criminal, who revealed how the Central Office police detectives protected bunco artists. His testimony showed that the police had alliances with gangs who dealt in counterfeit money and other swindles. Appo's testimony, filled with inside knowledge of how visitors to New York were bilked, was aimed at "the buttons," whom he said usually wound up with at least half the take. He explained how the police scared off victims, usually called jays or guys in criminal jargon. When a jay complained of having been fleeced, the police would remind him that he had willingly involved himself in an illegal scheme, and that the smartest thing that he could do was to avoid arrest by catching the next train back to Yokelville. The arrangement had worked successfully for many years, Appo said, because the bunco artists only swindled out-of-towners. Appo instantly became a celebrity and later in the year played himself in a melodrama about downtown life, although he faced harassment from police who had become zealous to punish his misdeeds.

Another day Frank Clarke, a bunco man who had for some years been plying his trade elsewhere, returned to New York to supplement Appo's testimony. Clarke said that Paddy Divver's saloon had been the home base of a bunco gang, which deposited the day's take in Paddy's safe every night. Unfortunately for Police Justice Divver, this embarrassment came to light just as the *World* was bedeviling him with a series of articles about various shady transactions that had provided him with the basis of his sudden wealth.

A restaurateur said that a wardman visited him after he had complained to the Police Board that the police had not pursued a thief. "He told me he would fix me for it, and said that he would send me to prison," he testified before the committee. "I asked him why a thief should be protected and I persecuted. He said I would find out. The next day another detective called at my place and said, 'I'll fix you, you son-of-a-bitch, for complaining against a policeman.'" The usual acquittal resulted when the accused patrolman appeared before the Police Board. The restaurateur said that the police harassed him so mercilessly in the weeks that followed that he was financially ruined.

"This is indeed pathetic," Goff said.

"It is an outrage," said Senator Bradley.

One day Goff subpoenaed a number of Bohemian saloonkeepers of the upper East Side, who—after prodding and threats—admitted that the main purpose of their Bohemian Saloonkeepers Association was to collect money to pay off the cops so that they could open on Sundays. One of the witnesses said he did not know the name of the precinct captain; he just called him "The Pantata." He explained that the Czech word meant "father-in-law" or "father of all things." The delighted Goff continued to use the word for the rest of the day. The next day men were addressing each other on the street as Pantata.

By this point New Yorkers had become convinced that there had never been anything like the Lexow hearings. They clamored to get in, although the hearings were being held in a poorly ventilated little courtroom and June was unseasonably torrid. Everybody would push closer and closer, trying to fit more people into the benches. They were most fascinated by the roles that saloonkeepers, gamblers and madames were playing in the drama of the city. Goff said that news clippings of the hearings were being sent daily to Emile Zola in the hope that the great French novelist would be interested in weaving a wondrous tale out of the lives of these ordinary people.

The committee also heard from Harry Hill, who had been a local celebrity with a famous concert saloon on Houston Street. John L. Sullivan, the former heavyweight champion, had knocked out his first opponent on Hill's stage. Hill, who no longer lived in New York, returned to tell how a rapacious captain had forced him out of the city. Hill had been paying faithfully, and had taken pains to keep his place orderly and decorous, but the captain—who had acquired the gambling fever—became more demanding as his IOUs mounted. The captain accosted Hill one day with a demand for a thousand dollars, which Hill paid. Two weeks later, Hill said, the captain wanted another $800. When Hill refused to pay the captain drove him out of town. Hill discovered that he could not open a saloon in Brooklyn because he "had gone back on the buttons."

It would be pleasant to suppose that Goff's witnesses acted out of a civic-minded spirit, but spite lurked so blatantly beneath their testimony that their obvious aim was to give the police their come-uppance. Were Zola to spin this tale it would be a novel of avarice and revenge. They were ordinary people of the kind who inspired Zola's observation that in every man's soul "there is a hog asleep"—people untouched by the suffused glow in which Emma Goldman wished to bathe her life.

Many of the witnesses were women. Rarely did women appear before government entities, yet in 1894, soon after suffragists stepped before the State Constitutional Convention, prostitutes and madames testified to the Lexow Committee.

The madames showed a pluckiness that should have brought blushes to the cheeks of the cautious merchants who were so reluctant to take a public stand. Goff's high-toned assistant Jerome was able to get forthright answers out of Julia Haddady, a tall blonde Hungarian who seemed unfazed by fears of police retaliation. Haddady had been running a cafe in Allen Street, where she had "girl waiters." During her first week in business Wardman Levy arrested her on charges of selling liquor without a license and for running a disorderly house. When the case was dropped Levy called on her to claim that his testimony had gotten her off easy and that things would continue to go well provided she "did the right thing." She commenced giving him $15 every month.

"Did not Levy himself have a house at 32 Stanton Street, and were there not girls in it, and was it not generally considered in the neighborhood to be a house of ill repute?" Jerome asked.

She said that she understood that a brothel in the neighborhood belonged to the wardman, and that some of her girl waiters had worked in it.

A more reluctant witness was Bessie Butler, a comely brunette who ran a brothel on Eldridge Street in the shadow of the precinct station. When she was subpoenaed she ran to her protector, Silver Dollar Smith.

"But why should you go to him for advice?" asked Senator Lexow.

"Why shouldn't I go to him?" she responded.

"He is your friend, then?" Jerome asked.

"Everyone is Silver Dollar's friend," she said.

"He is an engaging fellow," Jerome said. "I had the honor to meet him several years ago, when I prosecuted him for bribery. And the jury stood eleven to one for conviction."

Sometimes the women needed coaxing to get them started. They would begin with blanket denials, then a Parkhurst agent would be put on the seat, who would testify that just the previous day the women had admitted paying the police. After that they often decided to come clean. That was how Goff persuaded

Evelyn Bell to admit that she had been paying the police $150 a month for more than ten years. At the end of the day Miss Bell promised to come back, but she promptly disappeared.

The spirit of revenge burned almost visibly in Henry Hoffman, and his attitude could be discerned in his hard-walk stride to the stand. The young tough, who was losing his hair, had served a prison term for burglary and until recently he had been operating a brothel in the Eldridge Street precinct.

According to Hoffman, the man to see in the precinct was Philip Wissig, a former Tammany Assemblyman and go-between for the local whorehouses. Hoffman went to Wissig's saloon at Grand and Forsyth streets to talk about getting into the business, and rented a building from Wissig. He paid the initiation fee, began paying the monthly protection money, and set up shop. For a while everything went okay. Whenever Central Office detectives were sent from Headquarters to look through the area, Hoffman received word from the Eldridge Street precinct to lay low. Whenever any of Hoffman's girls were arrested he stopped by to give Wissig some money, and they were promptly released.

Then trouble developed. One night Captain Devery was walking past his place in civilian clothes when Kate McCarthy, one of Hoffman's eight whores, propositioned the captain from a window. The next morning a policeman called on Hoffman and said the captain wanted to see him.

"I went to the station house and the Captain was very friendly until I told him who I was. Then he said, 'You bastard, one of your cows called me up last night! I'd like to take you by the neck and throw you out.' I said, 'Well, Captain, nobody knew it was you, it's no harm,' but he was furious."

Two days later Wardman Glennon came around and said that because the Captain had been insulted Hoffman would have to pay an extra $10 per month to continue operations.

"Did you have any trouble at all?" Moss asked.

"Yes, once. I had a woman there whose brother kept bothering me, trying to get money from her. So I threw him downstairs. Wardman Glennon came around to the house and said, 'If he comes round again you let me know and we'll give him six months.' That cost me $10. I gave the money to Glennon, for he said he would have to square with the old man."

"Did you run your house publicly?" Lexow asked.

"Oh, yes. Two or three times policemen pulled two or three girls off the stoop. I paid Wissig $5 for each one and he bailed them out. They would have got a month or two, but I paid Wissig $25 apiece and he got them off for me."

In January, after Captain Devery left the precinct, Hoffman's place was raided. His lawyer took money from him to fix the case, but Hoffman was convicted and served two months on Blackwell's Island. He was still angry about being double-crossed and mocked for paying money and doing time anyway. Nobody in any of the surrounding whorehouses had suffered a like fate.

"Do you remember last August when Dr. Parkhurst called on the police to close 50 houses in your district?"

"Yes. I read it in the papers."

"And do you remember that the police captain, inspector and other officials denied that any houses were there?" Moss asked.

"Yes, and they lied."

"Were they receiving your money at that time?"

"Yes," he said belligerently.

During that period, he added, five Central Office detectives came to his house and caught five of his girls in the hallway, but said they would let him go this time.

"And Captain Devery reported that there was no violation of the law at your place?"

"So I read in the newspapers."

"How do you account for the police making such reports?" Senator O'Connor asked.

"By the revenue!" Goff interjected.

Moss hastened to add that at Devery's trial, "Superintendent Byrnes testified that his detectives from Headquarters had gone through the district day after day and could not find any disorderly houses."

* * *

Revenge also animated Lena Cohen. Hardly the glamorous madame of a titillating novel, the heavily built Mrs. Cohen looked and dressed more like a scrubwoman. She told a story to the committee that depicted the police as salesmen for the vice trade and herself as a victim.

William Travers Jerome conducted the questioning of the madame from East Houston Street. The aristocratic young attorney began by trying to ask Senator Lexow: "Will you please explain that this witness has the protection of—"

"Protection!" the woman broke in. "My God, I've paid enough money for protection which I never got. I hope I'll get it here."

Lena Cohen said she had engaged four prostitutes and opened her Lower East Side brothel the previous September. Jerome asked if the precinct ward men had ever visited her. She smiled bitterly as she replied that Wardmen Farrell and Brennan had stopped by frequently. She had visited the Union Market precinct station on several occasions to talk with Captain Jacob Seibert.

Lena claimed that the two detective wardmen had recruited her as a madame, had advised her on the basics of brothel-keeping and had encouraged her to stay in the business when she faltered. She was initiated in the business when she and her husband met with the wardmen in a saloon and were told that opening would cost them $500.

The woman spoke English with a thick accent, and the spectators and committee members leaned forward to catch every word.

"I then said to my husband, 'What am I to do? I have not got such a sum of money. Where am I to get it?' My husband said to me, 'My dear wife, I will tell you where to get this money. You must borrow it.' So I went to a friend of my husband's and borrowed $500. I had to give a mortgage on my furniture in order to get the money."

She returned to the saloon with the money, whereupon the wardmen told her that her monthly payment would be $50. She said that she told the ward detectives that she might not be able to pay all of it on the first of the month because her rent fell due on that date and asked to pay half then and half on the fifteenth. They agreed to those terms. Farrell called on October 1 and she began the monthly payments. He also stopped by frequently at night because he was "keeping company" with one of her boarders. She said that she became anxious when she read in the papers that brothels were being raided, and she went to Farrell, who told her she had nothing to worry about.

But the protection money so depleted the till that she had trouble surviving. When she told Farrell that she would have to close, he urged her to see the Captain. She went to the station house and told Captain Siebert she was broke. He persuaded her to stay open and warned against letting in the Parkhurst men. She tried a while longer, but could not make a profit. "Besides," she said, turning to the senators, "I wanted to live a decent life." Tittering broke out in the courtroom. Lexow banged the gavel and reproved the audience.

After she quit the business the wardmen raided her, out of malice, in February and again in March. She had been a prisoner in the Tombs, awaiting trial, since March 27.

"And you don't feel friendly toward Farrell and Brennan now, I suppose?" asked former Surrogate Ransom, who was representing the police that day while Nicoll attended the Constitutional Convention.

Before the witness could reply, Senator Lexow indignantly observed: "I don't think that any member of this committee imagines she could feel friendly toward them if she is a human being."

Ransom thought for a moment, then remarked, "I agree with you."

36

MALE PREROGATIVES

A s ever the liquor interests were working to defeat the suffragists.
When the woman's movement began a half-century earlier in upstate
New York, its leaders found that among its enemies the Rum Power was the most
unrelenting. Over the succeeding years it bested the ladies in every match. As
the suffragists slogged their way through the unseasonably sultry June, they continued to keep their cause in the newspapers, yet began to fear that the struggle
would end like all the others, with defeat at the hands of the liquor bottlers, beer
distributors and saloonkeepers.

Morris Tekulsky, a delegate to the Constitutional Convention and a
spokesman for saloon interests, was a formidable foe who knew Albany like the
back of his hand. For years he had patrolled the Capitol's Golden Corridor and
was acquainted with the political players. After signing the 1892 Excise Bill,
Governor Flower had sent the pen and penholder to Tekulsky, who framed them
for display in his saloon (which he had purchased from Paddy Divver when the
latter became a Police Justice in 1890).

To the suffragists Tekulsky represented not only economic interests but male
prerogatives. From their standpoint, "separate spheres" and "the protection of
women" camouflaged the political question of whether men would keep the
privileges that they guarded under the name of "personal liberty."

During the long struggle between male personal liberty and women's rights, history shifted the scenery and conditions. The women's movement began as a class
action on behalf of married women. In those antebellum days women found themselves stripped of rights when they married. A single woman could own property,
but a married woman *became* property—the property of her husband. Under the

291

law her business was owned by her husband, as were her earnings if she were employed. She had no right to make decisions about her children, get a divorce, or visit her children if he divorced her and took the children, as was his right.

Even in those early days, the liquor interests and male rights were linked, for in a majority of instances the friction between husband and wife was caused or aggravated by drink. When Stanton and Anthony began their work, a woman cursed with a drunken and abusive husband was at his mercy. He had the right to take money she had earned and spend it at a saloon, then come home and beat her and the children. Such was the predicament of thousands of women in the State of New York.

Having few alternatives, many women who hoped to further the rights of womanhood enlisted in the temperance movement. That began a long standoff between the woman's movement and the Rum Power.

"Let us petition our state government," Elizabeth Cady Stanton said at a temperance convention in 1852, "to modify the laws affecting marriage and the custody of children, that the drunkard shall have no claims on wife or child." Four years later, at a woman's rights convention, Stanton wrote that because husbands legally owned wives, marriage "stripped womankind of true virtue, dignity and nobility."

Temperance women raised the divorce issue cautiously, not in fear of men but because it might scare off women. And the most delicate question, which most women were reluctant to raise, was the husband's prerogative over the body of his wife—that is, sex upon demand. Stanton and Anthony and other women's rights advocates discussed the matter at length privately. And when Anthony raised it publicly, the *Utica Evening Herald* slapped her down:

"With a degree of impiety which was both startling and disgusting, this shrewish maiden counseled the numerous wives and mothers present to separate from their husbands whenever they became intemperate, and particularly not to allow the said husbands to add another child to the family."[1]

A half-century later, the saloon had become the fortress of male prerogatives. Women saw themselves as victims of these liberties—in the home, and in the streets where women had to fend off the unwelcome advances of drunken men (including drunken cops) after dark.

* * *

As the city's problems intensified and multiplied, women fashioned the argument for suffrage in terms of the city's collective life. They argued that public administration of large cities had become a demanding task, and that many men, with the weighty cares of business upon them, could not devote the necessary time to it; the hour had arrived for women to lend a hand.

They wanted to improve public life in new directions, such as the welfare of children. Hardly a school in the city was properly ventilated, and yet men were seemingly unconcerned that children sat through the day breathing noxious and stale air.

They also had begun to speak up on such issues as clean streets, a clean transit system, the banning of public spitting, and other matters of public delicacy. A few years earlier, a group of women had formed the Ladies' Health Protective Association in an effort to abate "the stable problem" and their efforts received little help from men, some of whom mocked them as The Hen Sanitarians. Their association fought the fertilizer businesses that packaged horse manure without regard for hygiene, and brought to public attention the plight of children living near stables and fertilizer operations who were more prone to respiratory disorders than children who lived at a further remove. These were health issues that most men failed to address. "What is a city but a large house in which we all live together?" asked a suffragist during the petition campaign. "Good city government is good housekeeping."

Public-minded women maintained that they were more effective and sensitive than were men in dealing with prostitutes, and women had insisted upon the employment of matrons in precinct stations to protect women who were in custody. They also had begun to campaign for the hiring of women as sanitary inspectors, for women on the school board, for women doctors in public institutions and for female representation in the management of all institutions involving women and children.

This infusion of women into selected departments of public life was happening in other cities as well. In Chicago, Jane Addams and her companions had established Hull House to do the work of the twentieth-century city. A similar passion for engagement burned in many New York women, from the suffragists to Emma Goldman to Lillian Wald, who was establishing the operation that later became known as the Henry Street Settlement. Many of them were sheltered daughters of the privileged who had grown uncomfortable and troubled about their role in life and restless to make themselves useful.

Their key argument for the vote and for entering public life was that the moral force of women would become a leavening element in a society too exclusively male in its outlook. Their approach was ameliorative; like Parkhurst, they were hopeful about improving the city, sensed the presence of virtue in the society, and hoped to foster that virtue as an engine for progress.

Women's influence, they said, would counter the forces that fostered crime, disease, immorality, poverty, and corruption, all of which could be traced to the power of the saloons. Without female influence, they argued, the city was a bedraggled sight—the public sphere that men had made.

37

TOOTH AND CLAW

After presenting a cavalcade of bunco artists, prostitutes, saloonkeepers and gamblers, Goff turned to lesser-known sources of police revenue. Succeeding witnesses disclosed that the police regularly extracted payments from sidewalk vendors, bootblacks, cabdrivers, produce wagons, shipping companies, and lemonade stands. The buttons, they testified, took one third of the gate receipts for prizefights, which were illegal in the city. They said that shopkeepers gave the cops money twice a year not to be hassled about blocking the sidewalks during deliveries. A building contractor testified that cops shook money out of him by threatening to find violations that would keep him in court instead of on the job. Another witness said the police took payoffs from hack drivers to let them break into carriage lines at the society balls. The police, according to testimony, even stopped in to dun money from private parties in rented halls so as to overlook the 1 A.M. time limit for serving alcohol. As in the case of the pushcart peddlers, the police crossed the line from corruption into what the twentieth century would call a protection racket.

By the middle of June everyone was talking about the reputations that Goff had demolished. The rapid exit of Boss Croker engendered rumors that other leading Tammany figures, including Police Board President Jimmy Martin, might join him at the Carlsbad mud baths in order to avoid a mud bath at home.

New Yorkers took a perverse civic pride in the hullabaloo. They enjoyed living in a metropolis where even scandal was so oversized that the whole nation, indeed the whole world, avidly kept up with the hearings. Goff reported that a prominent Parisian journalist had been attending the hearings to gather material for a book, and added: "He told me this investigation was creating a decided stir among the police of Paris, who, he said, were astounded at learning that the New York police could levy such enormous tribute."

Those who had been skeptical and unfriendly to the committee's intentions had shifted their ground. In March Dana's *Sun* mocked the Lexow Committee's arrival as mere political shenanigans. But by mid-June the newspaper was beating the drum for a relentless investigation. "Are these things really true," a *Sun* editorial asked on June 6, "or is it all a horrible nightmare that affrights and numbs the senses?"

One telling sign of the power of the hearings was the turnabout of Senator Jacob Cantor. A well-known bachelor about town known for having a way with showgirls, Senator Cantor jumped on the bandwagon and worked thereafter as a valuable committee member.

One morning Senator Jake told reporters that a retired cop doing work on his house in Harlem had admitted that he had paid to get on the force in 1867, and that twenty years later when the cop wanted to switch to lighter duty on the police court squad he paid for his transfer. Cantor stressed that the wrongdoing being uncovered could not be blamed exclusively on Tammany, because police corruption could be traced back a quarter-century, during which anti-Tammany Democrats and Republicans had also been culpable.

"That shows that this business of paying to get on the force has been in vogue for many years," the Harlem Senator said. "Now there's a living witness."

Whoever was to blame, the reputation of the Police Department was sinking, and not just in the city. A letter to the editor from a Pennsylvanian, for example, expressed trepidation about coming to New York. "I am more afraid of the police than I am of the bunco and green goods men," it stated. "Would you advise me to stay at home?"

Old foes of the police were emboldened to speak up. Back from his Blackwell's Island visit with Emma Goldman, John Swinton charged that police brutality was rarely reported for fear of retaliation and "that hundreds of persons are killed by the police of this city every year in one way or another and that many of these cases appear in the weekly reports of the Health Department under the head of 'Suicides and other violent deaths.'"

Swinton's exaggerations reflected the emotions of a public boiling over with indignation, and as the days wore on its mood changed to a loss of trust in the police. Some judges cautioned the public to keep a sense of balance, that the rot touched only a small cadre of police, but the conspiratorial silence that enveloped the force suggested that the guilt could be spread more broadly.

From pulpits, from editorial pages, from exclusive Fifth Avenue clubs to Third District saloons, New Yorkers could talk of little else. When would Clubber be called to the stand? What did Byrnes think of these revelations? Would any high-ranking cop, after the shambles that had been made of Justice Roesch, demand the right to defend himself?

* * *

One morning the courtroom was buzzing more than usual. Goff was talking with reporters about the likelihood of a summer break. Tammany Hall was insisting that the hearings continue through July and August, and the Senators had professed their willingness to go on all summer long. But Goff wanted a long recess. It would be difficult, he pointed out, to round up witnesses during the summer. One of the reporters asked if any political advantages colored his wish to break for the summer and resume during the election season. Goff denied any political motives and advised the reporters that he, Jerome, and Moss would be working as hard as ever straight through to September.

What had everyone worked up, however, was the news that Judge Martine had dropped charges against Lena Cohen for her public service in testifying before the Lexow Committee, and she had been released from jail!

That surprise brought District Attorney John Fellows to the witness chair to issue a warning. Now, the elegant D.A. said, half the men and women in the city's jails were clamoring to take the witness stand. It was their ticket to freedom. Fellows called it a sad day for the forces of law and order.

Nicoll rose to support his successor as D.A. "The impression has gone abroad among 4,000 policemen," he said solemnly, "that this committee will protect any witness who swears against the police. Policemen are honestly afraid to arrest lawbreakers in many cases."

"Oh, no," exclaimed Lexow.

"You have paralyzed the police force," Nicoll continued, looking worried. "The impression has gone out that the police will be punished if they dare to interfere with disorderly houses, whose proprietors have only to come here and testify against them."

"The testimony here shows," Lexow hotly responded, "that the police don't close up the houses and take money for not closing them up."

A strong outburst of applause reverberated around the room, silenced by Lexow's gavel.

"We'll have to call in the militia to police the city!" Nicoll exclaimed. "I learn that one of the witnesses here has resumed business at the old stand."

"Why don't the police arrest him then?" asked Senator O'Connor.

* * *

Where Nicoll saw a crestfallen and forlorn police force, Goff saw a band of insolent and ruthless men conniving to sabotage his investigation—and with some success.

The police, he contended, had been chasing, pushing out, shooing off, or bribing Madames, prostitutes and gamblers to leave the city, keeping potential witnesses out of the grasp of the Lexow Committee.

One day in late June, Goff emphasized his point. On that morning spectators at the hearing found a half-dozen women seated in the seats reserved for witnesses, dressed fashionably in black set off by white shirtwaists and colorful ribbons. When the hearing was called to order, Goff rose, surveyed the line of witnesses and called out the names of several women—the madames of various Tenderloin fancy houses. When no one responded Goff explained that the madames had fled. Therefore the subpoenas had been served on the assembled women, housekeepers who answered the doorbells. One by one Goff called them to the stand. Each testified, some indignantly and some with trembling, that the lady in question was gone.

"Mrs. DeForest left town about three weeks ago," said one of them. "She left on account of her health. I think she went to Europe. (Much laughter.) I don't know what has become of the girls."

Another housekeeper said she worked for "Miss Carrie."

"Were there girls in that house during the two years you have been there?" Goff asked.

"Well, there were lady boarders." (More laughter)

Goff browbeat and ridiculed several housekeepers with only token resistance until he came up against Ada Clinton, who kept house for Addie Shaw's brothel. Miss Clinton showed her disdain by saying whatever occurred to her at the moment. Goff grew ruddy in the face and began to flounder; masterful in dealing with hostility, he was unbalanced by flightiness. But eventually Goff managed to trip her up, and she admitted that the house had recently been raided, although she had testified a few minutes earlier that no policeman had ever entered the place.

Being caught in a lie seemed a matter of complete indifference to Miss Clinton, and Goff's manner became so fierce that Senator O'Connor advised him to take it a little easier on the woman.

"A witness of this kind," Goff responded, "should only get the treatment she deserves. Now, if you kept such a respectable house, how is it that you were arrested?"

The witness sighed that she did not know.

"What policeman arrested you?"

"Officer Cash, the ward man of the precinct," she replied. She said that she had been taken to Jefferson Market Court the next day and discharged.

"Get a subpoena for Officer Cash right away," Goff said to an assistant, then turned back to a suddenly blushing witness. "And did you not think it an outrage," he asked in a honeyed tone, "that you, a decent woman, living in a respectable house, should be arrested at a late hour of the night and dragged off to the police station?"

"I didn't think it was right; of course I didn't."

"I am to understand, then, that you never complained against the policeman who perpetrated this outrage on you?"

Ada Clinton replied that she had never made such complaint.

"Of course," Goff said with a smile, "when you consider what a great wrong has been done you, you would be perfectly willing to prefer a charge against the fellow."

The witness nodded affirmatively.

"All right, then," Goff shouted. "Here," he said, turning to Jerome, "take this woman to Police Headquarters and have her make out a charge of false arrest and imprisonment against Officer Cash of the Nineteenth Precinct."

Jerome led the witness, now pale and not so saucy, from the courtroom. "Of course," said Goff sharply to his colleague, "you will bring her back here again this afternoon."

During the streetcar ride downtown to Police Headquarters, Jerome warned her that Officer Cash would defend himself with proof, that a dozen witnesses could testify to the notorious nature of Addie Shaw's house, and that she could be indicted for perjury. At the door of Police Headquarters she changed her mind.

After the lunch recess, Ada Clinton came back to the witness stand looking far more thoughtful than she had been at the morning session.

"I testified this morning to some things that were not true, and I am very sorry for it," Mrs. Clinton said. "I was afraid that some harm would come to me. It has been understood among girls of my class that if they came before this committee and told the truth the police would make them suffer."

"A great many houses have been closed up since the committee came here?" Goff asked.

"Yes, sir."

"When Mrs. Shaw went away her impression was that if she gave any testimony she would have to close her house?"

"Yes, sir."

She said that Mrs. Shaw ordinarily kept ten girls, and that she had no idea how much Mrs. Shaw paid the police. She had never seen the madame give money to a policeman nor had the matter ever been discussed. She recalled, however, that about four months earlier, after having kept her house closed for some time, Mrs. Shaw came in one day looking triumphant and said, "Now I can open my house again."

After Senator O'Connor advised the witness to notify Goff at once if anyone attempted to interfere with her, Goff railed against police efforts to thwart the committee's investigations. Some of the spectators, however, thought that Goff had matched the police in audacity. He had brought off his bluff with such dash that he had overwhelmed the defense, who had been too awed or had not thought quickly enough to protest against the virtual kidnapping of Miss Clinton. His nerve and Jerome's mixture of threats and cajolery had worked.

* * *

Goff contended that the police had mounted an organized effort to interfere with the investigation, and produced witnesses to show that cops were harassing those who had testified and advising those who had not yet testified to "scram." Several major witnesses had disappeared, and Jerome said the police had managed to whisk one witness away after he had entered the courthouse.

Various witnesses testified that a member of the Tammany Hall General Committee had been threatened with a beating if he testified about payoffs for police appointments, that a former brothel-keeper had been assured that he would be sent to Sing Sing on planted evidence if he told what he knew, and that the police had organized a boycott of a Harlem tailor who had testified about payments made by applicants for substitutes to take their Civil Service police examinations for them. During one hearing Goff reported a rumor that five police captains had raised a $20,000 fund to bribe witnesses. The lengths to which they were willing to go, Goff proclaimed, explained why no one had ever come up with anything solid against the police.

Parkhurst agents complained to reporters about being trailed by the police. Arthur Dennett said he had been sent out with a subpoena for John Heise, a police station idler and stoolpigeon who collected protection money from the brothels for the police. Goff particularly wanted this witness: as a political associate of Barney Rourke, the Tammany saloonkeeper, Heise would have furnished a direct line between police corruption and Tammany Hall. But Heise managed to slip away. Dennett said two men trailed him, and that by the time he reached the Heise flat, the stoolpigeon "had skedaddled." Dennett learned that Heise's trunk had been shipped to New Jersey and he feared that Heise had sailed from the Hoboken pier for Europe.

Meanwhile the united front of the police did not crack. On the stand, their minds went blank, they could remember nothing, and if any of their fellow officers was doing anything fishy they were unaware of it.

And so the tooth-and-nail struggle continued at every level. The stakes were high, and men pressed every advantage to the utmost. And there were casualties who retreated from the field, like John McClave, hiding at his Connecticut harbor estate. The once-dapper Police Commissioner had become careless in his dress and distant in his thoughts. He lay about all day in his nightclothes, staring into space and trembling, while his doctors whispered that he would never recover if he did not give himself up completely to rest and rehabilitation.

* * *

The visit of the Swintons had changed things for Emma Goldman. John Swinton was so significant a figure that the head matron, who had been unfriendly, began to favor her with special privileges. Emma was even allowed to slip out to walk freely about Blackwell's Island, inhaling the harbor breezes.

People active in the New York scene were corresponding with her, including Arthur Brisbane, a reporter for the *World*, who expressed an interest in getting together with Goldman upon her release.

The warden overlooked the rules on limits for visitors in her case, and when her lover Ed Brady came (smuggling in Anarchist newspapers), arrangements were made for private visits.

One Sunday Ed brought along Voltairine DeCleyre, a Philadelphia anarchist active in the campaign to reduce Sasha Berkman's sentence. Goldman later wrote in her memoirs that most women in the movement treated her with antagonism and jealousy because men found her attractive. She was hoping that DeCleyre would be different, that she would be a female comrade, a kindred spirit with whom to share inmost thoughts and feelings.

But they were far apart in outlook. DeCleyre maintained that the place of Anarchists was among the poor and disinherited, and regarded Goldman's views as chic diversions for fashionable radicals. Goldman was taken with the idea that "the pioneers of new thought rarely come from the ranks of the workers" but "generally emanate from the so-called respectable classes." To limit one's activity to the masses was, she said, "contrary to the spirit of anarchism," which builds "not on classes, but on men and women." After two meetings the two Anarchist women became hostile rivals.

While she continued to revere Sasha for his heroism, Emma Goldman had abandoned his central tenet—the wisdom of the people. She saw no more legitimacy in the people than she did in any other authority. In the Old World she had seen her father defeated in a local election because he was a Jew and because he had failed to provide enough vodka for the debased and brutalized peasantry. She was inclined to place even less faith in Americans, who had rejected Sasha. Nor did she have any special faith in the wisdom of women, and believed that if they did win suffrage, most of them would vote as their husbands or sweethearts instructed them.

In her last months at the penitentiary, she was chafing to get back into the fray, but on a new basis. A new vision of liberation had become the central image of Goldman's career.

38

THE COMMITTEE
ADJOURNS

On the last day before the summer recess, the atmosphere in the hearing room was the same as ever—hot, late in starting, with Moss and Jerome combing the spectator seats, papers in hand, determining whether the witnesses had responded to subpoenas and checking names.

At the defense table DeLancey Nicoll's face was dark with anger. He turned over the papers on his desk impatiently as he listened to what Senator "Uncle Dan" Bradley was telling reporters. "You can put me down as making this prophecy," the Brooklyn Democrat said. "There will not be three police captains in power in this city after November next out of the entire lot who are now in command in the city precincts."

Visibly annoyed, Nicoll said that he intended to oppose a summer adjournment. Bradley responded that such was his right, but the committee would adjourn anyhow.

"Well, it will only be over my dead body," Nicoll said.

Ambling over to the circle of reporters that had formed around Nicoll and Bradley, Goff gave the official reasons for a summer recess. So many people would be away, he said, that his subpoena servers would not be able "to secure enough witnesses to keep the committee busy from day to day." Joining the clutch of talkers and listeners, Assistant Counsel Jerome added that Tammany Hall wanted the probe to drone on through the summer so that the public would become bored with it by the time the election campaign came around.

Goff ducked into the judge's chambers with the Senators to convince them of the good sense of a recess. The Irish lawyer wanted the opportunity to build an inventory of evidence that he needed to stage an impressive set of hearings in the fall. Everyone expected him to get what he wanted; although the Senators were formally in charge, Goff controlled the investigation, pursuing his own course and calling whatever witnesses he chose. The "committee to the counsel," as some reporters called it, was resigned to its subsidiary role.

* * *

In the closing days Goff had continued to astound the public with new sources of police graft. On this last morning he honed in on how the police harassed East Side saloonkeepers with raids until they bought Hollywood Whiskey, in which Clubber Williams had an interest. And he showed how the police extracted money out of humble retired seamen who owned sailmaking shops along the East River. They advertised their businesses by means of cloth banners that flapped from the upper windows of their little South Street shops.

"Did you ever pay the police for the privilege of having your sign out there?" Goff asked the first witness.

"I have, sir."

"How often?"

"Ten or fifteen times. We had to pay the police five dollars a year for the privilege of having our flag strung out over the street. I came to pay it the first time because I was fined for having the flag out there without a permit. In fact, I was fined twice, and each time cost me seven-fifty. After that a policeman told me that he could fix it for me if I'd give him a little money. I gave him five dollars, and that became the yearly tariff thereafter."

He was a picturesque old salt, with gnarled hands, a full head of white hair and a weatherbeaten, craggy face highlighted by prominent cheekbones. After six grueling weeks of hearings, Goff's skills as a ringmaster were as much in evidence as ever. He put other sailmakers on the stand to corroborate the first witness's account.

"I have subpoenaed these witnesses," said Goff, "because Senator O'Connor asked the other day if there was anything at all in New York City which the police did not levy a tax upon. Now here is something new."

"They would tax the air we breathe if they had a way to do it," O'Connor observed.

* * *

The committee then broke for lunch with the Senator's comment ringing like a summation of police venality. Charges had also been made that the police had found an even more scurrilous way to squeeze money out of victims: by planting evidence. Two women testified in the closing days that the police had framed them.

Chairman Lexow himself translated for Henrietta Hensing, a stout, florid woman who spoke only German. She and her husband kept a respectable twenty-room boardinghouse on Fourth Avenue, Mrs. Hensing testified, renting only to married couples and single men. When they had been in business for only a few days, she was visited by Wardman Hock, the precinct detective who had hounded Augusta Thurow. She told Hock, who spoke German, that she had just come to America and wanted him to protect her. Spectators hissed at the mention of Herr Hock, who had turned up so often in the testimony that he had become established in the public mind as a melodramatic villain whose knock invariably involved blackmail.

She said that she paid Herr Hock some money, but that it failed to keep her out of trouble, for shortly after New Year's Day, police raided the boarding house on the charge that her rooms were being used for immoral purposes.

Then, as Mrs. Hensing told it, the hand of every cop she met was itchy for Das Geld. A bribe went to the desk sergeant to accept her bond. Her lawyer extracted money from her to pay off the ward detectives so that their testimony would end in a dismissal, which it did. However, after the case was dismissed one of the detectives complained to her that the lawyer had not paid him as promised, and shortly thereafter the Hensings were raided again. Silver Dollar Smith then entered the picture, offering a package deal—bail, lawyer, bribed detectives and acquittal all for one price.

Louise Miller similarly claimed innocence. The police of the Fifth Street Station repeatedly raided her boardinghouse, arresting respectable tenants solely for the purpose of extortion. The price for release from custody was five dollars. Mrs. Miller also paid them off for good riddance, but they returned to make more arrests and to demand more money. The last time she was arrested, she said, a policeman charged that she made him an improper proposition. "That was impossible," said the thin, pallid woman. "I can bring testimony to that from my physicians. I have been very sick for eight months." Her illness, however, had not kept her out of the Tombs, where she had spent several weeks.

The testimony of Hensing and Miller was made more credible because Parkhurst agents had uncovered several instances in the Lower East Side of people falsely accused of running a brothel for the purpose of shaking money out of them.

During the lunch break the talk may have centered on other matters, like the Pullman strike outside Chicago, or the assassination of French President Carnot, stabbed in his carriage by an Italian anarchist. Yet whatever else was discussed, the absent Parkhurst's gallantry and sense of purpose were being called to mind. Especially since it had become apparent that working people liked him, newspapers spoke of making him the reform candidate for mayor. Two years had completely changed the public attitude toward the Presbyterian pastor, and the men and women who were taking brave risks were following his example.

* * *

After lunch, a storm broke. Senator Lexow read a note from the Board of Police Commissioners informing him that the Board was preparing to begin its own investigation of the charges brought out during the hearings. The Police Board's disciplinary hearings would begin as soon as the Lexow Committee recessed for the summer.

Goff blasted the Board's hearings as a sham. He said some of his witnesses had already fled because they were afraid that they might be called before the Police Board.

"It is at least a strange, unaccountable and incomprehensible proceeding," Goff said, complaining that the Board, which had been criminally inactive for twenty years, now chose to bestir itself at the very moment that such activity would be harmful.

"Why," exclaimed Senator O'Connor, "three of the Commissioners themselves have been charged before this committee."

"Just so," Goff said. "That a body charged with malfeasance in office should sit in judgment upon others before their own skirts are cleared is something inconsistent with any ideas of common justice. They will hunt up witnesses and subject them to severe cross-examination and other annoyances. It is very hard, you know, to get businessmen to come into court, and their action in this matter will make it only the harder for us when we resume work in the fall."

Opposing the adjournment, Nicoll called the committee irresponsible for not giving the accused a chance to reply to accusations. "You have received the testimony of perjurers, forgers, brothel keepers and self-confessed criminals, and eagerly received their revengeful stories, and have scattered such testimony broadcast before the people," he said. "You have admitted hearsay as the basis of attack against public officers. You have taken from the Tombs and promised immunity to—"

"Hold on," Lexow interrupted, "if it is unfortunately the fact that the police have had business partnerships with the criminals you have mentioned, then that unfortunate fact must remain. We have got such witnesses together as best we could."

"This testimony has created a distrust in the Police Department and created a lack of morale therein," Nicoll said. "You know that you have denied offers made by those who stand accused before you to take the stand."

"On the contrary," Lexow said sarcastically, "we went out of our way and invited Police Justice Divver to take the stand."

"I do not refer to Justice Divver," Nicoll shot back. "I refer to Captain Cross, who sat here while a disreputable woman was testifying against him. And on the specious ground that it would interfere with the plans of your counsel, you denied him the right to be heard—a right accorded by every tribunal to the meanest criminal. And that's the condition in which you propose to leave the matter for two months and a half."

"Do you dispute the fact, Mr. Nicoll, that these evils have long existed?" asked Lexow. "At least that they have been known in the department and to the public, and now do you seek to urge all that as an excuse against our adjournment when for ten years or more this state of affairs has been allowed to exist in this city?"

The crowded courtroom burst into applause at Lexow's remark, and would not stop even when the Chairman rapped the gavel repeatedly.

"Are these men hired to do this?" cried Nicoll, turning about and glaring at the spectators. "This is a most unseemly exhibition."

"No," exclaimed Goff, rising. "It is a wail from the great body of citizens of this great city. It is but a faint expression of the intense feeling that is sweeping over Manhattan Island against the corrupt practices that have been exposed by this committee."

This brought on another outburst of applause. Nicoll made himself heard above the uproar.

"You propose," he shouted, "to leave the Police Department resting under the stain and stigma of these charges without a chance of vindication! We are reaching a period of the year when crime is rampant. But what do you care? You are going away to mountains and lakes and cool breezes, leaving the city in charge of a demoralized police force. I protest in the name of justice and fair play. Mr. Goff says that there are no witnesses at hand. But there are plenty right here, demanding an opportunity to be heard. In the face of all this, then, you made the cool proposition that while you adjourn the department shall do nothing. Why, sirs, it is the duty of the department to investigate these charges! You may go, but they must do something in your absence!"

After that several people attempted to speak at once. The winner was Frank Moss, who waved a handful of papers—reports, he said, of captains who had commanded the Eldridge and Fifth Street precincts. Every month, he said, the Parkhurst Society had sent the Police Board the addresses of disorderly houses in these precincts, and every month the precinct captains and Inspectors had returned reports calling Parkhurst a liar and a disgrace to the clergy. "During all this time," he said, "the Board of Police Commissioners did nothing to check on the truth of these claims except to send the people accused out to investigate themselves and to find themselves innocent of all charges." He read some excerpts from these reports, which quoted such experts as Wardman Glennon and Wardman Hock—names that had become synonyms for graft and brought gales of laughter from the spectators. He incited more laughter by reading from reports of Inspector Williams and Inspector McAvoy on the absence of vice in various precincts.

"Do you understand, Mr. Nicoll, our doubts that the Police Commission will conduct a serious inquiry?" Lexow asked. "I am surprised that the Police Department now make it their excuse to investigate the evidence brought out before this committee, because we have developed facts which they have professed not to believe. There can be no plan of action so calculated to cripple this investigation as to proceed as the Police Board propose to do. One of the reasons why we have not taken an absolute adjournment is to prevent any intimidation of our witnesses. We have heard that our witnesses are already being hounded and harassed. If it is true, then it appears to me that the criticism passed upon the heads of the department applies to the whole force—yes, the whole force!"

* * *

On that note the Lexow Club shut down until September. Although the blue wall of silence had not been cracked, the investigation had been a triumph. Only two months earlier the city's wise men had predicted that nothing would come of the hearings. Now the people who had fashioned the success of the probe, chiefly Goff and the Parkhurst agents, were hailed as miracle workers.

Before the hearings had recommenced in May, Goff had tacked to the wall behind his desk a composite lithograph of New York's police commanders. Byrnes occupied the center, the four inspectors decorated the corners, and oval photos of the precinct captains encircled the face of the Superintendent. As each of the pictured figures in the Department had been accused of some transgression over the course of the next six weeks, Goff had playfully attached little red seals, the kind affixed to legal documents, on their brows, and by the time the hearings closed a third of the faces on the lithograph were decorated with scarlet wafers.

Goff and his assistants had accomplished these wonders through hard work and perseverance, but the crucial thing had been to establish the credibility of the committee. Promises were made to protect witnesses and the public had to see the promises kept before the committee was trusted. When the people saw that the committee kept its word they were emboldened, and by the middle of June were arriving at the Parkhurst Society office every day with information, volunteering affidavits to a corps of clerks. Goff, who once could not find a single witness except Granger willing to testify, now found himself with too many.

Many of the informants knew remarkably little of solid worth, and Jerome told the press that "the hardest work now before us is to separate the wheat from the chaff."[1]

Even before the hearings ended a new subject of discourse had begun to enliven the saloons and clubs uptown and down: what were Goff's intentions? Some said he wanted to be Mayor; others that he intended to run against his foe, Recorder Smyth, who was coming up for re-election in November.

Those who followed the hearings attributed the committee's success to daring, to the rancor of old enmities, to the love of revenge, to single-minded dedication, and not least to ambition.

* * *

And how had the suffragists fared? They had made a valiant effort in collecting half-million petition signatures, the best showing ever in the cause of votes for women. Nevertheless their plea to the Constitutional Convention had been unheeded, they did not have the vote, and the depletion of their ranks with the coming of the summer, as many of them departed for Newport, the Berkshires, Buzzard's Bay or the New Jersey shore, was a telling indication of how completely they remained an uptown movement.

Over the course of the spring they had found their call for the involvement of women in public affairs answered with stinging irony. At the Lexow hearings women had become involved in public issues to an extent never seen before in the city, and the appearance of their fallen sisters as witnesses raised issues that most of the suffragists had never before contemplated.

The suffrage campaign, played against the Lexow hearings day after day, raised a new question: how would this city be different if women shared in its management?

The old question—whether public life was too rough for women—was beside the point, because in the city the wolf would come to the door anyway, as it had already for Hensing and Miller, and as it had for countless downtown women who on beginning their odyssey to the city had never intended to become prostitutes.

There was an expectation in many quarters that women in public life would bring about the further evolution of society. "Now, I am not the prophet nor the son of a prophet, but I am willing to undertake a prediction just the same," a male sympathizer told women at a gathering in a Fifth Avenue parlor. "I am certain that if women are allowed to have a voice in the affairs of the nations of this earth, we may, before another century, sink our battleships and call in our standing armies, because force will have ceased to rule the world."[2]

Many women shared the faith that their entry into public life would illuminate the Twentieth Century. Any suffragist who rode a Third Avenue elevated train downtown that June would see that women had a common bond that transcended the differences of uptown and downtown.

The first thing that she would learn about her humbler sisters was their love of flowers—an array of flowers and plants, nourished and cherished in nearly every household in the poorer neighborhoods, down the East Side and far south of 14th Street. They bloomed on window ledges as a touch of grace in the midst of gloom, struggling for sunlight between the trestles of the elevated railroad. Often the receptacle was a tomato can, and there was something in its homeliness more touching than the costly jardinières in which the Fifth Avenue women kept their Easter lilies, violets and pansies. It was not a craving for display that cultivated these flowers of the tenements, but a love of beauty, a refusal to be crushed by hard lives and mean streets. These flowers expressed the spirit and style of women, and it was just this—the spirit that always puts something special in the lunch pail, the style of what Parkhurst called God's favorite sex—that was absent from the public life of New York.

The quality that they had to offer public life was not innocence but femininity. Their innocence—which men praised so highly in their attempt to keep women out of public life—would be discarded as they abandoned frivolity to take on a life of purpose, to become involved with the work of the city.

The testimony of the women at the Lexow hearings showed that the new woman of the coming century would also need to develop militancy—that if (as Parkhurst liked to say) it were the duty of the police to watch the people and the duty of the people to watch the police, it was also the duty of the women to watch the men.

MARVELOUS TRANSFORMATIONS

Summer 1894

39

AMERICA! AMERICA!

The United States lured me not merely as a land of milk and honey, but also, and perhaps chiefly, as one of mystery, of fantastic experiences, of marvelous transformations. To leave my native place and to seek my fortune in that distant, weird world seemed to be just the kind of sensational adventure my heart was hankering for.

—Abraham Cahan, *The Rise of David Levinsky*, 1917

When the shimmering heat in the lower East Side cooled a bit in the July evenings, the Jewish girls came out to sit on the stoops or to jump rope. "Boys—and girls—together," they sang as the rope looped in the twilight, "me—and Mamie—O'Rourke—tripped—the light—fantastic—on the—sidewalks—of—New York."

The parents of the Jewish girls had come from hamlets in Eastern Europe that lay along muddy roads that led the traveler back into the Middle Ages, but the children knew nothing of the traditions or culture of that life. They knew about the sidewalks of New York; they knew Daisy would look sweet upon the seat of a bicycle built for two. And their parents never spoke of returning to those East European villages.

Two hundred thousand East European Jews were crammed into the Lower East Side, and they were there to stay. They had their own theaters, where King David spoke Yiddish, waved a tin sword and wore a gold-paper crown. They shouted advice to the actors, and when the hero demanded to know where the heroine was hiding, someone in the second row would tell him.

In letters to their friends and relatives abroad they wrote about the plays that they had seen, and of a woman who wore an ostrich feather in her hat. They had heard scratchy voices come out of a telephone, had ascended in an elevator, had drunk out of a water fountain. They had gone up the Hudson on Dry Dollar Sullivan's excursion boats to a landing where men wrestled and drank beer and ate clams. The streets were not made of gold, but at twilight, as the girls skipped rope, the streetlamps threw a golden glow. They were as poor as ever, but they knew someone who had become rich. The people back in the hamlets read the letters and kept on coming.

* * *

Emma Goldman had arrived in the vanguard of the immigrant wave. Brimming with optimism, she and her half-sister Helena set out for the New World in December of 1885. Like their fellow-passengers in steerage they knew nothing of the geography of America, and although they had heard of New York they were not clear where it stood in relation to the rest of the United States. They were equipped only with a satchel of catch-phrases—the land of opportunity, the land of liberty, the Golden Land. For immigrants America was an idealized place of wonders and miracles, the place where everyone believed in progress, where tomorrow would be better than today.

Some of the immigrants brought along a few shards of knowledge. They knew that poor men returned to their villages in frock coats and high hats, with their beards trimmed or shaved, with trunks and bags full of belongings, sparkling with diamond pins, rings and gold chains, amazing their open-mouthed landsmen with the transmutation that America had wrought in Mordecai, now known as Max. Some knew that there were many ways of getting rich in America, that some men made fortunes as desperadoes and that men were even paid to vote. Some had heard that schools were free and that all children, rich or poor, were educated in them, and that adults were invited to attend night classes. Some knew that Jews did not need a permit to live in a particular place or to travel from one place to another, that a Jew was protected and restricted by the same laws as everyone else.

When Emma and Helena reached New York harbor, they stood pressed against each other, looking at the deep-scooped harbor as it emerged from the mist. The pedestal was still awaiting the unassembled Statue of Liberty, although Emma would recount the moment in her luxuriant memoirs with the completed Statue wheeled in for scenic effect. "Ah, there she was," Emma wrote, "the symbol of hope, of freedom, of opportunity! She held her torch high to light the way to the free country, the asylum for the oppressed of all lands." All their fellow-immigrants were rejoicing that the journey had ended at last, after their crowded ordeal in the steamer's gamy steerage section. Some of them had dreams of riches, others of finding safety, others of adventures, while others were coming to rejoin their families. Their expectations were vague. But Emma knew exactly why she had come. She was looking for a place where people did not have to bow and scrape before authority. And although she sometimes missed her parents, she also felt that she had escaped from her father's rages and her mother's coldness.

* * *

With Helena, Emma joined their married sister, Lena, at her home in Rochester. Emma found that German Jews who had emigrated two generations earlier "had done okay" in America. They lived in nice neighborhoods and controlled Rochester's garment trade. Leopold Garson owned the clothing factory in which Emma found work. He was chairman of the United Jewish Charities of Rochester, yet he paid his workers as little as he could, and probably worried that the loud and rough ways of the newer arrivals might reflect poorly on Jews. The owners supported each other in setting wage rates for workers who, being barely civilized, could thrive on a pittance. Some owners even warned that it might harm the workers to overpay them.

Used to the relaxed atmosphere that prevailed in Russian factories, Emma was displeased with working conditions; talking and singing were forbidden, discipline was onerous, and the workers were always being yelled at to work faster. All the workers thought they were paid too little, but she was one of the few who screwed up the courage to complain. Perhaps it was youthful naiveté that led Emma to think that a big philanthropist like her boss would understand that she wanted to contribute a bit more money to Lena, who was pregnant and would need it. Emma also wanted to make extra money so that she might occasionally buy a book, attend a theater and otherwise expand her horizons. But when she went to his office she was not invited to sit, and the scowling Garson told her that she expected too much and that she should go elsewhere if she were not satisfied in his factory. Worse yet, she wrote in a letter to a friend, her boss "insisted on the pleasures the young female wage slaves could give him—he had them or out they went."

Was America so different after all? "Instead of one Tsar, she found scores of them," wrote Hippolyte Havel, an early acolyte. "The Cossack was replaced by the policeman with the heavy club, and instead of the Russian chinovnik there was the far more inhuman slave-driver of the factory."[1] In Russia her mother had tried to fob her off in a loveless arranged marriage, and in Rochester as in

St. Petersburg sex was the only power that women possessed. Here as there she was a nobody working long hours for low pay in a factory. She was irked by the provincialism of American life, its demand that all conform to its standards, its busybody interest in everyone's doings—a set of social restrictions as stifling in its way as the laws of Russia.

Disillusioned with Americans, whom she regarded as empty people like Garson, concerned only with appearances, propriety, and material success, Goldman groped for an alternative. She attended lectures of visiting Socialists but found their political philosophy too mundane, and chiefly concerned with replacing the present rulers with themselves. Eventually she was led to the Anarchists, who were drawn in more heroic proportions. Fearless of public censure, they dared greatly. All of them were immigrants, transplanted to this frivolous country in which, as she saw it, the majority tyrannized the exceptional beings who tried to rise above them. She read Johann Most's newspaper and dreamed of leading Anarchist parades; when the Haymarket Anarchists were placed on trial in Chicago, she read their outpourings of contempt for the entire system of judges, laws and prisons, and came to realize, as Havel put it, "that no mercy could be expected from the ruling class, that between the Tsarism of Russia and the plutocracy of America there was no difference save in name."

In time Emma's parents migrated to America and came to live in Rochester, and one evening in 1887 she and Helena walked over to visit them. Inside other visitors were discussing the executions that day of four of the Haymarket ringleaders.

"What's all this lament about?" a woman said with a laugh. "The men were murderers. It is well they were hanged."

Goldman sprang at the woman's throat and tried to choke her. When she was restrained, she grabbed a pitcher from the table and dashed water into the woman's face. "Out," she cried, "Out, or I will kill you!" The frightened woman backed away and ran out the door.

Rochester's Jews denounced this ungovernable woman. Her father said her shameless ways had disgraced the family. Emma left for New York City, where her rebellious nature could flower. But everything that happened to her in the metropolis deepened her disappointment in America, a land of hollow promises. When her disenchantment obliged her to protest, she was arrested, and then convicted by a jury imbued with the outlook of a nation that attempted, as she put it, to make life "uniform, gray, and monotonous as the desert." America sent her away to Blackwell's Island to shut her up.

As she practiced her English while checking and sorting the drugs in the medicine chest of the prison dispensary, Emma Goldman reviewed her standing in her adopted land. Once she had dared to hope that America was fertile ground. In the nations of Europe old ideas prevailed. Smelling of vodka and garlic, the peasants clung to their outmoded religion, their superstitions, and their hatred of intellectuals. America seemed promising—a place where tradition enjoyed no special favor, especially in New York, where people scoffed at yesterday's ideas.

Yet Anarchism was less a force in this country than in European nations. The Jews were more interested in going to dance halls than to Anarchist meeting halls. Men who had been attracted to Anarchism in Germany spent their time at Coney Island or at cockfights. America's bosses were aware that most people permanently remained children and could be amused by silly diversions. America was a frivolous place where serious ideas were not respected, a materialistic land where only the dollar spoke with authority.

* * *

Other Jewish immigrants denounced the snares and false values of America. Men esteemed in their Eastern European hamlets for their learning and piety were nobodies in New York, while others who had neglected their studies of the Torah had become alrightniks and were spoken of as big men. Erudition meant nothing here, only success. In America it did not matter whether one became rich by back-breaking work over many years of self-denial, or whether one won a fortune on the turn of a card; it was the Almighty Dollar that mattered. Some

Silver Dollar Smith

of the whores who beckoned to passing men from windows on Broome Street and Allen Street had sailed from Hamburg with high hopes; Americans despised them not for being whores, but for being failures. Other women who sold their favors for high prices were celebrated in the gossip sheets and welcomed effusively when they entered exclusive restaurants.

Nevertheless the attraction of America grew stronger. Wherever Jews gathered in Russia, outside synagogues or at coach stops, they talked of America. People with relatives in the new land read their letters aloud to neighbors—with marvelous tales of how the fire laddies had put out a blaze in a six-story tenement; and of Silver Dollar

Smith's saloon on Essex Street, where hundreds of glittering silver dollars were soldered to the walls, ceilings and floors. Children played at emigrating. As the Jews groaned under the oppression of the Czar, some of them even thought of it as the Promised Land.

* * *

The Jews were expelled from Moscow in 1891. Grand Duke Sergius, Governor of Moscow and brother of the Czar, was administering the forced conversion of Jews to the Russian Orthodox faith. Jews were deported from Moscow into districts where Orthodox priests and secret police could keep a close watch on them. Thousands of Jews became beggars and wanderers. Homeless people were starving in the streets. Some Jews mustered up their numbers and foraged in groups. Some smuggled themselves across borders and swam rivers. Some headed for places where it was rumored that the regime was milder.

Among those fleeing that year was the Urchittel family. They left their friends, they looked at scenes never to be seen again, and fearing the unknown but hoping for a better life they went to Hamburg, the northern port city of Germany that was the embarkation point for thousands of Russian Jewish immigrants. It was a city of fleecers, confidence men, white slavers, thugs, money-changers. Many refugees arriving there were unable to leave because of bureaucratic complications; while they waited they were cheated at overpriced lodgings and their meager belongings were stolen. Mrs. Urchittel's husband died during their stay in Hamburg, so that she arrived in America in steerage, a destitute widow with four children. They had left Russia seeking who knows what—riches, freedom, tranquility, a table arrayed with delicacies and a steaming samovar—but they arrived concerned chiefly with survival.

Although Caela Urchittel did not speak any English, she was a determined woman, fiercely protective of her children, and she was an attractive woman which, whatever the justice of it, counts for something in the world. United Hebrew Charities lent Mrs. Urchittel money so that she could set up a boarding house and guided her in the dizzying experience of adjusting to American life, where Jewish men wore short coats just like the freethinkers.

Through scrimping Mrs. Urchittel managed to save $600 from her boarding house but quickly lost it in another business venture, a restaurant in Brooklyn. While this business was failing one of her children died. Another was severely burned in an accident. Once again she called upon the organized forces of American Jewry to aid her in her distress, and her plea was heard.

It was soon after Captain Devery was transferred to the Eldridge Street station that Caela Urchittel opened a little cigar and candy store in his precinct, on

Ridge Street near the corner of Broome. Some of the Jewish girls who skipped rope in the evenings came to look in her window, where she kept glistening glass jars filled with fruit gums, malt balls, toffees and other colorful kinds of candies. Mrs. Urchittel lived in the back of the tiny store with her three surviving children, two girls and a boy.

The second day she was in the store, as she told it later, "a man came in and, taking a paper of tobacco, wanted me to trust him for it. I insisted upon his paying for it, and then he gave me a quarter, at the same time making an insulting proposition, to which I paid no attention, simply giving him his change." The next day the same man identified himself as a ward detective from the Eldridge Street police station, said he had a warrant for her arrest, and demanded $50. She refused to give him any money and said that if he came in again she would chase him out with a broom.

At midnight another ward detective came to her store. He accused her of prostitution and said he knew she had saved $600 out of the business. He said he wanted $50 or else he would arrest her. In spite of her protestations and the wails of her children, he made her go out into the street with him. Two blocks away Max Hochstim was waiting. She knew that Hochstim was a powerful political figure with Tammany Hall. She appealed to her fellow Jew for protection, but Hochstim told her that he had already done her a great favor by reducing the detective's demand from $75. Hochstim would fix it for her for only $50, plus $10 a month to be paid thereafter.

She insisted that she had no money. She was dragged from corner to corner through the streets and into the Eldridge Street precinct station and then into the Delancey Street station, while both wardmen continued to demand money and told her that she would never be released until she gave them $50. After several hours of torment she gave them $25 which she had hidden on her person. They took it and released her but warned her that it was not enough and that they would be back for more.

Early the following morning a detective returned to the store and renewed the demand, warning that otherwise she would be sent to prison and would never see her children again. She fell to her knees in supplication. "I begged him not to take me away, that I am not able to give him any more money. The little children cried to him, 'Don't take mamma away,' but he only said 'Come along,' and I had to go."

She was turned over to another wardman and one of Hochstim's thugs, who dragged her around with them while they visited several men in an unsuccessful attempt to come up with $50 by selling her store. Finally they gave up, and the wardman said to the thug, "That bad woman don't want to give the money.

Take her to the court." She was taken to the station house, and the next day was arraigned.

While she was waiting for her case to be heard a detective told her that her children had been taken away, but that if she would give him $50 he would save her even then. She had come to find life, liberty, and the pursuit of happiness, but destiny had blown her into the Lower East Side, where she had fallen into a den of wolves.

* * *

America was no place for a Jew, said the learned rabbis of Europe. Boarders living in cramped quarters made advances to married women. The Yiddish newspapers of New York were filled with advertisements inquiring after the whereabouts of men who had deserted their wives and children. Jewish men who had tearfully vowed to send for their wives and family as soon as possible were passing themselves off as bachelors to seek the favors of women. The young people were interested only in developing an air of American smartness. The young men wanted to learn the angles, smoke cigarettes and talk out of the sides of their mouths. The young women wanted to wear fashionable clothes that flattered their shapes. As Sholem Asch wrote, "there awoke a yearning for unshackled liberty, and their fathers' piety became a matter of jest."[2]

Some of the learned rabbis would say that Mrs. Urchittel had been thoroughly warned and got what she deserved. Some had forbidden their flock to emigrate to that land of evil spirits, where the wrath of the Lord took the shape of tornadoes that blew people to Gehenna. Rabbi Israel Meir Ha-Kohen, the most distinguished moralist of the Continental rabbis, said it was better to endure persecution in Russia than to lose one's soul in America. He prophesied that the Lord's punishment upon a careless people would strike down the innocent with the guilty. Those who had to go to America, he said, should leave their families behind and return to them. "A man must move away from any place which causes turning away from the way of the Lord," said the great rabbi, "even if he knows for certain that he will have great economic success there."[3]

Nevertheless something about America attracted the Jews. Maybe it was nothing more than the loosening of sexual rules. In Eastern Europe men and women sat in different parts of the synagogue. Here they worked together in the sweatshops, and hugged and kissed during the lunch break. Men who had averted their eyes from a passing woman in Russia became bold in addressing women, and women who had been shy sought romance. The young people went to dance halls and danced with people to whom they had not been introduced, and they did not need matchmakers to arrange marriages for them.

There were too many attractions to count, and as the United Hebrew Charities noted, the immigrants were "dazzled by the brilliancy of the city."[4] Immigrants felt emboldened. "Forget your past, your customs, your ideals," advised a guidebook for Jewish immigrants. "Do not take a moment's rest. Run, do, work and keep your own good in mind."[5] Their agile minds were quick to discern an opening and fill it, like making the rounds of the sweatshops with soda, making three-quarters of a cent on each bottle sold.

They enjoyed hearing Emma Goldman speak at rallies, for they liked arguing social issues, but when she had told them that America was like Russia, they laughed. Russia was torpid and stultified; America crackled with nervous energy. In spite of disappointments, most immigrants were convinced that they were in a new world with new rules, and that they too would be changed from Mordecai to Max. Despite what the Anarchists said, they did not feel like victims in the grip of a demonic system but like riders on a merry-go-round. They had come to a place where everything was random, where the wheel of fortune was spun every day and everyone expected his number to come up—a land that would try anything, accept anything, absorb anything. They knew that it could be cruel and dangerous—a land where anything is possible was bound to have goblins and witches—but that it was an enchanted place.

They lived in the same tenement houses in which the Irish had lived before them, and two generations earlier German immigrants had choked these same streets. And like the Irish and Germans before them, the Jews found that the initial attraction did not fade but grew stronger, that America was irresistible.

40

CITY OF SURPRISES

For those who had joined the exodus from the lands ruled by the Czar, the most striking thing about America was that nothing ever stayed the same for long. They were accustomed to a rate of change measured in generations, and the American pace was breathtaking. Boarders moved in and moved out. The sweatshop moved to a new rookery every three months, and every time it moved the production system was reorganized. The workforce was doubled for two months, then everyone was laid off. The workers struck for shorter hours and the bosses gave in, then figured out a subterfuge to force the pay scales down. Old buildings came down, taller buildings replaced them. Gaslighting went out, incandescent lighting came in. Even the songs changed quickly; in June everybody would be singing a song, and in July everybody would sing a new song, and the old song was tossed in the dust bin.

Some of the older Jews still emotionally inhabited the old world, reading the Yiddish periodicals for news of Russia—a dismal record of pogroms, catastrophes, and epidemics—and seeking out the landsmen of their former Russian hamlets to worry together about those they had left behind. But the younger people had been borne through the unrest, hard times, rallies, and police clubbings of the summer of 1893, and lived with both feet in the Lower East Side.

Since by direct contact they knew the police involved in the hearings, the immigrant Jews were fascinated when the Lexow Committee took aim at the downtown precincts, and praise of Goff resounded through many a garment union meeting. And like the rest of the city they were astonished to discover that the Police Board, which had scoffed for so long at Parkhurst's charges, had embarked on a campaign to look into police wrongdoing.

* * *

Early in July, Francis Wellman, who as Assistant District Attorney had secured the convictions of Billy McGlory and Charlie Gardner, began a stint as special counsel to the Police Board, with the purpose of getting miscreant cops dismissed from the force.

Wellman first turned his attention to "sidewalk rental" cases—bribes that retail merchants paid to the police so as to remain free of harassment while unloading goods or displaying them for sale on the sidewalk. Wellman thought that his work would stand up solidly against reversal because it was based on the testimony of reputable businessmen, while the Lexow Committee evidence would crumble because it was based on the suspect testimony of gamblers, whores and brothel keepers.

But Wellman had guessed wrong. The store owners were afraid to testify against the police, and when Wellman managed to force an affidavit out of a storekeeper, he would be back three days later, desperate to renege while his lawyer complained that the thumbscrews had been put to his client. So Wellman pursued another line of attack—he went after Police Captain Michael Doherty and two of his wardmen.

Doherty did not think that the Police Board would give any weight to the testimony of a whorehouse keeper, and it took a visit to Board President Martin to convince the fat captain that Wellman was serious. When the hearing began, the defense made no attempt to deny that Captain Doherty took money from Augusta Thurow, but stressed that he had raided her boarding-house indefatigably. The Police Board hearing gave the Captain a chance at last to defend his record—which he did despite heavy sweating in the midsummer heat. Mopping his brow frequently, he said he had attempted to break up Mrs. Thurow's operation, but that she "was one of those women you couldn't drive out."

On cross-examination, the Captain was questioned about his wife's unaccountable wealth. While he plugged along on the modest $2,750 annual salary of a Captain, Mrs. Doherty had paid off the $18,000 mortgage on their house, which she owned. She also owned property in Brooklyn as well as an impressive coach. In addition there was a joint bank account of $30,000. Asked to explain his fortune, Captain Doherty responded with a tale of Wall Street plunging that began with $1,200 made in three days on an investment of $200 and became ever more incredible. The shadowy figure who had made all this money for the Captain was a high-stakes gambler whose whereabouts were unknown. Doherty professed to know nothing of what stocks his money had been invested in, and admitted that stocks were a mystery to him.

The wardmen of the precinct were also inordinately rich. One of them testified that his fortune resulted from a series of wildly lucky bets at the track. Following these hearings the Police Board dismissed Captain Doherty from the force, the first captain to be fired in nineteen years, and dismissed Wardmen Hock and Meehan as well.

* * *

All over town men, and even women, reacted to the testimony with chuckles or indignation, debated about who told the truth and who lied, and whether Superintendent Byrnes had been as excluded from the process as it appeared. They speculated on the motives of the Police Board in conducting the hearings, and why Captain Doherty, an out-and-out Tammany cop, had been chosen as "the fall guy." Some said the hearings reflected a struggle for dominance between the more reform-minded Tammany faction and the anti-reform Croker loyalists. Others claimed that Jimmy Martin was deliberately holding flawed hearings so that the cops would win reinstatement on appeal.

The hearings puzzled many of the Jews of the Lower East Side. From their vantage point, in the shadow of the Essex Market Court House, Tammany Hall and the police were the same thing, more or less. Silver Dollar Smith and Max Hochstim were Tammany Hall, and the police did their bidding, worked with them, enforced for them. So why would Tammany harm itself?

Long grown used to regarding government as a hostile force to be placated and undermined, some immigrants had trouble understanding the concept of a true investigation. Others, eager to exhibit their urban smartness, dismissed it as a trick. Some did not grasp the distinction between the Lexow Committee and the Police Board. But when the leaders of garment worker unions discussed the cases at rallies and when the pushcart peddlers mulled over the matter during the course of a hot summer afternoon, bit by bit the Jews were groping toward an understanding of the way the city worked.

* * *

For them it was a lesson in how Americans thought. In addition to being a political system, a mode of living, and a secular faith, Democracy was also a way of thinking. The two Americans that immigrants knew about, if they knew about any, were Abraham Lincoln and Thomas Edison—men with a New World mentality alien to the thinking processes of Old World villages.

When President Lincoln said upon becoming president that he had no intention of freeing the slaves and two years later freed them, that was a consequence of democracy. Lincoln kept changing his intentions all the time, yet he was revered as a great democratic hero because he always kept his eye on the ball.

Thomas Edison also thought in the American style. He had studied as rigorously as any Talmudic scholar, but instead of examining eternal truths Edison studied change. Early in his career he vowed never to waste his time in the development of an unwanted invention, and before he developed the electric-light industry he studied it in terms of public acceptance. He was determined to assess its reception, in terms of its appeal in lower costs, cleanliness and safety; and he proceeded to develop the industry—its lights, motors, circuitry, dynamos, and central generating stations—after he concluded that the public could be persuaded to support the replacement of gaslighting by electrical light and power. Now incandescent lighting was changing the face of New York.

And Jimmy Martin thought like an American. Jimmy had been protecting his protégés on the police force for years, but he sensed that as of the summer of 1894, thanks to Parkhurst and the Lexow Committee, the atmosphere in the city had changed. Suddenly Jimmy Martin had been seized by an urge to ferret out police malefactors, and he wheeled about in the opposite direction. Newspaper editorials did not condemn his inconsistency or hypocrisy—they congratulated him on getting a job done.

As the immigrants tried to understand democratic thinking, another surprise came: the appointment of Michael Kerwin to the Police Board to replace John McClave, who resigned on the advice of his doctors.

Some Croker loyalists were irked that again the Mayor had chosen a Republican handpicked by Boss Platt. Reformers also disapproved of Kerwin, a shady figure who had been fired from various jobs for incompetence and plotting, and had been accused of swindling the Republican Campaign Committee when he headed an Irish-American political club. But for novices in American politics the startling thing about Kerwin was his attitude.

"I believe that the two Tammany Commissioners will work hard to carry out the laws," Kerwin said in taking office. "I don't doubt that Dr. Parkhurst has accomplished some good, but when you lay bare the vices of a city you are likely to hurt the morals of the public."

Kerwin was completely at ease with his Tammany Hall colleagues on the Police Board, and in fact would be welcomed if he chose to join the Wigwam, just as Silver Dollar Smith, once a Republican, had painlessly switched his allegiance to Tammany. The concept that rival political parties were virtually interchangeable was a surprise for immigrants; in Europe political parties were based on ideologies, while in America political parties were based on winning. Tammany speakers came to the social clubs of the Lower East Side to court Jews with jobs; so did the Republicans. One of Kerwin's chief duties as a Platt lieutenant was to solicit saloonkeepers with the argument that the Republicans could protect them more thoroughly than could Tammany. In America, political parties imitated each other's successes. If it worked for one party, the other party tried it too.

The immigrants had always thought in terms imposed by formulas, chiefly Orthodox Judaism or radical political philosophy. They had thought of purity as more important than power. American thought looked for its answers in the society, and the answers changed as the society changed.

Back in their Old World villages, the immigrants had heard about liberty and rule by the people, but only in America did they realize the implications— that this kind of government is mercurial, that democracy rides upon the back of change.

Some immigrants failed to understand that, and never would; but others picked up the rhythms of America, its infectious energy and its restless ways. Once they got the beat, they quickly picked up the melody and harmony.

* * *

The drama of the Police Board hearings produced a windfall for the press. Instead of slowing down in the doldrums of August, the hearings picked up additional excitement, and despite the punishing heat, reporters jammed into the hearing room day after day.

On a day early in the month, Superintendent Byrnes walked into Wellman's office and closed the door tight. They talked in private for a long time, and when the door opened again Byrnes walked out to his carriage, went back to Mulberry Street and filed charges against Big Bill Devery.

Again the city was rocked back on its heels. Captain Devery was regarded as the most invulnerable cop on the force. Only months earlier his trial had rallied the forces of Tammany and the Police Department in his defense, and after his acquittal he had been carried like a hero out of the courtroom on the shoulders of his fellow officers.

The Croker loyalists were angry that Big Bill was under fire. The Tammany Police Commissioners, after they got over their initial shock, were dismayed. But Byrnes and Wellman had pressed the issue, and now the Police Board would be forced to sit in judgment on Devery.

This unexpected turn of events proved too much for Captain Devery. He developed headaches, complained of insomnia, had the sensation that his head was about to burst, spoke anxiously and responded to questions with bizarre answers. On hearing the medical report the betting was that Big Bill would wiggle his way out of this one.

* * *

Quickly, Wellman marshaled his evidence against Big Bill. He had his gallery of cathouse operators—Henry Hoffman, Katie Shubert, Carl Werner, Charles Prien, Rhoda Sanford—safely hidden in crevices, some of them in the country, and he was using a dozen or so private detectives to keep them under surveillance.

He could not guarantee, however, that he could protect them for long from the police, so he wanted to bring them to the witness stand only once. With that consideration uppermost, the Police Commission decided to try several officers jointly, building the hearings around the witnesses rather than around the police officers. The accused would include Big Bill Devery; Captain Adam Cross, who had preceded Devery as precinct commander, and three ward detectives of the precinct. In effect, the newspapers said, Wellman was bringing the Eldridge Street precinct up on charges.

When the hearings began on August 10, Police Board President Jimmy Martin opened proceedings by calling out the name of Captain William S. Devery. A silence followed. Then, rising heavily, a lawyer made a motion for adjournment. He read affidavits from two physicians declaring that the captain was suffering from cerebral neurasthenia, in common parlance brain fever, and was unable to appear for trial. Then he read an affidavit of Annie Devery, declaring that she had found a notice of the pending trial thrust under the front door of their house, and had withheld the notice from her husband on the direction of the captain's personal physician who feared that it would inflict further mental damage upon the captain.

President Jimmy Martin announced that the hearings would continue despite defense objections. Since the Captain had refused to submit to a medical examination ordered by the Police Board, he had already provided grounds for dismissal, and around the precincts it was whispered that Devery would rather be dismissed than face a hearing.

After the first day of testimony newspaper readers surmised that this case would not end with a triumphal procession for Big Bill. When Wellman pulled his witnesses out of seclusion and plunked them on the stand, their testimony was unequivocal; the witnesses admitted much of what they had denied during the Lexow hearings and added fresh details to their accounts.

Late in the month the Board dismissed Captains Devery and Cross and three wardmen for offenses committed in the Eldridge Street precinct. The *Herald* congratulated the Police Board with a headline that said WELL DONE, and the *World* commented: "Whatever the motives of the Commissioners may have been, they have freed the city from the scandal and the danger of continuing guilty men in office."[1]

* * *

While the hearings continued at Police Headquarters the precinct was also facing scrutiny in criminal court. Jeremiah Levy, an Eldridge Street precinct wardman, was charged with taking bribes from a saloonkeeper who had been operating a concert hall without a license. The precinct detective's lawyer was Abraham Levy (no relation); and one of the jurors, unrelated to either of the other two Levys, was Raphael Levy.

After long deliberation, the jury remained hopelessly deadlocked, nine for conviction and three (including Raphael Levy) for acquittal.

When the immigrants realized that police officials were called to terms for their actions, the Americanization process for which Parkhurst hoped was underway. Having lived without justice for so long, Eastern European Jews were astonished to find justice not as a far-off event toward which the world was moving, but an immediate possibility.

In a small irony, one of the first cops to be caught in the snare of justice was a Jew. Near the end of the Lexow hearings testimony had been heard against a Jewish police captain; and sitting on the committee listening to the testimony was a Jewish State Senator. In most of the Eastern European countries, Jews did not practice law nor did they serve on juries, nor in legislatures, and there were no Jewish cops. The Russian code contained at least 650 special laws regarding the Jews; America had none. For Detective Levy, as for his fellow non-Jewish cops, America was truly the land of opportunity.

41

THE NEW
EMMA GOLDMAN

Emma Goldman was released from the Island in early August, and on a hot night soon thereafter she spoke at a Bowery theater. New York's Anarchists greeted their Queen with cheers.

"Here I am again," she announced, speaking English. "You see they couldn't take my life, even for speaking freely. It was the right of free speech that was prosecuted, not Emma Goldman. And now that I have been punished are we going to keep quiet because the police and our law officers tell us to? No! A thousand times no! Better death first! Our first fight, since it has been forced upon us, must be the fight for free speech. That sounds funny, in the land of the free, doesn't it? But that is the issue, and we must meet it."[1]

Her lover, Ed Brady, had come with her, and as they left Emma praised the spirit and grace of a young Italian woman who had spoken at the rally. Ed replied that her beauty, and her commitment to Anarchism, would quickly fade—that Latin women aged early, in body and spirit, particularly after they had children.

Emma responded that if she hoped to devote her life to Anarchism it would be best to avoid having children.

Nonsense, Ed responded—women are made for motherhood.

The glow that had surrounded their reunion faded instantly. They stopped walking as she turned angrily to face him. Emma asked whether he thought her a foolish babbler because she intended to work for her ideals instead of having children. She said that she thought that Ed had shared her ideas about the liberating power of love, but now it appeared that he wanted her only to clean his house and bear his children. Speaking in a blend of overwrought Jewish emotionalism and Russian loftiness, she said that she would fulfill her destiny to live by her ideals and to make her life deep and rich. Breaking away from him, she walked back to her apartment alone.

She was appalled. Never before had she heard such views from Ed. He had tried to talk her out of her campaigning in the Lower East Side the previous summer, but that argument was framed in terms of concern for her health. Now, to her horror, he was speaking in the accents of male possessiveness.

* * *

In order to formulate her new message of liberation, Goldman had to free herself from the grip of her two early mentors, Most and Berkman. Johann Most reveled in the destructiveness of Anarchism; despite her fits of rage, Emma Goldman was not a destroyer. Sasha Berkman raised the fist of self-immolation; despite her admiration for his dedication, Emma Goldman was not a fanatic.

She had come to see that Most, who took the podium to preach the upheaval of all economic arrangements, was in his domestic arrangements the quaintest of old-fashioned Germans. He wanted a woman to light his pipe, mop his floors and cook his meals. He had not even acknowledged that Emma might have opinions of her own, and the independence of her views had led to their breakup.

She had also come to realize how deeply Berkman's self-denial repelled her. He had self-righteously disapproved of her exhibitionistic dancing and her craving to lead parades. They had argued because he objected to buying flowers while a worker's family remained hungry. Like Most, he oppressed her sense of beauty and fulfillment, and she intended to blossom.

That summer Emma Goldman was fashioning her own brand of Anarchism, adapted from Thoreau. She believed that government lacked integrity and possessed less force than the power of a single determined individual. Laws were useless, for they had never made anyone more just. She said that it was a lie that the State was needed to control crime, for the State was the real criminal, stealing in the form of taxes, killing in the form of war and capital punishment, yet failing to deter crime. Had laws for mine safety ended mine accidents, or had they just opened up another opportunity for graft? Had laws against child labor ended the exploitation of children? Of course not. Laws were cooked up for another purpose altogether—to make sheep out of men.

When she arrived for dinner with Ed Brady and Justus Schwab at the upper West Side apartment of the Swintons, the old radical showed them his collection of curios. The resplendent samovar on the sideboard was a gift from Russian exiles, in recognition of Swinton's work on behalf of Russian freedom. French Communards who had escaped after the collapse of the Paris Commune of 1871 had sent an exquisite set of Sevres. Hungarian separatists had sent peasant embroidery, and other tokens and gifts of appreciation adorned the home of the great libertarian. Emma was impressed; she had never seen a place so simply yet so beautifully furnished.

Since they had visited her on the Island, Emma had drawn closer to the Swintons. As serious Americans, she regarded them as rarities. With them she had discussed other serious Americans, like Emerson, who regarded all government as tyranny, and Jefferson, who called government a necessary evil. From them she had learned of American experiments in communal living.

Swinton took issue with the article that she had written in the *World* about conditions in the penitentiary. Emma had assailed a matron for taking rations from starved white women and giving them as extras to a group of black women who were her pet prisoners. Swinton concluded that Goldman was exhibiting the standard white prejudices. Goldman protested that she would have complained just as loudly if black women had been robbed of their rations to give to white women. "But you should not have emphasized this partiality," Swinton said. "We white people have committed so many crimes against the Negro that no amount of extra kindness can atone for them. The matron is no doubt a beast, but I forgive her much for her sympathy with the poor Negro prisoners."

"But she was not moved by such considerations!" Goldman said. "She was kind because she could use them in every despicable way."

During dinner, Swinton spoke of the part that Americans had played in trying to save the Haymarket Anarchists from the gallows. He talked about Americans who had courageously stood for unpopular causes. "The evening with the Swintons showed me a new angle of my adopted country," she later wrote. "John Swinton made me see that Americans, once aroused, were as capable of idealism and sacrifice as my Russian heroes and heroines."

On their way back downtown she told Ed and Justus that she would no longer speak in Yiddish, that language of gossips in which lofty thoughts could hardly be expressed. She had learned English well enough to devote all her efforts to winning over the only group that could bring about real social change—the Americans.

* * *

Ed thought that Emma would fulfill herself more completely if she took up a vocation and balanced her interest in radical ideas with a life as his wife and mother of his children. He said that he was not trying to dominate her, but her impetuous nature made him fear for her safety. He hoped that motherhood might soften her ardor.

Emma responded that she had decided not to have children. She had a condition that would make childbirth dangerous. Furthermore, she had suffered an abusive childhood, and worried about the legions of unwanted waifs already in the world. She continued to hope that Ed could accept her right to a life of her own.

One aspect of personal growth, in her view, was "free love." Goldman insisted that a union between a man and a woman should be regarded as provisional and should be ended when it became unsatisfactory. Lovers should not own each other and should set and live by their own rules rather than to seek the sanction of society in formal marriage.

The issues between Emma and Ed remained unresolved, but they decided to live together in a Greenwich Village flat. Emma commandeered a room for her private use, with a desk and a couch for sleeping. A steady stream of visitors came to the apartment, where she spoke of "freedom, the right to self-expression, everybody's right to beautiful, radiant things."[2] They were a new circle of followers, since many of her old allies took issue with her new causes; some found her flamboyant, self-indulgent, and not committed to issues of the working people.

Completely American in her individualism, she was European in her contempt for American styles and rhythms. Where some saw an America that was ever-changing and would absorb anything, Emma Goldman saw a lack of principles, a hollow center, a craven compromise. Where some saw democracy, she saw pandering to the masses.

At the age of twenty-five, this was the place to which Emma Goldman had progressed. She had thought herself in complete control of her life, but the city and the nation, New York and America, had changed her circuitry. In two years of rapid transformation the city had changed, Parkhurst had changed, the prostitutes had changed, and Emma Goldman had been swept along in the current.

She had become a new being with a vision of unlimited possibilities of self-realization—a vision irrelevant to the immigrants packed into the back halls of downtown saloons, but one that excited American parlor radicals.

42

COMMITMENTS

While the immigrants of the Lower East Side followed the Police Board hearings, another investigation was going on out of the public view.

No records exist to show the course of investigation, but timing suggests that Goff, Dennett, and the Parkhurst agents were developing the evidence during the summer, following the trail of a *World* article about an unnamed sergeant who had paid a bribe to be promoted to captain.

Eventually Goff and his aides came up with more: that the bribe amounted to $15,000, that the money had been raised by a group of saloonkeepers, that it had happened late in 1891 in the Eldridge Street precinct, and that the cop in question was Tim Creeden.

Many of the Jews who lived in the precinct were acquainted with Creeden, who had been desk sergeant at the Eldridge Street station house. He had bright blue eyes, a moustache and a full head of snow-white hair. Spry and trim, tall and well-knit, he cut a fine figure. And Timothy Creeden was a gentlemanly sort. One of his sons was a lawyer, another was studying in Rome for the priesthood, and he had two more in colleges in the city, at New York University and St. Francis Xavier College. Creeden's four daughters were still living at home.

At the age of thirteen young Tim had come over from Ireland, where some of his kin were engaged in revolutionary struggle, and found work in a factory in Manhattan. He belonged to a volunteer fire company, and one night the wheel of a fire engine ran over him, crushing his right leg. After two months in the hospital he walked out on crutches and as soon as possible he enlisted in the Union Army. He served in twenty-three battles in the Civil War, and on October 13, 1863, at Second Manassas, a bullet wounded him in his left shoulder. Left on the

Captain Timothy J. Creeden

battlefield to die, he crawled thirteen miles along the railroad line to Manassas Junction where he was found. He spent months in a hospital, and after his recovery he joined the Police Department. Dutiful service had earned five gold service stripes for his sleeve, but Creeden was so mannerly and unwilling to seize advantages that after twenty-seven years on the force he was still a desk sergeant.

For many years he had been passed up for a captaincy because he did not stand in with the right people. When he first took the Civil Service examination for Captain, he was advised that he would get the promotion only by paying for it. The price then was $6,000 and he rejected the proposition outright.

But his hair grew whiter and his financial needs greater, while others less qualified than he grew rich in fat precincts. Time and temptation wore away his resolve.

One day in the waning year of 1891, just before the Sage explosion, Creeden stepped through the swinging doors of a dark and uninviting Forsyth Street saloon. Oversized beer casks and liquor barrels crowded much of the floor space of the front room, and a fringe of customers of the lower social orders stood drinking glumly at the bar. He had come to see his friend, Barney Rourke, the political kingpin of the district.

Rourke rarely mingled out front with the gaptoothed customers whose coins filled his coffers, but was usually elsewhere in the building, with his ear cocked to make sure that his bartender was regularly ringing the cash register. On this day the stocky little Irish saloonkeeper was probably sitting in a back room, thrashing out various political affairs with a few henchmen, when the sergeant strode up and asked for private audience with his friend.

If that were the case, the two would have adjourned to Rourke's private sitting room with the Brussels carpet, where the big deals were made. There Sergeant Creeden explained the purpose of his visit. He had an opportunity to be promoted to Captain. The appointment would come from Police Commissioner Voorhis. But the price was too high for him—$12,000.

Rourke nodded and said he could help.

Within a few days Rourke called together a group of saloonkeepers that included his protégés Silver Dollar Smith and Dry Dollar Sullivan. They were willing to back Creeden. Yet as Rourke worked on the fundraising the terms of the agreement were changed.

These events took place at a time when Tammany Hall had not yet completely won control of "the Thoid." The Wigwam was contending against an assortment of political freebooters, including the Voorhis Democrats, an anti-Tammany Democratic club. Its leader, John Voorhis, commanded considerable patronage as a Police Commissioner.

Before he went to Rourke, Sergeant Creeden had been to see the Voorhis faction about being sponsored for a promotion. He had not dealt directly with Police Commissioner Voorhis; that was not the way these things were done. He had contacted a political broker of the district, John Reppenhagen, a dwarfish saloonkeeper who served as a district captain for Voorhis, and was the man to see about police appointments and promotions coming through Voorhis. After talking with the beetle-browed Reppenhagen at his Broome Street saloon, Creeden thought that he had a deal.

A few days after his talk with Rourke, the silver-haired officer was on desk duty at the Eldridge Street precinct station when he looked up to find the strange Reppenhagen, barely five feet tall, on the other side of the desk. Pale green eyes peered at Creeden from beneath a low forehead. Sidling closer, the little saloonkeeper whispered in a German accent that another sergeant had also offered $12,000 for the promotion and that if Creeden wanted to outbid his competitor the new price was $15,000.

After thinking it over for a day or so, Creeden asked if he could be guaranteed assignment to the Eldridge Street precinct. When Reppenhagen agreed to this stipulation, Creeden said that he would "have to consult my friends again, and lay the new proposition before them, and they would decide it." Then Creeden went back to Rourke, who agreed to raise the higher figure.

Creeden's backers met in Rourke's saloon, subscribed $15,000, and turned the sum over to one of their number who in early January of 1892 placed the money in a bank. The next day the bankbook was shown to Reppenhagen. A week later Creeden was appointed Captain.

But Creeden was sent to the Old Slip precinct—an assignment so unpromising that his creditors were concerned that he might not be able to raise the money to repay them. The new captain felt that he had been cheated out of the ripest plum in the city, but told Rourke "that I would have to stand the loss if there was any difference in the precincts." In a hastily convened meeting, the subscribers acceded to Creeden's wishes, and the check was turned over to Reppenhagen. By the summer of 1894 the loan had been repaid in full.

* * *

A second story was also unfolding that summer. Just a few days after the theater rally for the Anarchist Diva, about forty men and women were holding a quarrelsome session in the office of the architectural firm of Thorp & Knowles on West Twenty-fourth Street. The moving force of the meeting was Mary Sallade, who owned a building on the street. She operated a dressmaking shop on the ground floor and lived in one of the upstairs apartments, renting others to tenants. The strong-minded Mrs. Sallade aimed to rid the block of prostitutes.

Mrs. Cox, who kept a boarding house across the street, was indignant to hear her tenants called such names. She called them "theatrical people of the first water," and threatened to sue Mrs. Sallade for slander.

W.H. Tobin, a lawyer who represented another boardinghouse owner, said his client, a widow with young children, sympathized with Mrs. Sallade's campaign to clean up the block, but that this building was the widow's only source of revenue. "We tried to rent for a long time to decent people, but no one would take the house," he said. "It is impossible to get respectable people so long as the police refuse their cooperation in keeping the neighborhood clean. My client can't afford to let it remain vacant."

Another lawyer representing property owners admitted that some tenants were damaged goods. "But the notoriety arising from Mrs. Sallade's crusade has completely ruined this block for residence purposes," he said. "Even if every shady person in the block were to be cleared out tonight no respectable tenants could be induced to move in."

Mrs. Sallade, a tall and commanding woman in her mid-fifties, responded that the condition of the neighborhood had become unendurable, even Captain Schmittberger admitting that there were not many houses in the block "in which some man was not keeping a woman, or some woman a man." She said that drunken men made obscene propositions to her as she walked along her own block and that sometimes carousing men and women rang her bell by mistake.

Despite the protests of Mrs. Cox, by the time the meeting ended Mrs. Sallade had founded the West Twenty-fourth Street Property Owners Protective Association, and the Parkhurst forces had a new ally.

Through the summer she kept the issue alive. In her meetings with property owners and journalists she said that she had received no cooperation from officials—that Justice Hogan had ducked out on her when she tried to talk with him, and that Captain Schmittberger apparently thought she could be guyed by his pretenses of sympathy for her case.

She worked closely with Parkhurst agents obtaining evidence, on one occasion checking into a boarding house with Agent John Lemmon and ordering alcoholic drinks in their room before leaving. She also appeared as a witness in Police Court against a prostitute arrested as a result of Lemmon's investigations.

Mrs. Sallade admitted that she had linked up with the Parkhurst Society and the City Vigilance League out of desperation, for she made it a rule to steer clear of politics. With a laugh the thrice-divorced matron disclaimed newspaper accounts that described her as "a woman Parkhurst," and said she had no interest in improving anyone's morals. Mrs. Sallade explained that she had paid $30,000 for the building five years earlier, and had been disappointed to see that while real estate had shot up in other parts of the city, hers had not gained any value. "I'm interested solely in improving the value of my property," she said.

* * *

Through that summer changes sped past in the lives of the immigrant Jews. As steerage passengers they had been awed by the prospect of the fabulous country, and once they had arrived America had engraved itself upon them in a thousand ways—by means of its protean nature, its diversions, even by means of its

Yiddish periodicals, a prized feature of life in the New World that had been forbidden under Czarist rule.

America had fastened a stronger hold on them in a few years than had Mother Russia over several centuries. They had come to live in a dynamic society and the world that they had left behind seemed insipid and static.

They began to see that freedom and democracy were, like everything else in this country, in flux and unfinished. They had left a place where government was in the hands of a shadowy coterie and had found a government conducted in the open. The Lexow and Police Board hearings showed them the workings of the American system of checks and balances, of specific and limited power. And they understood—strident orators of the United Hebrew Trade Unions proclaimed it to them—that here it was the people who brought about changes. Their leaders reminded them that they were fashioning a new life not through the generosity of the owners of the garment factories but through their own collective efforts.

But they had not found paradise. Their journey had exposed them again to prejudice, injustice and oppression; yet that had only made their new lives deeper and more significant.

* * *

Something was expected of the Jews—a sign of commitment to their new land— and, as they had in the case of the pushcart peddlers, the Jews continued to show themselves equal to that demand. One night the City Vigilance League promoted a rally in support of the Kievents, the Jewish couple falsely accused and convicted of robbery in their saloon. As Rebecca Kievent completed her sentence, Jews of the Lower East Side called for her husband's release, and a petition was circulated asking for a pardon for the saloonkeeper.

Little has been preserved of what was said at that rally, but Frank Moss wrote that fervent speeches were made about the love of liberty. Speakers urged the audience to sign the petition and to defy the spies of the Essex Market Courthouse bail-bond gang that were planted among them.

Moss complimented them "upon their rare exhibition of bravery—a bravery which had not been equaled at that time in any part of the city." They seemed at that moment to be truer Americans than were the merchants who paid blackmail without protest and could not be persuaded to supply evidence against the blue-coats who had shaken them down. Yet these bearded and exotic men, only slightly acquainted with democracy, had risked their heads, their fortunes, and their sacred honor to protest injustice.

* * *

At summer's end, on Ridge Street near Broome, another family now operated what had been Mrs. Urchittel's candy store. Evenings under the streetlights the children would push their noses against the window to see the glittering glass jars filled with various kinds of bright candies—jujubes, red and black licorice sticks, bull's eyes, peppermints. Life went on as if the earth had swallowed up Caela Urchittel.

All summer she haunted the offices of the Parkhurst Society. Dressed in rags and perpetually overcome by grief, she spoke in Yiddish and always closed with the refrain, "Mine shildren! Mine shildren!"

"I could not understand her," Moss said, "and, supposing her to be one of the cranks that were so persistent at that time, tried to avoid her." Shaking with sorrow, and speaking no English, she could not make herself coherent to the trustee of the Parkhurst Society. But she continued to show up. One day Moss found that he could not get past her in the hall, and she babbled words that he did not understand. Then she fell to her knees, kissed his hand, and wet it with her tears. He still did not know what she was saying but was touched by her anguish. As he worked on through the day he touched his hand where she had kissed it, and he asked the Parkhurst agents to have a Yiddish interpreter present the next day.

The next morning Caela Urchittel was brought into the office and sat in a chair while an interpreter translated what she said and a stenographer took it down. "It was too frightful to believe," Moss said. "I was tempted to throw the translation away." But there was something about the woman; he felt as if her lips and tears had burned his hand; and he had Parkhurst agents investigate the story.

When she owned a candy store on the Lower East Side in the Eldridge Street precinct Mrs. Urchittel had been victimized by the police, who had accused her falsely of being a prostitute.

The night that they arrested her they led her about the streets for three hours, from midnight until three in the morning, insisting that she give them money or they would send her to jail and take her children from her. They accused her of having money hidden in her stocking. In desperation she sat at the corner of Essex and Rivington and took off her stocking and showed them that she had no money in it. "Still the officer persisted," Moss said. "He understood the financial instincts of the race. She had twenty-five dollars in her bosom, which she finally gave him, and he divided the money with Hochstim. They sent her home with a warning to prepare fifty dollars."

When she failed to come up with more money the following day she was arrested, and a case was made against her. They coached two police stoolpigeons to testify that they had had sex with her for pocket change. Despite her protestations and the testimony of a citizen that one of the lads had offered to renege on his testimony for fifty dollars, the court convicted her. The Special Sessions Justices—a Tammany trinity of Joseph Koch, Hogan and Divver—could not or would not see through the false accusations of tainted witnesses. Unable to pay the fine imposed, she was sent to the Tombs. Her home was broken up and her good name trampled in the dust. Her brother succeeded in selling the store for sixty-five dollars and paid the fine, so that she was released after serving some time in the Tombs. When she was discharged she found her children gone. She had no idea what had happened to them, but she began to search for them.

Having classified her as an unfit mother, the Society for the Prevention of Cruelty to Children had whisked her children away. Had Mrs. Urchittel spoken acceptable English, had she known how to navigate through American institutions, she might have located them quickly, but she was inarticulate in English and inexperienced in American ways. Nevertheless she eventually traced them to the Orphan Asylum at 151st Street and 10th Avenue. Unaware of legal niceties, she begged the people there to hand over her children, but they paid no attention to her. "None would hear me," she told Moss. "Grieved to the depths of my heart, seeing myself bereaved of my dear children, I fell sick, and laid six months in the Sixty-Sixth Street Hospital, and had to undergo a great operation." After leaving the hospital she made further vain attempts to get the children back. Then she went to the offices of the Society for the Prevention of Crime in search of Dr. Parkhurst, the scourge of police corruption. After many attempts she managed to get through to Moss. As summer ended the Society's agents were chasing the facts while Moss was trying to get Mrs. Urchittel's children back.

* * *

Through the summer Goff and Moss worked on behind the scenes.

In evaluating which testimony would prove the most telling, they believed they had in Caela Urchittel a witness who took the case against the police beyond corruption into police oppression and savagery. They had to consider timing, pacing, and public impact, for the Lexow Committee was ready to reconvene in a city about to have a mayoral election. If the evidence were skillfully presented and the stories convincingly told, if the hearings were well-covered, if the forces of reform could be corralled into a united effort; if, in other words, everything came together, the days ahead held the promise of an exciting campaign in which Tammany Hall faced the trouncing of its life. The curtain was about to go back up, and gentlemen were advised to hold onto their hats, for the high kicking was ready to start.

VIII

INSPIRED SOLDIERY

Fall 1894

43

"HOW FARES
THE CITY?"

*Everything that has been done in the way of reclaiming the
world has been done by inspired soldiery.*

—Parkhurst, *My Forty Years in New York*

On the night of September 6 the steamer bringing Charles and Nellie
Parkhurst back to New York from their summer-long vacation docked in
Quarantine. The ship-news reporters found him, as ever, cheerfully theatrical.
He said he had no ambition to run for mayor, but hoped that he could add his
mite to a united campaign of anti-Tammany forces lined up behind a single
standard-bearer.

On the same night a group of reform-minded gents were convening at Madison Square Garden with exactly that purpose in mind. At this initial meeting they
did not suggest candidates for office, but organized and chose officers as the
Committee of Seventy. Their collective title was nostalgic, for a group of reformers had closed ranks two decades earlier to battle Boss Tweed under the same
name. And, as they had twenty years earlier—for some of these brokers, bankers,
importers and retail merchants were veterans of the earlier anti-Tammany campaign—they filled the night with condemnation of high tax rates and nepotism.
"When Tweed was convicted we thought Tammany was dead," one said, "but
that was a mistake. We will do better this time."[1]

Under the same silvery moon, Goff and Moss gathered material for the reopening of the Lexow hearings. Moss was trying to determine the identities of
the two policemen who had bedeviled Caela Urchittel on an earlier frightful
night in the Lower East Side.

And with the same undertone of a coming confrontation, neighborhood organizations, typified by Mary Sallade's West Twenty-fourth Street Association, were burgeoning block by block up the east side and west side.

Hammering pianos, chiming clocks, snatches of song, the cackle of nighthags, horseshoes and iron-rimmed wheels ringing on cobblestones, a fire-bell summoning a hose company to a blaze—all the sounds of a city that stayed up late called the hastening dawn to make it snappy, New Yorkers had no time to waste on slow sunrises.

* * *

The pastor began his campaign the next morning. When and how he got together with his fellow trustees of the Society for the Prevention of Crime is unrecorded but, given his sense of urgency, it seems likely that it occurred forthwith, in his gaslit study, perhaps as the servants unpacked the trunks and Nellie Parkhurst began looking through the mail in the parlor. In that case the scene might be something like this: the two trustees, balding Frank Moss and graying Thaddeus Kenneson, would exchange familiar greetings with the maid. There would be the clopping of shoes on the stairs, hails of greeting and handshakes for the returned traveler as they entered his study, perhaps some chuckles over the perils of brain fever. Then Parkhurst would bring them quickly to brass tacks. "And now, good friends," he would declaim in his Elizabethan-drama style, "what news bring you? How fares the city?"

The next sound would be their briefcases snapping open, as they dug out the files that he would use in the culminating stage of his campaign.

Thus armed, Parkhurst plunged immediately into the jangle of a crowded agenda, attending a mind-numbing series of meetings, and answering, with secretarial help, one hundred letters a day. He typed up rapid-fire commentaries on passing events, including a regular column for a daily newspaper, and read a half-dozen newspapers every day. He restricted himself to three to five speeches a week. While riding this whirligig he found the time to minister to his flock with such attentive care that there is not on record a single protest from a congregant that he was devoting too much of his time to public matters and not enough to his pastoral duties. The pace never told on him, and to each demand he presented himself at his highest pitch of responsiveness. Some may have suspected that he was wearing one of those electrical belts advertised in magazines, the ones that were supposed to invigorate a man by passing an electrical current through him. He attributed his energy to his annual three-month vacation, which kept him going for the other nine months. Whatever the source, he thrived on a merciless schedule.

Parkhurst's optimism was buoyed by the growing number of neighborhood associations that were trying to compel the police to enforce the law. On East Thirteenth Street petitions were being circulated to revoke the license of the infamous Hotel Europe. Other campaigns had begun on a block of West Seventeenth Street and on West Thirty-ninth Street between Seventh and Eighth Avenues. The City Vigilance League, which Parkhurst had formed for just such a purpose, was offering help to these grassroots movements. When Parkhurst read the clippings about these organizations it could not escape his notice that women were leading most of them, and he took particular interest in the travail of Kate Monahan.

Mrs. Monahan lived on West Seventeenth Street, next to a boarding house rented to prostitutes. When she first began to admonish the police to do something about the vice on her block, some of them humored her, others argued with her, and one just walked away while she was speaking. When Mrs. Monahan took her case to Police Inspector McAvoy and to Captain Donahue, the precinct commander, they took offense at her entreaties. "I can't make the police do their duty," she said. "I've been outraged and insulted by these disreputable characters who live at Mrs. Giles' boarding house, and duped, deceived, laughed at and insulted by the police." She added that women sat in the back yard smoking cigarettes and that from time to time beaten bloody men were thrown out of

Kate Monahan
"I Hope There Won't Be Any Trouble."

the building. The noisy house kept her own lodgers awake. By repeated protest she had managed to pester the cops into bringing Madame Giles to police court.

"The night before the hearing Mrs. Giles came in front of my house and began to swing the gate back and forth violently," Mrs. Monahan said. "When I came to the window she began to yell out taunts. 'So I'm to be summoned to court tomorrow!' she screamed, laughing in a most aggravating way. 'Oh, yes, I'm to be sent to prison. Oh, yes, I'm to go to Sing Sing for ten years!'"

The next day Kate Monahan discovered why she had been mocked with such assurance. She had been directed to appear at court at half past ten. She was there by ten, but the gateman would not let her approach the desk until her case was called.

Hour after hour Mrs. Monahan sat there, watching the mill of justice grind slowly and looking around for Mrs. Giles. Finally, after court was adjourned for the day, she was permitted to approach Justice Hogan.

"You are too late, madam," he said. "You were not present when the case was called, and I had to dismiss Mrs. Giles."

"Justice Hogan!" the woman exclaimed, shaking her finger in his face, "I was here half an hour before the appointed time. Justice Hogan, you have deceived me." Hogan stood up and fled to his chamber, while court attendants hustled her out to the street.

That evening the Giles boarders celebrated. They threw lobster shells, wine bottles, whiskey bottles, soiled underwear and a mattress into Kate Monahan's back yard, keeping up the racket until dawn.

But that was not the end of it. On another September night soon thereafter Parkhurst walked over to a rally at the Eighteenth Street Methodist Episcopal Church. When he arrived, its pastor was speaking from the pulpit. Stopping as the listeners burst into applause for the new arrival, Rev. Dr. John Wilson said that Parkhurst had long been one of his heroes, but that he had also come to admire a heroine of his Chelsea neighborhood—Kate Monahan.

Because she was a poor woman and lacked schooling, said the tall fiery Wilson, the police assumed that she could be scared by a show of temper or jayed by a pretense of concern. Inspector McAvoy had ordered her out of his office, and Captain Donahue had tried to paint her as "touched with religion," not quite right in the head. But this fearless lady had stood fast in the face of ridicule and bullying. She had been working unceasingly to end the nightly abomination of her neighborhood, and had even chased some of the bad women out. A woman who had been operating a disorderly house had called on Mrs. Monahan and asked her to let up. She whined that she could not support her family in any other way and had trouble raising the money to pay the police. "Why do you want to squeeze me to the wall?" she cried despairingly. "Don't you know that every time you complain they raise the ante on me?" Mrs. Monahan said she did not want to make anyone's life any harder, but that the madame was raising her children in a house of sin.

Pastor Wilson read letters he had sent to Inspector McAvoy and Captain Donahue inviting them to speak in their own behalf. "If either of these gentlemen is present he will please come forward," the pastor inquired. No response came.

Most cops, Wilson said, were too honest to buy promotions, too noble to offer protection to thieves, gamblers and madames for part of the swag. "There is a wolf police, however, and the signs are that the animal has gotten loose in the sixteenth precinct, and we are here to see what we are going to do about it."

Wilson received strong applause, and then Parkhurst was welcomed as a conquering hero. Quickly he launched into an acerbic critique of a new report by Byrnes that said prostitution and gambling had been curtailed in the city, but the Sunday closing laws were being violated as blithely as ever.

"Byrnes has, with lavish and generous hand, distributed the responsibility for police dereliction among the entire force, with the exception of the Superintendent himself," he said. Yet the man headed a Department "which has been demonstrated as thoroughly and intrinsically rotten." Given such a shoddy record, he asked, could Byrnes exempt himself?

It was one of those nights in which Parkhurst slipped into the humorous mode—a condition that befell him against his will, since laughter from the audience annoyed him, and sometimes he would even admonish the spectators for their levity, yet would continue to put his case in an amusing way.

"Mr. Byrnes has said that it is impossible to enforce the law against opening saloons on Sunday," he said. "Well, I don't know. It hasn't been tried yet." Everyone laughed at the note of comic earnest. "If the edict were to proceed from Mulberry Street on Saturday, and it were known that the edict was backed by the entire power of this municipality, there wouldn't be a side or front door open on the following Sabbath. The police of this city can do all they try to do. I want to see them try."

His bitterness against the police had grown. None had stepped forward at this moment of crisis, and he despised their cowardice. He kept that feeling unexpressed, but when Wilson spoke of the many good cops on the force Parkhurst did not join in the praise.

* * *

Over at the courthouse, the Lexow hearings resumed to consuming public interest. Waiting crowds carried on excitedly about the prospect of watching Goff roast a cop on the griddle. For the few who got in, it was the best show in town.

Despite his daunting timetable, Parkhurst tried to stop by every day to take in part of the testimony. Seats were more in demand than ever, but a space at a special table was held in reserve for Parkhurst. One day in early September he slipped in to hear the testimony of Carl Werner, back for a return visit.

The former brothelkeeper said the police had been dogging his footsteps ever since that June day that he had taken the stand to admit paying protection to Captain Devery.

Everyone below the line expected the police to exact punishment from Lexow witnesses for daring to testify. Several male witnesses who had been haphazard in their marital support found themselves explaining to Civil Justices why they had fallen behind in their payments. Some of the saloonkeepers who had testified about police corruption were arrested for excise violations while on every side the Sunday commerce of other saloonkeepers remained untroubled. Werner was among those who had felt the pressure of strict law enforcement.

After his first Lexow appearance, Werner had opened a saloon under an assumed name in another precinct. The police nevertheless found him, and raided his place one Sunday for excise violations. Two days later he was charged with attempted bribery of the arresting officer, Patrolman Henry Cohen, and soon found himself locked up for a long stay. As Parkhurst entered the Lexow hearing room, Werner was denying to the committee that he had tried to bribe anyone.

"I got the necessary bail and was out two days when two detectives came to me and told me I had been surrendered by my bondsman," he testified. "I was told that the police made it too hot for the man who went on my bond." When his friends found other bondsmen for him, the police scared them off as well, and for the past month Werner had been shut up in The Tombs.

"Is it your object, Mr. Goff, to prove interference with our witness?" Senator Lexow asked.

"That's just it," Goff said, "interference and intimidation."

Patrolman Cohen was called to the stand and asked what happened when he saw Werner in the courthouse.

"Werner came up to me and slipped something in my hand," the cop said. "He had told me the day before that he wanted me to be easy in testifying against his barkeeper."

All the spectators, including Parkhurst, listened intently. Growing visibly uneasy at the prospect of facing off against Goff, the witness testified that he felt something in his hand, then opened it up to find a five-dollar bill.

"Now, officer, stand up and show your hand," Goff said. "I want to see just how this was done."

The policeman stood up as requested and showed how he had been standing at the time.

"Ah," said Goff, "I see that your right hand extends backward, and while the fingers of your left hand remain tightly closed those of your right hand are opened as if expecting something. Is this from force of habit?"

Howls of laughter broke out. The policeman looked confused, but he stood in place as he had been instructed.

"Now, sir," Goff continued, "as soon as you felt a soft substance falling into your right hand your fingers closed upon it mechanically, as it were?"

"Yes, sir."

This time even Parkhurst joined in the laughter.

The cop was then put through another demonstration. Jerome handed Goff a five-dollar bill, who placed it in the policeman's hand. By what appeared to be reflex the fingers closed upon the money, and once again the spectators howled. The bill was handed back to Jerome.

"The first time on record a five-dollar bill ever came back from a policeman," Senator Bradley said.

After a week of Lexow sessions, the picture in Goff's office had been adorned with three more red seals on the foreheads of police captains, and a half-dozen wardmen had been slapped with the tarbrush. Senator Lexow praised Goff for the glorious curtain-raiser he had presented.

44

A VOLATILE BREW

Tammany Hall owed its comeback in politics after the death of Tweed to its protection of immigrants, ordinary downtown blokes, and saloonkeepers. With the election campaign ready to begin, the Wigwam found itself suddenly under attack as the oppressor of all three of its core constituencies.

The saloonkeepers were fuming because Byrnes had resumed the practice that Tammany's Police Commissioners had ordered him to halt two years earlier—sending out plainclothes cops to make arrests for Sunday sales of alcoholic beverages. On the first Monday after Byrnes' directive went into effect, Police Justices were faced with 240 Sunday sales arrests, the highest total in the city's history. By the time the first bundle of afternoon newspapers was tossed out of the delivery wagon, the Retail Liquor Dealers Association, which had paid good money to the campaign chest of Tammany Hall to avoid such problems, was attacking Byrnes vigorously.

Condemning his methods as tyrannical and "un-American," they charged that plainclothes "spying" inevitably led to police blackmail. Speaking for the industry, Morris Tekulsky suggested that if Byrnes liked to employ spies, he ought to try them on vice operations. Had Byrnes applied the same zeal to suppressing dives, gambling and prostitution that he showed for harassing honest liquor dealers, Tekulsky said, New York would not be staring at "the spectacle of a police force reeking with extortion, oppression and blackmail." His attack signaled that Tammany ought not to count on the powerful saloonkeeper voting bloc in the coming election.

* * *

At every session of the Lexow hearings, the ordinary downtown blokes were re-minded that the Wigwam had never attempted to curb the police. On October 2, Goff laid before them a panorama of excesses that police brutality had reached in a Tammany administration.

That morning the benches were packed with uniformed police officers, all present under the duress of subpoena. As Goff spoke to the committee mem-bers, he turned to glare at the assembled cops. "The air of the trial room at Po-lice Headquarters is blue with perjury," he charged, with stoolpigeons corrobo-rating the lies of the cops for whom they worked. Over the preceding three years, he noted, only one cop had been dismissed from the force for assault upon a citizen. He laid the blame at the feet of the Police Commissioners for their inat-tention to police violence. The police had no reason to fear any consequences for their brutality except for an occasional small fine.

Ninety cops, each of whom had been convicted of assault, listened as Goff cited particulars. At first they reacted sheepishly as Goff called them one by one to the stand and withered them with his sarcastic contempt. They slinked away from the witness chair with red faces as he elaborated on how they had beaten victims—a newsboy, a Civil War veteran, a young girl—and then terrorized the families of the victims into dropping charges. But as the day wore on their au-dacity returned. It began with the testimony of a wagon driver who walked to the stand with his head swathed in bandages. When Goff asked whether he had re-cently had an experience with the police, the cops roared with delight. They were further amused by a story of how a policeman threatened to shoot a street-car conductor when asked to pay the fare. And they found hilarious a police-man's grinning description of how he had pulled a prostitute by the hair, thrown her to the floor, and held a loaded revolver against her head. Chairman Lexow pounded his gavel, but they laughed at that too, and in defiance they stamped their feet, sending a dust cloud through the courtroom.

The committee members sat, flabbergasted, until Lexow's tenor voice cut through the uproar. "This is no laughing matter!" he said, pounding the gavel again. Over the next few days, comments and letters in the press showed that the common people of the city—the ones whose heads were bloodied—had heard everything.

* * *

As for Tammany protection of immigrants, the case of Caela Urchittel had blown up in the faces of the cops and their Tammany supporters. After her day on the stand editors scrambled for all the information they could get about the immi-grant woman who had gone to jail and lost her children as the result of police perjury. Senator O'Connor said that the restoration of her good name in itself made the Senate investigation worthwhile. "If this was a sample of the method of treatment accorded to people in that condition by the police of this city," Lexow said in a letter to Moss, "they could not be found fault with for becoming anarchists." And Senator Bradley told reporters: "This is the most important case thus far. We should have the names of those detectives."

Moss had worked out the chronology of Mrs. Urchittel's nightmarish ordeal, the three hours during which she was interrogated first at one precinct station and then another. He believed that the two precinct stations were Delancey Street and Eldridge Street.

He told reporters that the case had sped through the courts with suspicious haste, that she had been convicted on the evidence of two stoolpigeons who were always on call to testify to whatever the police asked of them, and that he was still working on the identities of the police who were responsible.

Reporters found Mrs. Urchittel in a tenement on Orchard Street—a dark hole with hardly a stick of furniture. She had tried to brighten it in the hope that her children would be returned to her, but they would have to sit on old boxes, sleep on heaps of straw, and their table would consist of boards propped across a crate. They would have no place to wash, and the few clothes they owned would hang on nails in the walls. Their roof leaked and soon their broken windows would let in the wintry blasts. They would have to live among prostitutes and thieves, wife-beaters and drunkards. All around them neighbors would sicken and die of tuberculosis, cholera, and typhus. Nevertheless with her children back in her home it would be a paradise.

She tried to explain that she had gone to the shelter to visit her children but had been barred from seeing them. Checking with the Hebrew Sheltering Guardian Society, the reporters learned that she had gone to the facility on a non-visiting day.

Moss was helping her to get her children back, but he said that the Society for the Prevention of Cruelty to Children was putting up resistance. He said that the woman was trying to eke out a living by selling candy on Broadway and was struggling to establish a home and to convince the authorities to release her children to her. On the day after her appearance at the hearings, he added, two men stopped at her stand and threatened, in Yiddish, that if she testified any further against Max Hochstim she would go to prison for five years.

* * *

To saloonkeepers, ordinary blokes, and immigrants, Tammany had taken on the aspect of an oppressor of the people. And Tammany knew just who deserved the blame for bringing about this disaster. For two years Parkhurst had been driving a wedge between Tammany and its constituencies. Now he was preparing to go on the campaign trail, his pockets stuffed with notes and affidavits, as enemy of the police and champion of the people. He was ready to tell of a pushcart peddler who after testifying against the police had been hounded from one precinct to another until he was arrested for obstructing the sidewalk. He would tell about an old woman who set up a newspaper stand outside an empty store and was badgered by a cop for five dollars, arrested when she would not pay it, and charged with a trumped-up complaint. These and countless other instances, he said, betrayed the inhumanity of the police and behind them the heartlessness of Tammany Hall.

Speaking at a neighborhood association meeting, the pastor told the story of Jared Flagg, who was being blamed for the prostitution that infested a city block in Chelsea near Kate Monahan's. The police told residents that they were powerless to stop it while Flagg, a real estate agent for most of the tenements on the block, continued to rent apartments to disreputable women.

Flagg claimed that Captain John J. Donahue had summoned him to the precinct house and told him that he would have to "do the square thing" or shoo the whores out of his flats. Flagg said he replied that giving a bribe was as much a crime as taking one and that he would investigate his tenants and dispossess the bad ones.

In the next few days, he said, he had evicted or started proceedings against twelve tenants, but he had taken pity on a girl of eighteen years who had been coaxed to the city by a fast-talking slicker who had since abandoned her. Flagg agreed to let her stay until she had contacted her parents and made arrangements to go home. That evening he told the Captain of this special arrangement; that night the girl's flat was raided and she was taken to jail.

What had happened to the Tammany Hall that stood by the poor and unfortunate? Now it appeared that Tammany had taken control of the courts and police in order to persecute the helpless. Wherever he spoke, Parkhurst pressed these issues.

* * *

If Tammany had abandoned the powerless, the leaders of the anti-Tammany forces had a problem in identifying with the downtrodden. The Committee of Seventy was well stocked with bankers, corporate lawyers, retired judges, fashionable pastors, and wealthy merchants—men like John Crosby Brown of Brown Brothers (a member of Parkhurst's congregation) and J. P. Morgan, the financier. The committee had William B. Hornblower, whom President Cleveland had nominated (unsuccessfully) for the U.S. Supreme Court; and George L. Rives, the son of a former Ambassador to France, who, in addition to public service as a trustee of the Astor and Lenox libraries and member of the Municipal Art Commission, wrote articles on literature, history and law. Another member was Horace Porter, Civil War General, railroad executive, diplomat, and a member of President Grant's cabinet. They represented the class that downtown people called The Gold-Plated Holies, and it's likely that none of them had ever been tattooed or rushed the growler.

And they were marching against the rascals and racetrack touts of Tammany with all their familiar attitudes intact. One of the Holies spoke of their adversaries as "the community's refuse."[1] Another spoke of their aim to wrest government from "the despotic control of a handful of foreigners"[2] and restore the city to the keeping of the responsible and intelligent elite. They were preparing to wage the same campaign that had been fought against Tweed. But Tweed was dead and Little Old New York was gone, and the Seventy misread the volatile political atmosphere of 1894.

Although they had a few well-to-do assimilated Jews, there was not a single downtown Russian Jew in the Seventy, nor an Irish Catholic, nor a representative of a labor organization. Their political base did not extend to the lower reaches of the city. What did a wayward girl shivering in a jail cell, waiting for money from home, care about the Seventy's concern for the rise in bonded indebtedness, and its deleterious effect on foreign investors? They failed to hear new voices of urban life—including labor unions, immigrants and suffragists—clamoring in the city.

Parkhurst did not differ with the aims of the Seventy. He favored "good government" through a professional business administration and Civil Service reform, and giving public jobs to the capable rather than to those with pull. For two years he had been calling upon "the better people" to roll up their sleeves and get in the public arena. But Parkhurst had developed a feel for life below 14th Street. Unlike most of the Seventy, he could reach this constituency; ordinary blokes had little use for reformers, whom they regarded as cold desiccated types, but they trusted Parkhurst and greeted him warmly. At a number of rallies under the auspices of the City Vigilance League, he said the city needed a mayor "with a closet in his heart for the working people."

* * *

And not the least of Tammany's problems were the women. It was ironic that Parkhurst had a sense of how to appeal to women in the effort, because he had never supported woman suffrage, yet they came out to hear him.

One night Parkhurst took the elevated with a few of his friends to speak on behalf of a reform candidate at a Bronx church. Manhattan dwellers thought of the Bronx, then called "the annexed district," as a region populated chiefly by goats, but when the pastor arrived he found the church crowded and the excitement as high as at a Union Square rally. The pews were jammed with people, with extra chairs set up in the aisles for overflow—and a third of the audience was female.

Parkhurst acknowledged the amazing interest that women were showing in the political campaign, and suggested that it grew out of their concern about the salvation of the city and the moral precepts of its leaders. This was appropriate, he said, because the nurture of children was their sphere, but he warned them that they did not fully appreciate "the enfeebling and blackening influences upon their boys and young men resulting from the conditions under which we are now living." He blamed the depravity of the city on a Tammany government that included a murderer at the head of a city department and a Police Justice "who was not always in a coherent state of mind." Afterward a lot of women rushed forward to ask him about matters that had come up in the Lexow hearings.

This outpouring of interest among women whenever Parkhurst spoke gathered force in the days that followed; on some nights women made up a majority of the pastor's audience, a phenomenon entirely new to city politics. Several women's organizations invited him to address them, and he accepted with alacrity.

Some men complained that the pastor skirted the edges of decency in his discussions with women, but the women liked his frankness. More than most men of his time, Parkhurst was accustomed to working with women, who were active in church matters, missionary societies, and charitable associations. He admired their dedication and effectiveness, and did not share the prevalent male view that women were capricious and pusillanimous in their judgment. On the contrary, his only negative attitude about working with women was that some, he felt, tilted toward fanaticism.

* * *

The Committee of Seventy was trying to unite the city's diverse forces with an election ticket to oppose Tammany. But they would never have been able to do it without Parkhurst's help.

Neither Republican Boss Platt nor William Grace, who led the only significant anti-Tammany Democratic organization, had yet embraced the movement, and reformers feared that Tammany, as it had done so adroitly in the past, might strike another bargain with one of these two sly dogs. Former Mayor Grace contended that a Democrat should head the ticket because New York was a Democratic city, while Platt insisted that he would be unable to persuade his troops to work unless the mayoral candidate was a Republican. Unity would not be easy.

Early in October, the Seventy suggested Goff as the candidate for Mayor. Over the next few days the Goff candidacy picked up steam. The German-American Reform Union backed him, and Grace lauded Goff as a hero, suggesting that "even Tammany should feel grateful to him" for cleansing the organization.

Parkhurst did not object, but he was troubled. Fearing that Goff would be physically unable to serve as Lexow Committee counsel and run for mayor at the same time, the pastor believed that the effectiveness of the Lexow Committee would be impaired.

That worry ended soon. The Goff express came to a halt when it transpired that he was unacceptable to Platt. Goff notified the Committee of Seventy that he would not accept the nomination without Republican support.

After several names were floated, including Theodore Roosevelt's, at Morgan's urging the Seventy chose William L. Strong, president of the Central National Bank.

Morgan talked Platt's key political allies into going along. Although Strong had never been a Platt man, the Easy Boss accepted the choice. Having complained that Goff was not a Republican, Platt knew that Parkhurst would cast him as an obstructionist were he to complain that Strong was not the Republican he wanted. After Platt's men reached a secret bargain with Strong that Republicans would get key jobs in a Strong administration, Platt gave his blessing.

Still it looked as if Grace, commanding the only viable Democratic group outside of Tammany, intended to run his own candidates. Although he had wanted to stay out of the selection process, Parkhurst moved quickly.

He met with Charles S. Fairchild, chairman of the Grace organization and former Secretary of the Treasury, and pulled out all the stops. He noted that if Tammany could keep its enemies divided it would win, that it had managed to divide its opponents over the last several elections, and warned that in such a case he would condemn the Grace Democrats as collaborators in the Tammany victory. "Am I to understand that you and Mr. Grace and your associates think more of your little political organization than you do of the tremendous interests of New York City?" he scolded. "If you do, then God have mercy on you."[3]

A few days later the Grace faction nominated the anti-Tammany fusion ticket as its own. "I can readily conceive how difficult it was to adjust the competing demands made upon you by loyalty to party and loyalty to city," an overjoyed

Parkhurst wrote to Fairchild, "but the heartiness with which Mr. Grace, and a large majority of those associated with him in last evening's conference, threw the weight of their voice and influence on the side of our municipal exigencies, is suggestive of a degree of municipal loyalty for which I had not given him credit either in my own estimation or in my public utterances."[4]

The Madison Square preacher, a supposed amateur, had made victory possible. Both Platt and Grace knew that, if they refused to join the coalition, Parkhurst would blame them for Tammany's win. He had outmaneuvered them and had put a united anti-Tammany ticket in the field.

* * *

Aware that it was in for a battle, Tammany reached outside its organization to put up Nathan Straus, the city's leading retailer, as its candidate for Mayor. Since it had become impolitic to do otherwise, Straus expressed approval of the Lexow Committee, but claimed that Tammany Hall was being unfairly maligned because "the testimony shows that the Republican members of the police force are just as deep in the mire as are the Democrats."[5] He also chided the committee for stretching out the hearings too long. "It is wrong, because the police force is thereby demoralized," Straus said. "It is wrong to have four thousand men under the ban because two hundred and fifty are black sheep."[6]

The pastor had what he had asked for: a one-on-one contest between a Tammany and an anti-Tammany ticket. "I believe that God has designs for this great city," he told a crowd at Amity Hall, "and I believe that he is for the regeneration of this great metropolis."

* * *

The Platt men on the Lexow Committee were becoming impatient. They said that madames, patrolmen, saloonkeepers, candy-store owners and other plain folks might be able to testify to a wealth of new police outrages, but it was time to "go up higher." One morning Senator Lexow asked Goff and Moss when some of the big fish would be grilled.

Moss responded that the major task was to reorganize the police force. "As the matter stands the entire force rests under suspicion, and if we decide to go up higher at this particular time we will not have done enough to show what members of the force are and what are not smirched by blackmail and corruption. It is our intention that this investigation should be so thorough that, as far as possible, every guilty man should be known—every guilty man at least who occupies more than a subordinate position—in order that those who are innocent may be exonerated."

Lexow was puzzled. "You don't mean to say that it becomes the province of this committee to pass upon individual cases?" he asked, reminding Moss that the committee's purpose was to recommend legislation, not "to uncover every instance of police wrongdoing in the city."[7]

Goff said that at the onset the investigation had run into "a brazen wall with no fissure in it" and had been successful only by digging for particulars. "We found," Goff said, "that such was the terrorism under which the people of New York were held by the police that they were afraid to come forward and testify, but that terrorism has been broken for the first time in the history of this city."[8]

* * *

Captain Max Schmittberger knew it was only a matter of time until his name bobbed up at the Lexow hearings. He had been worried all summer. When he took his family on a Long Island vacation he could not stop thinking about the Police Board hearings, and cut short his vacation to get back to the city.

Upon his return Max called upon a businessman friend, Gustave Wolf, asking him to go to the French Steamship Company and fix matters up. Wolf offered $1,000 to a company official to lose the steamship company books which contained the record of a $500 payment to Captain Schmittberger. This would be a big favor to the captain, Wolf explained, since the entry would otherwise be used against him if he were called before the Lexow Committee. But the official turned down the bribe.

After that the anxious Max alarmed his wife by walking the floors of his house all night. His thoughts churned in an effort to determine how he had gotten into this mess. As he reviewed his career on those insomniac nights, this is what he found.

* * *

Max had been working as a baker when a couple of Tammany men took a liking to him and offered to get him on the force, free. After his appointment, Max was often chosen for decorative posts, for he was a good-looking cop. And, at the beginning, he was also an innocent young man.

His first night beat was in a Negro neighborhood with singing, dancing, occasional razor fights and six brothels to a block. One evening as he was walking his beat a young woman came running down the steps, pressed something in his hand and ran back in. It was a ten-dollar bill. Not knowing what to make of this, he showed it to a veteran cop.

The veteran explained that every once in a while the brothels passed a little money to the cop on the beat, to keep him smiling. Schmittberger took the bill to his captain, who told him that he didn't take "chicken-feed" from low-level members of the department.

Max quickly learned about hush money and about the particulars of patrolling Negro neighborhoods. For example, brothels had a racket called "the panel game"—entering the room of assignation by means of a sliding panel and taking the john's wallet. White pimps usually took only a couple of bills so that the customer would be unaware that his wallet had been touched. Not so the Negroes. White men were reluctant to let the police know that they had crossed the color line, so they seldom raised a fuss if they were robbed. Banking on such a reaction, the black pimps cleaned out their wallets.

The police feared that such practices might disturb the smooth course of commerce, so it fell to Max to urge restraint. He developed a network of informants and became the reigning expert on Negro vice. Max knew just about everything that was happening in the black enclaves, and was so feared that black mothers would quiet their children by threatening that "Officer Max'll come and ketch you."

* * *

Schmittberger's avarice eventually lost all restraint, and he began to take even from his brother cops.

His greed came to light during a Lexow hearing in October, as Goff probed into payments that the French Steamship Company routinely paid to cops on the docks to overlook small infractions of regulations and to take special care of cargo. Although illegal and against police regulations, the practice was of such long standing that the police had come to regard it as a legitimate stipend which they called "dinner money."

Breaking down the resistance of an official of the French line, Goff shook Schmittberger's name out of him. It was revealed as well that the Captain had gone to the steamship companies and appropriated for himself the "dinner money" that was customarily paid to the patrolmen.

A week after these revelations, Captain Max found himself in front of a Grand Jury, in danger of indictment. But he was not powerless. He had vast stores of knowledge about corruption on the force—information that could save him from serving time in Sing Sing with men he had sent up the river.

One day he stopped at the Superintendent's suite of offices, and talked privately in the inner office with Byrnes about spilling the beans to the Lexow Committee.

* * *

All of the trouble that was traceable to Parkhurst, all of the volatility that he had created, all of the disturbance that was blowing through the streets of New York that Autumn were a direct product of his commitment to the kingdom of God. Many Protestant clergymen of his time spoke favorably of preserving the United States as a Christian nation, by which they meant diminishing the influence of Catholics and Jews; but when Parkhurst spoke of a Christian nation, he meant something entirely different: he meant fostering the coming of the kingdom of God. That kingdom, true to the vision of Jesus in proclaiming it, would be open and inclusive. In the course of producing justice, human rights and democracy it would also upset the powerful and raise the lowly.

In addition to having something of First Century Jewish prophecy in it, his view of the world also had something military. Parkhurst was in his heart a Christian knight and his approach was chivalric. The hymns he had learned as a child swelled with the metaphors of battle, and to him the Holy Spirit was a virile force. The bass line of his religion was the rumble of the church on the march, his Christianity not a theology but a power bursting into the world to transform it.

For him bringing in the kingdom was the main purpose of the church, which he regarded as "a recruiting station to fit and equip for service." Theological concepts, philosophical ideas, denominational disputes would be of no help on the battlefield.

Helping to bring in the kingdom of God was a huge job, but he was up to it. Christianity began in First Century Palestine as a great disturbance and in nineteenth-century New York it was stirring again. Even his adversaries would agree to that.

45

"TO HELL
WITH REFORM!"

With the competing tickets filled out, the election campaign began to roll. Stumping for any anti-Tammany candidate who asked him, Parkhurst charged that Tammany misrule had degraded the city.

He frequently attacked Philip Wissig, Tammany candidate for the Assembly, reminding his listeners of the seamy record brought to light at the Lexow hearings of "Foul-mouthed Phil" as a thug, a trafficker in vice, and a leading figure in the Essex Market Courthouse gang.

Several years earlier Wissig, then an Assemblyman, had been expelled from Tammany Hall for notorious comments against woman suffrage. His speech, which had driven several women from the Assembly Chamber, was so scurrilous that it had been expunged from the record and so indefensible that even his fellow Tammany legislators demanded punishment. But that, Parkhurst said, occurred while Tammany Hall still preserved a modicum of decency; the new Tammany had restored Wissig to favor and placed him on the ticket.

Other targets were Justice Paddy Divver, Justice Barney Martin and his brother Police Board President Jimmy Martin, and Silver Dollar Smith. Parkhurst related their histories—their ties to the Whyos, bunco artists and vice lords and ladies—as a collective portrait of Tammany Hall.

A major judicial error reinforced Parkhurst's message. One afternoon in the Second District, Police Justice Divver staggered, drunk and belligerent, into Tekulsky's saloon. He accused Tekulsky of maligning his leadership.

"That is not so, Justice Divver," Tekulsky angrily replied. "Someone has been lying to you." Divver cursed and threw a punch at the Jewish saloonkeeper, missing widely. Tekulsky responded with a punch to Divver's nose. The Police Justice

threw his hat away and tried to buck Tekulsky with his head in the nose, then threw a
kick at him. Tekulsky hit him again, knocking him down and out.

Within hours the newspapers were
spreading the word that Justice Divver, seldom to be found on the bench these days,
had turned up drunk in the afternoon to
pick a fight in a saloon—the same saloon
that he had once owned and in which he
used to store the ill-gotten gains of bunco
men. It was so scandalous that everybody
was making jokes about it.

Tekulsky Leads with His Right

Another target of Parkhurst's scorn was
Recorder Smyth, who was running for reelection as the city's chief criminal
judge. The pastor recalled to his audiences that for many years Smyth had failed
to alert the city to the entrenched nature of police corruption, and for that matter had never skipped an opportunity to enhance the impression that the police
were immaculately clean. "Now that is a pretty serious matter in view of what has
been brought to light during the past six months," Parkhurst noted.

Articles about the coming election were being published all over the world,
he said, and contributions were being mailed from such faraway places as Tas-
mania and Persia. He read to his listeners extracts from European newspapers
about New York, including one from a Berlin newspaper that covered the uprising against Tammany as well as the Lexow hearings.

"What we have to labor for is not a mere local regeneration," he told crowds.
"We must have in mind the mighty country, of which New York is the throbbing
heart."[1]

* * *

The heat was too much for Straus. The cultivated German Jew quit the campaign,
and Hugh Grant took his place as the Tammany candidate for mayor. At first this
was regarded as a disaster for Tammany, but many of the braves were happy about
changing horses in midrace, more comfortable with the hale-fellow-well-met Grant
than with one who, although he had served as a Parks Commissioner, was not a
Tammany regular and gave off the stuffy aura of social uplift.

Ex-Mayor Grant spoke of cleaning up Tammany, but he began and ended by
dropping Wissig from the ticket. He found no fault with others, including Silver
Dollar Smith as an Aldermanic candidate.

Grant represented just what Tammany stood for—the right of every male to rush the growler on Sunday, whether the silk stockings liked it or not. Feeling more at ease, Tammany braves began to strike back at Parkhurst, who was cursed as an anti-Irish "foreigner" from New England. Tammany speakers called him Boss Parkhurst and claimed that he was directing all the moves of the Committee of Seventy, "fulminating edicts and manifestoes in his rectory."[2] They also went after Goff, who they said had pulled wires to get the Lexow job, so that he might face off against his enemy Recorder Smyth in this coming election.

"To you men of Tammany Hall," one speaker said, "who are maligned in the public press, who are termed scoundrels and blacklegs, who are classed with petty thieves and lawbreakers, to you I appeal to rise this fall and under the banner of our noble and high-minded leader, meet all this calumny at the polls."[3]

* * *

Now Tammany could be itself, and even Max Hochstim came out to campaign. "Boys, we're in trouble," Hochstim said at a rally. "If we lose the election we lose our jobs. And jobs, you know, are hard to get right now. Them reformers have given us a bad name. We have to elect our Aldermen to hold our jobs, or we don't eat."

He took a sip of water. "The Second District has come up with the slogan, 'A glass of beer on Sunday for the workingman.' This is all right for the Irish. It is not a slogan for Jews. We need a good issue, a good slogan to get out the Jewish vote. Anyone got ideas?"

Julius Melkin, a process server, arose to reply. "I have a slogan," he said. "Jews have not been getting political jobs. Everything goes to the Irish. Where do you see a Jewish copper, a Jewish fireman, a Jewish street cleaner, a horsecar driver or conductor? To get out the vote we must demand our rights. What kind of blokes are we to keep taking it on the chin? I have the slogan which will get out the vote for Tammany: 'Jobs for Jews.'"

The assembled applauded vigorously. Hochstim turned to the crowd. "Boys, we will beat them uptown bums yet. Get busy, go out and scratch. To hell with Reform!"

* * *

As Tammany dropped its pretenses, the women of the city lined up against saloon politics. At a hall at Ninety-sixth Street and Amsterdam Avenue, the Women's Auxiliary Anti-Tammany Organization was formed. "We want clean streets, a beautiful city, managed by good, clean men," said one of the organizers. "We want to see the Star Spangled Banner floating over every schoolhouse the year round. Women don't like to live in dirty places. We want clean homes, and why not clean out of office all the dirty men?"[4]

"We will endeavor to make it bad form for any man to admit, let alone boast, of fealty to the infamous Tammany organization," said another speaker. "Close your parlors on such men, just as you would not acknowledge the greeting of a man known to consort with women of ill fame."

The group announced a boycott of Tammany tradesmen, and uptown merchants began to place signs in their windows offering "Anti-Tammany chickens, 18 cents a pound, Anti-Tammany eggs 17 for a quarter, Anti-Tammany Pork 12 cents a pound."

But the Committee of Seventy and its candidates continued to stress male-oriented issues. William Strong, the banker who was the anti-Tammany candidate for mayor, was talking about tax rates and the Dock Board, and how to further develop New York as the financial capital, and the audiences that came out to hear him were almost 100 percent male.

Parkhurst plugged on, working for "a public vote on the Ten Commandments." When Josephine Shaw Lowell wrote a letter commending his attempts to involve women, Parkhurst prevailed upon her to visit him at the rectory. Mrs. Lowell was active in prison reform and had a reputation as a superb organizer, and he had already decided that she was the one to head a woman's reform organization. She had no intention of taking on such a task, and told him so when he broached the subject—but, as it so often happened, Parkhurst proved irresistible.

Through her network of contacts with women's organizations, Mrs. Lowell worked tirelessly at developing the Woman's Municipal League. She sent out postcards inviting women to a rally in Association Hall in mid-October, with Parkhurst as main speaker.

As women became more excited about the campaign, Parkhurst exhorted them to greater efforts. In his view, women understood better than men that when drunks become ill in the street the city suffers and that every evidence of caring enhances a city. He took issue with the view that social evils were subjects too indelicate for women, for the women were discussing them unblushingly, in parlors and on front stoops, with other women and with men, as freely as had ever been known in the city.

The Association Hall rally was crammed to the rafters with women. "This is not a political campaign," Parkhurst told them. "It is simply a warfare between that which is right and that which is wrong. In such a war, with lines so sharply drawn, I cannot conceive how anyone—yes, let us speak the words here— whether suffragists or anti-suffragists, can fail to enter into this work." His comment caused a ripple of laughter, which was drowned out by applause at the close of the sentence.

"Now what are you women going to do? Your influence is unbounded. You can make men do anything you want. By using that pleading and compulsory influence which you are so capable of doing you will be able to secure a large number of votes."

He called upon them also to influence the women of the East Side. "A woman called upon me this morning and told me of the singular condition of mind which exists among the women there. They have heard of the movement which has been started, but do not understand it, and they want to know if it will help them, or in any way relieve them from the slavery which oppresses them."

His speech was enthusiastically greeted, and afterward he engaged in a lively exchange with a group of suffragists. Some of the women said they refused to help because he had not supported their suffrage efforts; but others among them saw the campaign, as one of them put it, as "a preliminary skirmish to the great battle of suffrage, and that it will do more to make women realize their position, and to give them a better understanding of equal suffrage, and what would be accomplished by its means, than any other movement which could take place."

In an article for a British magazine, Lady Somerset predicted that this campaign would be remembered as the beginning of a political revolution that would end in woman suffrage. "I think that Dr. Parkhurst is beginning to understand that to fight this awful corruption which has been exposed in the city government he must have a strong reinforcement," she commented, "and this can only come from among the women."[5]

* * *

Parlor socialists, rosewater radicals, Tolstoyan pacifists, spiritualists, Theosophists and vegetarians—the types that wits called the Anti-Gravitational Society—all of them were turning out, along with reformers and suffragists, at dinner parties and afternoon salons, to see and hear Emma Goldman.

They found the famous Anarchist to be short, with wavy brown hair, and gray eyes encircled by spectacles. She was always neatly dressed in a shirtwaist and a sailor hat. She spoke with an accent, but was mastering English well. She was fleshy for one who had spent ten months in a penitentiary, but perhaps she had regained weight quickly, for obviously she enjoyed eating and liked wine.

Some left saying that she sounded like a fishwife. Nevertheless many testified to her power and her fire, and spoke of being in the presence of an elemental force. She radiated an aura of serene confidence, yet was not smug, and naturally accepted her role as center of the gathering.

She took direct issue with what she called Parkhurst's view of the role of women, telling her listeners that sex was a woman's sole commodity in this society. The prostitutes who sold it openly on the street were more honest than the women who bargained with it for a wedding ring and lifelong support. The difference between the two types of women was merely conventional, since both had sold their honor for a price. The rising divorce rate and the general ennui of married life showed that marriage as a lifelong partnership did not work. For her, marriage was a sordid pact arranged by hypocritical clergymen. Love and the mutual respect of equals for each other's freedom had nothing to do with such bargains.

Goldman characterized the conventions of society as examples of what she called the Spooks, or the Social Lie. Sexual taboos, religious observances, obedience to the State or to the family or to anything except one's own ideals was a sign of mental weakness. Everything that conventional society proclaimed as true was false. Social Lies were the morbid grip of the dead upon the living, binding people to the past. Marriage made a woman so dependent on her husband that she could hardly function outside the home, and she became careless in her appearance, clumsy in her movements, diffident in her decisions, cowardly in her judgment—a gossipy and petty nag that men came to loathe. She eventually became as flat, narrow and drab as her surroundings. Yet all of this was the consequence of what men wanted—woman's slavish acquiescence to his supposed superiority.

Goldman believed that the Spooks alienated people from their true selves and prevented them from growing. Even supposedly "emancipated women" remained entangled in respectability. For her America would never truly become the land of liberty until it rejected the very idea of authority.

The women asked what Emma Goldman thought about woman suffrage. Was she willing to join a campaign for voting rights?

Emma Goldman saw dim prospects for success in any attempts of women of the silk-stocking districts to do anything downtown. On several occasions she had visited one of the downtown settlement houses where the uptown women tried to improve the lot of the poor. She thought it laudable that women of the privileged classes took an interest in the well-being of the people of the Lower East Side. "Nevertheless the work of these ladies is merely palliative," the Anarchist said. "Teaching the poor to eat with a fork is all very well, but what good does it do if they have not the food? Let them first become the masters of life; they will then know how to eat and how to live." One young girl, the pet of the settlement, put on airs, sneering at the lack of refinement among her neighbors and friends. "They are creating snobbery," Miss Goldman said, "among the very people they are trying to help." Emma had attended the vulgar wedding of this girl, puffed up with the self-importance of a bride, and dressed in cheap finery. "When I congratulated her on choosing such a fine-looking fellow for her husband, she said that he was quite nice, though of course not of her sphere and that she was marrying beneath her station." The attentions of cultivated ladies, she concluded, produced more harm than good.

Emma Goldman expressed contempt for the suffrage movement. Even if it were successful, she asked, what could be expected of a voting woman populace? Women said voting would make them better Christians, better housekeepers, and better supporters of the State. Yet it was Christianity that condemned them to inferiority, it was the home that sapped their energy, and the State that demanded their foolish allegiance.

Wherever women secured the vote, she said, busybodies pried more puritanically into people's private lives. Women wanted the vote primarily as a weapon against saloons and brothels; women even wanted a moral criterion for voting so as to keep "bad women" from the polls. Nor did woman suffrage have any bearing on the plight of exploited workers; in fact many leading suffragists opposed labor unions. And some suffragists tied votes for women to a campaign against immigration, which, as Miss Anthony complained, had swollen the ranks of immigrant male voters, accustomed to "monarchical forms of government that do not understand our principles."[6] Goldman saw no reason to believe that women would purify politics, nor any evidence that conditions improved in places where women voted, and dismissed the suffrage movement as a parlor affair.

No longer interested in organizing or even in belonging to any kind of organization, Emma Goldman was forging a customized, individualistic political outlook. Its central motif would be her own integrity.

46

"AND THIS IS
NEW YORK IN
THE 19TH CENTURY!"

Every session of the Lexow hearings produced more evidence of a degraded city, but the low point was the day that Ambrose Hussey went on the stand.

Until recently he had been a wardman in the Delancey Street precinct. Goff intended to show that Hussey, working with Edwin Shalvey, wardman for the Eldridge Street precinct, and Max Hochstim, the Tammany saloonkeeper, had terrorized and framed a number of Jewish immigrants of the Lower East Side. A score of their victims were present and waiting to testify, but Hussey was called first.

As soon as he seated himself in the witness chair, Hussey began to glance anxiously to the left and right. When Frank Moss stood up and prepared to interrogate him, the cop smiled and pulled himself erect, perhaps relieved that he would not be facing Goff, who arrived after testimony began.

Before him on the counsel table Moss placed a file bulging with incriminating affidavits, more than he could use in a single day.

Hussey had good bearing and wore his uniform well. But as Moss questioned him about the arrest of Caela Urchittel, the long narrow face of the tall lithe cop began to flush and his wolfish smile disappeared.

Although he lacked Goff's brilliance, Moss proved himself competent as the witness damaged himself with bluster and contradictions. Moss showed that Hussey had framed Mrs. Urchittel on false charges of prostitution. Looking inept, the cop was forced to retract statements he had previously made in interrogatories and police court. He tried to blame another cop for having taken the money from Mrs. Urchittel; then, as his starched uniform wilted, Hussey tried to shift the blame to Joseph Block, his hired stoolpigeon. He claimed that if he were mistaken about Mrs. Urchittel he had been misled by the eighteen-year-old

Block. By this time Hussey looked like a blundering fool, and Senator O'Connor warned him to "come off it."

Then Moss put Mrs. Urchittel on the stand, an interpreter was called, and a long statement read that Moss had prepared to clear up some particulars of her previous testimony. It reiterated that Hochstim, the Tammany captain, and Hussey had dragged her around the streets until 3 A.M. demanding money, and had taken $25 from her. It said that two boys, one of them Joseph Block, "were engaged by Detective Hussey to testify against me. One said he had given me fifty cents and the other that he had paid forty cents, and that I had committed immoral acts." Mrs. Urchittel sobbed as this was read.

The statement continued: "While I was waiting in court Hussey came to me and told me that my children were taken away, but that if I would give him $50 he would save me even then. I cried aloud and was locked up in a dark cell."

"Mrs. Urchittel, are you certain that the man who took you around until three in the morning was Hussey?" Moss asked.

"That's him!" she shrieked.

Moss was prepared to follow with a series of witnesses to testify to her good character, but Senator O'Connor, serving as committee chairman in the absence of Lexow, asked him to abandon the effort since her character was not in question, noting that even the officers "who attacked it now seem to run away from that position."

* * *

By now both Goff and Parkhurst had arrived in the courtroom, in time to watch Moss switch to another shabby affair involving Hussey. He called Elias Mandel, owner of a small East Side eatery. The excitable Mandel said that Hussey had approached his wife, Katie Mandel, to demand protection money because he charged that gambling was being conducted in the restaurant. "He sent a young man named Block to my place afterward," Mandel said. "Block stays around Hochstim's saloon. Block ate a lot of meals at my place and owed me $40 for board." Block rented a room at the Mandels' and spied on them, reporting to Hussey that they were about to deposit $100 in a bank. Accompanied by Hochstim and Shalvey, Hussey came to the restaurant and demanded the money, claiming that it belonged to Block. When Mandel refused to hand it over, he was placed under arrest. On the way to the station his captors insisted on stopping at Hochstim's saloon, where they took money from his pocket, enjoyed a drink at his expense, and advised him that if he ever wanted to get out of custody he would have to use Hochstim as his bondsman.

"Allow me to state here that such is the condition of things around the Essex Market Police Court," Moss interjected, "that one or two men are autocrats there, and the prisoners are obliged to pay whatever these sharks may choose to demand. They will not permit other bondsmen to qualify there. The prisoners must either accept these sharks as bondsmen or remain in jail."

While Mandel was in custody, Hochstim showed up at the eatery claiming to be his bondsman and demanding money from Mrs. Mandel. The police rejected several persons who offered to go his bail, but Mandel refused to yield to pressure to get bail from Hochstim. Eventually he was brought in contact with Norberth Pfeffer, who managed somehow to get him out. When Mandel appeared before the Grand Jury the charges were dropped but, having left his restaurant unattended while in jail, his business was in ruins.

Katie Mandel next took the stand. Her testimony had barely begun when a commotion broke out in the rear of the hearing room, and fingers were pointed at Officer Hussey. Testimony ceased as Goff walked back and whispered at length with several people there. Then he returned to the front, asked Mrs. Mandel to step down for a moment, and took over the questioning.

"Officer Hussey," he called out loudly. The cop returned to the witness chair. For some time Goff did not speak, but stared at the officer, and silence stole over the courtroom.

"Now, sir," Goff said, "you have threatened to kill a man in this court. You are a policeman, and you wear a shield, and yet you have just told a person in this court room that you would put a bullet through his head."

"I didn't," came the faint response.

"Do you think you can come here and intimidate persons in this very court-room and before this committee?"

"But if you only knew his character," ventured Hussey. "I wish you were in that neighborhood. I—er—"

"Stop!" Goff shouted. "You have dared to threaten the life of Norberth Pfeffer. I want to know what you mean by it!"

The witness was unable to speak.

"Now, will you swear," said Goff, shaking his forefinger at the trembling witness, "that you did not say you would put a bullet in his head?"

"I'll swear I only said he was not fit to live."

"Will you swear that you did not use such threats to Pfeffer?"

"Yes, sir."

"Positively?"

"I—er—said, 'you are not fit to live' and er—'you are a dirty loafer.'"

NEW YORK HERALD, THURSDAY, OCTOBER 4, 1884—TWENTY PAGES

Hussey on the Stand
Some of the Persons Who Appeared before the Lexow Committee

"Now we will excuse you for a moment. I want to see if the City of New York is going to tolerate such work as this."

Pfeffer, a well-dressed young Jew, took the witness chair. He said that he had earned the animosity of Hussey and Hochstim because he had secured bail for Mandel. Pfeffer said that without provocation Hussey had leaned over and said clearly and distinctly, "You son of a bitch, I'll blow your brains out, I'll kill you like a dog."

Goff called three more witnesses, all of whom confirmed what Pfeffer said.

"Now, Hussey, just one word with you," Goff said in a commanding tone. "Take the stand again."

By this point Hussey looked sick and his bearing had changed to the sneaky look of a whipped dog. "I am under a doctor's care," he said as he passed Goff on the way to the stand. "I have a certificate."

Goff fastened his gaze upon the panicked witness and said: "Now, sir, you have heard the testimony of four witnesses, who stated that you used the words,

'I will put a bullet through your head, I will blow your brains out, I will kill you.' What have you to say for yourself?"

Hussey looked faint. He asked for a drink of water. It was handed to him. He made an attempt to swallow but failed. He looked at the ceiling for a time.

"I—I said nothing about killing. I only said you ain't fit to live."

"Are you prepared to swear that each of the four gentlemen who have testified here has sworn to a lie?"

"I—I didn't."

"Now either they are lying or you are. If what they said is true, you have sworn to a falsehood."

Goff repeated his question again and again. Hussey opened his mouth to speak but words failed him. After being asked several times, Hussey denied everything that the four witnesses had said. When Goff was through quizzing him the policeman looked ready to faint. "I am in a state of excitement," he said. "I don't often lose my head. This is all crooked work on me, I'll swear to that."

"Now you may go and get some fresh air. You will hear from us later."

* * *

A short break followed. Mrs. Urchittel, who had ended her testimony with an appeal to the committee to restore her children to her, took the opportunity to beg Moss for help. The embarrassed lawyer told her that he was doing the best he could and that she must be patient. She fell to her knees and prayed for God to speed his efforts and to protect him. Moss told committee members that every effort was being made to return the children to her, but that it was slow work under existing laws, which gave the Society for the Prevention of Cruelty to Children broad powers to take children from their homes and confine them in an institution.

Witnesses who had been called to testify against Hussey and Hochstim crowded around Moss, fearing personal injury when they left the building. Parkhurst approached Pfeffer, offering him sanctuary at the rectory if he feared bodily harm, but the young man said he was not afraid.

Then, as Moss took over the questioning again, Katie Mandel resumed her interrupted testimony. She related the torment she had endured in trying to find someone to go bail for her husband. Every time Pfeffer found one for her, she said, Hochstim's thugs would frighten the potential bondsman off. Hochstim told her that unless she gave him $100 he would send the word to the court to have her husband sent away for five years.

Mrs. Mandel spoke with great earnestness and the spectators listened with rapt attention. "I am living in a constant state of terror," she said, rising from the chair as tears welled in her eyes. "Men are constantly being assaulted in my neighborhood. I am afraid they will kill my husband." She said that since Pfeffer had helped her to get bail money Hochstim's men had beaten him twice.

Committee members advised her to call on Goff for protection if threatened, but she responded that when the damage was done it was usually too late to report anything.

"Your husband is safer now than he was before, madam," said Moss.

"Oh, thank you, sir," said the distressed woman. "But you do not know what we have suffered. My little child over there—he is only six years old. When my husband was arrested the child went with him over to the station house and remained with him in that cell for five days and nights, saying that he would not leave his papa alone in such a loathsome place." The tears brimmed over and fell from her eyes.

Silence followed her remarks. Senator O'Connor ventured to speak, but his voice was husky with emotion. The tears streamed down Moss's cheeks as he tried to say something, and with a gesture, he turned away.

"My God!" remarked Senator Bradley, wiping his eyes with a huge bandanna, "and this is New York in the nineteenth century!"

47

CAMPAIGNING

With three weeks until election, the reform forces were bubbling with confidence. They had the support of most of the newspapers and of the city's opinion makers. The uptown parlors were buzzing with excited talk, and money was coming in by the bushel. When the Committee of Seventy headquarters opened on Twenty-third Street the reform-minded poured in to shake the hand of W. Travers Jerome, its executive director, and to tell him that in their opinion it was all over but counting the ballots. Surely Officer Hussey's threat, which had shocked the city, had sealed Tammany's fate. Everyone they knew was voting for the anti-Tammany ticket.

But the decisive factor in the election would be the people they did not know, the hundreds of thousands of tenement men. Tammany claimed to represent the blokes who lived south of Fourteenth Street, and based its political message on the theme of us-against-them. The reformers were those uptown snobs who thought they were better than you.

When a Tammany captain walked into a saloon to buy drinks for the house, he would pat the customers on their backs and remind them of the jobs that had been given out. Smart buckos like themselves, he would tell the assembled drinkers, understood the smug arrogance of the Committee of Seventy—that no one could hold office without a pedigree. He counseled them to remember where they came from and to remain loyal to their friends.

Around the nation, since hard times had begun a year earlier, an anti-immigrant movement had been gaining strength. Among the Boston bluebloods it was called the Immigration Restriction League. In the Midwest, it took the shape of the American Protective Association, or A.P.A., which declared its hostility to Catholicism and deplored the growth of Irish power in cities. And in New York, Tammany charged, the movement was called the Committee of Seventy, the membership of which included Protestant pastors who sympathized with the A.P.A., according to Tammany Police Justice Thomas Grady. "The city is now against the Catholic," he told a Jewish audience in a downtown theater. "Next year it may be against the Hebrew, and in '96 a war may follow."

Tammany accused Strong, the anti-Tammany candidate for mayor, of anti-Catholic prejudice. A *Sun* article said that Strong had worked in 1880 against William Grace, then the Democratic candidate for mayor, because Grace was Catholic. It was also pointed out at rallies that Strong belonged to the Union League, which had blackballed a prominent Jew from membership.

Tammany charged the newspapers and the Protestant clergy with bigotry and claimed that Tammany's side of the story was not being told. In its anti-reform campaign, Tammany depicted its foes as the uptown people and their pastors, anti-immigrant forces, anti-Catholics, anti-Semites, suffragists, Prohibitionists, Puritans, and Parkhurst and his "hens," all looking down their noses at their presumed inferiors and pronouncing them unfit.

Justice Grady contended that Parkhurst, whom he called "the Presbyterian skirt-dancer," was interested only in notoriety, and recalled his midnight frolics in Hattie Adams' brothel. One evening at the Wigwam the pastor's name was invoked several times, and on each occasion a growl, at first low and menacing, then swelling into a roar, came from all parts of the hall.

* * *

Reform candidates were running for the Assembly and for the Board of Aldermen in downtown districts, but Strong ran an uptown campaign for mayor. In his absence Parkhurst became the standard-bearer for reform forces below the line, speaking in Bowery halls and Greenwich Village churches. At every downtown stop he said that Tammany was not the friend of the poor but its exploiter. He talked about how the police gouged sidewalk vendors. He talked about Silver Dollar Smith, the Tammany leader who, by creating the impression that it was necessary to pay him, squeezed "gate money," usually a dollar, out of every person who came to see a prisoner in the lockup at the Essex Market Court House. He told of "a voracious policeman" whom he saw lift a newspaper from the pile of a shivering little newsboy without paying for it and how that little boy walked over into a corner to indulge "in a little quiet and almost pardonable profanity."[1]

Wherever he went Parkhurst preached Americanization. "As long as we have in our city a Rome, a Berlin, a Belfast, or a Jerusalem, there can be no community interest among its citizens," he told a German group. "Race prejudices and affiliations must be swept aside if we would reform our municipal government."[2]

On some nights Parkhurst hopped about from one stop to another in the downtown districts, accompanied by his agents and bodyguards, telling the people that this was more than a municipal election—that it involved the future of the nation, because "the country cannot be saved unless the cities are saved."[3]

One night as Parkhurst left a hall on Broome Street for another a few blocks away, a cluster of rough-looking men in the rear of the hall crowded about the doorway. As the clergyman descended from the platform two of his bodyguard led the way, and the other two brought up the rear. As cheers went up for the departing orator a big fellow called out "Three cheers for Hattie Adams!" and pushed himself against Parkhurst. A bodyguard hurled him back into the crowd. Hundreds of people surrounded the pastor as he walked to his next engagement, and crowds gathered along the route to cheer him as the parade passed by.

He was welcomed among the trade union people, who enjoyed his playful pomposity, and he was at ease with them, presenting himself as the son of farmers and a product of the working people. Samuel Gompers, the president of the American Federation of Labor, appeared on several platforms with him. The union members prized his oratorical talent, although they joked that they would leave their Bibles at home and bring their dictionaries the next time they came to hear him.

* * *

When three thousand women rallied at Cooper Union, pledges were distributed at the door asking each signer to obtain ten votes for the anti-Tammany ticket, and leaflets handed out with each pledge stated that the A.P.A. question had nothing to do with the city election.

Mrs. Lowell, president of the Woman's Municipal League, said women were forced to step in because men were too wrapped up in their businesses to perform civic duties. "Women of New York," she said, "we have asked you to meet us today to hear again the story of the dishonor of our city, because we believe that if you could be made to realize how deep the disgrace is, your moral indignation would be so strong that no man outside the criminal class would dare publicly to support Tammany Hall." Next she introduced Parkhurst, whom she said "deserves the deep and lasting gratitude of every good man and woman in New York."

He said that he had just met with a Catholic prelate and a rabbi, and that both told him that their people were behind the movement. "This is not a movement against Catholicism!" he shouted. "It is a movement to rid our city of the devil of which it is possessed." The dishonor of the city was the work of such Tammany men as "Foul-Mouthed Phil" Wissig, the first casualty of the forces of womanhood, who had forced Tammany to drop him as a candidate. He also cited the opprobrious Police Justice Divver, "who has just taken part in a disgraceful row and who, I am glad to add, was well punched."

He said that Tammany would have to answer for the mistreatment of Caela Urchittel, who had come to this country to find freedom and instead had been oppressed. He read the translation of a letter from Mrs. Urchittel in which she spoke of her hope of regaining her children, and he again asked the women to stretch out a hand to the uneducated women of the city.

When the Committee of Seventy rallied in the same hall a few days later, it adopted Parkhurst's approach. Appealing to unity, a Catholic speaker said that Strong had opposed Grace in the 1880 campaign not because Grace was Catholic but solely on political grounds; and a Jewish speaker said that Strong had fought against the blackballing of Jews from the Union League.

Speakers emphasized that ordinary people had most to lose from the continued domination of the Wigwam. "We fight a band of political marauders," said one, "who have fastened themselves upon this city, who have been eating its heart's blood, whose oppression reaches the most humble woman in the community."

* * *

Nevertheless it was still the pastor himself who brought out the crowds in Jewish neighborhoods. They came despite the warnings of Jewish orthodoxy who said that the Jew survived only by strict adherence to tradition, and were critical of Parkhurst's calls for assimilation. The Orthodox advised their flock to let the uptown German Jews vote, since they already dressed their wives in revealing gowns and ate raw oysters. And they suspected Parkhurst to be a Christian missionary—today it was voting, tomorrow he would be calling them to Jesus.

Nevertheless, on Rutgers Square, on the East Side, a multitude stranded outside Harris's Assembly Rooms cheered as he appeared. The East Broadway hall was "packed to the point of suffocation," as one newspaper reported, and a large number of people were frustrated in their attempts to squeeze in. Cries of "Parkhurst! Parkhurst!" broke from the crowd in the hall, and when the preacher stood up he was unable to begin his speech for some time because of the cheers and applause. Noting that a Lexow witness had testified that he had bribed the police to have his store approved as a voter registration center, he pointed to a policeman in the room and said: "I dare say that our friend there in brass buttons would say that it is the usual thing, isn't it, now?"

Taken by surprise, the policeman nodded in assent, bringing on a tremendous outburst of laughter and applause.

When he told the story of Mrs. Urchittel, he reduced some of the crowd to sobbing and tears; a man in the rear shouted "Let us help her!" and started a collection of coins passed up to the pastor to be forwarded to her.

Parkhurst said that members of his own church had belonged to Tammany at one time, but that it had become absolutely corrupt. He said that it was a good sign that Superintendent Byrnes was clamping down on Tammany election fraud and sweeping through lodging houses in search of floaters, for it meant that the opportunistic Byrnes scented Tammany's defeat in the air. The only thing that could stop an anti-Tammany victory, he said, was election fraud, and he urged them to volunteer to aid the Good Government Club by doing everything possible to secure an honest vote.

When he tried to leave the people pressed about him, eager to shake his hand, and when he came down the steps the crowd outside surged toward him. A Socialist Labor meeting was being held in the square, but hundreds of people deserted the Socialist speakers and joined the crowd in front of the hall to cheer the enemy of corrupt government. A crowd of cheering people escorted Parkhurst to the end of the square. Some of the Jews ran ahead and then walked backward in order to get a good look at him. About one hundred of them walked along East Broadway to the Chatham Square station of the Third Avenue elevated, where as Parkhurst ascended the stairway they bade him goodbye with more cheers. "It was evident that they regarded him as their firm friend," the *Tribune* reported, "and were determined to show him what they thought of him."

The preacher was pleased by the welcome he received all over the downtown parts of the city, but he was especially heartened by the Jews, who appeared to understand American ways better than he had expected.

* * *

It seemed as if there were at least three Parkhursts leaving his shoeprints about the city that fall—east side and west, campaign rally and Lexow hearing, in dusty halls in the rear of saloons and in garlanded uptown parlors.

But some of his most important work was done in the rectory, where he was available to talk with anyone. Tenement dwellers and uptown swells rang his doorbell, and mingled in his parlor. He received callers every afternoon at five o'clock.

Those who came earlier in the day, except in cases of extreme urgency, were asked to return at the calling hour. A white-capped maid trotted to and from the door, seating people and cheerily assigning numbers to them. The preacher would hurry home, from a luncheon campaign speech, an afternoon on church business, or a few hours at the Lexow hearings, to meet with whomsoever asked to see him. Nobody, however shabby or disreputable, was turned away. Sometimes people who could not for their own safety be seen in his presence were sent upstairs. On some days secret callers were distributed, as in a vaudeville farce, in various parts of the house.

He would open the sliding doors leading from the parlor to the dining room and ask, "Who is first?" The caller would follow him into the dining room. If the interview involved delicate matters, the sliding doors would be closed tightly; if not, they would remain slightly ajar. When the interview ended the doctor would lead the way through the parlor and open the door leading to the street himself.

These conversations kept him in touch with what was happening. The meetings delivered nuggets of information to his doorstep, some handed over as a gift, and some imparted through an unguarded remark. Visits from reporters on almost a daily basis also kept him abreast of the events and trends of the city; they came to him for news, but invariably they exchanged information as well.

He found that reporters and ordinary folk, in contrast to the Committee of Seventy, were not at all sure that Tammany would be defeated. They pointed out that the saloonkeepers controlled 40,000 votes and although Tammany would not get all of them this time, none of them would go to the reformers. A similar prediction could be made for the 15,000 or so votes that adhered to the police; the cops were angry with Tammany but it was unlikely that many of those votes would be cast for Strong and Goff. Tammany's votes would be diminished but the anti-Tammany vote would not be correspondingly increased.

He heard unsettling reports that the Wigwam was dangling promises of city jobs before the people, especially to the Grace Democrats, who were tempted with the argument that a Republican mayor would have nothing for them. He heard that Tammany was calling upon contractors for donations—frying the fat, as politicians called the extraction of contributions. He heard that the Tammany campaign chest was filling up, that Mr. Ten Percent, the Tammany collector, was wending through City Hall every payday taking his tithe, that Tammany had called upon the gamblers for jumbo donations, and that Tammany candidates were paying higher rates than usual for being nominated—up to $30,000 for judgeships that encompassed a fourteen-year term. Tammany headquarters, it was said, was humming at a frantic pace.

Both reporters and ordinary citizens gave him their impressions of the reform candidate for mayor. Some of them praised Strong's intelligence and his republican virtue: despite his wealth, he had begun life as poor as anyone in the Third Ward. But Lincoln Steffens, the *Post* reporter who had become a frequent visitor to the rectory, thought Strong "the blundering, bullheaded sort" and regarded his obstinacy as a drawback.[4]

As for Byrnes, he seemed determined to strike a blow against election fraud, but did that determination stem from his love of righteousness, or out of a deal with the Republicans—with Strong or Platt—to cling to office?

As for the Women's Municipal League, Parkhurst's visitors remained unconvinced that the ladies would make much of a splash south of Fourteenth Street. Parkhurst was inclined to see their point after his wife made her initial political speech; under the auspices of the League, Nellie Parkhurst spoke to a dozen women in a sea of empty seats in a drafty downtown hall.

Having learned that sometimes even the foolish had useful information, Parkhurst listened to everyone with amazing endurance.

* * *

One recurring matter in Parkhurst's meetings with the people was police brutality. Far from having abated, the Lexow hearings had made matters worse, especially in the Lower East Side and especially against labor, since Joseph Barondess, head of the cloakmakers union, had been praising the Lexow Committee in speeches. The police were trailing Barondess, following him even to meetings outside the city. As labor unrest began to spread from one sweatshop to another an official of the Amalgamated Clothing Cutters warned his brothers to beware that "the police are smarting under the lash of the Lexow Committee."[5]

Clubbing was visited with special severity upon the cloakmakers after a series of walkouts began. When the strikers assembled at Rutgers Square to march to a rally in Union Square in mid-October, the carnage was particularly bloody. Barondess led the protests that followed and members of the Lexow Committee raised questions as to why the police resorted so quickly to violence.

Faced with these pressures from the Senate committee, Byrnes ordered an investigation of the charges of brutality, but he predetermined the outcome by appointing Inspector Williams to conduct the investigation. Not only did Clubber Williams favor the Strong Arm Squad approach to handling labor disputes, but he was also the most unabashed anti-Semite in the Department. Furthermore, it was well known to Steffens and other reporters who visited Parkhurst regularly that Byrnes thought that the strikers provoked attack and got what was coming to them. Therefore it seemed likely that the affair would be brushed off.

True to form, Inspector Williams closed the Rutgers Square affair by concluding that the strikers were damned liars. The union officials said Clubber advised them that they were wasting their time coming to his office, since he would never believe the word of a Jew.

By this point Parkhurst was working on the next phase of his campaign—developing a working relationship with women union leaders in the clothing trade. Working women, he had come to believe, were an untapped reservoir of enormous energy. He had seen the dedication with which the women of the Ladies' Branch of the Cloakmakers and Dressmakers Union fought for higher pay and better working conditions in the Lower East Side sweatshops. Yet, though they suffered under police abuse, they had rejected his attempts to interest them in the anti-Tammany struggle, and one of the women had told him, "What we are after is more money."

On October 20 the minister worked in the rectory while awaiting a visit from Madame Marie Louise David. Many of the philosophical Anarchists of the city congregated in her Greenwich Village salon, and he had asked the Frenchwoman to meet with him in the hope that he could thereby gain an introduction to the downtown women labor leaders.

When they settled down to talk he said that he hoped to bring some of these women into the Woman's Municipal League, to open the organization beyond the confines of the white-glove set.

Madame David warned Parkhurst that her bohemian comrades could be balky and might raise objections against working openly on behalf of a reformist movement. She assured him, however, that she could assemble a number of women who would be willing to consider his proposal. In the long run, she ventured, Anarchism would gain from the kind of alliance he proposed, for it would help to dispel the invidious notion that Anarchists were bomb-throwers. Scientific Anarchism, she informed him, "is founded on the life of Christ."

Parkhurst responded that it was time for all honest citizens of whatever stripe to cast aside their differences and unite "to overthrow that bribery and corruption which make it possible for the rich to gain special privileges which are denied to the poor." He told the madame that women were rallying all over the city against Tammany, and that factory girls, women clerks, office workers, and downtown mothers wanted good government just as much as did uptown women.

* * *

Not the least important of the visitors to his rectory were the Society agents who kept him current on what was happening among the neighborhood organizations. One of the trouble spots was West 39th Street between Seventh and Eighth Avenues, a block notorious as Soubrette's Row (a soubrette being a generic role for a young actress). It was a favorite stop for traveling men stopping in the city.

Parkhurst was interested in this block not only because the Woman's Municipal League had become involved in it, but also because the precinct captain was the most disagreeable and thoroughly disliked on the force. Lacking Devery's humor and Clubber's flair, Captain James Price was high-handed, officious, resentful of criticism, and frequently in trouble with Police Justices for his insolence. He had faced disciplinary hearings before the Police Commission on three separate occasions during the current year, the only Captain with that distinction, and on one occasion had been fined five days' pay.

Although slow to revolt, the West Thirty-ninth Street neighborhood had by this point reached a militant pitch. The owner of an apartment house said he had wasted fifteen months trying to get action from Captain Price, Inspector Williams, Superintendent Byrnes, and Police Commissioner Martin, but that within ninety days of seeing Parkhurst five indictments had been handed up by the Grand Jury and fifteen houses on the block had been vacated.

* * *

Darkness had already fallen one evening as Parkhurst led out the last caller while the maid placed a cloth on the dining-room table for dinner. He had not finished his dinner when the bodyguards arrived to take him to the Second Reformed Church, where he was scheduled to speak that night on behalf of the West Thirty-ninth Street Association.

On arriving at the church he plunged into the crowd that surrounded him, shaking hands as if he were running for office.

"I understood Captain Price was to be here?" Parkhurst asked.

"No, he will not be here," someone answered.

"Ah, ah, that's too bad, too bad," he said with regret. "I was going to make an allusion to him, and I thought I might be a little more free if he were here."

When the speeches began there was an air of expectancy among the crowd in the church, packed to the rafters, willing to listen to the other speakers but waiting for the main course. When Parkhurst's turn came, he did not disappoint them. "What you have got to do is to make your warfare steadily against the police," he said. "Don't allow yourselves to be consumed in passion against the lawbreakers. Let us have the kindest possible Christian feeling toward those unfortunates whose bad ancestry and untoward circumstances and influences have shifted into evil lives."

Beginning with a solicitous tenderness, he gradually worked his way into an attack on Byrnes, charging that the police were ignoring Byrnes's directives.

"Byrnes shows he is not the man for the place when he cannot sit in his office and make his will felt throughout the force," he said. Byrnes has lost the power to control the force, and the best thing he can do under such circumstances is to get out and make way for a man that can."

The preacher assured the audience that the Parkhurst Society had the goods on Soubrettes' Row. Just days earlier his detectives had gained admittance to one of the brothels, and he offered to read their report, although he noted that he would substitute fictitious names for the real ones. He patted his pocket, from which a sheaf of papers was sticking out. When his listeners shouted that they wanted to hear the report, he pulled out the papers. He explained that the madame, whom he called Mrs. Brown, had invited his agents inside, and then he commenced to read:

"As we entered the flat, which was on the first floor, we saw there was a policeman standing on the stoop. We asked Mrs. So-and-so, Mrs. Brown, what he was doing there. She said he had been placed there by Captain Price to watch these houses."

Everyone laughed—men and women too.

The madame, he reported, suggested that the policeman might want a drink, and that the agents invited him to join them. Accepting quickly, the policeman sat down on a chair, taking off his helmet and holding it so that it covered his shield, and ordered whiskey.

"Here's good luck to you," said the policeman, swallowing the drink. But still he held his helmet over his shield. Simulating tipsiness, one of the agents approached him, grabbing his helmet from his hands.

"Let's see how I'd look in a cap." He put the helmet on and pranced around the room, affording his associate an opportunity to read the number on the shield.

The audience guffawed and applauded in glee as Parkhurst pantomimed the action, and someone shouted, "Yes, that's the way the police protect us!"

Parkhurst looked down at the report and placed his finger on it. "His number was . . ." The pastor paused and looked out at the crowd, hanging on every word, and waiting with bated breath for a shield number that would mean nothing to them.

"Now I'm not going to tell you the number. (Laughter and groans.) But the man to whom it belongs will probably hear about it. Listen to this."

He began to read again of how the policeman got up and reclaimed his hat, saying that he must go out, since the roundsman was nearly due. Before he went one of the agents asked him why he was stationed at the door. He replied that there had been complaints about the flat to the captain and that they "had to make a bluff at watching it to please some of the people."

The resulting laughter and cheers stopped proceedings briefly. They were amused, but also impressed. By this point it seemed to New Yorkers that it was impossible to keep any mischief from the knowledge of Parkhurst, whose eyes and ears were everywhere.

CANDIDATE GOFF

In America it was said that a candidate ran for office, while the expression in England was that a candidate stood for office. As the New York campaign plunged onward toward Election Day, Parkhurst was running at top speed, although not a candidate, while John Goff, the most conspicuous figure on the anti-Tammany ticket, approached the end of October without having made a single speech. It might be said that he was standing for office.

But it could not have been otherwise. The lawyer was working incessantly, sometimes straight through the night, to squeeze every drop out of each session of the Lexow Club. The work had taken its toll. His thick hair and beard were sprinkled with gray. The concentration of his efforts for so many months had narrowed his chest and turned his shoulders forward, wrinkled his high and broad forehead, and sank his temples.

Not through campaigning but through his work as counsel Goff intended to win the office of Recorder. After dropping out of consideration for the mayoral spot, the anti-Tammany coalition had nominated him to oppose Smyth, the Tammany incumbent who had fined him for contempt a year earlier.

Some New Yorkers had expected that the Goff-Smyth matchup would be the hottest election contest, not only because of the note of mutual enmity in their rivalry, but because the winner would control the criminal courts for the following fourteen years, making the office arguably the most important on the ballot. Yet Smyth did not campaign either; regarding his office as too dignified to permit political speech making, Smyth confined his efforts solely to posters and advertising.

The newspapers tried to heat it up. The *World* and the *Post* devoted barrels of ink to intense scrutiny of Frederick Smyth's tenure as Recorder and raised questions about why he had ordered the release of a notorious forger and a number of low-level Tammany criminals. "One reason why the Police Department is rotten," the *World* commented, "is because it is supported in its course by the District Attorney's office, and because the Recorder of this city has not held as he should have held the District Attorney's office up to its duty."[1] When reporters attempted to dig up more on Smyth, District Attorney Fellows slammed the records shut. Asked to help the newspapers gain access to public records, Smyth joined the blockade.

As the Mayor was administrative head of the city's departments, the Recorder was administrative head of its courts. The office-holder had broad powers of oversight throughout the city's criminal justice system, including the District Attorney's office and the Grand Juries, the selection of which was in his hands. The Recorder could have disqualified Silver Dollar Smith and Hochstim as bail bondsmen and banished them from the Essex Market Court House. But Smyth never did anything wrong, and never did anything right. He operated in blinders, overlooking everything that went on around him, never raising a question about Tammany's misdeeds.

Having served as an Assistant District Attorney, Goff was acquainted with Smyth's narrow rectitude, and offered an opposing style. The voters knew that John Goff would make a zealous Recorder.

* * *

While Goff did not campaign actively for office, he was in a position to aid both his own cause and that of his fellow reformers by means of his selection and emphasis in presenting hearing testimony. In the days just preceding the election he was angling everything not only to make himself look good but to present witnesses who would make Tammany look bad.

With that aim in mind he made Police Commissioner John Sheehan dance on his griddle for five days. Some observers attributed the episode as a concession to the Platt men in the Lexow Club who were urging him to "go up higher," but Goff steered the hearings by his own lights, and obviously regarded the prolonged quizzing of Sheehan as the best political option open to him at the moment. It served as an emphatic reminder of the unqualified men whom Tammany Hall appointed to sensitive public positions.

Goff's questions established the chumminess of Sheehan and Inspector Clubber Williams. Commissioner Sheehan admitted that he had made efforts to get Clubber on the Police Board. Goff asked whether Sheehan recalled that, just prior to the Broome Street riot, Williams had denied that there were any brothels or gambling dens in Captain Devery's precinct.

"Do you remember," Goff continued, "that five of these very houses that Inspector Williams pronounced to be reputable were very shortly afterward raided by Dr. Parkhurst's agents, and that the keepers were all convicted in Special Sessions?"

"Yes, I do remember that, and I said to the Board that there must have been something wrong in Williams's report." This brought a ripple of spectator laughter.

"And you admit then that it was judicially determined that Williams was either an official liar or grossly negligent in his duties?"

"The Judges didn't declare him to be any such thing."

"But Inspector Williams said that these houses were reputable, and that Dr. Parkhurst was a liar. Now, the judges in Special Sessions declared that Parkhurst's report was true, and if that doesn't judicially declare Williams to be an official liar, what then was their decision?"

Sheehan hesitated for a moment, then said, "Maybe those disorderly houses were organized after Williams made his report."

"And who would organize disorderly houses for the purpose of proving Williams to be a liar?" Goff asked.

"The Society for the Prevention of Crime," Sheehan said hotly, "would be willing to do almost anything to run Williams down."

"Indeed! So then you are willing to go before the Legislature and the country as saying that the Society of which Dr. Parkhurst is president would be guilty of organizing houses of ill fame for the purpose of downing an inspector of police?"

"I say they would like to do anything to down him."

Sheehan's testimony established that he was unfamiliar with the location of precinct stations and was less informed about the status of several important police matters than was the average careful newspaper reader. After exposing his incompetence, Goff asked what Sheehan did to justify his salary since he appeared to do nothing and know nothing except a garble of misinformation. Sheehan left the stand the laughing-stock of New York, his testimony a refutation of those who extolled Croker's shrewd judgment of men.

* * *

Stories began to circulate that the Wigwam had made overtures to Goff about withdrawing as Lexow Committee counsel. One rumor had it that he had been offered $300,000 to quit. According to another tale making the rounds, Goff had been offered the nomination for mayor as the Grace Democrat candidate with a promise of Tammany backing. Goff refused to comment on any of these stories. One reporter suggested that he ought to deny the rumors if they were groundless "in the interest of fair play." Goff responded: "I have told everyone who has broached the subject to me that I would not say a word about it."

He also continued the efforts he had begun a year earlier to foil election violations. He assailed Tammany Police Justices, who had without authority released 800 vagrants sent to Blackwell's Island. "For what purpose this was done," Goff said, "I leave it to you to infer." Goff worked with Byrnes, who had his captains raid downtown lodging houses, pulling red-nosed and bedraggled tramps before Police Justices for election fraud.

Second only to Parkhurst in the public's affection, Goff was applauded every morning when he entered the hearing room. Unlike the pastor, however, Goff was a dealmaker. He had carved out a career as a lawyer in courthouses where the settlement was actively sought after. He fought with his fellow lawyers in the courtroom and then bargained with them over lunch. As an Assistant District Attorney he had worked closely with Byrnes and with some of the cops he was now investigating, and while he despised some of them he liked others. He numbered Tammany people among his friends, including Dr. Jenkins, who was Boss Croker's brother-in-law.

Making deals went with the Lexow Committee counsel's job; that was how confessions were extracted from witnesses, who were absolved from prosecution for their crimes in return for testimony. That was the deal, for example, that he offered to Madame Hermann to induce her to return to New York.

Matilda Hermann was one of the madames that the police had hustled out of town to keep her from the Lexow Committee's clutches. Goff especially wanted the testimony of Madame Hermann, who had paid more than $30,000 in blackmail to the police, and he sent agents to Toronto and then to Chicago to bring her back.

Although Matilda Hermann's story contained the standard ingredients of blackmail and protected vice, it blew up into something bigger when the returning party, which included the madame, a Goff agent, and the sergeant-at-arms of the Lexow Committee were detained under mysterious circumstances in Jersey City, just as they were about to board the ferry for New York.

For months Goff had been charging that the police would stop at nothing to interfere with the investigation, and now he claimed to have proof. He contended that the police had engineered the cooperation of their brother officers in Jersey City to jail a witness headed for the committee.

Goff burst into the courtroom that day brushing past the applause and cheers, his face flushed and brows knitted in anger.

"I told you several weeks ago that an important witness had been spirited away at midnight," he said. "She was barely dressed. A carriage stood in front of her door; she was thrust inside and rolled away. After considerable difficulty we succeeded in getting this woman to agree to testify here. She arrived in Jersey City this morning. Immediately upon her arrival she and all our men who accompanied her were arrested. A charge of disorderly conduct was trumped up. The police of Jersey City used threats and violent language to our men. The entire party was dragged before a police magistrate."

"Was it shown that your men were the servants of the Senate of this State?" Senator Lexow asked.

"Yes, they were so informed, but that made no difference. And understand me, Senators, this woman was a voluntary witness, and in spite of the fact that she wished to come before you and testify she was held in Jersey City and not allowed to do so."

If it were true that the police conspired to keep Matilda Hermann in a Jersey City jail so that she could not testify until after the election, they made a grievous error. The resulting uproar caused far more damage to their cause than they could ever have imagined. In much the same way that the activities of Officer Hussey in framing Mrs. Urchittel provided the ultimate in police oppression, the efforts expended on keeping Mrs. Hermann from testifying came to represent, for the people of New York, the ultimate in police audacity and arrogance.

*　*　*

The Matilda Hermann debacle was an extraordinary run of luck for Goff, but he never trusted to chance. To ensure that he would end the pre-election hearings with what vaudevillians called "a wow finish," Goff had been saving a witness under wraps—a short, stout gray-bearded physician who specialized as a "women's doctor." And Dr. Newton Whitehead had quite a story to tell.

On occasion Dr. Whitehead performed abortions. Although they were illegal, in one of his conferences with Goff he estimated that at least two hundred physicians in the city had performed abortions, almost all of them for unmarried women. Since respectable society regarded abortionists as "babykillers," an abortionist was bereft of friends and helpless in the clutches of the police—a goose ready for plucking. As abortions increased in the city, the police greedily pursued abortionists as a new source of revenue.

When he came to see Goff, late one night in April, Dr. Whitehead said in a fury that he been bled so white that he would confess everything, take his revenge on the police at any cost. And this is the story as the physician told it that night.

Dr. Whitehead was arrested for the first time on February 24, apparently by entrapment. While the doctor was in custody, on the way downtown to Mulberry Street on the Third Avenue Elevated, Detective Sergeant William Frink insisted that the suspect hire Emmanuel Friend as his lawyer. "I wanted to have Howe & Hummel," the doctor said, "but Mr. Frink said that Howe & Hummel were played out now, and that Friend was in with the people at headquarters."

The abortionist agreed to engage Friend, a Tammany clubhouse man whose specialty was defending brothels. (He had represented all of the madames arraigned in the Essex Market Court House on the day of the Broome Street riot.) Friend took $500 and Sergeant Frink took the same, with the understanding that Frink's memory would fail him and the case would be dismissed. But on the date of his hearing in the Jefferson Market Court House, Friend asked for $200 for the bondsman. When Dr. Whitehead protested that the bail bond fee had been included in his payments, Friend told him: "Doctor, I wouldn't make a kick for $200 but I only got fifty percent of it. I have to give half of it to the police. That's the way I get cases."

Sergeant Frink forgot a lot of things on the stand as agreed, and the Justice dismissed the case. Within weeks, however, Dr. Whitehead was twice more arrested, and the avarice he met on every side seemed limitless. The physician made payments to the police, to Friend, to other lawyers with clients who were ready to testify against him, to bail bondsmen, to midwives, and to Sergeant William O'Toole, in charge of the police contingent at the Jefferson Market Court House.

Dr. Whitehead suspected that Police Justice Joseph Koch was involved in the ring as well. On one occasion Dr. Whitehead refused to pay $750 in bail bond fees, demanding to be taken to the Tombs instead. Friend and Sergeant O'Toole begged him to reconsider, whispered together, came and went several times and eventually returned to announce hopefully that Justice Koch had reduced the bail and that the bail bond fee would be correspondingly reduced to $400. He paid it.

When Sergeant Frink rapped on his door to arrest him for the third time, on April 7, Dr. Whitehead complained at the prospect of spending another night in jail, and Frink offered to let him sleep comfortably at home, for fifty dollars. The deal was struck, with the physician promising to show up in Justice Koch's court the following morning.

But the abortionist was too angry to sleep. He knew that Goff was compiling evidence of police corruption while waiting for Sutherland to finish up his part of the Lexow investigation. Dr. Whitehead took a carriage to Goff's home and mapped out tactics with him until 1 A.M. Goff had saved this shocking story for the last. He intended to bring Dr. Whitehead before the Lexow Committee on November 3, the last session before the election. It had an election aspect, since Emmanuel Friend was campaign manager for Recorder Smyth.

* * *

But Goff wanted more. He wanted a full-hearted confession on the witness stand; he wanted a high-ranking police official sobbing for forgiveness, and showing where the bribes ended up. And he had two possible candidates.

The case of Captain Creeden, who had paid for his promotion, was not ready. Fortunately Goff had another Captain in an uncomfortable position, for in the middle of October the Grand Jury indicted Captain Schmittberger on charges of taking payoffs from steamship companies—the first indictment based directly on evidence developed at the Lexow hearings. Now Goff had all the leverage he needed to extract a public confession.

But before he made any deals with Goff, Captain Max went to his mentor Byrnes in search of guidance. The highest card that Max held was not an accounting of his own misdeeds but his inside knowledge of the crimes of his superiors. A repentant Captain ready to implicate those higher than himself ought to be worth a lot to Goff. He confided his secrets to Byrnes; for that matter he had been confiding in the Superintendent for some time, and Byrnes had looked to Max's interests. Now Max hoped that Byrnes would bargain on his behalf.

Schmittberger could show where the bribes went; he could testify authoritatively that there were established percentages in payoffs that a Captain distributed to his wardman for collecting them and to his Inspector who oversaw his work, 20 percent to the former, 25 percent to the latter, and that Inspectors McAvoy and Williams had taken these cuts. For example, when Byrnes transferred Max to the 88th Street precinct in the Big Shakeup of 1892, Schmittberger immediately sent his wardman to see Cornelius Parker, who had three horse rooms and ten numbers shops in the precinct. The price of protection for Parker was $800 a month; Captain Schmittberger kept $440 and gave $160 (20 percent) to his wardman and $200 (25 percent) to Inspector Williams.

Schmittberger also had evidence damaging to both Tammany Police Commissioners, Martin and Sheehan.

From May to December 1893, Captain Max had been commander at the West 47th Street precinct, a good assignment teeming with numbers shops and whorehouses. The precinct lay within the area that Jimmy Martin ruled as a Tammany district chief. Soon after Max settled in, Police Board President Martin instructed him to leave some of the whorehouses alone "until a school is built; then you can drive them out." Max, a member of the Tammany-based Pequod Club, was not eager to disobey someone who outranked him both in Tammany Hall and in the Police Department, but after receiving several complaints he sent his Wardman, Casey, on a fact-finding expedition to a brothel

Sheehan, Byrnes, and Martin

kept by Sadie West on West Fifty-first Street. Mrs. West refused to give Casey any satisfactory answers. Eventually she said to him, "Do you know Commissioner Martin?" Casey nodded. "You go and see Commissioner Martin," she said. "He will tell you who I am."

That night Schmittberger received a telephone call ordering him to report to Commissioner Martin at Mulberry Street in the morning. When he reported, Martin told him to send Casey "back there and make him apologize." Schmittberger protested that Casey was checking on a complaint from neighbors. "I don't care," Jimmy Martin responded. "You do as you're told. You send that man there and make him apologize to that lady." Schmittberger and Casey did as they were commanded.

Captain Schmittberger had also been embroiled in a dispute with Police Commissioner Sheehan. After Max had turned down several requests from a pair of sports who wanted to open a gambling den on Broadway between Forty-first and Forty-second Streets, one of the pair, a man named Proctor, came to see Max with a letter from Sheehan. The Police Commissioner asked Max to show his friend Proctor every consideration in any business endeavor that might engage his interest. (The only business in which Proctor was interested was gambling.) Max scurried downtown to confide in Byrnes about this contretemps. "Schmittberger, if you let that house open I'll break you," Byrnes told him. In the Pequod Club, where Tammany captains, brothel keepers and police captains hobnobbed in their off-hours, Commissioner Sheehan ordered Max to let Proctor run his operation without hindrance, contending that other gamblers were operating in the area and that the Captain was unfairly discriminating against his friend. Max responded that he was protecting Sheehan's good name, for Proctor was waving about Sheehan's letter of introduction and invoking the Commissioner's name in a compromising manner, and that he had orders from the Superintendent not to allow gambling, and would not risk facing charges of allowing gambling.

* * *

After Schmittberger was indicted, he went to Goff and told him about these events. With the advice of Byrnes, he was trying to trade his testimony for immunity, which in his case meant dropping of the charges. Max also hoped to have his standing on the police force protected, because he expected that the Police Commission would immediately dismiss him after he confessed to his misdeeds.

Schmittberger's approach to Goff introduced an important new element in the dealmaking—that Byrnes had brokered it, that the Superintendent himself delivered to Goff a Police Captain ready to name names and point fingers. How often Byrnes and Goff conferred, when the initial conference was held, and how much Byrnes helped steer Goff to other evidence was never spelled out, but it was later acknowledged that Byrnes cooperated with the Lexow Committee and was helpful in unspecified ways.

Byrnes knew that eventually he too would be taking the witness chair to give an accounting of his stewardship. So be it. But when that day came, Byrnes would have Goff and the Lexow Committee in his debt. The maxim that one hand washes the other had guided Byrnes throughout his police career, and with one significant exception—the intractable Parkhurst—he had pursued the policy of quid pro quo in his associations with felons, with Wall Street, and now with Goff, who in the following January might well be the Recorder.

Parkhurst was struggling for a new order, while Goff was working in the old system, in which some are punished while others bargain their way out of trouble. Byrnes felt at home in that system; he was used to dealing with men who could be seduced by power and success, who loved to wear long robes and sit in the councils of the mighty. Byrnes was willing to adjust to new circumstances in a new administration, but he expected that it would have some of the familiar old features.

49

THE BIG STORY

One day there were rumors of threats against Goff's life, on the next day a madame would flee to Europe, and on the following day prisoners at Sing Sing, convicted of fraud in the 1893 election, would warn others not to make the same mistake. Newspapers celebrated the heyday of journalism and New Yorkers read every word.

A reporter sent to cover the Lexow hearings had a good chance of writing the newspaper's lead story that day—unless the lead story turned out to be the political campaign, or Tom Byrnes and Jimmy Martin snarling at each other at a Police Commission meeting, or the indictment of a Police Captain. Often the newspapers would begin the day's Lexow coverage on the front page with a quick summary of the highlights, then jump inside for several columns of lengthy extracts from the testimony. On several occasions the *Sun* and the *World* devoted an entire front page to the hearings. But a mere retelling of the hearing testimony was never enough; a complete account had to include the comments of candidates on the hearings, police complaints of unfairness, neighborhood protests, brushes with the law of former Lexow witnesses, Parkhurst's views, the disappearances of various key figures, interviews with madames, sermons, comments from the bench, and speculative stories on what might happen next—often adding up to three full pages of coverage.

Everybody—preachers and newsboys, saloon philosophers and concert-hall comedians—had his own version of the story to tell, and New Yorkers savored the story's comic possibilities. They made up rhyme about the police captains who owned yachts, and corner lots. They laughed about Justice Divver's black eye and his tendency when tipsy to fall off his chair. At the Century Club, a member dressed as Parkhurst ran onstage during a performance and said: "Unless this show is made more indecent it must stop."[1]

Deep down, though, they were a sentimental lot, and their dearest moments were those that brought a lump to the throat and a tear to the eye—such as the scene enacted in the hearing room on an afternoon in the latter half of October.

* * *

When the children were ushered into the courtroom late in the afternoon, a witness was explaining how she had been released from Blackwell's Island in less than a month although she had been sentenced to six months as a prostitute. The Urchittel children—a tall girl of about thirteen years, a mite of a boy, and a tiny girl—gazed wide-eyed at the perfumed and bedecked woman and at the unfamiliar surroundings. Rows of silent men stared back at them from all sides, nodding solemnly or smiling with reassurance. The reporters took a measured look at them and scribbled on their notepads, while other men sketched their likenesses. The children were led to the front of the courtroom, where sat the members of the Lexow Committee, crowded together behind the judge's bench, and none smiling more broadly than the chubby Senator Jacob Cantor of Tammany Hall. Off in a corner sat their mother.

She waved timidly when she saw her children enter and take places in front of the committee. Then Caela Urchittel sobbed and had to restrain herself from springing forward to clutch them in her arms. But it was necessary for her to wait. The Hebrew Sheltering Guardian Society had surrendered the little ones to the care of the State Senate Investigating Committee, and before they could reach the arms of their mother certain formalities had to be observed.

Like her children, Caela Urchittel was neatly dressed. A benefactor had helped all of them, and the widow wore a new black gown and jacket and a new black bonnet with white-tipped plumes, although the clothing could not hide the wan features that marked her long ordeal. Mrs. Urchittel quivered with impatient excitement until the prostitute was finally excused.

Goff thanked the Hebrew society as well as Senator Cantor for his "very active part in bringing about this reconciliation." He concluded: "It affords me, Senators, in your name, great pleasure to give these children to their mother."

But not yet. Senator Lexow had to add a few words. As he orated Mrs. Urchittel, unable to contain herself any longer, cried out and sprang to her children, gathering them in her arms. They clustered about her and clung to her. There was a roar of applause. Tears rolled down the cheeks of many of the spectators.

Down sank Mrs. Urchittel on her knees, her right arm enfolding her babes as if they were a bouquet, her left raised heavenward. In a strange tongue she invoked the blessings of Jehovah on the kind gentlemen. She bade her children pray for them, and prayed for them herself right then and there. Then she began to thank them.

"That is all right, that is all right, my good woman," said the blushing Lexow. Senator Bradley pinched up some snuff, but even that movement did not conceal the mist in Uncle Dan's eyes.

A *World* editorial called the reunion "a happy ending to one of the saddest stories of wrong and persecution ever related before an American tribunal."[2]

* * *

Upstate the ongoing story was a fairy tale of the wicked city full of baggage thieves, white slavers who drugged the drinks of runaway young girls and dragged them away to a fate worse than death, and sidewalk vendors who sold expensive goods and then with sleight-of-hand substituted a cheap imitation at the moment of sale. Whenever they got home, the Republican Senators on the committee had many such whiz-bang anecdotes to tell to their constituents.

"We who live in the rural districts have looked with ever-increasing concern toward the great municipalities of the State as the danger spots of our liberties," Senator Lexow told the folks of Rockland County. "Vast concentrations of people within a small radius have produced new conditions not contemplated by our forefathers when they seared the young Republic upon the rock of individualism." After reciting a litany of abuses, including the triumph of boss rule over the public will and crime and immorality over purity and virtue, he concluded: "But one step further and anarchy is at the door knocking for entrance."

In more distant outposts, people like the LaGuardias, a family of New Yorkers transplanted to Arizona, read all about it. Every week they went into town to pick up a Sunday edition of the *World*. Their eleven-year-old son, Fiorello (later to become one of New York's greatest mayors), devoured every available word about the Lexow hearings, the activities of the Parkhurst Society, and the reports of the newspaper's own dogged journalists. "Unlike boys who grew up in the city and who heard from childhood about such things as graft and corruption, the amazing disclosures hit me like a shock," he later wrote. "I could not understand how the people of the greatest city in the country could put up with the vice and crime that existed there."

Urbanites read of the doings in New York with the shock of recognition. Journalists from newspapers around the nation had been sent to New York to "write up the hearings," and their dispatches reminded city dwellers that Chicago also had protected brothels and gambling dens, that Denver's police courts also bore looking into, that a Philadelphia preacher was taking lessons from Parkhurst.

Depending upon where it was read and who read it, the big story of New York that fall was interpreted as a lesson in what happened when the Irish took over city government; or about the need to keep the undesirable immigrants of Eastern and Southern Europe out; or about the growing power of saloons in cities across the nation; or about the changing morality that was emerging with the coming of a new century.

Parkhurst too saw the story from his own perspective.

Community as he had known it in the Berkshire Mountains was absent from the city. This was not the city upon a hill, the city of Pilgrims who had pledged mutual support during their voyage over the sea. Nor did this city have the same spirit as did the town of Lenox where Parkhurst had tended his first pastorate; where Parkhurst had preached on the text from First Corinthians: "Let no man seek his own; but every man another's wealth." Nor was this one of the little towns of Eastern Europe where the Jews awaited the Messiah. There was no easy unity to which the orator could appeal, the unity of faith, kinship, or shared visions. This was the American Metropolis, where the devil took the hindmost, a city of cross-purposes and contradictions. Yet somehow this place of unconnected people had to be made to work, because this was what America was going to be like in the time to come.

"And we won't be a successful municipality," Parkhurst told a crowd one October night, "until the chasms are bridged. How many of my audience know aught of the life below Fourteenth Street? Do any of you know that the persons down there have responsive hearts and souls and sympathies, and that when the right word is spoken, there is an echo?"

He described the cordial welcomes he had met in his visits to those neighborhoods. Nowhere, he said, did he encounter danger of physical violence. He sought to make permeable the divisions of society, he asked that poor persons be not just remembered in prayers but befriended, and he became irked when a burst of applause greeted these words.

"It's all very well," he shouted, "to sit here in a comfortable church and applaud a fine sentiment, but why don't you go down among these poor, oppressed, suffering citizens, who know naught of American institutions and ways, and clasp their hands in good fellowship? Then there would be assurance of a bright municipal future and of a city to be proud of and promise of a regenerated municipality."

He had visited their bare downtown missions and their third-floor synagogues, and he had found that one way to teach American institutions to the immigrants was to be a thorn in their sides—to overcome the resignation with which so many of them had always faced birth, death and the contumely of their betters. If the Anarchists could speak in militant terms, as a Soldier of the Lamb so could he.

In the neighborhoods below Fourteenth Street he called Tammany to account as a fraud that posed as a protector of the lowly. Over the years Tammany had been called upon to explain much, but never before had it been accused of exploiting widows and orphans. In the speeches that he made in the last days before the election he often mentioned Mary Sallade and Kate Monahan, and especially Caela Urchittel.

* * *

The preacher generated so much excitement downtown that even the Committee of Seventy saw the possibilities, and Strong went south of Fourteenth Street for a star-spangled night of ethnic campaigning. He spoke at a meeting in the Lower East Side, where he told the Jews that he had fought against the blackballing of a Jew from the Union League. From there he went to a meeting of Italians in the Bowery, where he said that the ballot would make them the equal of all other Americans. Then he went to a meeting in a German neighborhood, where he expressed support for a more liberal excise law and let it be known that he was German on his mother's side.

Strong was only one of the campaign attractions on the street that night. The reform candidate for Assembly in the Second District staged an extravaganza up the Bowery, occupying every corner from Chatham Square to Cooper Union. His speakers on wagons addressed crowds on the northwest and southwest corners of each cross street—a mile-long mass meeting, competing with Tammany candidates in several theaters along the Bowery and at Cooper Union.

In speeches that evening Parkhurst praised the courage of the immigrants who were volunteering as poll-watchers at every polling place in the downtown, determined to win the freedom that they sought.

Meanwhile a group of about twenty people, most of them women, waited in a ground-floor flat in Greenwich Village for Parkhurst to turn up. He had several engagements that night but he had promised that he would stop by, and at one point an assistant knocked to tell them that the minister, although running late, would keep his appointment.

The flat, its walls adorned with photographs and drawings of the Haymarket martyrs and other fire-breathing radicals, belonged to Madame Marie Louise David. The people, whom she had gathered to meet the pastor, rose out of a rootless fringe—political adventurers, bohemian drifters, and unknown artists and writers. While waiting for Parkhurst they diverted themselves by agreeing that Jay Gould had lacked the brains even of a grocery clerk.

When Parkhurst arrived he found an audience of deliberate oddities. In the styling of their hair, the flow of their garments, the attitudes in which they sat, they proclaimed a demand to be noticed. The pastor had come not only to enlist them in his cause, but also to exchange views with them. He had entered a hothouse of ideas, with an exotic plant in every pot. For some of his listeners the cross he wore as a lapel pin signified the Spanish Inquisition. Some, had they heard him preach on the values of the hearth, would have protested that marriage was an evil institution that held women and children hostage to drunken brutal men. In a sense this meeting was the exact opposite of the New England town meeting, where everyone shared certain basic premises. In the room in which he found himself, no two people shared the same view.

Those were the conditions under which he had to disseminate his message, and that room was a preview of the twentieth century, the kind of urban America in which he and they were destined to live. It would be a century in which the only shared vision was the will to be free, and it would have to be a century of coalitions based on the model of the anti-Tammany forces.

He said he had come to them because he hoped that they would agree that Tammany Hall's administration was illegitimate, since it oppressed the people. Whatever their differences, it was in their common interest that the city be preserved. One of the women replied that he was speaking the oratory of reform, but the reformers had overthrown Tweed, "and we know what followed."

Corruption had returned, Parkhurst concurred, but to stop it dead this time the Woman's Municipal League would remain permanently organized. "As for the work of the Society for the Prevention of Crime," he added, "I represent we will not have more than begun when election day has passed. That is in the direction of an answer to your question. Mr. Lexow told me today that there was a bill already drawn for submission to the Legislature making the Lexow Committee or one like it a permanent institution."

"We will have a meeting," said Madame David. "We have a speaker we can rely upon—Miss Emma Goldman." She smiled upon the dark corner where Goldman sat, and Parkhurst bent his gleaming spectacles to a doorway where a young woman sat in gloom and alone, as if not entirely committed to the spirit of the gathering.

"Why, is that Miss Goldman?" he exclaimed, arising and walking toward her. "I am very glad to meet you. I have heard of Miss Goldman."

"And I have heard of Dr. Parkhurst," she responded, bringing a chuckle to the group. "If I speak it is understood, of course, that I make no concessions," she added, rising to shake his hand. "I must maintain the principles in which I believe."

"As to that," he said, "I have gone among people of all creeds—among Hebrews, for instance, who do not believe in one part of the Bible in which I believe. I would consider it discourteous to them were I to attempt to make the occasion of my speaking among them on an entirely foreign topic an occasion for an effort to persuade them to my particular views on religious questions. I suppose you mean that you will, while holding to your principles, enter upon this movement for better municipal government, act and speak in the same spirit in which I have suggested?"

Goldman did not reply, but sat down at the table by his side and asked him his address and Goff's address and Moss' address, all of which she penciled in her notebook. Then the Doctor took her address and more discussion followed, as a result of which it was agreed that Parkhurst would contact some of the leaders of the Women's Municipal League to arrange for a meeting with the women Anarchists.

He said that he numbered himself among the people. "I was born in New England and lived on a farm," he said. "I am glad of it now, for I learned to work." He said he was raised on brown bread and pork and beans, and Emma Goldman said that was the kind of food they had on Blackwell's Island.

The Anarchists agreed to affiliate with the Woman's Municipal League, but only as an autonomous branch, and Emma Goldman had her way in insisting that the branch have no laws or rules of any sort, so that none might tyrannize over her.

Parkhurst had no reason for confidence that anything would come of his overture, but he had delivered it as persuasively as he knew how. In a daring political move, he had approached the radicals as serious players. Whether the Anarchists joined or sat in the gloom, anyone who looked at the temper of the city as the election approached had to concur that Parkhurst had taken the spirit of inclusion as far as it would go.

50

JUDGMENT DAY NEARS

With five days to election, Goff's griddle sizzled more audibly.

Goff charged that Morris Tekulsky as an official of the liquor dealers trade association had packed Grand Juries with men sympathetic to the saloon business. The unflustered Tekulsky denied that he wielded such power but admitted that he had sent in "names of reputable businessmen, so that we could get a proper Grand Jury."

J. P. Smith, editor of the *Wine and Spirits Gazette*, was next called to the witness chair to attest that Tekulsky was far too modest.

"In the early part of 1891," Smith said, "Mr. Tekulsky came to me and said that the liquor trade had not received proper consideration at the hands of the Grand Jury. He wanted me to give him some names, not liquor dealers, he said, but owners of real estate having saloons in their buildings. I asked him how he could arrange it. He said never mind that—that he could do so."

Lexow was shocked. "And this is a method," he asked, "by which those charged or about to be charged with the commission of crimes may pack the Grand Juries in their own interest?"

Goff informed the chairman that Parkhurst and Moss had protested a year earlier that a Grand Jury had been loaded with men friendly to the saloon interests—an accusation considered so outrageous that they "came within an ace of being indicted for it." Goff did not point out (although the newspapers did so for him) that the official in charge of forming Grand Jury panels was his rival, Recorder Smyth.

* * *

On the following morning, four days from election, the crowds pressing to get into the Lexow hearing filled the General Sessions building, the stairs outside and the adjoining sidewalks. They all wanted to see Madame Hermann, just released from New Jersey captivity.

Surrounded by Parkhurst detectives and wearing a professional smile, the tall, attractive brunette glided into the hearing room, and took the chair. The rapt crowd stirred as her gloved hands fluttered and her dark eyes roamed around the room.

Goff conducted the thirty-seven-year-old madame through a narrative covering her transactions with police officials from 1886 through 1892. Although Mrs. Hermann operated on a scale grander and fancier than did Lena Cohen and Augusta Thurow, the story of money passing from hand to hand was similar—initiation fees, emoluments to the cops on the corner, extra money to the sergeant on the desk to make sure that the bail was accepted and her girls released, and demands that grew ever more exorbitant until they forced her out of the trade.

When she received a subpoena to appear before the committee, she said, she wanted to testify but was frightened. She received threats that if she spilled the beans the police would send her to prison. Cops followed her wherever she went, threatening to arrest her. To hasten her flight, the police sent $1,700 by messenger to cover her expenses. The same messenger returned at 10 P.M. on a Sunday night and said someone from the police wanted to see her.

"Well, you didn't go out at that time of night to see a man in the street," Goff remarked.

"There were twelve men, Mr. Goff," she answered.

The twelve policemen saw to her departure on an odyssey that took her to Toronto and then to Chicago, where she stayed at a hotel filled with New York madames—all waiting for the Lexow Committee to leave New York. She said the police had paid them all to flee.

These police attempts to meddle with the committee's work were, according to an editorial headline in the *World*, "The Worst Outrage Yet."

Matilda Hermann testifies

* * *

But there was an even more shocking tale to come, and Goff called the abortionist Dr. Whitehead as a witness on the last day of pre-election testimony.

The spectators hung on every word of the physician's revelations of arrests and fixes. Near the end he told of an incident that happened in April when a woman came to his office seeking an abortion.

"I refused," the doctor testified. "I told her I had been blackmailed, and thought I would leave New York; that I was now held by a Justice to await the action of the Grand Jury." He smiled faintly. "She asked what Justice, and when I told her Justice Koch, she exclaimed, 'My God! He is the man who got me this way!'"

The packed courtroom burst into a roar of surprise.

The doctor said she told him this was the fifth time that Koch had impregnated her and that if Dr. Whitehead agreed to perform the operation she would talk to the Justice.

A few days later Justice Koch met in conference with the physician and his lawyer, Emmanuel Friend. According to Dr. Whitehead's testimony the Justice, looking chagrined, said to him: "Doctor, I am very sorry about this affair. I didn't know my girl had been to you." Then the Justice turned to the lawyer Friend and, in a confidential tone, added: "It's that Alexander woman, who made trouble for me before."

The physician's testimony sent shock waves through the city. One newspaper reported it under the headline "Villainy's Lowest Depths"; another, "The Foulest Revelations Of All." The *Post* demanded that Friend—Recorder Smyth's campaign manager—be disbarred.

"Of all the exposures that have shocked not only our city but the civilized world," Goff summed up, "I think the most terrible of all is the testimony of this afternoon. I think we have reached the climax of the horrible."

Sunday brought a wave of red-hot sermons. One pastor called the latest Lexow revelations "too horrible to be described." Another welcomed the coming election as "Judgment Day." A third said that the city was "upon the eve of a crisis greater than any through which we have been called upon to pass since the days of the Civil War."

At Madison Square Presbyterian Church two thousand people crammed themselves into pews, balcony and aisles built for half that number. Stating his case as vigorously as his strained vocal cords permitted, Parkhurst predicted that the effect of the election would be immeasurable, that a victory for reform would "create a thousand echoes far and wide across the continent." He suggested that nothing less than America's emerging role as a world power hung in the balance; for "if America, if New York, has not in its Christianity virile tension sufficient to subdue its own heathen and protect itself from its own outlaws, it will lack just those credentials needed to secure it hospitable reception and entertainment in Peking and Madagascar.

"A hundred years from today," he croaked, "history on this side and on the other side of the Atlantic will be in some measure what the momentous issues of this week make it."

Responding to the shock registered in respectable parlors for his overtures to Anarchists, he contrasted the Anarchist's forthright defiance of law to Tammany Hall's covert lawlessness.

"As a general principle the red-bannered procession is to be preferred, for then you know precisely who is who and what is what," he said. "Now, if there is anything that the Senate Committee has succeeded in demonstrating to this city, it is that the corporation of political reptiles that is administering this city has contempt for everything that is fixed and determined, and that the outward ceremonies of legality under which it conducts its operations are simply the thin and sneaking disguise with which it seeks to make its anarchical defiance of everything which is statutory—in other words, that the nerve and tissue of the system is anarchy in its essence . . . but tricked out in the millinery of legality."

After that, campaigning having ravaged his voice, Parkhurst spoke no more. But the rallies went on—in Union Square, Rutgers Square, Cooper Union and in theaters. Everybody knew that the uptown districts would go for the anti-Tammany ticket, but what would happen downtown? The answer to that question would determine the outcome.

Jewish speakers chided their listeners. If the people were trampled upon, they said, it was their own fault. They said that freedom was not a free gift but a prize, and that people unworthy of it would never win it. Those uncouth, thick-bearded men with unpronounceable names cheered mightily, and, although some of them were not even registered to vote, volunteered to watch the poll-watchers and to protect the men who were watching the poll-watchers.

* * *

At the rectory, Parkhurst explained to reporters his controversial overtures to the Anarchists. "They are bitterly opposed to Tammany Hall and are ready to work against it," he said. "It is not wise that any set of people holding extreme views should be left alone. It is by mingling with those who do not think as they do that temperance in sentiment is brought about."[1] He spent the rest of the day writing an appeal to be distributed in districts below the line, calling upon the ordinary people to forsake bossism and to vote for the anti-Tammany forces. "We call this a free country, and a good many Germans, Italians, Hebrews and Russians have come here because they wanted to find liberty," the pastor wrote in his flyer. "They find a statue of liberty down in the harbor, but no personal liberty up in the city."

When it was done, it was sent out to be translated into various languages, printed on circulars, and pasted on walls. With that his election work was over. If he had neglected to do anything, it was too late to remedy that now. It was time to take some hot water with lemon and honey and rest his vocal cords.

He saw auguries of victory. People with a feel for the public mood found the better element aroused, and the Tammany element despondent. Croker (back from Ireland and Europe) was disavowing any responsibility for defeat, and his Wigwam allies were nodding in glum agreement that Tammany was adrift without its leader.

But on the brink of the election the reform forces grew jittery. Rumors continued to fly over the transom. One had it that Tammany would somehow conspire to close many of the polls in unfriendly territory long before the legal closing time of four o'clock. It was said that the Tammany men were telling all the men south of Fourteenth Street that if Parkhurst's hens won the election, no man would ever get another glass of beer in New York City. And the most gnawing uncertainty for the reformers was the fidelity of the downtown Republican election inspectors, who in past elections had so often succumbed to bribery.

Parkhurst must have been edgy. He respected his foes; the Tammany braves might be testy and dispirited, but they had tenacity and they knew how to soldier.

* * *

He had a book to finish, and he had to work quickly. Scribner's publishing house had scheduled *Our Fight with Tammany* for release in February; and although there is no record of how Parkhurst occupied himself on election eve, it is likely that he was working at his desk, a towel wrapped protectively around his neck, typing the final touches into his manuscript.

Not affecting false modesty, Parkhurst acknowledged that he was the matrix of the anti-Tammany campaign, and his book demonstrated the difference that one person can make. Yet he left something out of it.

He had a quality that eluded description and defied definition. Journalists tried to convey it by writing of his "electrical presence" and his "brilliance." It was not magical, for it did not seek power over the gods; on the contrary, it brought about surrender to the community good. It was a charism that, like Mozart's magic flute, made everyone dance willy-nilly. This quality persuaded a

Grand Jury to turn its aim upon the police rather than to expend its ammunition on the retail purveyors of vice. The same quality had prevailed upon the Lexow Committee to put aside narrow political tactics and to conduct the intense investigation required to awaken the city.

What Parkhurst left out of his story was the power of his personality. But Goff spoke of it glowingly in recalling the days just before the Lexow investigation began:

"Everything was so discouraging. The outlook was exceedingly bad. The fate of previous investigating committees was before us. In our hands there was not a scintilla of evidence that would prove an act of corruption on the part of any member of the Police Department. The air was filled with rumors of political deals. Every man who spoke of the matter warned us of the danger that concerned such an attempt, and of the utter futility of making an effort to expose bribery and corruption in the Police Department.

"One voice rang out clear and above all others. It urged action. It foretold success. It appealed so eloquently that it was irresistible. That voice was the voice of Dr. Parkhurst." Goff said he reached an understanding with the Lexow Committee to become its counsel only through Parkhurst's efforts.

The gift occasionally failed—for one, it had not worked on Emma Goldman. But Parkhurst had used that gift to foster a woman's movement that the *World* called "perhaps the most remarkable that New York has ever known."[2] Then he took it downtown to try something unprecedented for a reformer—an appeal to Tammany's own constituency.

It had been a remarkable transformation for himself. Never a supporter of women's suffrage, he had reached out to women. Always calling for limits (although never a suspension) on immigration, he had welcomed men with strange-sounding names to the fold. Always an optimist, the practice of politics had evaporated all his hesitancies about what groups were suited to become Americans. In his sermons he had often spoken of a community of spirit and of bringing in the kingdom of God, and through his toil he had come to see that those who work to redeem the earth make up a community of spirit and all who work for that redemption will share in the benediction of the future.

* * *

The reader who comes upon a copy of *Our Fight with Tammany* will find it a scrapbook of sermons, speeches, and Parkhurst Society statements stamped with his evangelical style, excerpted news accounts and editorials, blended with stretches of narrative.

It has a Wigwam full of villains, but the lead villain is Tom Byrnes. His detectives shadow Parkhurst and Society agents. He accuses Gardner of blackmail while knowing that his men are doing the same thing, and instead of turning his efforts to scourging corruption from the Police Department, Byrnes leaves no stone unturned in his effort to destroy the Society. After a mob menaces Society agents on Broome Street, Byrnes turns the investigation over to Captain Devery and Inspector Williams, with predictable results. Appearing as a witness for Devery during Big Bill's criminal trial, Byrnes helps get the Captain acquitted. Parkhurst concluded that, had Byrnes crushed the Society as he intended, none of the remarkable events that made a Tammany defeat possible would have occurred.

Yet Byrnes cannot represent the Tammany-police nexus that operates in the city. Parkhurst gives that role to Captain Devery. When he is indicted the public sees—and here Parkhurst quotes a *Morning Advertiser* editorial that summarizes his theme—"that despite the power and strength of Tammany Hall, the people are even more powerful, when aroused, and the machinery of the law can be successfully invoked to work the reforms to which they are devoted."

The acquittal of Big Bill Devery is the turning-point of his narrative. It is an expensive victory for Tammany and the police. Because of the compelling strength of the case against Captain Devery, the acquittal shifts the sentiments of the public, which becomes convinced that the only way "by which right could be restored to its proper supremacy was by puncturing our iniquitous system to its vitals, and effecting its complete subversion."

As the pastor told it, the fight with Tammany is undertaken when District Attorney DeLancey Nicoll declines to cooperate with the Society because he objects to remarks that Parkhurst had made from the pulpit about his diligence and dedication. A bigger man, Parkhurst wrote, would have reacted in a public-spirited way, would have overlooked personal pique to work in tandem and to accept any assistance in the performance of his duty. The future of New York, Parkhurst said, hinged on that moment in the D.A.'s office. "Had Nicoll taken that attitude, the probability is that little more, comparatively speaking, would have been heard of our movement," he told his readers. Instead Nicoll tried to chasten the pastor by having him called before a Grand Jury. "Like a bird," he wrote, "we slip up on the wind that was blowing in our faces."

With a beginning, a villain, and a turning point, all Parkhurst lacked was an ending. For better or worse, that would be supplied tomorrow. He had done all he could. Now it was up to the people.

51

SWEET VICTORY

From the outset the signs forecast calamity for Tammany. By late morning, when the gamblers gathered at the St. James Hotel on Madison Square to broker bets on the outcome, the odds were running two to one in favor of the reform ticket of Strong and Goff, and the smart boys were saying maybe a 40,000-vote margin.

Everything was going wrong for Tammany, and it could not be set right by stuffing the ballot boxes. That remedy was unavailable; Superintendent Byrnes had summoned every precinct commander to his office for final election instructions and, in a finesse that caught everyone, including the Police Commission, by surprise, he had made drastic reassignments for election-day duty. All the captains and their key men were shuffled off to unfamiliar precincts where they lacked any ties to the local Tammany leaders. It was the most massive (albeit temporary) reassignment in the history of the Department, with 2,000 policemen, or half the force, ordered to report to a new precinct.

Byrnes had also obtained court warrants for the arrest of seven hundred illegally registered men. "It is likely," he said, "that most of those men have managed to learn that the police have been getting evidence against them, and the men may not try to vote, but if they do they will be arrested promptly."[1]

By mid-morning the police courts were inundated with floaters accused of ballot violations, while goo-goo poll-watchers assured cops that they intended to press charges. Conscious of the close scrutiny to which both the public and Byrnes were subjecting them, the police were making extraordinary efforts to enforce the election laws. In most cases the Police Justices eventually released the accused men, but the threat of arrest was discouraging interest in election fraud.

Byrnes had cast his lot with the anti-Tammany forces, and took the wind out of Tammany's sails.

But that was not the main problem. The way the gamblers figured it, the key to the election lay in the rumors of dissension heard all over downtown. If the defections proved as extensive as the signs suggested, Tammany was on thin ice. Downtown braves were griping that Croker had enriched himself and then deserted them, so why should they knock on doors and get out the vote? Surly saloonkeepers were not standing their customers to a drink "on Tammany." Police families had decided that since Police Board President Jimmy Martin had not stood by them, they would sit this one out.

The most conspicuous symptom of Tammany's dim prospects was the disarray in the Second District, which had always furnished Tammany's biggest cornucopia of votes. In recent years Paddy Divver had performed miracles, even raising up the dead to vote. But Justice Divver was holed up in his Long Island mansion in an alcoholic haze, and Divverdom lay forsaken.

The most telling sign of all was the lack of spirit; it looked as if all the starch had been boiled out of Tammany. According to the gamblers, it was not that the reformers had proven themselves masters of election wizardry but that the Tammany braves were letting it slip through their fingers.

Tammany's worst fears were realized as soon as the returns began to trickle in. The Wigwam emptied early, the braves slipping out singly and in small groups to drown their sorrows in drink. Many of them drifted to The Bowery, where they lurched about, demoralized. Nothing chilled them more than the prospect of reform, which for them meant the end of loyalty and trust and the reign of the cold, bloodless Simon Pures.

* * *

Within a couple of hours it was clear that Strong and Goff would win the election, and the anti-Tammany forces went on a spree. Horns honked in Harlem, blasted along Broadway and shrieked in the Bowery. Impromptu parades that began with a trio of tipsy strutters grew to the size of a regiment, with flags flying. The night was filled with laughter and voices hoarse with cheering, and a din of loud, excited voices filled the hotel lobbies and corridors. The men who had won big election bets ordered lobster in Sherry's, Delmonico's, and the St. James as waiters flew about trying to keep up with the orders.

Young men stood about with their sweethearts on Grand Street, where bulletin boards were posted with the latest returns. Four young men came sailing along arm in arm and piled into the crowd as if rushing the line in a football game, chanting, "Rip along! Skip along! We voted for Strong!" Theatergoers were kept current on the returns by means of announcements between the acts, and everywhere the news of Tammany defeat was greeted with huzzahs and applause.

In Herald Square, a magic-lantern man in a wagon was projecting slides on a huge white sheet hung from the south front of the *Herald* building. One slide that set the crowd to whooping announced TAMMANY HALL HAS CLOSED ITS DOORS AND PUT UP A SIGN, TO LET. As winners and losers were declared their portraits were thrown on the screen. The crowd hissed Grant and Smyth and cheered a drawing of Parkhurst. Every few minutes cable cars and elevated trains poured more people into the square.

Farther downtown, a sea of thousands upon thousands of men stretching across City Hall Park watched a stereopticon project the news on the facade of the Pulitzer Building, the tallest in the city. Inside the twenty-story building, men who mattered—shapers of opinion, writers and thinkers, Wall Street moguls, leading clergymen, heads of insurance companies and leaders of labor unions—were gathered together, trading observations as the returns came in.

Pulitzer was not there; he was cruising the seas in his yacht, *Liberty*, in a quest for relief from the hundred ailments that beset him like a nineteenth-century Job. Nevertheless he was gratified that the newsroom of his newspaper, "that mightiest engine of progress, that foremost power for good," was serving that evening as a field headquarters for the anti-Tammany powers of the city.

Political pundits were astonished at the interest women showed in the ballot results and the familiarity with which they discussed them. A large number of women were welcomed when they turned up at the Pulitzer Building to study the totals. They were not permitted, however, to mingle with the men. Lifted by elevator, they were escorted to two large rooms where the tallies were supplied to them in separate accommodations.

When the magic lantern beamed up the letters that said GOFF GOES UP HIGHER on the wall of the Pulitzer Building, the joyous wail bounded between the newspaper building and the City Hall and Hall of Records, back and forth in a triumphant echo that drowned out every other sound. As the crowd reached the acme of enthusiasm somebody saw a shining mane of white hair and shouted: "There he is! Hurrah for John W. Goff!"

Escorted by a policeman and surrounded by friends, Goff edged his way toward the doorway. A roar erupted as the crowd caught sight of him and surged forward, pinning the police against the walls of the building. Goff got within the entranceway in the nick of time. A great tossing mass of hands was reaching out to grasp him. In another second he would have been captured and lifted aloft on the shoulders of the crowd. His face flushed, his eyes dancing, Goff turned and faced the people as soon as he was safely within the portal. He lifted his head and bowed again and again as a roar broke loose.

Inside, men who only months earlier had predicted that political machines would tighten their grasp in the coming century, that corrupt city governments would strangle democracy, and that it was merely quixotic for a lone man to stand in the way of the juggernaut, were bubbling with cheer, their optimism restored. Parkhurst's comments about the national and global effects of the campaign intrigued them, and they were buzzing about the scope and breadth of the victory. They sauntered up to congratulate Parkhurst as if he had won the election. One ear cocked to the roaring of the crowd outside, the jubilant pastor savored the attention. "Isn't it glorious?" he asked his well-wishers, blinking both eyes at once, "Isn't it superb?"

* * *

That afternoon he had made a tour of Lower East Side polling places. He had lived for years with misgivings about whether immigrants, especially the Irish and Jewish immigrants, were promising material to become Americans. When he visited the Jewish districts that afternoon that afternoon he realized what a thoroughly peaceful, earnest class they were, as mindful of their public duties, he said, as they were of the Law and the Sabbath. Many of them had read his flyer about Mrs. Urchittel and the Statue of Liberty; and everything that they said demonstrated that they understood how American politics worked and that they were committed to making it work in accordance with the Ten Commandments.

The statue of the woman towering three hundred feet above the water was for him a militant figure. Although it is commonly regarded as a sign of welcome to immigrants, the statue's meaning is conveyed in its full title, "Liberty Enlightening the World." It is a beacon—an elaboration of the theme of the Puritans who came to the shores of the New World to carry out an "errand in the wilderness"; to set up a righteous government, a city upon a hill, with the eyes of the world upon it. Parkhurst was embarked on the same errand—reshaping liberty for an urban model, a New York Liberty that would dazzle the world.

* * *

When all the ballots were counted, the reform forces had won a famous victory. Strong polled 151,000 votes, winning by a margin of 43,000. Goff had won even more decisively; with 155,000 votes, he defeated the incumbent Recorder by 53,000. City Republicans usually considered themselves lucky to send three or four Assemblymen to Albany; in the coming year they would have a majority in the city of seventeen Republicans to thirteen Democrats. Republicans won control of the Board of Aldermen, and the losers included Silver Dollar Smith.

Recorder Smyth attributed his defeat to the poor general showing of Democrats, as voters around the nation blamed hard times on President Cleveland. In a front-page editorial cartoon, the *World* depicted a dead Tammany Tiger with an arrow in its chest labeled "The World." Never fettered by excessive modesty, Pulitzer's paper claimed that its exposure of Tammany knavery had brought the Lexow Committee to town. Platt was certain that he was the chief architect of victory. Rev. R. S. MacArthur regarded the results as an endorsement of the American Protective Association and a repudiation of Catholicism.

But Parkhurst credited the victory to the people, with a bow to the women, who had kept the issue of municipal virtue continuously before the public, and "in great part to the awakening of the foreign-born citizens." He added, "Thousands of them went to the polls yesterday independently to exercise for the first time since they came here their rights as American citizens."[2] No one suggested, although in hindsight it seems possible, that the election results reflected the joy of New York at the reunion of Caela Urchittel with her children.

Whatever the analysis, the results were unambiguous. "Now may the people of this city give themselves up to unbounded jubilation and thanksgiving," wrote the *Herald*. "New York is redeemed and will be regenerated." Hosannas burst forth from Protestant pulpits all over the city and the Doxology sung with renewed spirit.

Parkhurst was the toast of New York. His name was emblazoned across the American horizon. European papers were filled with accounts of the anti-Tammany uprising. British newspapers sent reporters to interview him. Religious bodies adopted resolutions in his praise. New Yorkers expressed their gratitude in the newspapers every day with letters suggesting all manner of testimonials.

A public discussion began on how best to pay him homage—by endowing a chair in a university, establishing a home for fallen women, commissioning a public statue of the reverend. Letters suggested that the statue should stand across the street from Tammany Hall, on perpetual alert. A prominent artist sculpted a bas-relief of Parkhurst, with forty copies to be cast. The pastor turned down an offer from Mayor-elect Strong to serve on the Police Board.

Letters and telegrams poured into the rectory from all over the continent. "People in Savannah, in Chicago, in San Francisco and in Montreal," he said, "are saying that if we can root out and overcome official corruption here in New York, they can do the same in their cities. The effect of our triumph is to be far-reaching."[3]

52

ON WITH THE FIGHT?

The Lexow hearings were expected to resume on the same exciting note on which they were adjourned just prior to the election, and they lived up to expectations. Goff kept the sessions packed with drama, providing the two most important confessions of the hearings.

The first came from Captain Timothy Creeden, who confessed to paying the dwarfish saloonkeeper Reppenhagen for his promotion. Then Captain Schmittberger took the stand to confess that he collected from gamblers and prostitutes and passed money up to his superiors, including Inspectors Williams and McAvoy. His testimony depicted a corrupt and predatory Police Department, with everyone in on the plunder except Byrnes, a lone pillar of probity. His testimony confirmed that the Parkhurst Society had been on target two years earlier when it set its sights on indictments for Devery, Williams, and Schmittberger.

Max's sweeping testimony, implicating so many police officials, shocked the city. For days New Yorkers could talk about little else. False rumors abounded that various police officials had fled the country, that more confessions were imminent, that Captains and Sergeants were shouldering each other out of the way to get to Goff's office first. The testimony of Captain Schmittberger raised expectations that Inspector Williams and possibly Commissioners Martin and Sheehan would be indicted for their attempts to interfere in his precinct. That would be going higher up indeed.

Legislators praised the results and assured New Yorkers that they would return the Lexow Committee for an encore performance to probe into other city departments. Newspapers around the nation and even Tammany men extolled the committee.

For the moment it looked as if public passion might burn the canker out of the Police Department. The Police Board resumed disciplinary hearings against several cops for neglect of duty, with Byrnes bringing in fresh charges every few days. Worried police were entering and leaving Grand Jury sessions and interrogatories were typed up by the ream in the District Attorney's offices. A police captain was convicted of extorting a basket of peaches from a merchant. Calling the pettiness of the bribe immaterial, the Judge imposed a prison term, sending shivers down the spines of a score of other police officers under investigation. The newspapers were filled with rumors of forthcoming confessions. Public support of police reform seemed more solid than ever. But the mind of Parkhurst did not rest easy, and he voiced his concern at his own testimonial dinner.

Organized by Sunshine Erving under the auspices of the City Vigilance League, the dinner brought out Good Government people, labor leaders, lawyers, clergymen—and a considerable number of women, who were seated separately, in the gallery. "We feel more than ever," joked General Horace Porter, glancing up at them, "the force of the passage in Scripture that men should set their affections upon things above." All the speakers hailed the victory and added warm testimonials to the preacher. Goff spoke of how he had learned first to esteem Parkhurst, then to love him, and brought a tear to the pastor's eye.

Near the end Parkhurst was called upon to speak—and the occasion changed from celebration to warning, as he concentrated his fire upon bossism and the unrepentant Police Department.

"We will keep a watchful eye and a sharp thought on everything that goes on in our municipality," he said on behalf of the vigilance league, "and just as hard as you and I have jumped on Tammany Hall, just so hard will we jump on the Republican Party if they need it." There were still, he told the crowd, "sly enemies standing in the way."

"There isn't much to prefer between a boss of one political complexion and a boss of another political complexion, for they both are unquestionably and thoroughly destructive," he continued. "The boss is the most cunningly devised scheme that has yet been invented for the purpose of crushing out and drying up individual manly personality, and you and I will fight the boss, no matter what may be his pretension to respectability—the more respectable he is the more damnably dangerous he is."

He told them to watch their representatives at Albany. "Make it your civic religion to keep your eye on them and remind them of the fact that they do not represent themselves, but you, and that they are your servants."

As for the police, he said, he had come to the conclusion that the old department should be legislated out of existence, and the dependable men reappointed, for "as long as any of the old hands are kept the old system will creep back again."

* * *

Close on the heels of Parkhurst's warning, Lexow showed signs of weariness when the *World* asked him if he intended to go up higher. "I don't see how it can go much higher than it has gone," the chairman sighed, noting that the committee had already placed three Police Commissioners on the stand.[1] Senator O'Connor concurred. "I believe we have accomplished as much as we can hope for, and I don't see any use of wasting any more time," said the Binghamton Republican. "Senator Lexow and myself want to close the investigation tomorrow."[2] It was time for the committee to get back to Albany and write its report, in which it would make legislative recommendations for the reform of the police force.

When the committee members and staff showed one morning at the courthouse they found Parkhurst waiting in the corridor to speak with them. He received assurances from four sources—Lexow, O'Connor, Goff, and Moss—that Byrnes would be summoned to the witness chair. That failed to calm the pastor, who predicted that Byrnes would not appear on the same terms as the other police witnesses, but would be treated as a pontificating expert, providing critiques and suggesting reforms. This, he said, would bestow not a red seal but a stamp of approval on the Byrnes forehead. Lexow responded that the committee was not in the vindication business. "No evidence has been presented here against Superintendent Byrnes, therefore what is there to question him about?" Lexow asked. "I don't think that Dr. Parkhurst's position is logical."[3]

Meanwhile the Great Detective seemed zealous for reform. He would summon his Inspectors to his office to thump his fist and squint, demanding strict enforcement of excise laws. He shook up his captains again, making six shifts in precinct commands. "If I can have my own way and carry out my plans," Byrnes promised, "this police force will be unrecognizable as the old one in six months from now, and in a year's time it will be the finest and most efficient body of police in the world."[4]

Thus the stage was set for the Lexow Committee's big finale. Advance news stories noted that the Superintendent enjoyed the support of financial moguls and Fifth Avenue club members, as well as Boss Platt and former Mayor Grace, leader of the anti-Tammany Democrats; and the press expected, as the *Herald* put it, that Byrnes would "emerge from the ordeal unscathed."

Parkhurst took the seat at his reserved table to watch how Goff would play it. At first the Recorder-elect deferred to Byrnes as an expert witness whose opinions weighed heavily in preparing a bill for the reorganization of the force. Goff then began to ask some delicate questions about the sources of the Great Detective's rumored wealth—which amounted to about $350,000, an impressive sum for a public servant on a good but hardly princely salary. Byrnes, prepared for the questions, pulled out a paper of dollar amounts from his jacket pocket.

"After I was assigned to the detective bureau and reorganized that bureau," Byrnes explained, "it brought me in contact with persons that were large investors and operators in Wall Street. They have advised me in speculations." Then straightforwardly and without apology he told of how Jay Gould had taken charge of his fortune.

Other Wall Street men whom he had been able to help with "blackmailing letters and things like that" had advised him in the stock market, he said, but Gould had taken direct control of his money. Whenever Gould made an inside stock market killing some of Byrnes's money was in it as well. He had come prepared with an accounting, having asked George Gould to provide him with a statement of what Jay Gould had made for him, and it came to about $185,000. Since his father's death George Gould had made Byrnes another $40,000.

"So that we have it, superintendent," Goff asked, "that the extraordinary good fortune that has followed you in the stock market is slightly due to the protection, care and judgment of your influential friends?"

"Nothing else in the world." As Goff closed this phase of the questioning, the Superintendent dropped the easy, offhand manner in which he had described his financial bonanza and sat bolt upright in the chair. Crisply he began to delineate the steps he had taken to stop crime. "During my term of service as Superintendent of Police," he said, "there have been three times as many arrests as for a similar period before my appointment."

"Was not the increase of the arrests due to the efforts of Dr. Parkhurst?" Goff asked.

"He was a good auxiliary force. I want to do him credit, although he has given me a dash whenever he could. Dr. Parkhurst bred a public sentiment which has rendered the good work of this committee possible."

Having established himself as the hero, he went on to point out the villains of the melodrama. His lynx eyes closing to slits, he told of his tribulations heading a police force "honeycombed with abuses." He had tried faithfully to promote the good and punish the bad, but was blocked because "my witnesses were discredited by the Board of Police Commissioners, by the District Attorney's office and by the Grand Jury. Where is your corroboration? they would ask."

Byrnes contended that despite the resistance of the Commission he had nevertheless rung in some reforms. By the frequent shuffling of captains in precincts where vice abounded he had hindered the opportunities of criminals to make deals with the police. "My action in driving these persons from pillar to post and keeping them constantly on the move has made it possible for this Committee to accomplish its work," he said. "There's another thing I wish to say right here— that had I not driven these lawbreakers from place to place they would not have testified. Every witness who has appeared before this committee has in one way or another admitted that he was practically driven to turn upon the police. He paid for protection only to have his scheme defeated by a transfer of officers. This drove him to the committee."

Twice, he said, he had considered retiring but was dissuaded by a sense of civic duty that kept him going although the Commissioners never slackened in their attempts to break him. "I have been trying to enforce the law, and with the Commissioners on one side and Dr. Parkhurst on the other, I have had a lively time of it."

Near the close of his testimony he announced that he had sent a letter to Mayor-elect Strong offering to resign. The crowded room was rapt in silence as he drew it from his pocket and handed a carbon copy to Senator Lexow, who read it to the audience.

The reorganization of the Department mattered far more, he said, than his own future. "I would not have been in this department for thirty-two years unless I had hoped for this promised reorganization," Byrnes said. "If the last election had resulted differently, then I should have lost hope."

With that the audience burst into cheers which continued until Lexow restored order with his gavel.

As Byrnes left the stand the committee cleared up odds and ends, including closing speeches, but the shouts and applause for the Superintendent were still ringing in the ears of Parkhurst.

He returned to his rectory disappointed. Politicians had their own way of doing things, and public life was never free of ironies, but he did not place much confidence in a reformed police department in the hands of Tom Byrnes. It was not for such an outcome that he had put the agents and files of the Society at the service of the Lexow Committee. He suspected that Platt, about to take control of both the legislative and executive branches of the State Government, was lurking in the wings, and a deal with Byrnes was in the works. It was bruited about in Albany that when the police bills were tailored—the proposed legislation that would be the fruit of the Lexow Committee's loom—they would be cut to fit Byrnes.

* * *

Their work done, the Senators of the Lexow Club rushed back to Albany. Over the next two weeks, Chairman Lexow wrote and issued a final report.

As a summary of the weeks of testimony that poured out of the hearings, the Lexow Report was succinct and evenhanded. But when he came to recommendations, Chairman Lexow kept his eye screwed upon the undue influence of Tammany Hall in the Police Department—those partisan activities that had been scrutinized during Sutherland's brief tenure as counsel to the committee. The report even attributed the election victory over Tammany Hall not to a public uprising but to an honestly conducted election, which, because of Tammany's control of the Police Department, had been unknown in the city in recent years.

Based on these priorities and assumptions, the Lexow Report concluded that the Police Department could be fixed up good as new with the adoption of Platt's old standby remedy—a Bipartisan Police Bill for a four-member Police Commission, two from each party. After months of arm-twisting and tears, after scores of witnesses had risked their lives and livelihoods, the committee's solution was the same one that had been proposed the previous spring and vetoed by a previous Governor. But now both the governor and the legislature were fitted out in Platt's livery. The Republican members of the committee endorsed the report with Senator O'Connor, Platt's new Senate Majority Leader, looking over their shoulders.

The reformers groaned at the word from Albany. The City Club, the Good Government Clubs, the Union League Club, all felt betrayed. Senator Lexow had sat at their banquet tables and had been toasted by their speakers, and now he had reverted to form as a creature of Platt. The *World* called the report "a complete surrender." Reformers said that Platt wanted to further entrench the practice of dividing up appointments on an equal basis and perpetuate an atmosphere in which each Commissioner protected "his men" against charges of wrongdoing. Parkhurst said the only recommendation he liked in the report was the proposal to change the title of the executive head of the force from Superintendent to Chief of Police.

Platt responded by calling the reformers "ambitious busybodies trying to boss this Legislature."[5] He had press packets made up with readymade editorials belittling the pastor as a self-seeking political boss, and had them mailed off to upstate Republican newspapers.

Anxious lest victory be snatched from their grasp, the reform forces of the city were holding rallies every few days to mobilize opposition to Platt's call for a Bipartisan Board. "Haven't I been justified in saying that I'd rather fight five Crokers than one Platt?" Parkhurst told an audience at East River Park. "We are now worse off than we were six months ago."[6]

The turn of events embittered him. "Right here," Parkhurst said at a rally, "I want to take back something I said some time ago—I thought that nine-tenths of the police were honest, noble men. I take that back. The Lexow investigation has shown the force to be corrupt and demoralized, and if there had been many honest men on the force they would have taken advantage of the recent opportunity to tell the truth."[7] When a fat cop came lumbering down the aisle during one of his speeches the pastor remarked upon his resemblance to a pig. Several people in the audience took exception to the pastor's outburst.

Appalled at his vehemence, many of the ministers who were late to join forces with Parkhurst were early to part with him. As the relations between the Easy Boss and the preacher grew abominable, Platt announced that he was quitting the Madison Square Presbyterian Church (which he never attended anyway). The Platts joined the Marble Collegiate Reformed Church, where the pastor welcomed him as the sort of respectable political leader that the city required and expressed shock at having heard Parkhurst compare this gentleman unfavorably with a lowlife like Croker.

Parkhurst said he would rather stick with the existing Police Commission system, however imperfect, than to see Platt's scheme imposed upon the city. Relations were deteriorating, and were about to get worse.

* * *

With several of his fellow-reformers, Parkhurst rode the express to Albany to testify before the Cities Committee of the State Senate on the Bipartisan Police Board Bill.

Upon his arrival in the Senate Chamber the only members of the Lexow Committee to welcome him were its two Democrats, Bradley and Cantor, both of whom had declined to endorse the Lexow Report and had written minority reports of their own. Senator Lexow did not exchange greetings with the pastor or even glance his way.

Lexow had broken with his erstwhile reform allies. He had called the Parkhurst Society's attack on the committee's work "the most damnable piece of insolence I ever saw," charged that a small group of reformers presumed to speak for the city, and called Parkhurst "an insulting jackanapes."[8]

Parkhurst said that the committee had misread the message of the voters—that the anti-Tammany fusion ticket expressed popular sentiment for non-partisan city government. He said there was "no more honest reason for introducing the element of partisanship or bipartisanship into a police commission than we should feel in introducing it into the agency of a banking or manufacturing corporation." The people, he went on, did not want four Police Commissioners—they wanted a single one who could be held accountable for his actions.

Parkhurst called for extreme measures to flush bad cops out of the department—a bill that would fire all police above a certain grade, "say that of sergeant," with the vacancies to be filled "by a board of special commissioners acting with the Mayor." The lower grades should also be subject to wholesale dismissal—and the good men rehired, to begin on a new basis in a new department.

In his earnestness Parkhurst passed up chances to be ingratiating, but did not belittle the Republican members of the committee. After he left the chamber the insults began. The men sent to present the Platt view called the pastor from Madison Square a crank. Edward Lauterbach, the State Republican chairman, brought cheers from the gallery when he declared that madhouses were full of people who believed in nonpartisanship in public affairs. "I am here," Lauterbach proclaimed, "to represent the machine politicians who work at politics from January 1 to December 31 and have the impudence to ask that we not be turned down at the demand of a lot of amateur clubs who represent nobody." One speaker brought laughter and applause when he mocked the preacher who surrounded himself with "old ladies in bloomers."[9]

* * *

A wave of support for Byrnes followed his testimony before the Lexow Committee. Senator O'Connor discerned "a desire in the public mind to have the Superintendent reorganize the Department."[10] Editorials praised Byrnes's intentions for reform, and Mayor Strong expressed confidence in his stewardship—all of which threw the pastor into momentary dejection. "What took me two years of hard work to accomplish," he exclaimed to a reporter, "that man Byrnes, with all the resources and knowledge at his command, could have done in a week!"[11]

He wrote a scathing attack on the Lexow Committee for its gentle treatment of the Superintendent. Late in the day he alighted from a carriage at Moss' office where the other two trustees read and approved the statement on behalf of the Society. Parkhurst then read it fiercely to reporters. The committee, he said, "flinched at the crisis" and "stumbled just at the completion of their work." The statement said in part:

"Wherever they have stuck in their fork they have found rot, and whether Byrnes be rotten or not he has been in rot for thirty-one years and has been the executive head of rot for the last two years. The presumption therefore was against him, so that the indisposition to handle him thoroughly must have been grounded in some other consideration than that of his presumable innocence."

Parkhurst accused the committee of making a deal with Byrnes that if he uncovered some of his associates he would not be called, or if called would "be allowed to use the stand as a histrionic opportunity for incriminating his official associates and celebrating his own personal and official innocence." He even lashed out at Goff. "If I had been a lawyer of Mr. Goff's ability," he lamented, "I would have put Byrnes on that toasting iron, and I would have guaranteed to broil out of him all of his official reputability inside of one day's session."[12]

Back to his old self, Parkhurst set to work with the intention of changing public opinion. He began to exploit the Superintendent's admission that Jay Gould had made him a fortune, bestowed upon him for private services rendered while Byrnes was filling the office of a public servant. Within days several of the dailies had reexamined Byrnes's testimony, and on closer inspection had become disturbed. Steffens of the *Post* summed it up in a letter to his father: "Dr. Parkhurst spoke out loud, my editor altered his position and condemned Byrnes. The *Tribune* followed the lead, and several other journals came out first tentatively, then vigorously for a complete change."

"A system cannot be sound or wholesome which permits a police officer to accumulate a fortune of $300,000 in a few years through gifts or 'points' from rich men," the *Post* commented. Byrnes, the newspaper went on, had allowed himself "to be secretly hired by wealthy men to devote to their service powers or talents which he owes to the community." Using police power to extricate rich men from scrapes might be forgiven, the editorialist added, but taking money for it was inexcusable.[13] The *World* also had second thoughts, calling Byrnes unfit as shown by "his own admissions on the witness stand."[14]

Parkhurst pressed his case with Mayor Strong at a dinner at the home of the *Post* editor. As Byrnes came under shelling in the editorial columns, the Committee of Seventy, the Chamber of Commerce and the City Club reversed themselves, canceling their support of Byrnes. Mayor Strong, who had at first declined to accept Byrnes's resignation, began to examine suggestions for a replacement.

The pastor continued to make it hot for Byrnes. When a Special Grand Jury was empanelled to examine criminal charges of neglect of duty leveled against various cops, Parkhurst attempted to get the Superintendent indicted. After hearing Parkhurst the Grand Jury also took testimony from the adventuress Zella Nicolaus about Byrnes's extraordinary measures to expel her from the city so that she would cease annoying George Gould. Parkhurst's agents had found the temptress and brought her back to the city, with the understanding that the Parkhurst Society would pay her bills.

A Special Grand Jury met continuously for more than a month, from early January to mid-February, then resumed its labors in March for an additional week. Upon completion of its work it issued indictments against Inspector McLaughlin—head of the detective bureau and Byrnes's most trusted ally—and seven captains, including Devery and Price. The former was indicted for extorting money from a construction company as a guarantee against harassment, the latter for prying money from Jared Flagg, the rental agent for Soubrette's Row.

Even more damning than the indictments, the most sweeping in the history of the city, was the jury's complaints about police obstruction. "They whose duty it was to aid in detecting crime have united to prevent its detection," the Grand Jury declared in a presentment. The investigating body surmised that witnesses coming before them were being intimidated by the police, while other witnesses were unable to conceal their conviction that hindering the investigation was to their advantage. "During our entire session," the jury ruefully observed, "no police official, high or low, has volunteered one particle of aid, nor has any evidence whatever been forthcoming from police circles, except such as has been drawn from unwilling witnesses and under persistent effort."

The Grand Jury cast doubt on Byrnes' ability to lead. "The enjoyment by the executive head of the force," it stated, "of a considerable fortune accumulated as the result of favors granted in recognition of the performance of official duty may well have caused demoralization in the force under his command."

* * *

In Albany the State Legislature adopted Platt's bill for a Bipartisan Police Commission. Even before the Governor signed the bill, Mayor Strong broke with Platt by firing Kerwin and Murray, the two Platt members of the Police Commission, and appointing new members, including Theodore Roosevelt as Board President.

The burly Roosevelt bounded upon the stage eager to shake things up. Having inherited many cases of alleged misconduct not yet heard, Roosevelt pressed for hearings. He wanted to dismiss the policemen and let the courts decide how far the Commission could go in kicking out unsuitable men. He advised high-ranking police officials to apply immediately for retirement and a pension, or face charges.

The chief targets were Byrnes and Clubber. Steffens, one of Roosevelt's inner circle, wrote in the *Post* on May 24 that "the preponderating forces in the Board have settled finally into the conviction that a complete reform of the department will be impossible as long as these two men are in it."

Inspector Williams went quickly. Keeping up his blustering hooey to the last, Clubber told reporters that "the story that I was forced out by the Police Board is a God-damned lie."[15]

By the following day it transpired that Byrnes too was willing to retire. His friends urged him to resist, but if he refused to go quietly, Roosevelt was ready to try him on charges of breaking department rules in rendering private services to the Gould family. Byrnes offered to leave if not openly attacked.

Within days Byrnes retired on a pension of $3,000 a year. As agreed, the Board spoke not a disparaging word, but his resignation was accepted with neither thanks nor praise for the man who was regarded for nearly two decades as the foremost detective in America. He departed forlornly, shaking hands ceremoniously with aides and gathering up his belongings. When he walked out of Headquarters for the last time, the legend reduced at last to human size, an era ended in New York.

53

WINDS OF CHANGE

Tammany had been defeated but not eliminated. Out of power yet a force to be reckoned with, the braves regrouped, preparing to outlast their foes. "These reformers are like honeybees," they told each other, "they sting you once, then they die." The cops hardened their resistance, criminal trials and Police Board hearings failing to crack the blue wall of silence.

But for the time being, the reforms stood firm. Holding police accountable to higher standards, the new Police Commission made a discernible difference in changing the atmosphere of the city. The Board ordered liquor laws enforced, and ensured that police made arrests. With the Commission watching closely, the alliance between police and vice had to operate with more restraint. The Strong administration ousted Police Justices Divver, Grady, and Hogan and improved the atmosphere in the police courts; and Recorder Goff saw to it that Silver Dollar Smith and Max Hochstim were persona non grata in the Essex Market Court House.

* * *

As the spirit of reform took wing, the range of issues widened. New York was filled with the voices of citizens at meetings of the Board of Aldermen, at rallies, and in letters to the editor, raising new issues—one of them a controversy over the shameful state of tenements. Reporters found basements awash in several inches of water and pestilential conditions on the floors above. By midyear some of the worst buildings in Mulberry Bend were condemned and plans were underway to build a small park on the site. One of the remarkable aspects of the new public agitation was that much of it was led by women, and that many of the women had been introduced to civic activity by involvement in the election campaign or in neighborhood associations fostered by the City Vigilance League.

As women became more active in public life, they tended to stress a set of issues different from those that concerned men. In Chicago the women of Hull House and in New York the women of what became the Henry Street settlement were demanding cleaner streets and public sanitation, drinking fountains, public bathhouses, parks, and lodging houses for the homeless. It was not surprising, therefore, that one of the earliest and brightest accomplishments of the Strong administration was a cleaner city by means of a refurbished Streets Department; or that the Mayor quickly appointed a woman as a District School Inspector.

* * *

Parkhurst welcomed these changes, but he looked beyond them, having always seen his mission in terms of the coming century. He took the train for Chicago where he was greeted as a visiting hero. Wherever he appeared men cheered and women waved handkerchiefs while he explained how to see past the whorehouses and gambling dens to the root cause—a corrupt police and government.

And God knows, said those who shook his hand, Chicago needed the same kind of shakeup that he had applied to New York. Widespread corruption, protection of vice, political influence in the Police Department, police officers becoming unaccountably rich, Grand Juries packed with friends of the machine— the similarities were so obvious that a Chicago Alderman had sat in on several sessions of the Lexow Committee hearings to pick up pointers for the Chicago Common Council's own police investigation.

He told Chicagoans that if it could be done in New York it could be done anywhere; and he continued to encourage people to see the Parkhurst crusade as a prototype of a decentralized but national movement.

That spring his example was being taken to heart all over America. The outpouring that greeted him in Chicago demonstrated the national view that Parkhurst had plumbed the depths of what was called "the municipal problem" and that the cleanup of New York was the latest example of American practical know-how. Said the *Herald*: "Boss-ridden cities, which have worn the shackles of slavery so long that freedom seemed a hopeless dream, have taken courage from New York's example and are rising in their might to throw off the yoke."[1] The president of Johns Hopkins University called New York "a sort of teachers' college where other cities may learn both what to do and what not to do."[2]

The winds of reform began to blow across America. A Committee of Public Safety investigated election fraud in St. Louis, where the police had shielded ballot-stuffers, floaters and repeaters. A Municipal League arose to battle the protection of gambling and prostitution in Denver. The Law and Order League of Connecticut employed agents in the manner of the Parkhurst Society to look into corruption in the New Haven police courts. City governing bodies were asking State Legislatures to give their cities "the Lexow treatment." The New York newspapers referred to the leading spokesmen for such crusades as the Brooklyn or the San Francisco or the Chicago Parkhurst.

So the task that remained for Parkhurst was to keep the public taut. For a long time and at the top of his lungs he had exhorted the people to seize their power, and his message bespoke his vision of democracy, for like Jefferson he associated liberty with a vigilant public. To him struggle was not the price paid for democracy, but its essence, and he exulted in it as he did in the bracing liquor of mountain-climbing. "Municipal ground will always have to be a battlefield," he wrote in the conclusion of his book, "and may the God of battles multiply his champions, solidify their ranks, put might into their arms, chivalry into their hearts, and crown us all with a steady and widening victory."

* * *

While militancy and change ruled the streets, a quiet vigil was kept at Mount Sinai Hospital, where Caela Urchittel lay dying. The joyous reunion with her children had been followed by a poignantly brief life together, and the strain of her ordeal had toppled her precarious health. Moss had arranged for the children to be returned to the Hebrew Home that had sheltered them during their separation from their mother.

On several afternoons Parkhurst sat at her bedside. There were between them so many barriers—Christian and Jew, native-born and immigrant, learned and ignorant, man and woman—that it is hard to surmise what she made of him. She must have been honored by his visits, and despite the language barrier he may have conveyed to her his conviction that her odyssey to America had a providential purpose. She knew that rallies had been held for her, that immigrant Jews had shouted her name, that collections of pennies had been taken up for her, that men had raised their fists and vowed revenge on her behalf, that crowds had been urged to hearken to her plight, that society women and prostitutes had shed tears for her and for her suffering children. Was she too listless to understand that she and Parkhurst were linked? Or was she sharp to the last, aware on her deathbed that she had played a key role in a drama with villains, heroes and a promised land?

EPILOGUE
[1898 and After]

"What is government itself but the greatest of all reflections on human nature?"

—James Madison, *Federalist Papers*

Time whirled on, fashions changed, new songs became old chestnuts, and the new century loomed close. In 1898 Emma Goldman took her message coast to coast. "I demand the independence of woman, her right to support herself; to live for herself; to love whomever she pleases, or as many as she pleases," she boldly told audiences. "I demand freedom for both sexes, freedom of action, freedom in love and freedom in motherhood."[1] She frowned past her listeners, challenging the official powers in one city after another to halt her cross-country tour of America's heartland.

She still called herself an Anarchist, and spoke to immigrant audiences at demonstrations, protest meetings, picnics, and lectures arranged by radical unionists. But the distance between Emma and working people continued to widen. Labor leaders regarded her as a lethal ingredient in their struggle for public sympathy; the membership objected not only to her ideas but also to a confrontational style that assumed that all opinions contrary to hers were ridiculous.

After studying nursing in Vienna, she had returned to New York and began to work as a midwife on the Lower East Side. Horrified by the bondage of poor women to their reproductive organs, Emma Goldman advocated birth control. She shocked the nation but, like Parkhurst, respectability only appeared as a hindrance to her. Seeing an alternative to being worn out by a dozen pregnancies, women began to respond—middle-class women first, the message gradually reaching working-class women as well.

Her lecture-hall audiences enjoyed her blasts at American conformity, and her insistence that people had the right to live exactly as they wanted. Everything that hindered human growth had to be rooted out so that every individual could reach the peak of self-expression through love, the only "inspiring, elevating basis for a new race, a new world."

One of her crowd-pleasers was "Sex, the Great Element of Creative Art," in which she spoke of the power of the libido over all aspects of life and argued that sexual inhibition not only harmed health but repressed creativity. When Oscar Wilde went on trial in England for sexual deviance she sprang to his defense, proclaiming sex as entirely a private matter into which nobody—neither church, state nor fellow citizens—had a right to intrude.

She remained a stormy petrel. The *San Francisco Call* proposed that she be "hanged by the neck until dead and considerably longer." But Goldman believed that her tour was successful. "Even the most conservative clubs and organizations, that only a few years ago would have refused to listen to a professed Anarchist, are now inviting Anarchist lecturers," she told an interviewer. "They have learned that conservatism is fast losing ground, and that nothing but advanced and radical ideas meet with popular approval."[2] She thought that the coming century, now almost within her grasp, would embrace the values of Emma Goldman.

* * *

In New York the skyscrapers grew taller. A fickle public weary of goo-goo virtue voted Tammany Hall back into power, raising the cry of To Hell with Reform. Boss Croker rushed back to command the Wigwam when victory looked likely—a victory that he owed to his old ally Platt, who divided anti-Tammany forces by running a Republican ticket.

Roosevelt, the former Police Board President, joined forces with Platt and attacked Parkhurst as an "idiot," a "goose," and a "dishonest lunatic." And although the former divekeeper Billy McGlory became an evangelical preacher, the sinful city roared on with legendary energy.

Most of the cops who had been admonished before the Lexow Committee and dismissed by the Police Board were back in uniform. Those who had been tried in criminal court had been acquitted, on the basis that their accusers—abortionists, prostitutes and gamblers—were unreliable witnesses. Others escaped by means of negligence, oversight, misplaced confidence, politics, judicial error, bribery, or a combination of the foregoing. Few suffered more than the momentary chagrin of public disclosure of their misdeeds, and now that they were back on top they banded together to bar Captain Schmittberger from marching in the police parade.

Captain Creeden retired on a pension. Clubber Williams remained a malign influence for many years after his retirement, particularly as an advisor of Police Lieutenant Charles Becker, who became the center of a later police scandal. A supposedly repentant Hussey was forgiven for threatening the life of a witness at the Lexow hearings and eventually became a corrupt Inspector. Byrnes became general manager of the burglary insurance department of the United States Casualty Company, and died a wealthy man.

Croker installed his favorite cop, Big Bill Devery, as Chief of Police. All restraints were tossed aside as the Devery era eclipsed anything previously seen in the city in the way of corruption, and the brothels and gambling dens flourished.

Dry Dollar Sullivan, now called Big Tim, controlled vice and gambling interests below Fourteenth Street. Max Hochstim was developing prostitution into an organized operation, or, as the twentieth century called it, a racket. Protected by Sullivan, Hochstim imported women into the city as whores for the Lower East Side, then expanded citywide, and then extended operations to Newark and Philadelphia, marking the first instance of an inter-city crime organization in America.

Prohibition offered new vistas to organized crime, and the cops yielded readily to the blandishments of gangsters. Every twenty years or so a monstrous scandal rocked the police force, hearings were held, the public recoiled in shock. The police hunkered down, rode it out, kept their lips buttoned, and the storm passed, as it does to this day.

* * *

W. Travers Jerome became a crusading District Attorney. Frank Moss served both as a Police Commissioner and an Assistant District Attorney. Judge Goff, although he became a gloomy bully during his years on the bench—one lawyer called him "that saintlike son-of-a-bitch"[3]—proved to be uncompromisingly honest.

The effects of the Parkhurst crusade lived on in the city. Neighborhood associations made it uncomfortable for the police. Italian priests in Little Italy led a revolt against the padrone system. Protestant ministers aided in campaigns for inspected meat, untainted milk, and decent housing for the poor. Refuting the predictions that immigrants would depress the labor market, workers emulated the tenacity of the Jewish garment workers to win themselves a living wage and more humane working conditions. Women kept up their fight to win the vote and demanded clean streets and good schools. The days of public torpor were over.

Ever the optimist, Parkhurst argued that the Tammany regime was so incautious and the blemishes of the administration so visible that victory in the next mayoral election was assured. The struggle for the soul of New York was subject to setbacks, but he would take his case to the people, who kept the passion for liberty and democracy in their hearts. Calling regularly for help upon the God of Battles, Parkhurst remained as president of the Society until 1908 and fought on even after that. He died in a fall from a porch roof in 1933, at the age of ninety-one, while sleepwalking.

In his autobiography Lincoln Steffens, a witness to many stirring events in the history of the city, credited the pastor with setting in motion the juggernaut that "led up to the whole period of muckraking and the development of the Progressive party." Although he cannot be closely identified with the Pure Food and Drug Act, the popular election of Senators, Child Labor Laws, tenement reform, woman suffrage, and some of the other fruits of progressivism in the early twentieth century, Parkhurst's vision of the American Revolution as a living tradition broadened and deepened America's concept of democracy. He restored popular efforts to make government accountable, and pioneered in the methods of direct participation that reshaped democracy in the context of a new kind of community—the urban, regulated, interdependent society that grew up near the end of the Nineteenth Century, and in which most of the people in the world now live. His investigation of the police stimulated newspaper efforts in the same direction, making 1892 as good a date as any to mark the birth of the muckraking school of journalism. And his efforts to apply the concept of the kingdom of God to social problems began the movement of Protestant activism that came to be known as the Social Gospel.

* * *

After World War I Emma Goldman was deported as an undesirable alien. While visiting the United States on a visa in 1934, she wrote to her former lover, the ex-prisoner Berkman, that "there is still the spirit of adventure, there is something refreshing and stimulating in the air . . . America brings out adventure, innovations, experimental daring which, except for Russia, no European country does."[4] She lived her last years in Canada, and often she would prevail upon a young friend to drive her to the border, where the old Anarchist would sit looking across to the United States of America, tears streaming from her eyes.

NOTES AND SOURCES

A PERSONAL NOTE

After reading a brief account of the Parkhurst crusade in a history of New York, I knew right away that I was going to write a book about it.

It didn't take much searching to discover that my way was clear, that nobody had ever done a book on this subject. And, combing through old books, magazines, and newspapers in pursuit of more information about Parkhurst, I came to realize that the clergyman's story was a significant chapter in American history—that the reform spirit with which we entered the twentieth century could be traced back to Charles Parkhurst's sermon of February 1892. And as I spooled through New York newspapers of the early 1890s I also became fascinated by the emergence of Emma Goldman as a radical voice on the Lower East Side. There were countless connections between the two stories. Both Parkhurst and Goldman were working the same territory; both were courageous, charismatic, brilliant, visionary, and given to histrionics. Both began their missions with a misstep that set them on widely divergent paths. I had a hunch that they had met and eventually I found evidence of a meeting. Using Goldman's story as a subplot threw light on the Parkhurst story, with the added irony that Goldman has become an icon of our culture while Parkhurst has disappeared from our history. Thus this book began to take shape.

Research is like police duty in at least one way—both are marked by long stretches of boredom punctuated by moments of intense excitement. During those bursts of excitement, musty old records speak as if time has suddenly been abolished. Putting up with the drudgery, the researcher gets high on the surprises. And sometimes there are surprises of another sort. For example, when I read that brief piece about Parkhurst in that history of New York—the one that whetted my appetite for more—June and I were vacationing in the Berkshire Mountains of Massachusetts. Later I learned to my delight that Parkhurst had lived in those same mountains before coming to New York, and that the impressive Congregational church on the hill in Lenox, which June and I had passed dozens of times, was the very church in which he had served as pastor. We were asking about the church on another trip to Lenox when the owners of our bed and breakfast told us that we were dawdling over morning coffee on former church property—in a house that probably served as rectory for Dr. and Mrs. Parkhurst. As people used to say in the Sixties, Oh wow.

One day during my researches, at the Rockland County Historical Association, I found, in a manila folder, a photocopy of M. R. Werner's *New Yorker* article on the Parkhurst Crusade, published in the 1950s. Instantly I recalled the eager interest with which I had read it several lost decades ago, and remembered that I had completely forgotten about it. Was this forgotten article the hidden source of my excitement about coming across the story in the New York history book so many years later? Research is as weird and unaccountable as everything else in the world. Some will see in these events merely a series of random coincidences; others, a sign of the oceanic otherness of the mind. Parkhurst himself would have seen a sign of divine purpose that collides with, as he put it, our overemphasis on the agency of free will. Purpose, he would say, is not primarily based on conscious intent.

SOURCES

Werner's article, which later appeared as a chapter in his book, *It Happened in New York*, is a fine piece of writing. And in acknowledging another source of inspiration I cannot recommend too highly Irving Howe's *World of Our Fathers*, which in its deft sketches of life on the Lower East Side, its literary flourish and its political and sociological analysis is a masterpiece of historical writing.

It was a time-travel adventure to read the New York newspapers of the 1890s, which provide an almost novelistic depiction of life in the city and the day-to-day concerns of its citizens. The coverage of the Parkhurst campaign from beginning to end, especially the work of the *World* and the *Herald*, is of a high order. The daily papers painted the scene, captured the drama and explained the issues with vivacity and enterprise. Although I read a portion of the official transcripts of the Lexow Committee, I continued to rely on newspaper accounts for lively coverage of the daily proceedings that ranged far beyond the testimony.

Another wonderful source was Parkhurst himself. His sermons and books, as well as the comments of his contemporaries, testify to his uncanny and sure-footed sense of leadership, his flexibility and inclusiveness, and his Christian sense of purpose. I came to admire his first-rate mind, his playful heart, and his winning soulfulness. He was sometimes pompous and prim but never smug, and I hope that readers can see past the culture-bound nineteenth century prejudices that he carried—and partially overcame—to see the chivalric heart that beat so ardently. He told his version of the story with modesty in *Our Fight with Tammany*. I also gained insights from reading *My Forty Years in New York*, in which he has more to say about his early experience and his basic values, and *Three Gates on a Side*, a collection of powerful sermons.

Other valuable sources included the New-York Historical Society, which has Parkhurst letters in other people's collections as well as records of the Society for the Prevention of Crime and the papers of Hugh Grant. The Rare Books Collection at Columbia has other records of the Society for the Prevention of Crime, papers of Lincoln Steffens, and much material on Pulitzer and the *World*. The Historical Society of Rockland County (N.Y.) has papers that illuminate the relationship of Lexow and Platt. Material about Anarchists, including Emma Goldman, was found at the Houghton Library at Harvard University. The Early Mayors' Papers of the New York Municipal Archives were also useful, and included affidavits of Parkhurst Society agents in connection with what the newspapers called the Broome Street Riot.

Charles Gardner's book, *The Doctor and the Devils*, published in 1894, is a colorful guide to the initial stages of the Parkhurst crusade, although not completely reliable. News stories of the trials, for example, show that his narration is often chronologically incorrect; and his account of their visit to a flophouse bears close resemblance to a Jacob Riis article in the *Tribune* of Jan. 31, 1892.

Goldman's autobiography, *Living My Life*, has to be read warily as far as this period in her life is concerned. Most of her early papers were lost and she relied on a faulty memory. She wrote, for example, that on the afternoon of the shooting, Stein rushed into her room with a newspaper headlined: "YOUNG MAN BY THE NAME OF ALEXANDER BERGMAN [sic] SHOOTS FRICK." (Every headline I've seen identifies the celebrated victim, and leaves the identification of the then-obscure assailant to the text of the story.) Her memory is also selective, leaving out what she would rather the reader not know, and forgetting the storm of condemnation that followed Berkman's deed.

I have made some additional comments of warning about inaccuracies in the works of Gardner, Goldman, Rovere and Steffens in the notes that follow.

SOURCES BY CHAPTER

I have referred to books by the author's name except when several works of the author are cited in the bibliography, in which case I use the title as the citation.

In referring to oft-cited texts, I have used OFWT for *Our Fight with Tammany*, MFYNY for *My Forty Years in New York*, and LML for *Living My Life*. I have minimized footnotes, but have used them, chiefly for specific quotes, when to do otherwise would unduly entangle the reader.

Prologue: Winter 1891–1892

The eviction material, including the dialogue, comes from newspaper accounts, notably *World*, March 20, 1892 (New York's Evictions). The portrait of the rich comes from many sources, especially *Herald*, Jan. 10, 1892 (Ballrooms of the Four Hundred) and *World*, Apr. 29, 1894 (Mecca of Millionaires), as well as Cowles, which is also the source of McAllister's comment on respectable poverty. Specifics about the Vanderbilt mansion are from *World*, Dec. 18, 1892. The dynamiting narrative is from newspapers, notably *Herald*, Dec. 5, 1891. The precautions that the rich took after the bombing is from *Times*, Jan. 3, 1892.

1. McAllister.
2. *North American Review*, June 1892.
3. Quoted in Moss.
4. E. L. Godkin in *The Nation*, Jan. 19, 1893.

Chapter 1

None of the news stories about McGlory's arrest and trial described the activities in his saloon. I have adapted the description of activities in an earlier McGlory saloon called Armory Hall on Hester Street. The description comes from a *Cincinnati Enquirer* account found in Howe and Hummel, as do the description of McGlory and the quote from the police detective. Since Recorder Smyth said he had never before heard such nauseating testimony as he had in this case, perhaps the Armory Hall description understates the case, but it will have to do. A key source of information is *Post*, Dec. 31, 1891, on McGlory.

Parkhurst later claimed to be astonished by the press reaction. "No notice was given of its delivery," he wrote in MFYNY, "and it did not occur to the preacher that it would excite particular interest or create any marked impression." This is a puzzling comment, since the sermon was thoroughly covered in the newspapers of the following day. The complete sermon is in OFWT.

1. *Times*, June 13, 1892.
2. *In Danger.*
3. *Herald*, Jan. 5, 1892.
4. *Herald*, Jan. 12, 1892.
5. *Herald*, Feb. 16, 1892.
6. *Herald*, Feb. 16, 1892.
7. *Sun*, Feb. 17, 1892.
8. *Mail & Express*, Feb. 23, 1892.
9. OFWT.

Chapter 2

The survey of Bowery saloons is from Harlow, the description of typical saloons from Breen. Material on political saloons comes from many sources, one good one being the *Herald*, Oct. 14, 1994. The phrase "goo-goos" became common a little later than 1892, since the spread of the Good Government clubs commenced after the formation of the City Club later in the year. The meeting with Nicoll and the meetings with Whitney are in OFWT. That Parkhurst suspected that Tammany Hall issued a directive to Nicoll to discredit him comes from Gardner. Whitney, an important ally, died in the summer of 1892.

Chapter 3

This is mostly from Gardner, with help from Moss, Brown, Howe & Hummel (*In Danger*) and news accounts of the trials. Parkhurst's sermons show that he believed in a personal Satan. The Windsor Garden was notorious; one angry letter about its activities appears in the *Mail & Express*, Jan. 7, 1992. The thoughts on mountain climbing are from the *Swiss Guide*.

The fact that they walked to Maria Andrea's after visiting Hattie Adams' is provided in Andrea trial testimony in the *Herald*, May 10, 1992.

Chapter 4

Parkhurst's background and his difficulties with the New York Presbytery are from MFYNY. The quote from Chickering Hall and the reporter's comments are from *The Making of an American*. The sermon scene is from Gardner, newspaper accounts, and OFWT.

Chapter 5

Hattie Adams' visit to the rectory is recounted in *Herald* of Mar. 19, 1892. What Parkhurst told the March Grand Jury is in OFWT, as is the fact that he changed the jury's focus from Madames to the police. See also *Herald* of Apr. 2, 1892. Smith's Grand Jury appearance is reported in *Herald* of Apr. 1, 1892. The mass transfer of police captains is in *Herald* of Apr. 20, 1892 (Lightning Strikes Hard in the Police Department). *Tribune* of Jan. 10, 1892 helps to explain the Detective Bureau and Byrnes' own career (Byrnes' New Men). See also the Byrnes obituaries in *Times* and *Herald* of May 8, 1910. The progress of excise bills in the Legislature and Sunday sales issues are well-covered in *Tribune*.

1. *Herald*, Mar. 15, 1892.
2. *Herald*, Mar. 19, 1892.
3. *World*, Mar. 16, 1892.
4. *World*, Mar. 16, 1892.
5. *Herald*, Apr. 2, 1892.
6. *Herald*, June 6, 1892 (quoting Rev. David Burrell).
7. *Tribune*, Apr. 5, 1892.
8. *Post*, Apr. 20, 1892.
9. *Herald*, Apr. 16, 1892.
10. *Post*, Apr. 20, 1892.
11. *Tribune*, May 2, 1892.
12. *Tribune*, May 3, 1892.
13. *World*, May 3, 1892.
14. *Herald*, May 3, 1892.
15. *World*, May 16, 1892.

Chapter 6

The press covered the dispossess hearings and criminal trials. The Parkhurst sermon is in *Tribune* of May 2, 1892.

Richard H. Rovere in *Howe & Hummel* (1947) asserts that Byrnes persuaded Howe & Hummel to have Hattie Adams plead not guilty. Then, according to his account, Parkhurst would have to take the stand and compromise himself by testifying about the sexual antics he had watched. According to Rovere, Byrnes and the criminal lawyers figured that would scare Parkhurst back to Massachusetts.

But Rovere's analysis is leaky, since Parkhurst had already shown himself ready to testify at the dispossess hearings, held prior to the criminal trials. It also seems unlikely that Byrnes gave legal tips to Howe & Hummel. And why would Howe & Hummel want to scare Parkhurst from New York? His investigations brought business to the firm.

Testimony in the Adams and Andrea trials is from Gardner, *Times* of May 6, 1892 (Once More Before Jurors) and *Sun* of May 10, 1892 (Young Erving Broke Down).

Gardner went out of his way in his 1894 book to state that when the women were chosen for the circus, Parkhurst chose his first. Without underscoring it in the text, the mischievous detective left evidence in his book that he perjured himself in the Andrea trial to shield Parkhurst. (Unless he told the truth in court and embellished the tale in the book.) According to Gardner it was determined in a meeting at Moss's office before the Andrea trial that the witnesses should try to counter "all attempts to show that the Doctor had witnessed French vice, for fear that the District Attorney . . . would try to bring out the point that we were committing a misdemeanor in witnessing the exhibition."

The Catholic anti-Parkhurst comments are from Walsh; the former Chaplain who thought Parkhurst had gone mad is from *Sun* of May 13, 1892. Parkhurst's comments on the effect of the trials is from OFWT. The comments on Parkhurst's views are based on an interview with him in *Herald* of Feb. 4, 1892.

1. Walsh.
2. *Sun*, Apr. 7, 1892.

Chapter 7

The Scottish Rite Hall speech is from *Tribune* and *Sun* of May 13, 1892. Other material, including the Parkhurst Society's caution about a rally, comes from OFWT. The Cooper Union rally material is from *Herald* and *Tribune* of May 27, 1892 and Gardner.

Parkhurst did not oppose immigration but favored a go-slow policy. In a sermon of Oct. 9, 1892, he declared that the three great evils (all urban) of the age were crime, unchecked immigration, and corruption. He used the phrase about the less developed races in correspondence with the president of the Liberal Immigration League in 1911.

1. *World*, Dec. 11, 1892.
2. *Christian Union*, Feb. 10, 1890.
3. Quoted in Hofstadter.

Chapter 8

Clubber material comes from many sources, especially *Tribune* of Nov. 20, 1892. Crime in the old days is covered in Asbury and Moss, and the Whyo material comes from Asbury and *Herald* of Dec. 27, 1891. I have combined parade material from *World* of June 1, 1892 and *Tribune* of June 1, 1893. (The Madison Square Presbyterian Church stood on Madison Avenue, present site of the Metropolitan Life building.)

1. *Herald*, Jan. 23, 1888.
2. *Tribune*, Oct. 6, 1889.
3. *Herald*, Apr. 24. 1888.

Chapter 9

Mostly from biographies of Goldman, including LML, Berkman's memoirs, and news accounts. Modest Stein was known at this time as Aronstamm. I have called him by the name he later adopted.

Most's remarks and speech are in *Times* of Apr. 21, 1892. The quote about dynamite, made by Albert Parsons, is from *The Haymarket Tragedy*, the description of Fourteenth Street prostitutes from *Herald* of Feb. 1, 1893. The Parkhurst imitator is reported in *Tribune* of July 3, 1892. The song parody is from *It Happened in New York*. "Entertainment For Man and Beast" was the proud boast of Harry Hill's famous concert saloon, out of business by 1892. (Hill testified at the Lexow hearings.) A letter of Dyer Daniel Lum in the Houghton Library at Harvard mentions celebrating at Justus Schwab's saloon over the shooting of Frick.

1. *Times*, Apr. 10, 1892.
2. *North American Review*, July 1894 (Byrnes article).
3. *World*, July 7, 1892.
4. LML.
5. *Times*, July 28, 1892.
6. *Times* and *Herald*, July 28, 1892.
7. Drinnon (page 82).

Chapter 10

Mostly news accounts. Good sources include *Herald* of July 17, 1892 (Tammany Hall Chiefs) and of Aug. 7, 1892 (Tammany Leaders Who Make Up the Chosen Thirty). On Croker, see interviews in *World* of Jan. 17, 1892 and Feb. 21, 1892, and *Tribune* of Jan. 6, 1893 (King Croker's Iron Hand).

The *Post* was a steady source of anti-Tammany material. Its astute observation about Republican surrender to Tammany in the city election campaign was in an editorial of Oct. 24, 1892.

Platt's private deal with Gilroy, confirmed long after the election, is from *Tribune* of Oct. 30, 1897. The conflict between Martin and Byrnes is detailed in the latter's testimony before the Lexow Committee on Dec. 29, 1894. Martin's account agrees but is somewhat more subdued, and also came from a Lexow appearance. Croker's break with Grant is reported in *World* of Jan. 5, 1893 and May 27, 1894. Breen reports that Grant shed tears.

Election coverage is completely from newspapers. See especially the story on selling votes in *Herald* of Oct. 30, 1892 (Found a Place Among the Army of Colonizers). On Rourke see *World* of Apr. 19, 1892 (B. Rourke Still Supreme); on Tim Sullivan see *World* of Dec. 15, 1892. The Commonwealth Club debate is in *Times* of Jan. 28, 1893 (Tammany and Democracy).

1. *North American Review*, Feb. 1892 (article signed by Croker).
2. *Herald*, Nov. 4, 1892.
3. *Times* editorial, Oct. 19, 1892.
4. Lexow hearing of Dec. 30, 1894.
5. *Herald*, July 17, 1892.

Chapter 11

Several biographies of Goldman were consulted for a picture of her situation in 1892. All of them play down the hostility that she aroused even in radical circles (expressed, for instance, in the New York *Volks-Zeitung*, the leading American Marxist newspaper of the time). The newspapers quoted numerous radical leaders and union officials who condemned her celebration of the shooting. Johann Most's fears about prosecution and/or deportation influenced his flip-flop on revolutionary violence, expressed in various issues of *Freiheit* and cited in Trautmann. Drinnon says Goldman and Stein decided to blow up the courthouse. Goldman's intention to leave America is noted in a letter of Oct. 8, 1892 in Max Metzkow Papers, Houghton Library. Goldman's quotes are from LML.

1. Stead.
2. Rischin (page 5).

Chapter 12

News accounts, including obituaries, furnish material on Gould's death. His burial is covered in *World* of Dec. 7, 1892 (Placed in the Tomb). Threats against

Gould are also in newspapers; see especially *Herald* of Jan. 18, 1892 (Crank Landauer May Be "AB 33"). For the earlier attempted blackmail see *Herald* of Nov. 15, 1881 (Colonel Welles in Tears). A later anarchist bomb threat, common at the time, is in the *Herald* of Feb. 9, 1894; its target happens to be Chauncey Depew. Fears about public plunder are set forth in *Herald* of Apr. 22, 1888.

Banquet details are from *Sun* of Jan. 15, 1893. *Sun's* comments on the millennium were printed Jan. 14, 1893. Silver Dollar's views are in *World* of Dec. 31, 1892. As for Croker's deal with the saloonkeepers, Tekulsky boasted of it in an interview in *Tribune* of Sept. 11, 1893, John P. Smith outlined it in *World* of May 27, 1894, and the Lexow Committee testimony of Jimmy Martin, Sheehan and Shalvey all attest to it. Parkhurst's remarks on the Vigilance League are from *Herald* of Nov. 24, 1892.

1. *World*, Dec. 3, 1892.
2. *Herald*, July 29, 1894.

Chapter 13

The main sources are the Gardner trial, press accounts and Moss. Parkhurst's views on the grand design of American history and Providence from MFYNY (see also Cremin), his comments on Tammany from OFWT. The police court stories are from press accounts and from Brown. Also see Steffens' chapter on "The Underworld" in his autobiography.

Essex Market Courthouse material is from press accounts and from Moss, whose book is larded with paternalistic bias regarding Jews (and Italians). Hochstim's malaprop is reported in Asbury, who mistakenly identifies Hochstim as a lawyer. Moss and press accounts were used for the gambling operations material. The confrontation of Gardner and Devery over wine is from testimony at Gardner's trial.

Newspapers of December 1892 covered the Byrnes-Parkhurst rift. Steffens' story of Byrnes is from his autobiography. Much of the Byrnes view is in *World* of Dec. 7, 1892 (Byrnes Attacks Parkhurst). For evidence that Byrnes was galled by Parkhurst's refusal to work with him, see his remarks in *Herald* of Dec. 9, 1892 (Byrnes Preaches Back at Chief Parkhurst). Parkhurst's response was also well-covered, as in *Herald* of Dec. 8, 1892 (Parkhurst Gives the Lie Direct).

1. Godkin article (Criminal Politics).
2. Parkhurst article (Is Christianity Declining?).
3. *Times*, Dec. 10, 1892.
4. *Times*, Dec. 10, 1892.

Chapter 14

The police disciplinary hearing is from newspaper coverage, especially *World* of Jan. 16, 1893, which is also the source of the view that "the Parkhurst crusade" made the hearing necessary. Williams' career was thoroughly aired in his Lexow Committee appearance. Other accounts are in *Herald* of Dec. 29, 1894 and *World* of Jan. 16, 1893. Inspector McLaughlin's real estate transactions are in *Sun* of Jan. 14, 1893 (Police Buy Corner Lots); other accounts of the personal finances of police come from Lexow hearings. Brown is a good source of Tenderloin lore. The story about the watch-stealers is an oft-told tale. Harlow places it at Broadway and 42nd street about 1890. The Clifton-Gardner dialogue is from Clifton's testimony at Gardner arraignment of Dec. 6, 1892, covered in all the dailies.

1. *Herald*, Jan. 13, 1893.
2. OFWT (press statement of Aug. 10, 1893).

Chapter 15

Mostly from the trial transcript and news accounts. Parkhurst's closing comments are in OFWT.

Chapter 16

On bunco and greengoods, see *Herald* of Jan. 25, 1888 and Lexow hearings of June 14, June 19, Sept. 11 and Sept. 12, 1894.

The Thurow story, including dialogue, comes from her Lexow testimony of June 4, 1894. The contempt of court material is in *Times* of Feb. 15 and Feb. 21, 1893.

Barney Martin's checkered past is reported in *World* of Apr. 29, 1894. Croker's sudden wealth was much discussed in the press. He responded in an interview in *Herald* of Dec. 17, 1893 (Croker to His Critics). All of Parkhurst's comments and the material about the choice of the Eldridge Street district, including the quotes, come from OFWT.

1. *Times*, Feb. 10, 1893.
2. *Times*, Dec. 10, 1892.
3. *World* editorial, Dec. 8, 1892.
4. Lexow hearings, Dec. 21, 1894.

Chapter 17

Roosevelt used the expression "ethnic turnover" in his *History of the City of New York* [1891]. Moss comments and color material on the precinct are from his book. *World* of May 22, 1892 reports on the Lower East Side and includes the quote about the family with seven boarders.

Schmittberger's Lexow testimony of Dec. 21, 1894 establishes that the great days of the Tenderloin were over, that Eldridge Street precinct was now the prize of the city.

Werner kept a place on Delancey Street in 1893. His comments are from Lexow hearing of June 13, 1894. Sanford's comments are from *Herald* of Aug. 17, 1894, when she appeared before the Police Board. Lexow hearings established that Tammany cops did not buy promotions, but were given them for services rendered. Steffens material is from his autobiography.

1. *World*, Dec. 15, 1892.

Chapter 18

Devery's remarks about the plight of the workers is in *World* of Aug. 18, 1893. The Pythagoras Hall episode is in *World* of Aug. 23, 1893, Devery's advice to troublemakers from *World* of Aug. 19, 1893. Most's denial of having been horsewhipped is in *World* of Aug. 1, 1893. The scene with Goldman's speech about the Walhalla Hall attack, including quotes, comes from *Herald* and *World* of Aug. 19, 1893. Barondess' conversation with Devery is in *World* of Aug. 20, 1893. Byrnes' remarks in *Herald* of Aug. 25, 1893. *World*'s comments on free speech are a composite of editorials of Aug. 23 and Sept. 2, 1893, and *Tribune* editorial was published Aug. 26, 1893. The train ride with Sergeant Jacobs (and his career as a brothelkeeper) is from LML. Jacobs's surveillance of labor through spies was revealed in the affidavit of a union worker, published in *World* of Oct. 17, 1894. The fact that he met his informants in a Bowery restaurant is in the *Herald* of Feb. 28, 1895. For more on Jacobs see Moss. Goldman's views on socialism vs. anarchism are dealt with in LML.

1. Higham.
2. Quoted in *Herald*, July 28, 1892.
3. *Herald*, Aug. 19, 1893.
4. *World*, Aug. 19, 1893.

Chapter 19

The October 1893 report of the Society for the Prevention of Crime contains much material on Devery's precinct, including arrest statistics for prostitution. Parkhurst's belief that Devery had to pay to get the precinct is from OFWT. Devery's responses are in *World* of Aug. 11 and Aug. 12, 1893. The Police Board reaction was widely reported. McClave's comment is in OFWT. Clubber's comments are in *Tribune* of Oct. 21, 1893. The *Post* editorial appeared on Aug. 11, 1893, the anti-Parkhurst *World* editorial on Sept. 25, 1893. Information on the purging of Parkhurst agents is in *Times* of Feb. 13, 1893 (Parkhurst Men Discharged), and Parkhurst's comments on the resulting increase in effectiveness is in OFWT.

The shakedown of Hester Street pushcart peddlers is covered in *Herald* of Jan. 4, Jan. 15, Jan. 16, Feb. 16 and Oct. 28, 1894.

Broome Street incident comes from *Herald* and *World* accounts of Oct. 29, 1893 (no reporters were eyewitnesses), OFWT, Moss, and affidavits in Early Mayor's Papers in New York City Archives. Some of the background on Hochstim came as Lexow testimony on Oct. 30, 1894 (the Spitz case). Another source on Hochstim is *Herald* of Sept. 23, 1894 (Look At This, Mr. Lexow). Parkhurst's remarks on the assimilation of Jews comes from a National Liberal Immigration League booklet (cited in bibliography). Lemmon's experience at the lineup and Devery's remark to him are in his affidavit.

1. Moss.
2. OFWT.
3. *Herald*, Nov. 4, 1893.

Chapter 20

In LML Goldman continued to deny that she had shouted for insurrection and criminal behavior, but the evidence is against her. Her fellow-Anarchists agreed that Jacobs had quoted her accurately. And at a meeting in Newark, N.J., in that same month Goldman is quoted as having made the same insurrectionary remarks (see *Herald* of Aug. 22, 1893). She is also quoted in several news accounts as having made similar remarks at saloon meetings during the same period. Nellie Bly's interview with Goldman appeared in *World* of Sept. 17, 1893. Trial questions about her religion are quoted in Drinnon, and the *Times* editorial was published Oct. 11, 1893. The hostile journalistic comments are from *Herald* of Oct. 5, 1893 (Anarchist Emma's Riotous Words), and Judge Martine's sentencing comments are from *Herald* of Oct. 17, 1893.

Many versions of the "deaf and dumb brother-in-law," a bit of urban folklore, are reported in old newspapers. One example appears in *Tribune* of Nov. 29, 1892.

1. *World*, Nov. 9, 1893 (comment of Samuel Ordway).
2. Letter from Platt to C. C. Hickok, Aug. 10, 1893 (Lexow Papers).
3. *Herald*, Oct. 10, 1893.

Chapter 21

The Thurow material comes from her Lexow testimony.

Accounts of the Parkhurst-Nicoll meeting come from *Times* and *Herald* of Dec. 23, 1893, and the former paper contains Nicoll's assessment of Parkhurst. By the time the accounts appeared in the press Nicoll and Parkhurst were quarreling about what had been said. Nicoll's version differs from Parkhurst's in two important particulars. First: according to Nicoll, Parkhurst said he would think about working with Byrnes and added at a later conference that he would be glad to work with the Superintendent. The matter is moot since he and Byrnes never reached an accommodation, but Nicoll's version is not credible. And as to Parkhurst's recollection that Nicoll had suggested that Byrnes would be readier to join with Parkhurst were the Schmittberger case pressed rather than the Devery case, Nicoll flatly denied that he even hinted at such.

The "wave of purification" and the visits to the Parkhurst home were covered in the newspapers, and OFWT was also a helpful source. Parkhurst's comments on the "shallow pretense" of the police were in *Herald* of Dec. 6, 1893, and his remarks on revelations that prostitutes had made to him about being recruited are in OFWT.

Stories about the countermanding of Byrnes' orders were rife in the December 1893 papers; see *World* of Dec. 18, 1893 on his instructions to Devery to close a brothel. The material on Zella Nicolaus comes from several sources, especially *Herald* of Dec. 7, 1893. *World* of Mar. 5, 1894 published a comprehensive account of what happened at the P. Divver Association meeting and what prizes were offered. Croker's defense of Tammany and his comments about Fassett were in *Herald* of Dec. 17, 1893, and reports of threats to Parkhurst's life were in *Herald* of Oct. 31, 1893 (from which comes concluding quote) and *World* of Dec. 10, 1893.

1. *Herald*, Dec. 19, 1893.
2. *Herald*, Oct. 19, 1893.
3. *Herald*, Dec. 6, 1893.
4. *World*, Dec. 10, 1893.

5. *Herald*, Dec. 9, 1893.
6. *Tribune*, Feb. 25, 1894.
7. *Times*, Dec. 23, 1893.

Chapter 22

The Goldman material is from LML. The Kievents story, including Parkhurst's comments on "police rottenness," is told in *World* of May 7, 1893 (Parkhurst As a Champion) and in Moss, who writes of the rally for the couple. On police collections from pushcart peddlers, see notes above for "A Colossal Organization of Crime."

1. *World*, May 25, 1893.

Chapter 23

The Real Estate Exchange charges are in *Herald* of Jan. 9, 1894. New York City's dislike of Albany's rule was long-standing. For a typical reaction, see *Herald* editorial of Mar. 25, 1888. Senator Cantor's remarks are from *Herald* of Jan. 31, 1894. The police dinner and the remarks of Recorder Smyth were covered in dailies of Jan. 24, 1893.

The initial meetings of the Lexow Committee were thoroughly covered in the dailies. The description of Platt is from *Herald* of Sept. 25, 1892. Platt's aims can be found in the Lexow Papers of The Historical Society of Rockland County. His patronage arrangements with Croker are outlined in *World* of Jan. 1, 1894, and commentary about the likelihood of a deal with Croker are in *Herald* of Jan. 19, 1894. Interview with Parkhurst about the committee is in *Herald* of Feb. 5, 1894.

1. *Herald*, Nov. 4, 1893.
2. *Tribune*, May 8, 1892.
3. Henry A. Stimson Papers, letter of Mar. 22, 1894 (NY Historical Society).
4. *World*, Dec. 4, 1894.
5. *World*, Jan. 3, 1894.

Chapter 24

The Lexow Committee meetings were covered in the newspapers. The notes to Lexow from Platt and from Goff can be found in the Lexow Papers. The Tammany uproar was reported in newspapers and the note on Justice Divver's new home was in *World* of Mar. 19, 1894.

A *Times* article places Goff in Albany and meeting with the Lexow Committee on Feb. 28, 1894. Goff listed his meetings (and got the Albany date wrong) in *Herald* of Mar. 13, 1894, which is also the source of Senator Saxton's comments.

1. *Herald*, Feb. 6, 1894.
2. *Herald*, Feb. 6, 1894.
3. OFWT.
4. *Herald*, Feb. 4, 1894.
5. *Herald*, Feb. 9, 1894.
6. *World*, Jan. 14, 1894.
7. *Herald*, Mar. 4, 1894.
8. Platt letter to Lexow Mar. 2, 1894, Lexow Papers.

Chapter 25

The hearing on the Bipartisan Police Commission bill was covered in the dailies of Mar. 16, 1894. Parkhurst's promise of cooperation with the Committee is made in a letter of Feb. 25, 1894 in Lexow Papers. The train ride back from Albany is in OFWT and *Herald* of Mar. 17, 1894. Goff's account of his meeting with Parkhurst is in Godkin book. Parkhurst's confidence in the Committee was expressed in *Herald* of Mar. 18, 1894.

1. *Herald*, Mar. 16, 1894.

Chapter 26

The newspapers covered the hearings and the Goff-Sutherland dispute. Parkhurst's comment to Lexow about the distrust of his committee came to light during debate over the Lexow Report in 1895, and was reported in the press. Tekulsky testified on Mar. 26, 1894, Martin on Mar. 31, Apr. 6 and Apr. 7, 1894. Croker's resignation was widely reported. The story of his marital situation is in McGurrin. Platt's use of the hearings for the promotion of the Bipartisan Police Commission Bill is summed up in *Herald* of Apr. 1, 1895. For comments on Martin's wealth, see *Herald* of July 29, 1894.

1. *World*, Dec. 15, 1894.
2. *Tribune*, May 11, 1894.
3. *Herald*, May 8, 1894.

Chapter 27

Information about the operation of the Society for the Prevention of Crime comes from Moss, OFWT, Lexow hearings, and *World* of Mar. 25, 1894. Evidence that the Society covered the excise arrests closely and cited the expected arrest quotas is shown in their communications to the Police Commission (e.g. the August 1893 letter on the Eldridge Street Precinct). Trial coverage comes from *Herald* and *World* accounts. Speech at the Harlem church, and Nicoll's reply, is from news coverage of Apr. 11, 1894. This church was the leading Methodist church in the city, according to *Herald* of June 26, 1892.

1. *World*, Mar. 25, 1894.

Chapter 28

Most of this part of the story, including City Vigilance League dinner on Apr. 30, 1894, comes from news accounts. Parkhurst's remarks to workingmen were in *Tribune* of May 11, 1894. Mrs. Thurow's story is based on her Lexow testimony.

1. OFWT.

Chapter 29

Mostly newspaper accounts. *Sun* was especially diligent at covering the suffragist campaign. *Herald* comment on the veto ran May 19, 1894.

In his book Platt says he recommended Murray for the commission at Gilroy's request. An ongoing relationship between Tammany and Platt in conferring on Republican appointments is confirmed in a letter of Nov. 13, 1889. "Will you oblige me," Platt asks Mayor Grant, "before naming a successor to Hon. J. M. Paterson for Police Justice by giving me opportunity to confer with you on the subject . . . ?" (Hugh Grant Papers, New-York Historical Society)

Even before Croker quit as Tammany Boss, the press had reported angry exchanges with Mayor Gilroy (see *World* of Jan. 15, 1894), and commented that Gilroy was chafing under Croker's rule; various news accounts in April 1894 said Croker had threatened to resign from his Tammany *Post* during a quarrel with Gilroy.

1. *Sun*, Apr. 19, 1894.
2. *Tribune*, May 14, 1894.

Chapter 30

Mostly newspapers again. A phrenological examination of Goff was in *World* of Feb. 4, 1894. Goff's career and private life are outlined in *World* of Oct. 14, 1894 (Goff's Climb to Fame) and in Werner (*It Happened in New York*). Godkin book recounts Goff's difficulties in getting witnesses to testify. The concert hall operator's comment was quoted by Goff in *Herald* of June 4, 1894. The information about O'Kelly, Granger, and McClave comes in Lexow testimony.

1. Godkin, *Triumph of Reform*.

Chapter 31

Mostly from news accounts of the hearings and Godkin's book, *Triumph of Reform*.

Although proof eluded Goff because of the use of intermediaries, later testimony further suggested that McClave was taking payoffs for police appointments and promotions. When McClave resigned his secretary, Charles A. Grant, immediately left the city for a seaside residence in Asbury Park, NJ. Although Grant's salary was $1,800 a year, he owned real estate in the city to the amount of $75,000 to $100,000. Subpoena servers were unable to track down the elusive Grant.

1. *Herald*, June 7, 1894.

Chapter 32

Shopgirl comments were published in *Sun* of June 24, 1894. A key source of this chapter is comments of Elizabeth Cady Stanton in *Sun* of Apr. 19, 1894. Depew's comments were in *Sun* of Apr. 27, 1894.

Chapter 33

Goff's analysis of the effect of the McClave testimony and what came immediately afterward is in Godkin, *Triumph of Reform*. The hearing testimony and other descriptions are from newspaper coverage.

Chapter 34

Mostly comes from newspaper coverage. Roesch's initial denial was in *Tribune* of June 8, 1894; Dr. Jenkins' comment was in *Herald* of June 10, 1894. Silver Dollar Smith's comments were in *World* of June 13, 1894.

1. *Herald*, June 5, 1894.

Chapter 35

All from newspaper accounts of the hearings.

Chapter 36

The Gurko and Kraditor books were helpful in this examination of "personal liberty." The Stanton quotes come from Barry. The suffragist comment about good housekeeping is in *Times* of Aug. 19, 1894.

1. Barry, *Susan B. Anthony*.

Chapter 37

Mostly news coverage. Cantor's comments are from *Sun* of June 16, 1894. Goff's story of the Parisian journalist is in *Herald* of June 19, 1894. Letter from Scranton, PA, is in *Herald* of June 20, 1894. Swinton's letter is in *Herald* of June 16, 1894. Goff's rumor about police raising a bribery fund is in *World* of June 10, 1894. Ada Clinton's streetcar ride with Jerome was recounted in *Herald* of June 21, 1894, including quotations of what they said to each other, although no source is given. (An officer named Patrick H. Cash was mentioned in Moss's Lexow testimony of Oct. 2, 1894.)

Antipathy between Voltairine DeCleyre and Emma Goldman in *An American Anarchist* and in LML. DeCleyre's comments about intellectual fads are in *An American Anarchist*.

Chapter 38

Mostly newspaper coverage. Bradley comments are in *Herald* of June 18, 1894. For newspaper support for Parkhurst as May or, see *Evening Telegram* of June 6, 1894. O'Connor said in *World* of Dec. 21, 1894 that the Committee had never played an important role in the investigation. The red seals that Goff placed on the police lithograph are mentioned in *Sun* of June 17, 1894.

1. *Herald*, June 12, 1894.
2. *Sun*, Apr. 18, 1894 (remarks of Dr. Egbert Guernsey).

Chapter 39

Background material for part 7 comes from *World of Our Fathers*, Handlin, Rischin and Sanders. Goldman material comes from LML. Mrs. Urchittel's account of her arrest from an affidavit made to Moss, read at Lexow hearing of Oct. 3, 1894.

1. Anarchism (Havel's introduction).
2. Asch (America 1918).
3. Hertzberg.
4. Rischin (page 51).
5. Di yuden in America (Odessa, 1881), quoted in Handlin.

Chapter 40

All from newspaper coverage. Wellman revealed in *Herald* of Aug. 13, 1894 that he had hired private detectives to keep an eye on his witnesses. Kerwin quote is in *Times* of July 16, 1894.

1. *World*, Sept. 9, 1894.

Chapter 41

Mostly from LML and various Goldman biographies. The dinner argument with Swinton is from LML.

1. *Sun*, Aug. 20, 1894.
2. LML.

Chapter 42

Herald of Oct. 14, 1894 furnishes the description of Rourke bar. *World* article that led to the search for Creeden appeared on Dec. 12, 1893 (Police and Money). Creeden story is based on his Lexow testimony of Dec. 14, 1894. Actually he never said where he met with Rourke, but the saloon is the only likely possibility. Reppenhagen, while basically substantiating the story, differed in some details in his testimony. According to him the price was always $15,000, Creeden agreed from the first to pay that much for a promotion, and no promises had been made to him about what precinct he would command. As for being pressured about another sergeant bidding for the job, Reppenhagen knew nothing about it. According to him, Wiegand never made him an offer. "He [Creeden] told me that Wiegand was going to be appointed that day," Reppenhagen told the Committee, "and that if it could be stopped he would give $15,000 for the appointment. I said I would try to stop the appointment of Wiegand."

Herald and *Sun* of Aug. 15, 1894 tell of Mary Sallade's meeting in the architect's office. In his book Moss describes his meeting with Caela Urchittel and the details of her travail with the police are from that book and her affidavit to the Parkhurst Society.

Chapter 43

Many of these details come from a feature on Parkhurst's activities in *World* of Oct. 28, 1894 (Parkhurst's Daily Toil). His dramatic style of speech as used here is adapted slightly from a quote in *World* of Aug. 13, 1893. The arrival and departure of Parkhurst during Werner's testimony is in *Sun* of Sept. 13, 1894. The best stories on Mrs. Monahan are in *World* of Sept. 17, 1894 ("She Has Parkhurst Grit") and *Herald* of Sept. 18, 1894 ("Police Against Her"). Rally at the Eighteenth Street Methodist Episcopal Church is covered in *Herald* of Sept. 21, 1894. See also Lexow hearings of Oct. 3, 1894 and Oct. 11, 1894.

1. *Herald*, Oct. 26, 1894 (the speaker was Charles Stewart Smith).

Chapter 44

Some readers may be puzzled as to who the "anti-Tammany Democrats" were. Through much of the latter half of the nineteenth century there were in effect two separate Democratic organizations in the city, amounting in effect to two political parties. By the late 1880s Tammany Hall had once again become the dominant Democratic organization. The anti-Tammany organization was known from decade to decade by various names; in the 1890s it was officially called "The New York State Democracy" and informally known as "the Grace organization" or "the Grace faction" after its leader, ex-Mayor William Grace. Police Justice Voorhis (accused of wrongdoing in the promotion of Police Captain Creeden) belonged to that faction.

Tekulsky's comments are in *Herald* of Oct. 4, 1894. "Police brutality" day at Lexow hearings was Oct. 2, 1894. Several newspapers gave less initial coverage to the Urchittel story than it warranted when she testified on Sept. 12, 1894, and tried to correct their initial mistake with aggressive follow-up. The police were hounding Mrs. Urchittel, and through some undisclosed means Byrnes was induced to put a stop to it. Mrs. Urchittel testified again on Oct. 3, 1894, and Moss' disclosures of the new threats against her were made to the committee that same day. Lexow's letter to Moss, dated Sept. 14, 1894, is in Society for the Prevention of Crime Papers at the Rare Books Collection, Columbia University.

The Jared Flagg story ran for several days in the press; one account is in *Herald* of Oct. 1, 1894. Parkhurst comments in the Bronx (at Bethany Presbyterian Church) are in *Herald* of Sept. 26, 1894. Morgan's pressure on the Republicans to support Strong are recounted in *Herald* of Dec. 16, 1894. The pressure on Moss and Goff to "go up higher" came at the Lexow hearing of Oct. 16, 1894, and *Tribune* of Oct. 19, 1894 covers the continuing debate. *Herald* of Oct. 17, 1894 has Goff's comments on police silence. The Schmittberger material is from Steffens and Lexow hearings of Oct. 11, Oct. 18, and Schmittberger's testimony of Dec. 21, 1894. Attempts to bribe the steamship company official are related in Lexow hearing of Dec. 18, 1894.

Parkhurst's thoughts on the kingdom of God come from *Three Gates on a Side* and MFYNY; see also sermon in *Tribune* of May 2, 1892.

1. *Herald*, May 3, 1894 (comment of Albert Stickney).
2. *Times*, Mar. 29, 1894 (comment of Joseph Choate).
3. *Herald*, Oct. 10, 1894 (in a speech).
4. Fairchild papers, NY Historical Society.
5. *Herald*, Oct. 11, 1894.
6. *Herald*, Oct. 12, 1894.
7. *Tribune*, Oct. 19, 1894.
8. *Herald*, Oct. 17, 1894.

Chapter 45

The Tekulsky-Divver brawl of Oct. 17, 1894 was widely reported in newspapers. The *Herald* of Nov. 5, 1894 enumerates articles from around the *Tribune* on the Lexow hearings. Hochstim's remarks are from *World of Our Fathers*. The Association Hall rally of Oct. 12, 1894 was thoroughly covered. Goldman's anti-Parkhurst comments are paraphrased from her letter in *World* of Sept. 10, 1894; her views on marriage, voting and woman suffrage from *Anarchism*, her settlement house comments from LML.

1. *Herald*, Oct. 12, 1894.
2. *Herald*, Sept. 15, 1894.
3. *Herald*, Oct. 11, 1894.
4. *Herald*, Oct. 5, 1894.
5. *Tribune*, Oct. 8, 1894.
6. *Woman's Journal*, Sept. 1, 1894.

Chapter 46

All of this chapter comes from newspaper coverage and Moss.

Chapter 47

Grady's comments and Parkhurst's downtown campaign are in *Herald* of Oct. 24, 1894. The night Parkhurst was accosted is reported in *Herald* of Oct. 26, 1894 (In the Tiger's Lair). The Women's Municipal League rally was covered in *Tribune* of Oct. 20, 1894. The Rutgers Square scene comes from *Tribune* of Oct. 17, 1894. Police shadowing of Barondess is revealed in *World* of Oct. 17, 1894. *Tribune* of Oct. 14, 1894 reported on Clubber's investigation, the *Herald* of Oct. 13, 1894 on Parkhurst's contacts with women union leaders. The visit from Madame David is in *World* of Nov. 11, 1894, Parkhurst's busy schedule in *World* of Oct. 28, 1894. Parkhurst's evidence against Captain Price in newspapers of Sept. 25, 1894.

1. *Herald*, Oct. 24, 1894.
2. *Herald*, Oct. 31, 1894.
3. *World*, Apr. Nov. 94.
4. Letter of Feb. 16, 1895, Steffens Papers, Rare Books Collection, Columbia University.
5. *Sun*, July 9, 1894.

Chapter 48

Sheehan testified in late October. Tammany's overtures to Goff reported in *Tribune* of Oct. 8, 1894. Goff's attack on Tammany Police Justices was made at Lexow hearing of Oct. 16, 1894. Interception of Madame Hermann in New Jersey reported at hearing of Oct. 24, 1894. Dr. Whitehead testified Nov. 3, 1894. Schmittberger material is from his Lexow testimony on Dec. 21, 1894. Although there is no evidence of when he spoke with or reached agreement with Goff, it seems likely that it occurred prior to Election Day. Goff took all of the month of November off, and almost everything that occurred in December appears to have been based on spadework done earlier. The circumstantial evidence that Byrnes delivered Schmittberger is compelling. In the *World* of Dec. 21, 1894 both Lexow and O'Connor spoke glowingly of how helpful Byrnes had been to the investigation and, as O'Connor put it, "of service to Mr. Goff."

1. *World*, Oct. 22, 1894.

Chapter 49

The Urchittel reunion came at the Lexow hearing of Oct. 19, 1894. Lexow's comments on the city are from *Herald* of Dec. 12, 1894. LaGuardia quote is from his autobiography. Parkhurst commented on life below Fourteenth Street in *Herald* of Oct. 27, 1894. *World* gave an unattributed but credible account on Oct. 30, 1894 of the meeting of Parkhurst and Goldman. See also *World* of Nov. 11, 1894.

1. *World*, Jan. 19, 1895.
2. *World*, Oct. 2, 1894.

Chapter 50

Tekulsky and Smith testified on Nov. 1, 1894, Mrs. Hermann on Nov. 2, 1894, Dr. Whitehead on Nov. 3, 1894. Goff's comments on Parkhurst are from Godkin book.

1. *World*, Oct. 31, 1894.
2. *World*, Oct. 21, 1894.

Chapter 51

Parkhurst's tour of Lower East Side voting places and his comments on the awakening of the foreign-born are in *Tribune* of Nov. 8, 1894. His views on Christian inclusiveness can be found in MFYNY.

1. *Tribune*, Nov. 6, 1894.
2. *Tribune*, Nov. 8, 1894.
3. *Tribune*, Nov. 8, 1894.

Chapter 52

The City Vigilance League dinner of Nov. 27, 1894 was reported in all the dailies. Byrnes testified on Dec. 29, 1894. Platt's new church is reported in *Herald* of Dec. 27, 1894.

1. *World*, Dec. 8, 1894.
2. *World*, Dec. 22, 1894.
3. *World*, Dec. 21, 1894.
4. *World*, Jan. 13, 1895.
5. *Herald*, Dec. 4, 1894.
6. *Herald*, Feb. 8, 1895.
7. *Herald*, Jan. 18, 1895.
8. *Herald*, Jan. 31, 1895.
9. *Herald*, Feb. 7, 1895.

10. *World*, Dec. 21, 1894.
11. *Herald*, Dec. 31, 1894.
12. *Herald*, Jan. 1, 1895.
13. *Post*, Dec. 31, 1894.
14. *World*, Jan. 3, 1895.
15. Steffens (Autobiography).

Chapter 53

Parkhurst's attack on the Committee for its support of Byrnes is in *Herald*, Jan. 1, 1895. The Steffens comments come from a letter of Jan. 6, 1895 to his father in the Steffens Papers at Columbia Rare Books.

The Steffens autobiography, while colorful and useful, is highly inaccurate. It was written near the end of his life—a period in which he delights in referring to black people as niggers and extols the Soviet Union as the wave of the future ("I have seen the future and it works."). He apparently wrote the story of the Lexow investigation from memory; most of it is wrong. He spins it so that just about everything is Jerome's doing; Moss is unmentioned, Goff mentioned but once. He asserts that Schmittberger's testimony assured the defeat of Tammany, although a check of the dates would have shown him that Max appeared before the Committee after the election. He credits his friend Roosevelt with getting rid of Byrnes, a credit that should go to Parkhurst.

1. *Herald*, Jan. 13, 1895.
2. Tolman.

Epilogue: 1898 and After

For one instance of a labor group refusing to let Emma Goldman speak, see *Herald* of July 31, 1895. The closing anecdote on Goldman is from Falk.

1. *The Firebrand*, July 18, 1897.
2. Wexler.
3. Logan.
4. Solomon.

BIBLIOGRAPHY

BOOKS

Adams, Henry. *Democracy*. Gloucester, Mass.: Peter Smith, 1965.

Appletons' Dictionary of New York and Its Vicinity. New York: D. Appleton, 1892.

Armstrong, William M., ed. *The Gilded Age Letters of E. L. Godkin*. Albany: State University of New York Press, 1974.

———. *E. L. Godkin. A Biography*. Albany: State University of New York Press, 1978.

Asbury, Herbert. *The Gangs of New York*. Garden City, N.Y.: Garden City, 1928.

Astor, Gerald. *The New York Cops*. New York: Scribner's, 1971.

Avrich, Paul. *The Haymarket Tragedy*. Princeton, N.J.: Princeton University Press, 1984.

———. *An American Anarchist: The Life of Voltairine de Cleyre*. Princeton, N.J.: Princeton University Press, 1978.

Barrett, James Wyman. *Joseph Pulitzer and His World*. New York: Vanguard, 1941.

Barry, Kathleen. *Susan B. Anthony: A Biography of a Singular Feminist*. Bloomington, Ind.: First Books Library, 2000.

Bennett, D. R. M. *Anthony Comstock: His Career of Cruelty and Crime*. New York: Da Capo, 1971.

Berkman, Alexander. *Prison Memoirs of an Anarchist*. New York: Schocken, 1970.

Breen, Matthew P. *Thirty Years of New York Politics*. New York: Author, 1899.

Brown, Henry Collins. *In the Golden Nineties*. Hastings-on-Hudson, N.Y.: Valentine's Manual, 1928.

Burgoyne, Arthur G. *Homestead*. Pittsburgh: Hawthorne Engraving & Printing, 1893.

Byrnes, Thomas. *Professional Criminals of America*. New York: Chelsea House, 1969.

Cahan, Abraham. *The Rise of David Levinsky*. New York: Harper & Brothers, 1960.

Comstock, Anthony. *Traps for the Young*. Cambridge, Mass.: Belknap, 1967.

Cowles, Virginia. *The Astors*. New York: Knopf, 1979.

Cremin, Lawrence A. *American Education: The National Experience 1783–1876*. New York: Harper & Row, 1980.

Dreiser, Theodore. *The Titan*. New York: Horace Liveright, 1925.

Drinnon, Richard. *Rebel in Paradise: A Biography of Emma Goldman*. Chicago: University of Chicago Press, 1961.

Duis, Perry R. *The Saloon: Public Drinking in Chicago and Boston 1880–1920*. Urbana: University of Illinois Press, 1983.

Ellis, Edward Robb. *The Epic of New York City*. New York: Coward-McCann, 1966.

Falk, Candace. *Love, Anarchy, and Emma Goldman*. New York: Holt, Rinehart & Winston, 1984.

Gardner, Charles W. *The Doctor and the Devil, or The Midnight Adventures of Doctor Parkhurst*. New York: Vanguard, 1931.

Ginger, Ray. *Age of Excess*. New York: Macmillan, 1965.

Godkin, E. L. *The Triumph of Reform*. New York: Souvenir, 1895.

Goldman, Emma. *Living My Life*. New York: AMS, 1970.

——. *Anarchism and Other Essays*. New York: Mother Earth, 1910.

——. *The Social Significance of the Modern Drama*. Boston: Richard G. Badger, 1914.

Griffith, Elisabeth. *In Her Own Right: The Life of Elizabeth Cady Stanton*. New York: Oxford University Press, 1984.

Gurko, Miriam. *The Ladies of Seneca Falls: The Birth of the Civil Rights Movement*. New York: Macmillan, 1974.

Hammack, David C. *Power and Society: Greater New York at the Turn of the Century*. New York: Russell Sage Foundation, 1982.

Handlin, Oscar. *The Uprooted: Second Edition Enlarged*. Boston: Little, Brown, 1973.

Hapgood, Hutchins. *The Spirit of the Ghetto*. Preface and Notes by Harry Golden. New York: Funk & Wagnalls, 1965.

Harlow, Alvin F. *Old Bowery Days*. New York: D. Appleton, 1931.

Heaton, John L. *The Story of a Page*. New York: Harper & Bros, 1916.

Hertzberg, Arthur. *The Jews in America*. New York: Simon & Schuster, 1989.

Higham, John. *Strangers in the Land: Patterns of American Nativism 1860–1925*. Piscataway, N.J.: Rutgers University Press, 1988.

Howe, William, and Abe Hummel. *In Danger, or Life in New York*. New York: J. S. Ogilvie, 1888.

Howe, Irving. *World of Our Fathers*. New York: Simon & Schuster, 1976.

Howe, Irving, with Kenneth Libo. *How We Lived: A Documentary History of Immigrant Jews in America, 1880–1930*. New York: Richard Marek, 1979.

Hoyt, Edwin P. *The Goulds: A Social History*. New York: Weybright & Talley, 1969.

Kaplan, Justin. *Lincoln Steffens*. New York: Simon & Schuster, 1974.

Kraditor, Aileen S. *The Ideas of the Woman Suffrage Movement 1890–1920*. New York: Columbia University Press, 1965.

LaGuardia, Fiorello H. *The Making of an Insurgent: An Autobiography 1882–1919*. Philadelphia: Lippincott, 1948.

Logan, Andy. *Against the Evidence: The Becker-Rosenthal Affair*. New York: Avon Books, 1970.

Mamet, Edward. "An Analysis of Detective Organization in the New York City Police Department." Master's thesis, C. W. Post Center, Long Island University, 1977.

McGurrin, James. *Bourke Cockran: A Free Lance in American Politics*. New York: Scribner's, 1948.

Morton, Marian J. *Emma Goldman and the American Left: Nowhere at Home*. New York: Twayne, 1992.

Moss, Frank. *The American Metropolis*. New York: Peter Fenelon Collier, 1897.

Nevins, Allan. *The Evening Post: A Century of Journalism*. New York: Russell & Russell, 1968.

O'Brien, Frank M. *The Story of the Sun*. New York: George H. Doran, 1918.

Parkhurst, Rev. Charles. *My Forty Years in New York*. New York: Macmillan, 1923.

———. *Our Fight with Tammany*. New York: Scribner's, 1895.

———. *The Swiss Guide: An Allegory*. New York, 1895.

———. *Talks to Young Women*. New York: Century, 1897.

———. *Three Gates on a Side and Other Sermons*. New York: Fleming H. Revell, 1891.

Platt, Thomas Collier. *The Autobiography of Thomas Collier Platt*. New York: B. W. Dodge, 1910.

Richardson, James F. *The New York Police: Colonial Times to 1901*. New York: Oxford University Press, 1970.

Riis, Jacob A. *How the Other Half Lives*. New York: Dover, 1971.

———. *The Making of an American*. New York: Macmillan, 1957.

Riordan, William L. *Plunkitt of Tammany Hall*. New York: E. P. Dutton, 1963.

Rischin, Moses. *The Promised City: New York's Jews 1870–1914*. Cambridge, Mass.: Harvard University Press, 1962.

Rittenhouse, Mignon. *The Amazing Nellie Bly*. Freeport, N.Y.: Books for Libraries, 1971.

Rovere, Richard. *Howe and Hummel*. New York: Paperback Library, 1963.

Sanders, Ronald. *The Downtown Jews: Portraits of an Immigrant Generation*. New York: Harper & Row, 1969.

Savell, Isabelle K. *Politics in the Gilded Age in New York State and Rockland County: A Biography of Senator Clarence Lexow*. New City, N.Y.: Historical Society of Rockland County, 1984.

Schlereth, Thomas J. *Victorian America: Transformations in Everyday Life 1876–1915*. New York: Harper Collins, 1991.

Smith, Page. *As a City upon a Hill: The Town in American History*. New York: Knopf, 1966.

Solomon, Martha. *Emma Goldman*. Boston: Twayne, 1987.

Sproat, John G. *"The Best Men": Liberal Reformers in the Gilded Age*. New York: Oxford University Press, 1968.

Stead, W. T. *Satan's Invisible World Displayed*. New York: Arno, 1974.

Steffens, Lincoln. *The Autobiography of Lincoln Steffens*. New York: Harcourt, Brace, 1931.

——. *Letters of Lincoln Steffens*. New York: Harcourt Brace, 1938.

Strong, Josiah L. *The Twentieth Century City*. New York: Baker & Taylor, 1898.

Swanberg, W. A. *Pulitzer*. New York: Scribner's, 1967.

——. *Citizen Hearst*. New York: Bantam, 1963.

Tolman, William Howe. *Municipal Reform Movements in the United States*. New York: Fleming H. Revell, 1895.

Trautmann, Frederic. *The Voice of Terror: A Biography of Johann Most*. Westport, Conn.: Greenwood, 1980.

Werner, M. R. *It Happened in New York*. New York: Coward-McCann, 1957.

——. *Tammany Hall*. Westport, Conn.: Greenwood, 1970.

Wexler, Alice. *Emma Goldman: An Intimate Life*. New York: Pantheon, 1984.

White, William Allen. *Masks in a Pageant*. New York: Macmillan, 1928.

ARTICLES

Bellah, Robert N. "Civil Religion in America." *Daedalus*, Winter 1967.

Bocock, John Paul. "The Irish Conquest of Our Cities." *Forum* 17, April 1894.

Byrnes, Thomas. "How to Protect a City from Crime." *North American Review* 158, July 1894.

Carnegie, Andrew. "Wealth." *North American Review* 148, June 1889.

Chandler, The Honorable W. E. "Shall Immigration Be Suspended?" *North American Review* 156, January 1893.

Croker, Richard. "Tammany Hall and the Democracy." *North American Review* 154, February 1892.

Godkin, E. L. "Criminal Politics." *North American Review* 150, June 1890.

Kramer, Rita. "Well, What Are You Going to Do About It?: The Story of Boss Croker." *American Heritage* 24, no. 2, February 1973.

Merlino, S. "Italian Immigrants and Their Enslavement." *Forum* 15, April 1893.

Parkhurst, Charles H. "Is Christianity Declining?" *North American Review* 141, July 1885.

——. Correspondence between Rev. Dr. Charles H. Parkhurst and the president of the National Liberal Immigration League on the effects of present-day immigration. Published by the National Liberal Immigration League, New York, 1911.

Turner, George Kibbe. "The Daughters of the Poor." *McClure's*, November 1909.

Van Etten, Ida M. "Russian Jews as Desirable Immigrants." *Forum* 15, April 1893.

NEWSPAPERS

The New York Commercial Advertiser
The New York Evening Post
The New York Herald
The New York Mail & Express
The New York Sun
The New York Times
The New York Tribune
The New York World

TRANSCRIPTS

The People of the State of New York vs. Charles W. Gardner. Stenographer's minutes. New York, 1893.
Special Senate Committee to Investigate Police Matters in the City of New York, 1894.

INDEX

Brisbane, Arthur, 301
Broome Street "riot," 166–70
Brown, Jake, 282
Brown, John Crosby, 32, 356
Bryce, James, xx
Bunco games, 137–38, 285
Burrell, David, 63
Butler, Bessie, 287
Byrnes, Thomas, xix, 42, 61, 63, 69,
  71–72, 134–36, 182–83, 188, 288,
  387, 392, 415; and anarchists, 74, 75,
  80–81, 157, 159; becomes
  superintendent, 46; departmental
  investigations, 119, 121–23, 169–70,
  385, 422; and Devery, 230–31, 327;
  Gould family and, 99–101, 187, 429;
  Lexow Committee, 397–98, 423–25;
  liquor statutes and, 44–48, 353;
  Parkhurst Society, 112–17, 123,
  412–13; reshaping NYPD, 423, 427,
  429–30; retires, 430–31, 439; and
  Schmittberger, 362, 395, 397; and
  Tammany, 84, 89, 383

Callahan, Michael, 172
Calvary Methodist Episcopal Church,
  232
Cantor, Jacob, 201, 275, 295, 400, 427
Carnegie, Andrew, xvii, 75
Casey, Wardman, 395–96
Cash, police officer, 299
Century Club, 399
Chamber of Commerce, 188, 246, 251,
  275, 429
Cherry Hill, 19
Choate, Joseph, 140–41
Christian Union (magazine), 61
civil courts (NYC), xiii, 51, 283
City Club, 206, 426, 429
City Vigilance League, 103, 194, 227,
  233, 236, 339, 347, 357, 422, 434
Clan-na-Gael, 250

Clarke, Frank, 285
Cleveland, Grover, 89, 356
Clifton, Lillie, 112, 123–24, 128–30,
  132–35, 171
Clinton, Ada, 298–300
Cloakmakers and Dressmakers Union,
  Ladies' Branch, 386
Cohen, Henry, 350–51
Cohen, Lena, 289–90, 297
Committee of Seventy, 345, 356–57,
  358–59, 367, 368, 379–80, 382, 384,
  403, 429
Commonwealth Club, 91
Comstock, Anthony, 171
Connecticut Law and Order League, 435
Cooper Union, 62, 73, 381
Cox, Mrs., 338–39
Cranks, 100–101
Creeden, Timothy, 335–38, 395, 421, 439
Croker, Richard, 84–85, 88, 90–91, 103,
  107, 181, 209, 281, 283–84, 295,
  391, 411, 416, 438; defends
  Tammany, 188; new wealth, 142, 208,
  235; and Platt, 201–2, 204, 207, 236;
  resigns, 223–25, 247; and
  saloonkeepers, 48, 221–22
Crosby, Howard, 13, 70
Cross, Adam, 276, 328
Cross, Richard, 162
Crowley, Michael, 130, 132–33

Daly's gambling den, 59, 110–11, 113
David, Marie Louise, 386, 403–4
DeBarrios, Francesca, xvii
DeCleyre, Voltairine, 301
Delmonico's, 25, 85, 93, 127, 201
Dennett, Arthur, 227–29, 252, 274, 277,
  300, 335
Denver Municipal League, 435
Depew, Chauncey, 102, 269–270
Devery, William, 111, 113, 128–30,
  132–34, 184; as chief of police, 439;